How to Become a Law Enforcement Professional

How to Become a Law Enforcement Professional

FROM THE WRITTEN TEST TO THE PSYCHOLOGICAL EVALUATION

First Edition

TIFFANY MOREY

Southern Oregon University

SAN DIEGO

Bassim Hamadeh, CEO and Publisher
Alisa Munoz, Senior Project Editor
Casey Hands, Production Editor
Emely Villavicencio, Senior Graphic Designer
Greg Isales, Licensing Associate
Natalie Piccotti, Director of Marketing
Kassie Graves, Vice President of Editorial
Jamie Giganti, Director of Academic Publishing

Cover image: Copyright © 2016 iStockphoto LP/kali9.

Printed in the United States of America.

cognella® ACADEMIC PUBLISHING

3970 Sorrento Valley Blvd., Ste. 500, San Diego, CA 92121

BRIEF CONTENTS

CONTENTS

CHAPTER 6   What Is an Assessment Center?   243

CHAPTER 7   Why the Background Investigation Is Critical?   261

CHAPTER 8   What Is a Lie Detector Test?   284

CHAPTER 9   What Is the Psychological Evaluation?   293

ACTIVE LEARNING

This book has interactive activities available to complement your reading.

Your instructor may have customized the selection of activities available for your unique course. Please check with your professor to verify whether your class will access this content through the Cognella Active Learning portal (http://active.cognella.com) or through your home learning management system.

History of Law Enforcement

What Is the History of Law Enforcement Testing?

"Becoming a police officer is a choice. It's not something you're born into."

—Franchesca Ramsey

KEY TERMS

Rotten apple officer: A term to describe the rare officer who is deviant and corrupt.

Historical testing process: The law enforcement testing process before the 1960s to include the eight-step process of the job application, written test, physical fitness test, oral board interview, background investigation, medical/physical, chief/sheriff review, and, finally, hiring.

Matrons: A historical term to describe the duties a policewoman is associate with, such as working with women, juvenile delinquents, and abused children.

Pinkerton Detective Agency: One of the oldest and largest private investigative agency in the United States.

Marie Owens: In 1891, she was the first documented policewoman.

Lola Baldwin: In 1908, she was the second documented policewoman.

Alice Stebbins Wells: In 1910, she was the third documented policewoman and was instrumental in paving the way for future policewomen.

August Vollmer: Chief of police in Berkley, California, in the 1920s, is known as the father of American policing, and was an advocate for policewomen.

International Association of Women Police (IAWP): IAWP is a global organization for women in criminal justice professions.

International Association of Chiefs of Police (IACP): The IACP is the world's most significant and most influential professional association for the leaders of police departments.

Immutable characteristics: Characteristics a person has at birth and should not be asked to alter.

Attrition: When an agency has officers retire and replaces them with younger ones.

Furlough: Temporary unpaid leave employees take during a financial crisis.

CHAPTER LEARNING OBJECTIVES

After reading the chapter, you should have a good understanding of the following:

- The history of the law enforcement testing process before the 1980s
- The stereotypical police officer and how that changed in the mid-late 20th century
- How policewomen entered policing and their roles
- How minority officers entered policing and how police administrators controlled their duties
- The critical forces behind the changing landscape for policewomen and minority officers in the 1960s
- The federal employment laws and how they changed law enforcement testing
- How the millennium and the financial crisis of 2007 changed law enforcement testing

How Was Law Enforcement Testing Conducted Before the 1980s?

Law enforcement candidate recruiting and testing looks a lot different today than it did in the past. Many of the testing procedures utilized historically are still in use today; however, their operation and content are much different. Besides, many agencies have created new tests, and the requirements have changed.

This chapter will look at how policing has changed in the last 200 years and how that, in turn, has modernized the testing process for new candidates. Contemporary issues in policing have also rejuvenated the hiring process. Law enforcement agencies in the United States are now more aware of corruption and the **rotten apple officer**, which describes the rare officer who is a deviant and corrupt. Moreover, collectively these agencies are throwing everything at the hiring process, other than the kitchen sink, in order to ensure only those honest officers with high morals and ethics make the cut.

Historically there has always been a standardized testing process to be hired as a police officer. See Figure 1.1 for the eight-step historical law enforcement testing process.

The following is a quick overview of the **historical testing process**:

JOB APPLICATION: Individual agencies determine what information will be on the application and what the requirements are. The following list illustrates the requirements to apply:

- U.S. Citizen
- 21 years of age
- High school diploma or GED
- 5'7" for male candidates
- 5'2" for female candidates

WRITTEN TEST: The written test determines if the police candidate possesses the necessary skills to perform the job of a police officer.

Historical Look at the Law Enforcement Testing Process

FIGURE 1.1 The eight-step historical law enforcement testing process.

PHYSICAL FITNESS TEST: Most agencies referred to the military and utilized their physical fitness requirements. The following list illustrates the physical fitness requirements:

- 1.5-mile timed run
  - Different qualifying times for men and women
- Timed push-ups
  - Different qualifying times for men and women
- Timed sit-ups
  - Different qualifying times for men and women

ORAL BOARD INTERVIEW: The questions on the oral board were basic, and agencies would alter questions in order to hire specific candidates and would fail other candidates due to their sex, race, or other characteristics deemed inappropriate by the agency.

BACKGROUND CHECK: Agencies did a basic entry-level military background check on candidates.

MEDICAL EVALUATION/PHYSICAL: Officers were required to have basic physical requirements related to vision, hearing, and other tests to confirm the candidate was in excellent health.

CHIEF/SHERIFF REVIEW: If a candidate passed all these tests, the head of the agency would review the candidates and determine which to hire. The system created allowed the passing over of women and minorities since there were no federal laws to protect these classes of candidates.

The job of a police officer was more often handed out to those in the "good ol' boy club" or with prior military experience. Many officers were given a badge and a gun and started working on the street weeks or even months before attending a police academy. Historically, agencies have made many mistakes, and this would have topped the list. To place officers with no training in the line of fire was ludicrous. This testing process did not start seriously changing until the 1990s.

Policing before the 1980s was very different than it is today. Due to several factors, such as the passing of federal civil rights laws, affirmative action, and technology, changes occurred for the better. The law enforcement world has evolved and opened for many to whom it used to be sealed shut. These factors also influenced the new law enforcement testing process.

What Did a Stereotypical Police Officer Look Like in History?

From the late 19th century until the mid-1960s police officers in the United States fit a stereotypical mold (Figure 1.2). Historically police officers were White and male and were at least 5'7" tall. Women and minorities were allowed into the "good ol' boy club," sort of; however, their duties and powers were limited and outlined to fit the perceived notions of the period.

FIGURE 1.2 The stereotypical police officer in 1920, Houston Police Department.

Where Were the Policewomen?

The advent of women in policing is a relatively new occurrence. History does show women in policing as far back as 1820; however, this historical portrayal does not correlate with how women operate in the 21st century as officers. Trailblazer women in policing were **matrons** and performed matronly duties mostly with women and children. Policewomen wore skirts and were not allowed the full authority policemen had. They had prescribed duties in social work, interviewing abused and sexually assaulted children and females (this was the custom since male administrators felt that most females were uncomfortable talking to a male officer), investigating crimes at local skate parks, the theater, or any location where children congregated such as the local arcade.

Women did not start making strides in becoming accepted police officers until the mid to late 20th century. One of the many reasons policewomen were accepted was because of their employment with the Pinkerton Detective Agency and Wells Fargo. **The Pinkerton Detective Agency** is one of the oldest and largest private investigative agencies in the United States. According to More (1998), women took jobs as detectives, undercover agents, and spies for these two agencies and began to build their credibility. At the same time, social movements were gaining momentum in the United States and Great Britain. Leaders wanted reform, and one prominent platform was the need to change police practices by advocating for women in law enforcement.

According to Schulz (1995), there were *six eras of women in policing:*

1. Forerunners: The matrons, 1820–1899
2. The early policewomen, 1900–1928
3. Depression losses, 1929–1941
4. World War II, 1940s
5. Paving the way for patrol, 1950–1967
6. Women become crimefighters, 1968–present

The author of this guide, through education and experience as a woman officer in the 6th era, has changed the period for the 6th era and has added a 7th era: *women are accepted as coworkers, 2001–present.*

Schulz (1995) further delineates the history of women in policing and how women began making strides when the "initial demands for a limited, specialized role based on gender were replaced by demands for equality by later generations of women with totally different social histories and self-images" (p. 1).

Today, policewomen are given full powers as their male counterparts. They have the same job responsibilities and expectations. However, the process to full authority was not an easy one, and many women police officers still feel the playing field is not level, even in the 21st century. If it were not for the forerunners, women would never have the freedom and acceptance in the profession they have today.

Who Were the First Three Policewomen?

Before the 1950s women in policing were allowed to perform matronly duties only; social work type involvement was allowed, and generally this work was awarded to widows of police officers as a type of death benefit. According to Jones and Hornig (2017), three women were credited with being at the forefront of women in policing. The first was **Marie Owens** in 1891 (Figure 1.3). Marie Owens was hired in Chicago and was given the powers of arrest and the title of a detective sergeant. However, even though she was considered a star for her time, she was limited to investigating child labor law violations.

The second woman police officer, **Lola Baldwin**, was sworn in as a female detective, in Portland Oregon, on April 1, 1908 (Figure 1.4). Lola's duties included social work and crime prevention. She did not have arresting powers as women law enforcement officers have today. Moreover, her office was located at the YMCA, not at the police department along with the White male police officers.

Finally, the third woman police officer, **Alice Stebbins Wells,** was appointed as a police officer in Los Angeles in 1910 (Figure 1.5). According to Jones and Hornig (2017), Alice Stebbins Wells had arrest powers, "a telephone call box key, a rule book, a first aid book, and a policeman's badge." Alice Stebbins Wells is known for arguing for young female victims. She proposed that children who were abused or sexually assaulted did not want to confide in a male officer; instead, they were more comfortable confiding in a woman (Jones & Hornig, 2017). The police department even gave her a policewoman badge with the number 1 on it (Jones & Hornig, 2017). Officer Wells focused on crimes relating to social service and sensitive female issues. Officer Wells was one of the most respected female officers because of her efforts to promote other female officers. She was instrumental in the hiring of 16 policewomen across the

FIGURE 1.3 Marie Owens, first policewoman, 1891.

FIGURE 1.4 Lola Baldwin, second policewoman, 1908.

FIGURE 1.5 Alice Stebbins Wells, influential policewoman, 1910.

country and the formation of several policewomen associations (Jones & Hornig, 2017). Officer Wells worked hard and even started the **International Association of Women Police (IAWP)**, which is still in existence today. Officer Wells retired from the Los Angeles Police Department after 30 years of service.

Was August Vollmer an Advocate for Women Officers?

August Vollmer, who was the chief of police in Berkley, California, in the 1920s, and who is known as the father of modern American policing, also advocated for women officers. August Vollmer was ahead of his time because not many policemen, let alone police administrators, believed in policewomen and their fight for equality. August Vollmer believed in many concepts that police departments around the country still utilize. He even appointed *Elizabeth G. Lossing*, as the head of the crime prevention division. Lossing had a bachelor of science degree, which for the time was rare. She utilized community policing and problem-oriented policing concepts to solve the ongoing juvenile delinquency problems (More, 1998). Lossing was also ahead of her time with these two concepts. Community policing and problem-oriented policing would not become officially documented as a way of policing until the 1980s. Lossing was a leader and showed what women could do in police leadership roles. The techniques Lossing utilized are still prevalent in policing today (Figures 1.6 and 1.7).

FIGURE 1.6 Civilian Women's' Police Training Corps drill at NY Police Field Day, 1917–1918.

FIGURE 1.7 Women police reserves in police parade, 1918.

Did the IACP Define Women's Role in Policing?

The **International Association of Chiefs of Police (IACP)** is the world's most significant and most influential professional association for the leaders of police departments. Since its inception in 1893, the association has advanced leadership and professionalism in policing. Through research, training, and conferences, the association prepares police leaders to address the many policing challenges.

In 1922, during an annual IACP conference, the difference between women and men officers was a hot topic. According to Hale (1992), Hutzel (1933), and Walker (1977), it was decided women would be required to be confident and pleasant and have a solid education and formal training in social work to better understand how to conduct crime prevention. IACP passed a resolution supporting women in law enforcement; however, women had to display specific feminine characteristics without having any moral turpitude (More, 1998). Amazingly enough, their male counterparts did not have to demonstrate the same exacting standards (Figure 1.8).

How could police administrators be expected to change the status quo when the IACP, who set the standards for policing, dictated the continuation of policewomen and their matronly duties? It would be another 60 years before this way of thinking would change.

FIGURE 1.8 San Francisco Society Girls Red Cross ambulance drivers sworn in as policewomen to give them added authority, 1918.

What Were Policewomen in the 1920s and 1930s?

World War I provided the podium for women as police officers due to men engaged in military endeavors. As the men were involved in war-related activities, work still needed to be done. There weren't enough non-military men left at home; therefore, the windows were cracked and unbarred for women to slip quietly through.

According to the U.S. Census, in 1930 there were 1,534 women in public and private law enforcement agencies, and 10 years later the number swelled by 241 (Schulz, 1995). These numbers revealed the hiring of only an average of 24 policewomen each year. There would still be trials and tribulations since the public was not exactly ready to see women in the role as a crime fighter and being involved in fights and shootings. Women were seen either as wives, mothers, homemakers, or in unequivocal crannies (Figure 1.9).

FIGURE 1.9 1909 to 1932: policewoman training how to handcuff a prisoner.

FIGURE 1·10 Special police practice to guard New York's water supply, 1919.

It had been socially acceptable for women to fill the role in a social capacity; however, that role was changing dramatically, and it would take time and patience to accept it fully (Figure 1.10).

What Were Policewomen in the 1940s and 1950s?

With the advent of World War II, a new shift occurred that placed the law enforcement focus back on delinquency and issues of morality. *The reform era of policing was in full swing.* During this era, the crime control model was developed and policing became professional. Policewomen were still only allowed to work with juveniles and in the social areas of police work. At the end of World War II, women saw their assignments change; these new assignments included investigations, firearms training and qualification, and upgraded uniforms (Schulz, 1995).

Finally, women were breaking the chains that so held them into the stereotypical roles of social work. They were not fully accepted; however, the bowling ball was already rolling down the lane, and it would be impossible to stop it now. According to Schulz (1995), by 1950, there were 2,500 policewomen in America, which accounted for 1% of the population. The writing was on the wall that the landscape was continuing to change, and women were starting to trickle into other areas of policing other than the stereotypical matronly duties (Figure 1.11).

FIGURE 1·11 1941 to 1945: Women's Army Corps recruiting poster.

What Were Policewomen in the 1960s and 1970s?

The 1960s did not show much improvement in job assignments for a policewoman. However, by the end of the decade, some unbelievable shifts *would* occur. For the first time, women were allowed to work in the field with uniformed male officers. Before the 1960s, women could go into the field to investigate their matronly type duties; however, they were not allowed to venture in the field for the more traditional patrol duties. The District of Columbia Police and Miami Police Departments both utilized policewomen in field operations in 1965 (More, 1998). Even more shocking, in 1968, Indianapolis, Indiana, assigned two women to patrol as partners (Schulz, 1995).

Changes were occurring, and policewomen saw the light shining through in the cracks of the doors that had once been shut. The profound changes that occurred could be attributed directly to civil rights legislation, the women's rights movement, court cases, and due process issues. These changes gave women and people of color a step up in the law enforcement community. Discrimination was prevalent when it came to women and minorities in law enforcement, and before the 1960s it was seen but ignored.

Policewomen also started seeing the light on the horizon with respect to promotion. While in the past they had been denied or forbidden to seek promotion, they were now *not* tiptoeing away with their heads hung low. In 1961, *Felicia Shpritzer* and *Gertrude Schimmel*, took the New York City Police Department to court for the right to take the sergeant promotional exam. In 1964, they passed and were promoted, and then, after further litigation in 1967, they were the first two policewomen promoted to lieutenants (Schulz, 1995). It was unfortunate they had to pursue litigation for a right freely given to male officers; however, their continuing fight and fortitude made it possible for future policewomen to seek promotion in the 21st century.

In 1975, women represented only 2.2% of sworn officers in police departments (Martin & Jurik, 1996). Nationally, the numbers of policewomen in law enforcement were rising; however it was slight, and the total numbers of women in law enforcement showed a barely noticeable increase.

Did Policing Change for Women Post 1980?

By the 1980s it was clear that the role of a policewoman was expanding. The ever-so-long pencil skirt, a required uniform for the policewomen of yesteryear, was now replaced by pants. The changing uniform was a huge win, which can indeed be understood by any woman who is or has been a police officer. Patrol work is hard enough without having to wear a skirt.

Policewomen were now responding to calls for service on patrol along with their male cohorts and the line between male and female officers began to disappear. Policewomen were now expected to perform the same job duties and responsibilities. The only delineation left for the woman candidate testing for the position of a police officer was the physical fitness portion of the testing process. Some departments utilized two different requirements for this test. Depending on the candidates' sex and age, the requirements for the timed mile-and-a-half run, sit-ups, and push-ups would change.

Figure 1.12 illustrates that policewomen were making their mark in the police world. In 2007, the percent of full-time law enforcement officers in local police departments and sheriffs' offices who were women was almost 15%. The change was a 12.8% increase since 1975 and a 0.4% increase each year from 1975–2007.

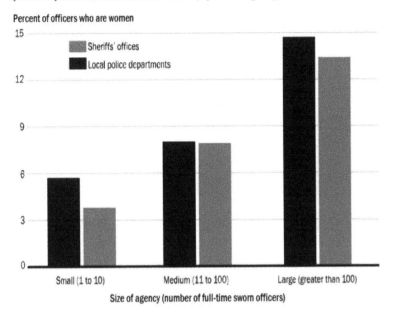

Percent of full-time sworn law enforcement officers who are women among local police departments and sheriffs' offices, by size of agency, 2007

FIGURE 1.12 Percent of women in local police departments and sheriffs' offices, 2007.

Figure 1.13 illustrates the percent and number of full-time policewomen in 13 of the largest police departments in the United States. In 2007, 27% of the Detroit Police Department were women officers, whereas Las Vegas Metropolitan Police Department had only 9% women officers.

Percent and number of full-time sworn officers who are women among the largest police departments, 1997 and 2007

Agency	Percent		Number	
	1997	2007	1997	2007
Detroit	22 %	27 %	880	829
Philadelphia	22	25	1,461	1,666
District of Columbia	25	23	904	916
Chicago	19	23	2,549	3,097
Los Angeles	17	19	1,644	1,779
Memphis	17	19	250	386
New York City	15	17	5,743	6,151
Dallas	16	17	444	527
San Francisco	15	16	303	378
Baltimore	14	16	432	485
Boston	13	14	275	293
Houston	12	13	637	656
Las Vegas Metro*	8	9	113	219

FIGURE 1.13 Percent/number of full-time sworn women officers, 1997–2007.

FIGURE 1.14 Sergeant Laurie Rich, White female, and Sherrine Freeman, minority female, White House police officers, 1987.

According to Langton (2010), by 2008 there were approximately 100,000 policewomen in federal, state, county, and municipal law enforcement agencies.

Although changes occurred with each new year, policewomen are still not seen as equals by all in law enforcement. In 2015, the president of the National Association of Women Law Enforcement Executives (NAWLEE), B.R. O'Connor, published a study conducted by NAWLEE and the International Association of the Chiefs of Police (IACP). It showed that the national average of women in policing is only 12%. The same study showed another disheartening fact that women make up less than 2% of chiefs of police or top administrators in law enforcement organizations across the country (O'Connor, 2015).

Progress was slow, and the overall numbers still showed a lack of policewomen in policing. The doors finally opened for the first time in the 1980s; however, even though they were not locked, the doors were not opened fully, making it difficult to walk through (Figure 1.14). By the new millennium the doors were propped open and yet the numbers did not rise respectively. What could be the reason? Does the law enforcement field only attract males due to the nature of the work? Alternatively, are numbers rising and more time needs to pass before women represent more fully? Whatever the reason, one thing is for sure: Because of the frontier policewomen paving the way, new roads opened are now navigated by new age policewomen.

POLICE STORY 1.1 **The Tough Road**

by Retired Lieutenant Tiffany L. Morey NLVPD, N. Las Vegas, Nevada

While I was testing for various police departments, I had ideas of grandeur. I was sure any law enforcement agency would want me. I knew I had to pass all the testing requirements put before me; however, I thought mistakenly that once I passed I would be a valued addition. During the time I was testing, I saw that policewomen were in the minority. I went on a ride-along, and on the shift there was only one policewoman, and other shifts had none. I mistakenly thought this meant that departments needed more policewomen and would welcome qualified women with open arms. I soon learned this was far from the truth. I had no prior experience in the military or in a correctional facility (the norm for this time). I did, however, know the chief of police and to this day I am sure his influence assisted me through the testing process (even though I would have passed the tests without his assistance, I don't know if "they"—the good ol' boys—would have allowed my access because of my sex).

Throughout the police academy, field training, and then during my first decade with the department, I saw discrimination rear its ugly head. Male coworkers threw my sex in my face, and many officers made it clear my place was in the home, raising children, and not on the street, side by side with them. There were double standards, and I had to prove my worth as an officer continually, many times at the risk of my safety and that of the public we contacted.

My first badge was labeled "policeman" (see Figure 1.15). Moreover, even after I tested for sergeant, I remember fellow officers gossiping that my promotion was due to my sex (even though I placed first on the promotion testing list after a written test, oral board interview, and assessment center). Once, I complained of how ill-fitted our male bullet-proof vests were, of how they did not fit the body of a policewoman. A decade later, after much trial and tribulation, the battle was won, and the policewomen at my department finally wore bullet-proof vests made for women.

As I entered my second decade in policing I began to notice a change. More and more women were testing and becoming police officers and were accepted in those positions by coworkers. The new standard was not if the candidate was a male, but instead if the candidate could do the job. That was fair, and I could see the new landscape on the horizon. Once I was promoted I made it my mission to be a valuable mentor to those policewomen who followed in my footsteps.

FIGURE 1.15 First police badge as a policewoman.

Where Were the Minority Policemen?

Most of the literature on the history of minorities in policing shows the involvement of women and Black men. There is little information about Latino or Asian American officers. What is common for all minority men in policing is that they were discriminated against and segregated into specific duties, just as women were. If the officer was a White male, that officer was allowed to be involved in the multifaceted world of policing. No matter the call, the White policeman had full authority; however, the same was not true for policewomen nor minority policemen. Most minority officers either filled a need or specific niche of policing or were only utilized in a volunteer role (Figure 1.16).

FIGURE 1.16 Volunteer civilian police, Amache Colorado, 1942.

Where Were Officers of Color?

The United States has had Black policemen employed in municipal/city police departments since 1861 (Johnson, 1947). Historically, Black policemen only policed other Black citizens. If Black citizens represented a neighborhood, Black policemen were chosen to work the area due to their cultural identification and insight into the plights of the neighborhood (Figure 1.17). The belief was that a Black policeman would be more effective working for a Black community and thereby alleviate police-community tension (see President's Commission on Law Enforcement and Administrative Justice, 1967; President's Commission on Civil Disorders, 1968).

The segregation of Black policemen occurred due to White citizens not accepting a Black policeman. In 1871, in Meridan, Mississippi, there was a riot when a Black policeman had a confrontation with a White citizen. A White official said "Negroes ought not be put in a position to discharge constabulary functions which it is proper for white men to exercise" (Wharton, 1947, pp. 167–168). In 1875, in Clinton, Mississippi, a shooting took place between Blacks and three Whites and approximately thirty Blacks were killed. Riots continued for 4 days after the killings, and Whites murdered another estimated 10 to 50 Black leaders (Wharton, 1947) (Figure 1.18).

According to Gosnell (1935), Black policemen felt that they were targets because they were Black and because the police department did not like Blacks. Problems of discrimination still existed in 1966 when Black policemen were still not voluntarily integrated and required a direct order from the head of the department to work White neighborhoods (National Center on Police and Community Relations, 1967).

The ebb and flow of discriminatory practices toward Black policemen would begin to change as they did for policewomen in the late 1960s. It would take significant lawsuits, civil rights actions, and new federal employment laws to begin the alterations. Noticeable transformations would not occur until 1971 when a report from the Commission on Civil Rights affirmed the need of more minority officers into law enforcement (Margolis, 1971).

FIGURE 1.17 Military police on guard duty at Fort Hamilton, New York, 1917.

FIGURE 1.18 Arlington County Division of Police, 1940.

CASE STUDY 1.1 A Black Policeman Discriminated Against in 1930

One Black policemen who tested for promotion was denied it due to his color. He shares his experience: "I passed all three examinations and was among the highest in my rating for patrol sergeant. After the examinations were graded the chief of police called me in and asked me to waive my right for promotion to patrol sergeant. He told me I didn't have to unless I wanted, but that if I did, he would look after me when it came time to appointments for detective sergeants. I hesitated. I didn't want to waive any right that was mine, but on the other hand, I knew that the chief would have the right to refuse me three times if I didn't waive the right. As he had promised to appoint me to detective sergeant, I thought better to get that job for sure than take a chance standing on my rights. So, I agreed to waive my right for promotion to patrol sergeant" (Gosnell, 1935, p. 263). The chief of police never did promote this Black policeman to detective sergeant.

Do you think Black officers still experience discrimination in promotional testing today? How? Conduct research to justify your answer.

What do you think would have happened if the Black officer in this case would not have waived his right for promotion?

Where Were Black Officers in the 1860s?

The acceptance of Black officers in the military and in federal law enforcement occurred regularly, unlike in local municipal police departments. According to Dulaneyu (2010), Blacks were first seen in the law enforcement arena as police officers, just before the civil war. Black policemen patrolled neighborhoods composed of Black citizens only. Black policemen could not arrest Whites, and in some cities these restrictions remained until the 1960s (Kuykendall & Burns, 1980) (Figure 1.19).

The first documented police department to hire a Black policeman was Washington, DC, in 1861 (Johnson, 1947). Then in 1872, the Chicago Police Department hired its first Black policeman (Sloan, 1965). The arrest of President U.S. Grant for driving too fast was big news. In 1873, he drove a team of horses at a dangerous pace, and a Black policeman arrested him (Landis, 1958). The arrest was unheard of at the time, and the officer did certainly face repercussions for his unorthodox behavior.

The following list illustrates cities that hired Black policemen before the 1890s:

- 1870: Galveston, Texas (Jefferson County Coordinating Council, 1953)
- 1871: Meridian, Mississippi (Wharton, 1947)
- 1873: Columbia and Charleston, South Carolina (Bennett, 1968)
- 1874: Philadelphia, Pennsylvania (Dubois, 1899)
- 1874: Jackson, Mississippi (Wharton, 1947; Bennett, 1968)
- 1875: Clinton, Mississippi (Wharton, 1947; Bennett, 1968)

Also, in 1874, Jackson, Mississippi hired its first Black chief of police (Wharton, 1947: Bennett, 1968). The hiring of a Black chief in a jurisdiction where the citizens were predominantly Black occurred to solve an issue. The city administrators hoped the new chief would be able to understand the neighborhood and the culture and restore order.

By 1890, in the United States, there were 74,629 watchmen, policemen, and firemen; of these, 2,019, were Black (Johnson, 1947) (Figure 1.20).

FIGURE 1.19 One of the first Black police officers, Colonel Charles Young.

FIGURE 1.20 1942 African Americans in military police.

Where Were Black Officers Post 1960?

The number of Black policemen in the United States from the 1890s–1920s remained steady. However, their duties did not change. Not unlike the policewoman, the Black policeman still fulfilled only a particular portion of a police officers required duties. From 1920-1930, Black policemen increased by 28%; however, this was only a less than 1% increase for the decade (Kuykendall & Burns, 1980). By 1952, 252 Black policemen were working in cities with a population over 5,000 (Guzman, 1952). In 1962, there was one Black policeman to every 1,361 Black residents, compared to one White policeman to every 443 White residents (*Ebony*, 1966).

It was not until 1948 that Memphis, Tennessee, employed a Black policeman. In Atlanta, Georgia, in 1948 Black policemen were still not allowed to wear uniforms during courtroom testimony and to and from work. They also were required to report to work at the Young Men's Christian Association in a Black neighborhood instead of the police department like White policemen. Because of this, community members in Georgia referred to Black policemen as YMCA cops (Thomas, 1967).

In 1966, officers were still segregated in their police cars by race. Black policemen only worked Black neighborhoods, and if a Black policeman happened to arrest a White suspect, a White policeman would be called to take over the arrest (U.S. Commission on Civil Rights, 1962, 1967) (Figure 1.21).

It is ridiculous to think that only 50 years ago discrimination was still occurring far and wide across America. Sadly, it was not the actions of a police administrator or even the IACP that changed the status quo. Instead, it would take significant steps to reverse the horrendous actions of law enforcement agencies across America.

FIGURE 1.21 1972 DC Metropolitan Police Department.

How Were Black Officers Finally Accepted Into the Policing World?

The race riots of the 1960s resulted in a demand for more Black police officers. Thanks in part to affirmative action and the Federal Civil Rights Act, minority police officers would be protected under federal law. Historically, a department could treat a minority officer however they wanted without fear of repercussion. Thanks to new laws these departments would be required to make the morally and ethically correct decision by hiring and promoting the person most qualified for the job. Although this new way of thinking would take a bit to catch on and many lawsuit judgments to be thoroughly understood, it was a start to a new beginning.

Where Were Latino and Asian American Officers?

The historical roots of minority officers are limited. Not unlike the roots of a redwood tree, they are hidden and often nonexistent. Policewomen and Black policemen have more historical documentation than any other minority.

One of the biggest obstacles for Latinos and Asian American officers has been the height requirement. Before the 1970s a policeman had to be at least 5'7" tall, and a policewoman had to be at least 5'2" tall. This screening device resulted in the disqualification of a disproportionately high number of persons from minority groups and therefore was under scrutiny by the Equal Employment Opportunity Commission (Talbert, 1974).

There is not much historical information before the 1970s for Latino officers. In 1972, the National Latino Peace Officers' Association formed. Asian American officers have even less historical information before the founding of the National Asian Peace Officers' Association, which began in 1980. These two associations marked the beginning of Latinos and Asian Americans representation in law enforcement (Figure 1.22).

According to Reaves, by 2013, there were 130,000 minority police officers in the United States. This was a 150% increase from 1987 when there were only 52,000. Minority officers made a 14–28% increase each year from 1987–2013 (2015).

FIGURE 1.22 Circa 1871–1907, U.S. Indian Police with a White man.

DECISION TIME BOX 1.1

One task required of police administrators is the continual review of department policies and procedures. Moreover, these must follow prescribed federal, state, and municipal laws. The rules must also be morally and ethically correct. Historically, police administrators have either turned their heads to discriminatory practices or openly condoned them.

If you were a police chief for a police department and heard about a sergeant who never gave the "good" patrol calls to a minority officer, what would you do? Outline the steps you would take to ensure that history did not repeat itself.

What About LGBTQ Officers?

We do not know a lot about the history of lesbian, gay, bisexual, transgender, and questioning (LGBTQ) people in policing. The main reason is that historically most LGBTQ officers did not openly admit to their sexual orientation (Belkin & McNichol, 2002), partly due to the fear of repercussions and harassment but also because their sexual orientation is no one's business.

Historically if an officer was LGBTQ it was grounds for dismissal; however, this type of discrimination is no longer officially condoned. Even though the law provides protection, the integration of LGBTQ officers into policing is at times stalled, even in the 21st century. Many departments enacted a zero-tolerance policy due to harassment and bullying of LGBTQs and homophobic actions (Belkin & McNichol, 2002). In 1982, a lawsuit was filed in Texas claiming denial of employment because of same-sex preferences (see *Childers v. Dallas Police Department*, 1982). Many other lawsuits have been filed against police departments for the same type of discrimination.

Times are changing, and the stone has been etched in Los Angeles, New York, and Seattle, where they are actively recruiting officers from the LGBTQ community (see *Childers v. Dallas Police Department*, 1982). Other police departments have created LGBTQ liaison units, staffed by officers who are openly LGBTQ, in an attempt to provide service to the community (Gay and Lesbian Liaison Unit, 2009).

LGBTQ officers have agonized over secrecy and acceptance. Changes have begun; however, there still exists homophobia and sexism. Just as policing needs policewomen and minority policemen, it also needs LGBTQ officers. Policing is about meeting the needs of the community served. As soon as people accept that we live in a society of unique individuals, the more attentive officers will be at meeting those needs.

CASE STUDY 1.2 Transgender Los Angeles Police Officer 2019

Deputy Austin Guastalli is one of a dozen officers who is transgender and works for the Los Angeles County Sheriff's Office. Guastalli transitioned from female to male while he was working for the sheriff's office. "I just want to do my job and live my life," said Guastalli, who is currently assigned to the Long Beach Courthouse, where he brings inmates to court. "I want to be like everyone else and be the best deputy sheriff I can be" (Gazzar, 2019).

According to Gazzar (2019), the sheriff's office has a policy that protects transgender officers. The Los Angeles County Sheriff's Office was the first in the nation to adopt a transgender policy. The policy was approved in July 2014, and it is a comprehensive policy for the protection and support of transgender officers. It addresses issues of transitioning on the job, privacy, and locker room/restroom use.

Deputy Guastalli's partner, Deputy Holt, met Guastalli after he had transitioned; therefore, he did not know that he was transgender. "Then I was proud to be his partner," Holt said. "He's opening doors for those who come after him" (Gazzar, 2019).

"I said I don't expect you to agree with me or share the same beliefs I have," Guastalli recalled. "I just want you to respect me and know that I'm a good partner regardless of your personal feelings about my transition" (Gazzar, 2019). Guastalli knows not everyone will be keen about his decisions, but the department policy has protected him from harassment for decisions he feels are his own. "I don't want to be separate. I just want to be equal and to just be seen that way" (Gazzar, 2019).

How Did Federal Employment Laws Change Law Enforcement Testing?

The reason the stereotypical historical policeman continued from the inception of law enforcement agencies in the United States in the mid-1800s until the mid-1960s was because nothing occurred to require anything different. Both private and public employers were free to create their benchmarks. If they did not like a candidate's sex or color, or for that matter any characteristic, the candidate was either denied or hired to provide only a specific set of duties. If the officer was ready for promotion, the candidate was told to wait and never revisit the subject. There was no *big brother* to look out for the minority officers. As with the Stanford Prison Experiment in 1971, and then the real abuse at *Abu Ghraib Prison* in 2003, if no rules are delineated and administration allows discriminatory behavior to occur or if administration disappears altogether, atrocious consequences will most certainly be on the menu.

Status quo was the way of it, and if anyone rocked the boat, they would find themselves harassed or even unemployed. However, some did decide to shake it up and did not accept what was the norm, and lawsuits were filed. These lawsuits pushed the pea-sized pebble off the cliff, and as it rolled down the mountain, it gained size and momentum that could do some damage. Moreover, the damage started as a small rock but would soon explode into something much more significant.

FACT BOX 1.1: STANFORD PRISON EXPERIMENT

In August 1971, Dr. Philip G. Zimbardo, in the Psychology Department, had an idea. He wanted to do a unique experiment. What Zimbardo did not plan for were the results. They were so outside the box and insane that they are still studied today. Zimbardo started by placing an ad in the paper looking for male college students to participate in a 2-week study on the psychology of power. The students chosen for the experiment were assigned as either a prisoner or as a prison guard. The Psychology Department hosted this experiment, and they used part of the building as a mock prison (Figure 1.23).

What marked this experiment was the fact that the student prison guards were given little to no training on what they were to do. Zimbardo intentionally wanted the prison guards to be depersonalized and authoritarian. He directed them to wear dark sunglasses when on duty. The prisoners were assigned to live in conditions that were humiliating and dehumanizing (Bornus, 2016).

The student prison guards immediately started to mistreat the student prisoners. They harassed them by forcing them to exercise, did not allow them to sleep, and humiliated them by forcing them to undress and stand naked in front of everyone. The experiment was supposed to go for 2 weeks; however, when Zimbardo saw the inhumane conditions and emotional breakdowns the prisoners were experiencing, he terminated it after 6 days (Bornus, 2016).

After an extensive review of the experiment, it was found that those in power, if given minimal to no instructions on how to do their job and are not supervised on their actions, disgustingly subject others to inhumane treatment. The lack of primary supervision was again replicated; however, it was not an experiment—it was in real life. In 2003, in the Iraq Abu Ghraib Prison, personnel of the U.S. Army and Central Intelligence Agency committed human rights violations to the prisoners (Figure 1.24). This is another example of what can occur when those in power are given little to no instructions and are not appropriately supervised.

The Stanford Prison Experiment and the abuse at Abu Ghraib Prison amplify what occurred to policewomen and minority officers during the mid-1860s until the 1970s. When those in power fail to train and supervise, and proper policies and procedures are not procured, bad things happen.

FIGURE 1.23 Stanford Prison Experiment.

FIGURE 1.24 Abu Ghraib Prison abuse.

What Did Title VII of the 1964 Civil Rights Act Do?

The 1960s and 70s saw not only ground-breaking lawsuits but also many new laws passed that changed the landscape of policing. The 1964 Civil Rights Act prohibited discrimination based on characteristics a person has when born. Protection under Title VII made it a federal violation for an employer to discriminate on the basis of **immutable characteristics** associated with race. If a person is discriminated against for their skin color, hair type or texture, or facial features, Title VII provided protections minorities never had before (Bell, 2004). The Equal Employment Opportunity Act (EEOA) established the Equal Employment Opportunity Commission (EEOC) to investigate any claims of discrimination.

FACT BOX 1.2: TITLE VII OF THE CIVIL RIGHTS ACT OF 1964

The following list illustrates how Title VII of the Civil Rights Act of 1964 prohibits discrimination on the basis of the following:

- Race and immutable characteristics associated with race: skin color, hair texture, certain facial features
- Color
- Religion
- Sex
- National origin
- Sexual orientation (Bell, 2004)

The 1964 Civil Rights Act extended its regulations to government agencies in 1972, which included law enforcement (Figure 1.25).

In 1969, President Richard M. Nixon also assisted in this effort by issuing Executive Order 11478, which prohibited discrimination in federal agencies because of race, color, sex, age, religion, national origin, or handicap. Another considerable step came in 1971 when the U.S. Civil Service Commission lifted the firearms exception, and women immediately saw the curtains lifted, and the official

FIGURE 1.25 1964 signing of the Civil Rights Act.

watermark of duty was complete. Several federal agencies, such as the U.S. Postal Inspection Service and the U.S. Secret Service began hiring women as special agents, and the Federal Bureau of Investigation joined in a year later (Archbold & Schultz, 2012).

Did the Hiring Frenzy of the New Millennium Change Law Enforcement Testing?

Near the end of the 1990s as the world prepared for the trials and tribulations of the new millennium, law enforcement agencies across the United States faced difficulties maintaining their workforce levels. Many things occurred to cause the perfect storm in which agencies lost a considerable percentage of their officers. The following list illustrates why agencies faced significant deficiencies in the workforce:

- Baby boomer retirements/attrition
- Military call-ups
- New generational expectations
- Organizational changes

What Happened to the Baby Boomer Generation?

The baby boomer generation included those people born after World War II, from 1946–1964. Since police officers are eligible for retirement after 25 years of service, by the millennium this generation of officers was ready to retire. The baby boomer generation was so large that the effects of the mass exodus was debilitating for some agencies. **Attrition**, which is the loss and replacement of officers, is something that agencies must always be ready for, with a plan of action. The millennium forced agencies to think outside the box in order to face the loss of so many officers at once. New York City Police Department faced the departure of baby boomer officers who had 20-plus years of service, and their answer was to offer bonuses and incentives to entice these officers to stay (Wilson et al., 2010).

What Happened to the Military Call-Ups?

As the United States becomes increasingly involved in wartime and peacekeeping efforts, military call-ups will always be a concern. This concern reared its head after the terrorist attacks of September 11, 2001. The hole caused in police staffing nationwide grew exponentially due to the number of police officers who dually served in the military. The numbers of officers who were called away to active duty swelled during the 12 months ending on June 20, 2003 (Hickman & Reaves, 2006). Departments not only lost valuable officers on the street but were also required to pay all benefits for those officers. This cost meant departments not only lost valuable personnel but an abundance of money.

The fallout from the turmoil created in the millennium was a peculiar conundrum. Agencies were slapped in the face with officer shortages and hastily countered with the following solutions:

- Expanded recruiting efforts
- Development of intense marketing plans
- Signing bonuses
- Relaxed qualifications

What Were the New Recruitment Efforts?

The expanded recruiting efforts included the creation of new *recruitment divisions* whose sole mission was to hire mountains of new police officers quickly. The turnstile was closing, and the agencies felt as though they had to run and jump high in order to get through. Officers assigned to these shiny new divisions enjoyed creating luring videos and appetizing brochures. There were also tasked with building attendance at career fairs across America, all in an effort to beat out the other agencies searching for the same new shiny police officers.

During this time the economy was healthy; therefore, the recruiting divisions were showered with healthy budgets to create reverent marketing plans. Sparkling billboards, polished television ads, and SWAG galore became each agency's benchmark, which it laid out in a plethora of confetti. Since every agency across the United States was facing the same shortages, innovative thinking on how to entice the most qualified candidates became the new game. In the end, money talks, and enticing signing bonuses were offered to ensure successful bewitching of the prize. Why wouldn't a candidate choose one department over another with a hefty $5,000 signing bonus?

Why Were the Qualifications Lowered?

The most frightening prospect of all occurred when somewhere, somehow, someone decided one action that would have long-lasting, devastating effects. When all the perks were exhausted, and the qualified candidates ebbed, the last resort was to open Pandora's box. Hindsight being 20/20, the thought never should have translated into action; however, it did. How were the agencies going to fill the open police officer positions? New recruiting divisions, check! Development of robust marketing plans, check! Offer signing bonuses, check! What was left? How could departments fill the gaps? The answer came too quickly and would haunt many agencies for years to come. The answer was the qualifications, they were lowered, and rotten apple officers slithered through the unguarded vault, in daylight, unhindered. The following list illustrates the three most common lowered qualifications:

- Background investigations
- Psychological evaluation
- Chief/sheriff review

Departments still conducted background investigations; however, issues that once would have terminated candidates were now overlooked. The psychological evaluation was also still conducted; however, during the chief/sheriff review, the recommendations made by the psychologist were not seen under the same microscope. Whereas agencies once would never have rolled the dice on a candidate who may or may not have specific personality issues, decisions were approved to do just that.

Did the Financial Crisis of 2007 Change Law Enforcement Testing?

In under a decade, agencies went from an insanity race of hiring, trying to replace the enormous numbers of openings, to the financial crisis of 2007. Police officers who had been hired in the years around the millennium were now trained and through probation. Many had just passed their fifth anniversary and were beginning to feel comfortable in their positions. When the crisis first hit, agencies responded by fighting to save every police officer position; after all, they had been won after what felt like a grudge match.

Those officers, safe in their positions, with over 10 years in the system, took **furloughs** by taking time off without pay and donating benefits. Emergency union meetings were held and the force rallied, all in hopes of saving every last officer's job. The magic ink that was written on the wall soon began to develop, and it was apparent that more extreme measures would have to be taken.

In Chicago, hundreds of jobs went unfilled, and officers who once rode as partners were now directed to ride in patrol vehicles alone (Associated Press, 2009). Chicago also instituted a "20-and-out" rule, which led to a deficit of officers on the department (Spielman, 2009). In North Las Vegas an entire detention center closed, forcing hundreds to seek employment elsewhere. Officers who lost their jobs also lost their homes, and many had to leave the state and move back in with their parents. Just 7 years earlier, these same agencies were scrambling, with huge budgets, pulling out all the stops to hire as many officers as they could.

What Was Good About the Financial Crisis?

The financial crisis resulted in the pulling back of the recruiting divisions. This crisis included all their new mandates since officers were now being laid off and there were no new hires. For upward of 5 years many departments froze the hiring of new police officers. The most positive consequence was once the economy started to recover so too did the qualifications that had been lowered. Agencies had time to see the repercussions of the relaxed qualifications through citizen complaints, excessive use of force incidents, and indecent behavior. Internal affairs stepped in and investigated these issues, and the rotten apple officers were fired; however, the damage done could not be unwound.

Why Can't Candidates Pass the Testing Process?

When the baby boomers retired, their numbers were never entirely replaced, since all subsequent generations could not fill the enormous losses. Compounding the matter was the fact that the new generation of candidates could not meet the minimum required qualifications. Snags with criminal records, prior drug use, relaxed physical fitness, and financial history issues were all common threads with this new generation (Raymond et al., 2005).

Drug use: In 2008, 50% of all high school seniors reported having smoked marijuana, and one in four reported using an illicit drug other than marijuana (Johnston et al., 2008).

Physical fitness: The obesity rate doubled in the past 3 decades for adolescents 12–19 years of age (Sturm et al., 2007).

Financial history: In 2001, credit card debt among Americans 18–24 years of age rose 104%. The average young American spends 30% of their annual income on debt subsidence (Draut & Silva, 2004).

Para-military nature of work: Policing is highly militaristic in that it functions within specific rigid parameters. The emphasis is on a chain-of-command hierarchy and is formal at its core. Many departments are strict on officer appearance by not allowing men to have long hair or beards, or requiring women to wear long hair up, and the tattoo policies remain stern. Scheduling is also a nightmare since the world of policing never slows or stops, it is a 24/7 institution where officers are married to their work. Changing generational preferences concerning off-duty life has also affected recruiting (Brand, 1999).

Increased competition was a factor when agencies were seeking to fill their workforce from a genus of the population who could not meet specific qualifications and characteristics. This unique pool was further delineated since there existed enormous competition looking for the same type of candidate. From the military to federal, state, county, and municipal agencies, along with the private sector, candidates have a plethora of options. With so many options, agencies found themselves fighting for the same top candidates.

After the September 2001 terrorist attacks against the United States, the expansion of private security positions stimulated a high demand (DeRugy, 2006; Kondrasuk, 2004). The military has also magnified enlistments, specifically among higher-educated recruits (Kane, 2005). Therefore, there is now a smaller pool of qualified candidates for the larger pool of careers.

Conclusions

Over the last 60 years, law enforcement has unmistakably had a makeover. The policeman badge was redesigned to read "police officer," and minority officers were no longer openly discriminated against; instead, they were actively recruited. Where once a male officer had to be at least 5'7" tall, today an agency would find itself up a creek without a paddle and violating a federal employment law with such a requirement.

Just because change has occurred does not mean the world of policing is all dandy and proper. Policewomen and minority officers are still underrepresented, and many in the policing world still believe women cannot do the job of a police officer. Therefore, change must be continual and those in prominent positions must never let their guard down to ensure equality.

Police work is multifaceted. No one officer can respond to the vast array of calls for service and handle them flawlessly. Many agencies have a multitude of different divisions, from motors to the mounted unit, SWAT, and narcotics. These divisions and many others require passion from its members in order to succeed, and having differences among the ranks is a good thing to ensure the divisions are filled with the best officers.

Law enforcement candidate recruiting and testing has also undergone its fair share of transformations. Mistakes have been made along the way; however, when looking at the importance of the job of a police officer, the testing process cannot be taken lightly. Every possible precaution must be taken to ensure that when the oath is taken, and the badge is pinned on, the officer chosen will uphold the great trust that is given to them.

SUMMARY OF CHAPTER 1

1. The law enforcement testing process looks radically different today than it did in the past.

2. Policewomen and minority officers faced many forms of discrimination, which kept them from the complete job of an officer. The federal employment laws of the 1960s nursed the broken landscape; however, the advancements since have not fixed the issues of equality in policing.

3. The hiring frenzy of the new millennium showed the rips in the fabric of the testing process; however, did the resolutions fix the issues or provide a Band-aid that is now failing?

DISCUSSION QUESTIONS

1. What are the significant differences between an officer from the late 19th century to officers in the 21st century?

2. Are policewomen accepted in the policing world today? Why?

3. Should there be more female police chiefs? Why?

4. Since the police hiring frenzy of the new millennium, do you think law enforcement agencies responded too radically by making the testing process too restrictive? If yes, what parts are too restrictive? If no, what parts do you agree are correctly given?

INTERNET EXERCISES

1. Using your preferred search engine, search "women police officers 1900," and enter the parameter for "images." What are the policewomen wearing? Are they wearing skirts? If there is more than one policewoman in the image, is the second (or third, or fourth) officer a male or female? What does this mean? In the search parameters, change 1900 to 1950

and answer the same questions. In the search parameters, change "women" to "Black" and answer the same questions.

2. Look up the following associations:

- International Association of Black Officers
- International Association of Latino Officers
- International Association of Women Officers

What do these associations have in common? How are they different? What do these associations offer their members?

See Active Learning for the Following:

- Practice quizzes
- eFlashcards
- Video links
- Cognella journal articles
- Answers to "Decision Time"
- News clips

References

Archbold, C. A., & Schulz, D. M. (2012). Research on women in policing: A look at the past, present, and future. *Sociology Compass, 6*(9), 694–706. https://doi.org/10.1111/j.1751-9020.2012.00501.x

Associated Press. (2009, June 24). Even cops losing their jobs in recession. NBC News. http://www.nbcnews.com/id/31530751/ns/us_news-life/t/even-cops-losing-their-jobs-recession/

Belkin, A., & McNichol, J. (2002). Pink and blue: Outcomes associated with the integration of open gay and lesbian personnel in the San Diego police department. *Police Quarterly, 2*(1), 63–95.

Bell, D. (2004). *Race, racism and American law* (6th ed.). Aspen.

Bennett, L. (1968). *Black Power U.S.A.: The human side of reconstruction, 1867–1877.* Penguin.

Bornus, D., (2016, May). The Stanford Prison Experiment, the fundamentals of a secure residential environment. *Corrections Today, 78*(3), 48–51.

Brand, D., (1999, August). The future of law enforcement recruiting: The impact of Generation X. *Police Chief, 8,* 53–63.

Childers v. Dallas Police Department, 671 F. 2d 1380.

DeRugy, V. (2006, December 14). Facts and figures about homeland security spending. American Enterprise Institute. http://www.aei.org/docLib/20061214_FactsandFigures.pdf

Draut, T., & Silva, J. (2004). *Generation broke: The growth of debt among young Americans.* Demos. http://archive.demos.org/pubs/Generation_Broke.pdg

DuBois, W. E. B. (1899). *The Philadelphia Negro.* University of Pennsylvania Press.

Dulaneyu, M. (2010). Black police in America. In R.G. Dunham & G. P. Alpert (Eds.), *Critical issues in policing*. Waveland Press.

Ebony. (Ed). (1966). *The Negro handbook*. Johnson Publishing.

Gazzar, B. (2019, February 2). *Transgender LA LEO is among many living their truth on force*. PoliceOne. https://www.policeone.com/police-heroes/articles/482837006-Transgender-LA-LEO-is-among-many-living-their-truth-on-force/

Gay and Lesbian Liaison Unit. (2009). *About the gay and lesbian liaison unit*. http://www.gllu.or/resources/index.htm#pubs

Gosnell, H. F. (1935). *Negro politicians: The rise of Negro politics in Chicago*. University of Chicago Press.

Guzman, J. P. (Ed.) (1952). *The Negro yearbook: A review of events affecting Negro life* (11th ed.). William H. Wise and Company.

Hale, D. C. (1992). Women in policing. In G. W. Cordner & D. C. Hale (Eds.), *What works in policing? Operations and administration examined* (125–141). Routledge.

Hickman, M, J., & Reaves, B. A. (2006). *Local Police Departments, 2003*. Bureau of Justice Statistics (NCJ 210118). http://bjs.ojp.usdoj.gov/index.cfm?ty=pbdetail&iid=1045

Hutzel, E. (1933). *The policewomen's handbook*. Columbia University Press.

Jefferson County Coordinating Council. (1953). *A study of Negro police*. Coordinating Council.

Johnson, C. S. (1947). *Into the mainstream: A survey of best practices in race relations in the South*. University of North Carolina Press.

Johnston, L. D., O'Malley, P. M., Bachman, J. G., & Schulenberg, J. E. (2008, December 11). *Various stimulant drugs show continuing gradual declines among teens in 2008, most illicit drugs hold steady*. University of Michigan News Service. http://monitoringthefuture.org/data/08data.html#2008data-drugs

Jones, J., & Hornig, C. (2017, September 12). *Alice Stebbins Wells: Meet the first woman police officer with arrest powers in the U.S.* Women You Should Know. https://womenyoushouldknow.net/alice-stebbins-wells-meet-first-woman-police-officer-arrest-powers-u-s/

Kane, T. (2005, November 3). *The demographics of military enlistment after 9/11*. Heritage Foundation. http://www.heritage.org/Research/Reports/2005/11/The-Demographics-of-Military-Enlistment-After-9-11

Kondrasuk, J. N. (2004). The effects of 9/11 and terrorism on human resource management: Recovery, reconsideration, and renewal. *Employee Responsibilities and Rights Journal, 16*(1), 25–35.

Kuykendall, J. L., & Bums, D. E. (1980). The Black police officer: An historical perspective. *Journal of Contemporary Criminal Justice, 1*(4), 4–12. https://doi.org/10.1177/104398628000100403

Landis, K. M. (1958). *Segregation in Washington*. National Committee on Segregation in the Nation's Capital.

Langton, L. (2010). *Women in law enforcement 1987–2008*. Bureau of Justice Statistics Crime Data Brief (NCJ 230521), 1–4. https://www.google.com/url?q=https://www.bjs.gov/content/pub/pdf/wle8708.pdf&sa=U&ved=0ahUKEwierOmB-ITgAhWqiVQKHezhCAYQFggFMAA&client=internal-uds-cse&cx=015849196504226064512:8qeg8tt4g1g&usg=AOvVaw2rq68afrprdebt4MQvWvTY

Margolis, R. (1971). *Who will wear the badge? A study of minority recruitment efforts in protective services*. Government Printing Office.

Martin, S. E., & Jurik, N. C. 1996. *Doing justice, doing gender: Women in law and criminal justice occupations*. Sage.

More, H. W. (1998). *Special topics in policing*. Anderson.

National Center on Police and Community Relations. (1967). *A national survey of police and community relations, Field Survey V, report of the President's Commission on Law Enforcement and Administration of Justice*, Government Printing Office.

O'Connor, B. R. (2015, January 9). Building trust and legitimacy. *NAWLEE Testimony, 21st*, 1–5.

President's Commission on Civil Disorders. (1968). *Report of the Advisory Commission on Civil Disorders*. Bantam Books.

President's Commission on Law Enforcement and Administration of Justice. (1967). *Task force report: The police*. Government Printing Office.

Reaves, B. (2015). *Local police departments. 2013: Personnel, policies, and practices*. Bureau of Justice Statistics, Law Enforcement Management and Administrative Statistics (LEMAS) Survey.

Schulz, D. M. (1995). *From social worker to crimefighter: Women in United States municipal policing*. Praeger.

Sloan, I. J. (1965). *The American Negro: A chronology and fact book*. Southern Regional Council.

Spielman, F. (2009, July 23). Early retirement for cops helps budget, not force. *Chicago Sun-Times*. http://www.suntimes.com/news/cityhall/1681991,chicago-cops-shortage-retirement-072309.article

Sturm, R., Ringel, J. S., Lakdawall, D. N., Bhattacharya, J., Goldman, D. P., Hurd, M., Joyce, G. F., Panis, C., & Andreyeva, T. (2007). *Obesity and disability: The shape of things to come*. RAND Corporation. http://www.rand.org/pubs/research_briefs/RB9043-1/

Talbert, T. L. (1974). A study of the police officer height requirement. *Public Personnel Management, 3*(2), 103–110. https://doi.org/10.1177/009102607400300203

Thomas, D. (1967, October 24). The Color Line-Why. *Denver Post Bonus*, 4–5.

U.S. Commission on Civil Rights. (1962). *Memphis, Tennessee, hearings, June, 1962*. Government Printing Office.

U.S. Commission on Civil Rights. (1967). *Employment, administration of justice and health services in Memphis Shelby, County, Tennessee*. State Advisory Committee.

Walker, S. (1977). *A critical history of police reform*. Lexington Books.

Wharton, V. L. (1947). *The Negro in Mississippi: 1865–1890*. University of North Carolina Press.

Wilson, J. M., Dalton, E., Scheer, C., & Grammich, C. A. (2010). *Police recruitment and retention for the new millennium: The state of knowledge*.

Image Credits

Fig. 1.9: Source: https://www.loc.gov/item/96514629/.

Fig. 1.10: Source: https://commons.wikimedia.org/wiki/File:Drills_-_Police_-_Special_police_drill_-_will_guard_aqueduct_-_NARA_-_26434598.jpg.

Fig. 1.11: Source: https://commons.wikimedia.org/wiki/File:%22Are_you_a_girl_with_a_star-spangled_heart%22_-_NARA_-_513876.jpg.

Fig. 1.12: Source: Lynn Langton, "Women in Law Enforcement, 1987–2008," Bureau of Justice Statistics Crime Data Brief, p. 2, 2010.

Fig. 1.13: Source: Lynn Langton, "Women in Law Enforcement, 1987–2008," Bureau of Justice Statistics Crime Data Brief, p. 2, 2010.

Fig. 1.14: Source: https://commons.wikimedia.org/wiki/File:Sergeant_Laurie_Rich,_white_female,_and_Sherrine_Freeman,_minority_female._(White_House_Police_Officers)_-_NARA_-_558657.tif.

Fig. 1.15: Source: North Las Vegas Police Department.

Fig. 1.16: Source: https://commons.wikimedia.org/wiki/File:Granada_Relocation_Center,_Amache,_Colorado._Volunteer_civilian_police,_such_as_this_patrolman,_gua_._._._-_NARA_-_539098.tif.

Fig. 1.17: Source: https://commons.wikimedia.org/wiki/File:Military_Administration_-_Military_Police_-_PHOTO_SHOWS_POLICE_ON_GUARD_duty_at_Fort_Hamilton,_New_York._1917_-_NARA_-_45500576.jpg.

Fig. 1.18: Source: https://commons.wikimedia.org/wiki/File:Arlington_County_Division_of_Police,_1940.png.

Fig. 1.19: Source: https://commons.wikimedia.org/wiki/File:COL._CHARLES_YOUNG_-_WEST_POINT_GRADUATE,_MILITARY_ATTACHE_TO_HAITI,_LIBERIA_-_NARA_-_535679.jpg.

Fig. 1.20: Source: https://commons.wikimedia.org/wiki/File:African-americans-wwii-002.jpg.

Fig. 1.21: Source: https://commons.wikimedia.org/wiki/File:President_Nixon_meeting_District_of_Columbia_Metropolitan_Police_Department_officers_to_congratulate_them_on_their_help..._-_NARA_-_194765.tiff.

Fig. 1.22: Source: https://commons.wikimedia.org/wiki/File:Members_of_U.S._Indian_Police,_with_white_man_-_NARA_-_523707.tif.

Fig. 1.23: Copyright © 2014 by Eric E. Castro, (CC BY 2.0) at https://commons.wikimedia.org/wiki/File:Plaque_Dedicated_to_the_Location_of_the_Stanford_Prison_Experiment.jpg.

Fig. 1.24: Source: https://commons.wikimedia.org/wiki/File:Abu_Ghraib_prison_abuse.jpg.

Fig. 1.25: Source: https://commons.wikimedia.org/wiki/File:Lyndon_Johnson_signing_Civil_Rights_Act,_July_2,_1964.jpg.

Careers in Law Enforcement

Is a Career in Law Enforcement for ME?

2

"The best way to predict the future is to create it."

—Abraham Lincoln

KEY TERMS

Agent: A commissioned or sworn employee of the federal government.

Cadet or explorer: An important stepping block as a volunteer with a law enforcement agency, where the focus is on education.

Civilian or noncommissioned/non-sworn employee: An employee at a law enforcement agency who does not have state-given arresting powers.

Commissioned or sworn: This terminology is utilized in the policing world to define a certified police officer with the powers of arrest.

Community service officers: A civilian/noncommissioned/non-sworn employees of a law enforcement agency.

Community supervision: Because of the Sentencing Reform Act of 1984, this term was created and utilized in the parole/probation reporting field, in addition to parole and probation.

Conservation law enforcement officer: A newly coined term for which identifies game wardens in the 21st century.

Deputy: A commissioned or sworn employee of a county.

Federal game warden: Commissioned/sworn law enforcement officer sworn to protect and service through conservation and protection while working with the U.S. Fish and Wildlife Service.

Gaming control agent/officer: A commissioned or sworn employee of a state gaming board.

Job announcement: A list posted by the hiring agency noting the required duties, responsibilities, educational requirements, and anything else the agency is requiring for the specified position.

Local jail population: A correctional or detention facility operated by a sheriff's office or police department, generally incarcerating individuals for less than 1 year before sentencing for an alleged crime.

Military prison population: Service personnel confined in a facility operated under the jurisdiction of U.S. military correctional authorities.

Park police officer: A civilian/noncommissioned/non-sworn employee who patrols identified parks for park violations.

Parole: A period when a person is released from prison and supervised per preset conditions.

Parolee: A person who is either under the conditions of parole or probation.

Police officer: A person who is a commissioned or sworn employee of a city police department.

Portfolio: Contains useful documents a candidate has collected to enhance a resume and includes items such as recommendation letters, thank-you letters, transcripts, certificates, and a sample research paper.

Prison population: Individuals who sentenced to a long-term confinement facility operated by a state or federal government.

Probation: Court-ordered supervision where the person is released and allowed into the community under preset conditions.

Recidivism: The tendency for a criminal to re-offend.

Reserve police officer: The definition varies depending on the law enforcement agency. Some agencies define a reserve officer as a retired police officer, who at some point in their career was a commissioned/sworn employee of a police department. This reserve officer is now employed either as a volunteer or part-time paid employee to assist with calls for service. The second type of reserve police officer is generally between 18–21 years of age and is looking to enter the world of policing. This position offers the reserve officer a foot in the door to learning the duties and responsibilities of a police officer while proving one's dedication and passion for the career.

School police officer: A commissioned/sworn law enforcement officer under the direction of a school district.

School resource officer (SRO): A commissioned/sworn law enforcement officer whose primary responsibility is the safety of the students as well as various crime prevention–related activities.

Social services: Careers in public service, generally provided by the government, nonprofit organizations, or other types of for-profit/private businesses. The community of social services are entities that ensure citizens are housed, fed, job trained, and have strong role models, thereby creating a healthy community.

State game warden: Commissioned/sworn law enforcement officers sworn to protect and service through conservation and protection while working as a state police officer and in conjunction with the state fish and wildlife division.

Strengths: Police officers must have specific strengths such as honesty, integrity, trustworthiness, responsibility, and physically and mentally fit.

Trooper: A person who is a commissioned or sworn employee of the state.

Weaknesses: Police officers must not have specific weaknesses such as issues with anger, a negative driving record, and a harmful level of dominance.

CHAPTER LEARNING OBJECTIVES

After reading the chapter, you should have a good understanding of the following:

- The difference between a commissioned/sworn position and a noncommissioned/non-sworn position at a law enforcement agency

- How to distinguish between law enforcement designators such as a police officer, a trooper, or a deputy
- Why jurisdiction is so important
- The difference between a jail and a prison
- How to recognize certain positive personality traits you have and certain personality traits that may cause concern for the future police officer candidate
- The differences between parole and probation
- The differences between a reserve officer and a cadet/explorer
- Some commissioned/sworn officer positions in law enforcement
- A portfolio and why is it so important
- Critical components needed before filling out an application
- How a candidate can get a certificate through NIMS for an online class and why is this an essential process for a future police candidate

I Think I Want to Be a Police Officer, or Do I?

Have you dreamt of being a police officer for as long as you can remember? When you were young and asked the inevitable question, "What do I want to be when I grow up?" did you solidly know the answer? Alternatively, were you a late bloomer? Did you graduate from high school, or earn your GED, or begin your college career or even begin working a job still not knowing the answer to such a question? No matter the answer, if the decision to go into the world of law enforcement (and make no mistake, it is a world!) is something that you are thinking about doing or have already decided to do, then welcome to the universe of law enforcement, where the blue line matters!

If you still are wondering, "Is this career right for me?" You are not alone. You should continue to ask questions. You have concerns. This is not a career for a superhero, because superheroes in real life die. Bullets do hit their target and can kill, and humans cannot fly, nor do they have superpowers to see future actions. Therefore, the way to stay alive in a career where one literally can be killed just because one is a cop is to train and never take on the persona of superiority of invincibility. Humans are not bulletproof. In order to stay alive and make it home after each shift, training is the name of the game. Safety is a top concern and should never leave the uniformed officer. There are evil people in the world intent on continuing to break the law and corrupt those around them. Are you ready to face such evilness? Are you ready to face your fears?

Moreover, one of the most challenging questions to answer is "Can you take a life to save a life?" Such a question is never easy to answer; however, these questions and more must be acknowledged. Before you go any further, answer them. If your answer is no, then you should look for a different career. This may sound harsh and cruel; however, it is indeed a kindness. Policing is not for everyone.

Are you ready to take a life? This question sounds awful, doesn't it? How could anyone ask such a question? Why not just ignore that particular question instead of throwing a coin into a babbling brook hoping it never comes to fruition? However, it could happen. You could find yourself in a position to have to make the ultimate decision, the ultimate sacrifice. How will you respond? Can you take a life? If you had to choose between saving the life of an innocent person or yourself, could you choose correctly?

Have you thought about the possibility of responding to a call where the victim was an 8-month old baby boy and the suspect was the uncle who had just raped his nephew? Would you be able to interview the suspect? Could you control your emotions? Do you believe a person is innocent until found guilty, and do you realize that will take place in a court of law, not out in the field? Are you able to remain neutral or be Switzerland regarding criminals that commit crimes? Alternatively, do you have certain strong religious or political beliefs? Are you able to close those personal feelings in a closet and not visit them while you are an officer? You have to be ready to see all the different types of human beings in many diverse situations. You will not agree with everyone and the time to voice your opinion on matters close to your heart will have no place in this field. You must be unbiased and open to everyone and everything. Are you ready to embrace this new way of life?

There are also many positives in the law enforcement world. Many university students who want a career in law enforcement chose to major or minor in psychology or communications. The reason for this is because police officers find themselves in situations where they must understand how the human mind works and how to best communicate with the citizens they serve. The more knowledge the officer has about the varied situations they will be placed in, the more they give to the field. The best officers are often the best communicators. When you add caring with confident communication skills, the results from such clear communication can be tantamount to a miracle.

Those who enter the world of law enforcement always start with a passion. It is generally a passion to help or save. Most understand that one person cannot solve everything; however, one person can make a difference. Those interested in policing want to make a difference. It is a service-oriented career. Whether an officer is assisting as a mediator between two neighbors who are arguing over loud music, helping first graders understand stranger danger, or responding to a robbery at a bank where the suspect has just shot and killed five people, future officers want to make a difference, no matter how small.

Do I Know Myself?

Some personal questions are easy to answer. What is your favorite color? What is your favorite movie or television show? How about your dream vehicle? These questions should cause enthusiasm, not stress. However, there are more profound more intrusive questions that can elicit distress. Make no mistake, the hiring process for police officers is not intended to cause torment and pain, yet inevitably questions are asked that do provoke the inner beast. Because of this, the future police officer candidate must ensure the answers to such uncomfortable questions are known, not hidden. The goal should be to open the book of yourself through the hiring process.

If you have asked and answered those awkward questions about yourself both about past behavior and future needs and desires, then you are ahead of the game. If you have not done so, then you should be prepared to spend some time doing just that. This chapter is designed to assist you through this process. Everyone can learn something new about themselves, and the law enforcement testing process should not be the avenue to which these items are tackled.

What you do *not* know about yourself can hurt you too. The job of a police officer is multidimensional. Just because you watch a cop television show or a law-related movie does not mean you know what the actual real-life job entails. All too often, candidates rely on what they see in the make-believe world to make serious future life decisions about themselves in real life. This can be a decision that can bite you in the future, especially during the law enforcement testing process. Instead of wasting your time and the time of a law enforcement agency during the months of testing, and being dumbfounded by the results, take the time to be self-aware today.

What Self-Assessment Tools Are Available?

The criminal justice career field is a very satisfying and enjoyable profession. Students who chose to major or minor in this field ponder which criminal justice vocation they want to pursue. As the professor asks which students are interested in law enforcement, in being an attorney, a social worker, parole/probation officer, in doing rehabilitation work, in being a game warden, a crime scene investigator, a forensic investigator, in having interest in the psychological aspects of the criminal mind or corrections, the inspiration is palpable as the thoughts of future careers fly through the air. Many students have no idea where they will land once they reach the elusive bachelor's degree. The options surrounding the field of criminal justice are endless. One cannot turn on a television without seeing a news story, a television show, movie, or even read a book without catching sight of some part of the criminal justice world. At some point, the students who do enter the criminal justice field will learn what fantasy is and what is not. However, this shock should come slowly instead of being thrown in one's face, and this is where self-assessment tools can help. By utilizing the following self-assessment tools, a picture will begin to emerge of the type of person the law enforcement world requires. While the world of policing is varied and requires a wide range of personality types, it does not fit well with everyone and is not a one-size-fits-all type of career. Therefore, by taking the time to complete the following self-assessments, one can learn where they fit in their future career plans.

SELF-ASSESSMENT 2.1: STRENGTHS AND WEAKNESSES

The following self-assessment is the beginning of self-awareness. This assessment can also be dually utilized during the oral board interview portion of the testing process. The questions of your greatest strengths and weaknesses are ubiquitous questions asked during an oral board interview. Therefore, when you are completing this first self-assessment, remember to save it and utilize it as a study guide for your oral board interview.

Instructions: On a piece of paper or via your computer or tablet in a writing program, answer the following questions:

1. List five of your strengths.
2. For each of the five strengths listed, explain in detail (at least 200 words for each strength) why it is a strength for you.
3. List five of your weaknesses.
4. For each of the five weaknesses listed, explain in detail (at least 200 words for each weakness) why it is a weakness for you.

Answer key:
STRENGTHS: There are no right answers to this self-assessment. This is purely for you to understand yourself better. Some keywords that might indicate you are on the path to becoming a

police officer include (but are not limited to) the following:

- Abstractedness
- Accountable
- Accepts criticism
- Adaptable
- Apprehension
- Approachable
- Attention to detail
- Communication skills (communicate/communicator)
- Community oriented
- Compassion (compassionate/empathy)
- Compromise (ability to)
- Conscientiousness
- Confident
- Dependable
- Emotional stability
- Ethical
- Good health
- Good level of dominance
- Honest (honesty)
- Humility
- Initiative
- Integrity
- Interpersonal skills
- Job success
- Liveliness
- Marital stability
- Mentally fit
- Negotiation
- Openness to change
- Patient
- Perceptive
- Perfectionism
- Physically fit
- Private

- Problem solver
- Reasoning
- Responsible
- Rule consciousness
- Self-reliant
- Sensitivity
- Service oriented (volunteer work)
- Socially bold
- Strong mental attitude
- Tension (to a certain level)
- Training mind-set
- Trustworthiness
- Vigilance
- Warmth
- Written communication skills

WEAKNESSES: There are no right answers to this self-assessment. This is purely for you to understand yourself better. Some keywords that might indicate you might have some obstacles to becoming a police officer include (but are not limited to) the following:

- Arrest record
- Specific types of mental/psychological disorders
- Cynical work attitude
- Issues with anger
- Negative attitude in a variety of situations or on a variety of issues
- Negative driving record
- Negative level of dominance
- Negative personality trait
- No work history
- Previous job firings
- Prior divorce
- Psychopathology (certain ones)
- Tension (over a certain level)

SELF-ASSESSMENT 2.2: CATTELL'S 16 PRIMARY FACTORS

One essential part of the law enforcement testing process is the psychological evaluation. Depending on the psychologist conducting the evaluation, a variety of tests can be utilized. The MMPI-2-RF Police Candidate Interpretive Report is the most commonly utilized personality evaluation. Some psychologists will also utilize Cattell's 16PF questionnaire. "The Sixteen Personality Factor Questionnaire (16PF) is a comprehensive measure of normal-range personality found to be effective in a variety of settings where an in-depth assessment of the who person is needed" (Cattell & Mead, 2008, p. 135). The 16PF questionnaire has been utilized to predict future behavior of candidates who are interested in a career in law enforcement (Cattell & Mead, 2008).

The following self-assessment of the 16PF is a tool to assist you in understanding your personality and how it relates to that of a police officer 16PF assessment.

Instructions: On a piece of paper or on your computer/tablet in a writing program or directly in Table 2.1, read the primary (low and high) and decide which you are. Next, fill in your responses for each of the 16 primary factors, whether your personality is low or high, and denote any of your specific personality traits listed.

TABLE 2.1   Questions: 16PF

Primary Factor	Low	High	You Are (Low or high and list specific characteristics):	Officers Are Seen Showing
Warmth	Reserved, impersonal, distant, cool, reserved, impersonal, detached, formal, aloof	Warm, outgoing, attentive to others, kind, easygoing, participates, likes people		Find answers at the end of the chapter
Reasoning	Concrete thinking, lower general mental capacity, less intelligent, unable to handle abstract problems	Abstract thinking, more intelligent, bright, higher general mental capacity, fast learner		Find answers at the end of the chapter
Emotional stability	Reactive, emotionally changeable, affected by feelings, emotionally less stable, easily upset	Emotionally stable, adaptive, mature, faces reality, calm		Find answers at the end of the chapter
Dominance	Deferential, cooperative, avoids conflict, submissive, humble, obedient, easily led, docile, accommodating	Dominant, forceful, assertive, aggressive, competitive, stubborn, bossy		Find answers at the end of the chapter
Liveliness	Serious, restrained, prudent, taciturn, introspective, silent	Lively, animated, spontaneous, enthusiastic, happy-go-lucky, cheerful, expressive, impulsive		Find answers at the end of the chapter
Rule consciousness	Expedient, nonconforming, disregards rules, self-indulgent	Rule conscious, dutiful, conscientious, conforming, moralistic, staid, rule bound		Find answers at the end of the chapter

Primary Factor	Low	High	You Are (Low or high and list specific characteristics):	Officers Are Seen Showing
Social boldness	Shy, threat sensitive, timid, hesitant, intimidated	Socially bold, venturesome, thick-skinned, uninhibited, can take stress		Find answers at the end of the chapter
Sensitivity	Utilitarian, objective, unsentimental, tough minded, self-reliant, no nonsense, rough	Sensitive, aesthetic, sentimental, tender minded, intuitive, refined		Find answers at the end of the chapter
Vigilance	Trusting, unsuspecting, accepting, unconditional, easy	Vigilant, suspicious, skeptical, wary, distrustful, oppositional		Find answers at the end of the chapter
Abstractedness	Grounded, practical, prosaic, solution oriented, steady, conventional	Abstracted, imaginative, absent minded, impractical, absorbed in ideas		Find answers at the end of the chapter
Private	Forthright, genuine, artless, open, guileless, naïve, unpretentious, involved	Private, discreet, non-disclosing, shrewd, polished, worldly, astute, diplomatic		Find answers at the end of the chapter
Apprehension	Self-assured, unworried, complacent, secure, free of guilt, confident, self-satisfied	Apprehensive, self-doubting, worried, guilt prone, insecure, worrying, self-blaming		Find answers at the end of the chapter
Openness to change	Traditional, attached to familiar, conservative, respects traditional ideas	Open to change, experimenting, liberal, analytical, critical, free thinking, flexibility		Find answers at the end of the chapter
Self-reliance	Group oriented, affiliative, a joiner and follower, dependent	Self-reliant, solitary, resourceful, individualistic, self-sufficient		Find answers at the end of the chapter
Perfectionism	Tolerates disorder, unexacting, flexible, undisciplined, lax, self-conflictive, impulsive, careless of social rules, uncontrolled	Perfectionist, organized, compulsive, self-disciplined, socially precise, exacting will power, control, self-sentimental		Find answers at the end of the chapter
Tension	Relaxed, placid, tranquil, torpid, patient, composed, low drive	Tense, high energy, impatient, driven, frustrated, overwrought, high drive, time driven		Find answers at the end of the chapter

Source: Changing Minds (n.d.).

Cattell's 16PF are very telling, especially when you have completed the table and you compare your specific personality traits with those of police officers. This alone is not telling of whether you will fit the mold of a police officer; it is just a guide to give you an idea. After completing this self-assessment, you should begin to have tools to give you an understanding of your personality.

According to Cattell and Mead (2008), when a police officer undergoes stress their response tends to be that of calmness and resilience. Officers also are responsible, self-disciplined, task focused, rule conscious, perfectionistic, practical, tough, pragmatic, tough minded, unsentimental, practical, bold, fearless, dominant (slightly), and traditional. In 2007, Herb Eber's sample of 30,700 officers showed that police officers showed these traits (Cattell & Mead, 2008).

SELF-ASSESSMENT 2.3: WHAT PERSONALITY TYPE DO I HAVE?

What type of personality trait do you have? Depending on our personality, our future behaviors can be, to a point, predicted. This is important in law enforcement, because if a person tends to overreact and become violent, then this person should not be a police officer. During the law enforcement testing process, future behaviors such as this are predicted. A violent person who is hired as a police officer might utilize excessive force on a suspect if they become too agitated. Therefore, this type of candidate would be passed over because they are a ticking time bomb. The testing agency may not want to roll the dice and hope that this person will do the right thing and not overreact; however, statistically speaking, such a person with that personality type will overreact and utilize excessive force, resulting in unknown injury to the citizen and unpreventable harm to the agency that hired such a personality.

Our personality types have been studied since the dawn of time. "From the four temperaments of the ancient civilizations to the latest advances in psychology, we have been driven to fit the variables and complexities of human personality into well-defined models" (16 Personalities, n.d.). Our personalities are derived from our experiences, our childhood, and our changing goals. The nature versus nurture theory can apply here as well. Therefore, when learning what types of personality characteristics we each have, one must allow for the unmalleable changes that occur throughout one's lifetime.

What do all those ISTP (-A/-T), ESTP (-A/-T), and so forth on the 16 personality types mean? The different letters behind each of the 16 personality types in Figure 2.1 are directly correlated to what personality types, are defined as the five personality aspects. "Mind, Energy, Nature, Tactics, and Identity," are the categories to which each personality type falls into (16 Personalities, n.d.). Therefore, the letters that follow each of the 16 personality types are in direct connection with the five aspects.

Instructions: See Table 2.2 for an overview of the 16 personality types, according to the 16 Personalities website.

Then go to the following website: https://www.16personalities.com/free-personality-test

Take the free personality test by NERIS Type Explorer.

Review your results to see what personality type you have and identify any issues that may be revealed.

TABLE 2.2   What Type of Personality Do I Have?

Type of Personality	Analysts	Diplomats	Sentinels	Explorers
Behaviors displayed	**Architect** INTJ (-A/-T) Outlines everything that occurs, creative	**Advocate** INFJ (-A/-T) Calm and mysterious, visionary	**Logistician** ISTJ (-A/-T) A realist and sensible, always on a mission to find the truth	**Virtuoso** ISTP (-A/-T) Explorer and researcher of every available mechanism to complete the job
Behaviors displayed	**Logician** INTP (-A/-T) Knowledge is power, always striving to learn more	**Mediator** INFP (-A/-T) Artistic, romantic type, always looking for a virtuous occasion	**Defender** ISFJ (-A/-T) Faithful to those they love and defend, very devoted	**Adventurer** ISFP (-A/-T) Fascinating and alluring, trying out innovations no matter the idea
Behaviors displayed	**Commander** ENTJ (-A/-T) Persistent leader, never says no, inventive	**Protagonist** ENFJ (-A/-T) Charming and captivating, almost magical in speaking	**Executive** ESTJ (-A/-T) Reliable leader, a mentor and manager of all things	**Entrepreneur** ESTP (-A/-T) Engaging and educated on news ways of living
Behaviors displayed	**Debater** ENTP (-A/-T) Intelligent, always looking for a debate to win	**Campaigner** ENFP (-A/-T) Zealous, animated, and passionate, always happy	**Consul** ESFJ (-A/-T) Universally accepted, ready to do whatever it takes for those around them	**Entertainer** ESFP (-A/-T) Impromptu, ready to jump into anything exciting, always ready to go

TABLE 2.3   Five Personality Aspects: Understanding the Letters Behind the Personality Types

Mind	Energy	Nature	Tactics	Identity
Introverted (I)	Observant (S)	Thinking (T)	Judging (J)	Assertive (A)
Extraverted (E)	Intuitive (I)	Feeling (F)	Prospecting (P)	Turbulent (T)

Source: 16 Personalities. (n.d.).

Results: The following personality traits have been identified as traits that could cause police officers issues on the job (Twersky-Glasner, 2005):

Undue suspiciousness
Anxiety
Sexual concerns
Depression
Phobic personality
Drugs and/or alcohol use
Family conflicts

Guardedness
Rigid type
Illness concerns
Excessive absences
Antisocial attitudes
Hyperactivity
Unusual experiences

SELF-ASSESSMENT 2.4: CAREER INTEREST SURVEY

The South Dakota Department of Labor and Regulation has a Career Interest Survey (SDCIS) that is free to the public and can be assessed on the Internet.

To complete the free career interest survey, go to https://dlr.sd.gov/lmic/menu_sdcis.aspx.

The survey is meant to assist individuals in identifying occupations that are of interest to them. The survey will identify primary, secondary, and third highest interest areas. The career interest areas are based on John Holland's career development model, or Holland codes (Hultman, n.d.).

SELF-ASSESSMENT 2.5: OPEN EXTENDED JUNGIAN TYPE SCALES

The "Open Extended Jungian Type Scales 1.2" by Eric Jorgenson is a personality test that will give the candidate a result that is comparative to the Myers–Briggs type indicator. After answering 32 questions, the candidate can find out if they are extroverted, introverted, intuitive, sensing, thinking, feeling, perceiving, or judging.

To complete the free personality test, download it at https://openpsychometrics.org/tests/OJTS/development/OEJTS1.2.pdf.

SELF-ASSESSMENT 2.6: THE BIG FIVE PERSONALITY TEST

The "Big Five" personality test will help the candidate understand why they act a certain way. The following descriptions will be identified:

- Extroversion
- Agreeableness
- Conscientiousness
- Neuroticism
- Openness to experience

To complete the free personality test, download it at https://openpsychometrics.org/printable/big-five-personality-test.pdf

What Careers Are Available in the Commissioned/Sworn Policing Field?

Careers in the policing field are tough to obtain. Merely walking into the local employment office or Human Resources Department, picking up an application, and waiting for the interview is a fairy tale in the policing world. Just as a high school student studies and prepares for the ACT or SAT and the university student studies and prepares for the LSAT, the police candidate must study and prepare for the law enforcement testing process or failure is almost guaranteed.

The term *law enforcement* is as all-encompassing as the term *criminal justice.* Careers available in the law enforcement realm are far and wide. The plethora of career options vary from being a police officer on the street to working in an office compiling crime analysis data or helping those recently released from prison reacclimate into society. Even in the policing world, the options available for the future police candidate are varied. Once one decides to enter the world of policing, the next step is to determine what type of policing According to Reaves (2015), 77% of the police officers in the United States work for a county or city agency, while only 14% are with federal agencies, and an even lower 9% work for a state agency. Why is the percentage so high for county and city agencies and so low for federal and state agencies? Do county or city agencies provide a different set of benefits? Do they pay more? Not always, some state agencies pay less than a county or city agency. Federal agencies tend to pay more. Therefore, if it is not the pay or benefits, what is the reason? The answer is simple.

According to Reaves (2015), the federal Bureau of Justice Statistics (BJS), who annually conducts many different types of surveys on police agencies in America, there are more than 15,000 cities/local/municipalities, county, and state agencies in the United States. These agencies employed over one million persons.

Most citizens have not had contact, of any kind, with a police officer. Some jurisdictions offer DARE (Drug Abuse Resistance Education) or GREAT (Gang Resistance Education and Training) classes to students during their younger schooling years, thereby exposing them to the real domain of policing. Yet others have had only a negative contact with a police officer, either through a traffic violation or some criminal law or civil violation. Either way, since the most common agencies are county and city agencies, it would stand to reason that the most common contact with police officers would be the same. Because of this, when the decision is made to enter law enforcement, the first place that most likely pops into mind when filling out a job application is with a respective county or city police department where the candidate is from.

What Is a Commissioned or Sworn Policing Position?

In the policing world, the terms **commissioned** and **sworn** are heard daily and are interchangeable terms. This terminology is utilized in the policing world to define a police officer who has been certified through the state as a commissioned or sworn police officer with the powers of arrest.

To those outside the blue line, they are confusing terms that are not understood. When a person decides to take on the world of policing, they first go through the arduous hiring process. Many qualified candidates are foregone due to scores that lack the numbers to qualify for consideration. Herein lies the reason behind this textbook. If the candidate utilizes this textbook fully, along with the accompanied university class, success is just beyond the horizon. Once hired, the police recruit (formerly the police candidate) enters the police academy. Once graduated from the academy, the police recruit is tested and takes an oath to uphold individual rights and is given the powers of arrest by the state. At this point, the police recruit officially becomes a commissioned or sworn police officer of the state. Therefore, when the terms *commissioned* or *sworn* are utilized, it is understood that the person who holds the title has arresting powers.

FACT BOX 2.1: POSSIBLE DIVISIONS WITHIN A LAW ENFORCEMENT AGENCY

All too often when a person decides they are ready for a career in law enforcement they generally stick with what they know. It is a tough career to break into; therefore, the safest retreat is with area law enforcement agencies. Candidates feel comfortable close to home, so why go any further than a quick car ride away? This may not seem like a bad idea, and hopefully all will turn out all right; however, due to the many facets of law enforcement, and the significant difference between agencies, it is of the utmost importance to slow down and do some quick and basic research.

A healthy budget is the name of the game, and the larger the agency, the more career options a future police officer will have. For example, if an officer decides to work for a smaller municipality, where the city population is under 20,000 residents, the respective police department will likely have under 30 police officers. Now, if community policing is what you are looking for, you chose correctly; however, if you were someday hoping to learn to fly a helicopter, or work on a K-9 patrol dog unit, you probably are barking up the wrong tree. Smaller departments do not have the budget nor enough officers to offer the more glamorous divisions like a homicide unit, CSI, or undercover narcotics. Moreover, police departments are busier when the crime rate is high, so if you currently live in a small city with low crime, that is great to live in, but not for a career in law enforcement, unless you want to focus on more of the community-related issues and solutions.

The following is a list of the possible divisions that can be found in a law enforcement agency. The list is not all inclusive, and one should understand that smaller police departments might only have one or two of these divisions, while a larger police department (Los Angeles Police Department or New York Police Department) may have all of the below divisions and more:

- Academy/Tac Officer
- Advocate section
- Air Support
- Auto Theft/(VIPER)
- Background Investigations
- Behavioral Health Unit
- Behavioral Science Services
- Bike Patrol
- Bike Theft Task Force
- Case Management
- Civil Department
- Community Outreach/Policing and Development/Relations section
- Community Services
- Computer Crimes
- Concealed Weapons Division
- Confidential Investigations Division
- Conflict Management
- Counter-Terrorism Unit
- Court Advocacy
- Crime Lab
- Crime Prevention Division
- Crime Scene Investigations (CSI)
- Criminal Intelligence Unit
- Crisis Negotiation
- Critical Incident Command/Stress Management
- Crowd Incident Command
- Data Analytics Unit
- Detective/Investigations (persons, property, major crimes such as homicide, rape, robbery, burglary, auto theft, DUII, domestic violence, cold cases, and so forth)
- Drugs Division
- Emergency Operations/Management
- Employee Services
- Explosives Disposal/Unit
- Family Services
- FBI Liaison Unit
- Fire
- Fish and Wildlife
- Fleet Liaison
- Forensic Evidence
- Forest Patrol
- Freedom of Information Section
- Fugitive Apprehension
- Gaming Enforcement
- Gangs/Gang Enforcement
- Graphics/Video Unit/Audio Visual
- Gun Task Force
- Harm Reduction/Offender Reentry

- Homeland Security Command
- Homeless Liaison
- Honor Guard
- Human Trafficking
- Information Technology
- Inmate and Support Services
- Innovation and Strategic Planning
- Intergovernmental Affairs
- Internal Affairs
- Joint Terrorism Task Force
- Legal Affairs/Services
- Lottery Security
- K-9 Unit
- Major Assaults/Family Violence/Major Offenders
- Management/Labor Affairs
- Marine Patrol Unit/Safety Unit
- Mental Health
- Microanalysis Unit
- Motors/Traffic Division
- Mounted Unit
- Narcotics
- Neighborhood Response Team
- New Affairs Unit/New Technology
- Office of Communications
- Office of Strategy/Planning
- Organizational Development
- Organized Crime
- Park Patrol
- Psychological Services
- Problem-Solving Unit (PSU)
- Professional Standards
- Project Management Team
- Public Information/Public Affairs

- Range Master
- Recruitment
- Regulatory Services
- Reserves
- Risk Management
- School Crossing
- School Resource/Visitation
- SCUBA/Underwater Unit
- Search and Rescue
- Senior Services
- Sex Offender Registration
- Sex Trafficking
- Social Media
- Special Events
- Special Operations/Emergency Team/Special Investigations
- State Athletic Commission
- Supervision/Management (Corporal, Sergeant, Lieutenant, Captain, Deputy Chief/Sheriff, Assistant Chief/Sheriff, Commander, Chief, Sheriff)
- SWAT
- Technical Services
- Training
- Transit Services
- Tribal Gaming
- VICE/Forfeiture Division
- Various Area Task Force (usually made up of various law enforcement agencies in the area, to sometimes include federal agencies too)
- Various Area Unit/Division (depends on the agency and the needs of the agency)
- Volunteer Management/Citizens
- Weighmaster
- Youth Services Division

CASE STUDY 2.1 The Differences Between a Small and a Large Police Department

The opportunities offered for police officers in different agencies can vary depending on many factors. The location, the type of agency, the population the agency has jurisdiction over (and receives tax monies for), and the size of the agency are all mitigating factors.

Instructions: Go to the website https://www.discoverpolicing.org/explore-the-field/search-the-agency-directory/#/.

1. City: Choose any city (or leave blank)
2. State: Choose any state (or leave blank)
3. Agency type: Leave blank
4. Minimum education: Leave blank
5. Agency size: Leave blank
6. Population served: 10,001–20,000

Next:

1. Click on the police departments that have 29 officers or less.
2. Write down the specialized units for each police department clicked on.
3. Do the previous steps for ten police departments.

Start the search over, this time enter in the following search criteria:

1. City: Choose any city (or leave blank)
2. State: Choose any state (or leave blank)
3. Agency type: Leave blank
4. Minimum education: Leave blank
5. Agency size: Leave blank
6. Population served: More than 1,000,000

Next:

1. Click on the police departments that have 3,000 officers or more.
2. Write down the specialized units for each police department clicked on.
3. Do the previous steps for ten police departments.

Questions for thought:

1. What did you notice was different about the types and number of specialized units for the smaller departments (less than 29 officers/population under 20,000) compared to the larger departments (over 3,000 officers/population over 1,000,000)?
2. Why do you think there was a difference in the types and number of specialized units between the smaller and larger departments?
3. Would you rather work for a smaller or larger department? Why?

Are All Those in Law Enforcement Referred to as "Police Officer?"

Commissioned or sworn employees are referred to as police officers. There are other terms in law enforcement, such as deputy, trooper, and an agent. These terms are not interchangeable, and there are different designations that identify the type of law enforcement agency the employee works for.

To understand the organizational layout of any one law enforcement agency can be difficult. There are similarities as a whole, depending on the type of agency; however, it must be understood that every police department is unique, so what is good for the goose is not always good for the gander, and differences do pop up from time to time. The following list identifies the different designations for different types of law enforcement officers across the United States and the designator for the top cop and primary uniform color(s). The following list is a guide, and it should be understood that certain agencies may not follow these prescribed "norms."

- **Police officer:** A commissioned or sworn employee of a city or municipality. The top cop is the chief of police and is appointed by the city manager, mayor, and city council. Examples of departments with police officers are Los Angeles Police Department, Portland Police Bureau, Chicago Police Department, Detroit Police Department, Houston Police Department, Philadelphia Police Department, San Diego Police Department, Columbus Ohio Police Department, and the Denver Police Department. However, not all city departments are organized the same. For example, the New York City Police Department has a senior sworn uniformed officer titled chief of police and also has a head civilian administrator titled police commissioner. *The primary uniform for a police officer is dark/navy blue.*
- **Deputy:** A commissioned or sworn employee of a county. The top cop is the sheriff and is an elected (by the people) position. Examples of departments with deputies include San Bernardino (California) Sheriff's Office, Coconino (Arizona) County Sheriff's Office, Nye (Nevada) County Sheriff's Office, Mojave (Arizona) County Sheriff's Office, Las Vegas, Metropolitan Police Department, Anne Arundel (Maryland) County Sheriff's Office, Essex (New Jersey) County Sheriff's Office, and Jackson (Oregon) County Sheriff's Office. *The primary uniform for a deputy is dark brown, tan, and/or dark green.*
- **Trooper:** A commissioned or sworn employee of the state. The top cop is the superintendent, commissioner, major, or colonel/director (depending on the state agency, the top designation can be unique) and is appointed by the governor. Examples of departments with troopers include Oregon State Police, Nevada Department of Public Safety (Nevada Highway Patrol), Virginia State Police, Massachusetts State Police, Pennsylvania State Police, Indiana State Police, Michigan State Police, and Delaware State Police. *The primary uniform is for a trooper is usually dark/navy blue with a campaign hat (a cowboy type hat with a flat brim).*
- **Agent:** A commissioned or sworn employee of the federal government. The top cop is a director and appointed (the person who appoints the top cop varies depending on the federal agency). Examples include the Federal Bureau of Investigation (FBI), Alcohol, Tobacco, and Firearms (ATF), Secret Service, Central Intelligence Agency (CIA), and Department of Homeland Security (DHS). *The primary uniform for an agent is a business suit, and if in the field different tactical equipment is utilized.*

Federal Law Enforcement

The federal arena of law enforcement careers is broad and vast. Agents working in federal law enforcement are not a part of a national police agency. Instead, federal law enforcement agencies are more of a national security organization, which partners with city, county, state, and other law enforcement agencies to solve threats that face the nation. The media often reports on how a local police department solved a national crime; photographs are broadcast in newspapers or on social media with local police officers apprehending criminals. However, behind the scenes exists one or more federal agencies that indubitably worked hand in hand with the local police department in solving the crime. All too often, federal agents take a back seat when it comes to the glamour side of apprehension and instead chose to let the local departments take all the credit.

The options in the federal law enforcement arena are almost endless, and the rewards outweigh most of the other local agencies. However, there is a catch, which centers on education and experience. Most law enforcement–related careers in the federal arena require a bachelor's degree at a minimum and depending on the type of degree could also require 3 years of related full-time work experience before the candidate can apply.

Candidates interested in the Federal Bureau of Investigation (FBI) as a special agent, for example, are looking at the following educational requirements:

- A bachelor's degree in either (a) accounting, (b) computer science, (c) information technology, (d) foreign language, or (e) law (only a criminal justice major if the candidate is planning on working full time for a law enforcement agency for at least 3 years before applying as a federal agent). These five entry programs must be identified by the candidate agent up application.
- OR a JD degree from an accredited law school
- OR a diversified bachelor's degree *and* 3 years of professional experience, OR a master's degree, or PhD along with 2 years of professional experience

FBI agents must

- be a U.S. citizen or a citizen of the Northern Mariana Islands;
- be 23 years of age to apply and younger than 37 years of age (upon appointment) and age waivers may be granted to eligible veterans older than 37;
- have a valid driver's license,

The FBI actively recruits for candidates that have the following skills:

- Accounting
- Computer science
- Diversified experience
- Finance
- Foreign language
- Information technology
- Investigation experience (as a detective with a local police department)
- Law experience
- Physical sciences

The duties of federal agents are also diverse. For example, agents with the Federal Bureau of Investigation (FBI), are required to do the following:

- Protect the United States from a terrorist attack, espionage attacks, cyber-based attacks, public corruption, civil rights decay, much white-collar crime, national and transnational criminal enterprises, and serious violent crime.

Just as a city police officer is responsible for enforcing city/municipal criminal codes/laws, a federal agent is responsible for enforcing federal codes/laws. However, a federal agent does not work the streets of a city responding to calls for service from citizens in the respective jurisdiction. Instead, federal agents work more like detectives in a local police department. The uniform of choice for daily duties is a business suit, and agents regularly work to gather evidence by investigating different crimes through their various computer tasks, making telephone calls, meeting with confidential informants, testifying in federal court, and executing search warrants.

Federal agents for the U.S. government are at the discretion of the federal government, meaning once a federal agent is hired, they are assigned to a specific federal office. This could be very exciting for some, never knowing where one would land in the United States, and could be a way to explore the nation. However, for others, this could be very stressful, since one's home location is always at the discretion of the federal government.

Different federal agencies, as with local police departments, offer different work environments for their agents. For example, the FBI enforces 200 categories of federal laws, unlike the Drug Enforcement Administration (DEA) and the Bureau of Alcohol, Tobacco, Firearms, and Explosives (ATF). Consequently, it is recommended that the candidate thoroughly study each of the federal agencies as to the opportunities offered.

BOX 2.2: FEDERAL JOB POSSIBILITIES

Federal job possibilities (this list is not comprehensive):

- Federal Bureau of Investigation (FBI): Agent, intelligence analysis, laboratory sciences, linguistics, security, information technology, human resources, general management
- Bureau of Alcohol, Tobacco, Firearms, and Explosives (ATF): Special agent, investigators, attorneys
- Drug Enforcement Administration (DEA): Special agent, diversion investigator, forensic scientist, intelligence researcher, 221 domestic offices in the United States, and 90 foreign offices in 69 countries
- Secret Service: Special agent, uniformed division officer, special officer
- Central Intelligence Agency (CIA)
- National Security Agency (NSA)
- United States Marshals Service (USMS): The nation's oldest federal law enforcement agency; deputy positions, administrative positions, and detention/aviation positions
- U.S. Army Criminal Investigation Command (CID)
- U.S. Army Counterintelligence
- Department of Agriculture: Office of Inspector General (USDA-OIG)
- U.S. Forest Service Law Enforcement & Investigations (USFS LEI)
- Department of Commerce: Office of Inspector General (DOC-OIG)
- Office of Security (DOC-OS)
- U.S. Commerce Department Police
- Office of Export Enforcement (OEE)
- National Institute of Standards and Technology Police
- Department of Commerce: Office for Law Enforcement (OLE)
- Department of Defense: Defense Criminal Investigative Service (DCIS)
- Pentagon Force Protection Agency (PFPA)
- U.S. Pentagon Police (USPPD)
- Department of Defense Police
- Defense Security Police

- Defense Security Service
- Defense Logistic Agency Police
- Defense Intelligence Agency Police
- National Geospatial-Intelligence Agency Police
- U.S. Army Military Police Corps
- Department of the Army Civilian Police
- U.S. Marine Corps Criminal Investigation Division (USMC CID)
- Master at arms (military police)
- Department of Navy Police
- Marine Corps Provost Marshal's Office (military police)
- U.S. Marine Corps Civilian Police
- U.S. Air Force Office of Special Investigations (AFOSI)
- U.S. Air Force security forces (military police)
- Department of the Air Force Police (civilian police)
- Office of Criminal Investigations: Department of Health and Human Services
- National Institutes of Health Police
- Department of Homeland Security
- U.S. Coast Guard (USCG)
- U.S. Coast Guard Investigative Service (CGIS)
- U.S. Customs and Border Protection (CBP)
- U.S. Border Patrol (USBP): Special agent, border patrol tactical unit, border patrol search trauma, rescue unit, and border patrol special response team
- Mount Weather Emergency Operations Center Police
- Office of Chief Security Officer (OCSO)
- U.S. Immigration and Customs Enforcement (ICE): Deportation officer, detention and deportation officer, special agent, immigration enforcement agent, intelligence positions, and investigative positions; the second largest investigative agency in the federal government; has employees in all 50 states and 47 countries. The largest investigative agency in the federal government
- Homeland Security Investigations (HIS)
- Federal Air Marshal Service (FAMS)
- Bureau of Indian Affairs Police
- Hoover Dam Police (Bureau of Reclamation Police)
- National Park Service Ranger
- U.S. Park Police
- U.S. Fish and Wildlife Service (USFWS)
- Division of Refuge Law Enforcement
- Department of Justice
- Federal Bureau of Prisons
- Bureau of Diplomatic Security
- Office of Odometer Fraud Investigation (OFI)
- Department of Treasury: Bureau of Engraving and Printing Police
- Financial Crimes Enforcement Network (FINCEN)
- Internal Revenue Service: Criminal Investigation Division (IRS-CI)
- United States Mint Police (USMP)
- Department of Veterans Affairs Police
- United States Capitol Police
- Marshall of the U.S. Supreme Court

- Office of Probation and Pretrial Services
- Central Intelligence Agency: Security Protective Service (CIA SPS)
- U.S. Environmental Protection Agency
- National Background Investigations Bureau (NBIB)
- U.S. Postal Inspection Service: Postal police
- National Zoological Park Police (NZPP)
- Amtrak police
- Federal Reserve police: Federal Reserve Board Police
- Tennessee Valley Authority Police (TVAP)

State Law Enforcement

Every state in the United States has some form of a state police agency. State police work for a state. State law enforcement agencies are responsible for traffic enforcement along highways and interstates. Many state agencies focus primarily on traffic enforcement, while others may focus on traffic and other general investigation duties. For example, in Oregon, the state police work for the state of Oregon and the department is Oregon State Police (OSP). OSP not only focuses on the traffic-related issues on the highways in Oregon but also has the following divisions: patrol services, criminal investigations, fish and wildlife, forensic services, field operations, SWAT/MRT, public

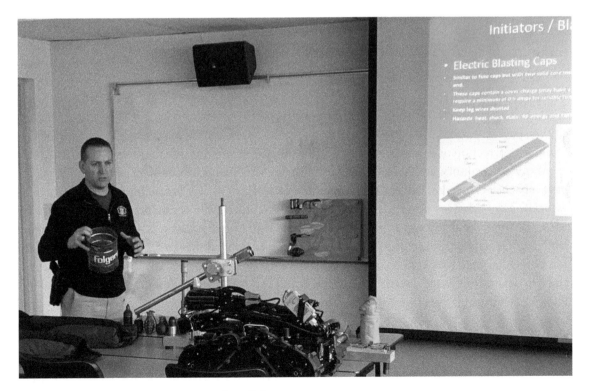

FIGURE 2.1 Oregon State Police trooper Brett Keller.

safety services, gaming bureau, lottery security, tribal gaming, training, state athletic commission, and an explosives unit. Figure 2.1 illustrates a state trooper operating an explosive unit robot.

State law enforcement agencies are empowered to provide service throughout the state. State law enforcement employees are generally called **troopers**, and the uniform is generally blue (navy and/or light blue); however, there are individual state highway patrol agencies that wear a combination of tan, dark brown, and dark green, such as California Highway Patrol. Most do, however, wear round tipped hats.

FIGURE 2.2 Uniform of a county sheriff's office, Sergeant DiCostanzo.

County Law Enforcement

According to the U.S. Department of Interior (2018), there are 3,142 counties in the United States. Each county has an elected sheriff, and **deputies** (i.e., police officers) work directly under the sheriff. Deputies are no different from any other city police officer other than the sheriff can be responsible for the courts and jails (i.e., correctional facility) in their respective county. However, there are also many city police departments that are responsible for jails, so it just depends on the department. Each state is divided into counties, and each county, depending on size, could have a sheriff's office. Figure 2.2 illustrates county deputy uniforms.

Municipal/city police work under a municipality or city. If a city has a government (i.e., mayor and city council members and a municipal code (misdemeanor laws for the city)), then the city can have city police. If a person works for a city, the designation is police officer. Some cities have a jail (i.e., correction or detention facility), while others are run through the sheriff and the county.

Many state, county, and municipal/city police departments do not require future candidates to have a bachelor's degree. Currently, many of the candidates testing for such positions do have an associate's or bachelor's degree, so although it is not required, the candidates are more desirable. Also, the trend for many law enforcement agencies is to require at least 2 years of college before applying. Generally, college degrees become a required educational background when an officer wants to enter management (i.e., sergeant, lieutenant, captain, commander, undersheriff, deputy chief, assistant chief, and so forth). Many chiefs and sheriffs have either a master's degree or PhD. Figure 2.3 illustrates a recruitment poster for a city police department.

Tribal Police Officer

According to the Bureau of Justice (BOJ) statistics, as of 2008, there are 178 law enforcement agencies operated by American Indian tribes. Just as with local city police departments, many tribal

FIGURE 2.3 "Are you ready?" poster.

agencies perform universal police duties; however, others only enforce natural resource laws (BOJ, 2008). These tribal law enforcement agencies have as little as two officers, and other communities, such as the Navajo Nation (250,000 population) in Arizona, have over 200 tribal officers (Tribal Court Clearing House, n.d.).

According to the National Congress of American Indians (NCAI), tribal officers have an involved jurisdictional authority because they answer to a complex set of authorities. There are only 2,380 tribal officers, to serve an estimated 1.4 million Indians over an area of 56 million acres of tribal land across the United States (Tribal Court Clearing House, n.d.). Talk about doing a lot with a little! To be a tribal officer, the candidate does not have to be of Indian ancestry. Figure 2.4 illustrates the crimes reported by tribal police in the five largest states with a tribal police department.

University Police Officer

University police and university/college public safety departments are unique and diverse entities. University police departments hire commissioned/sworn law enforcement officers. These officers have to meet the same requirements and receive the same type of police academy training. The state also swears them with arresting powers. As an example, the University of Nevada, Las Vegas (UNLV, n.d.) Police Services was created on June 11, 1965, when the Nevada Revised Statute

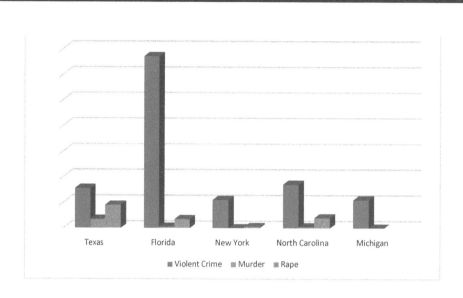

Tribal Law Enforcement. (n.d.). Retrieved February 21, 2019, from https://www.tribal-institute.org/lists/enforcement.htm

FIGURE 2.4 Tribal police crimes in the five largest states by population (Tribal Court Clearing House, n.d.).

396.325 became law, giving UNLV Board of Regents authority to create a police department for the university. The UNLV Police Services has the following divisions:

- Patrol (Auto, Bicycle, Cart, Foot)
- Communications and Dispatch
- Emergency Preparedness
- Community Engagement
- Investigations
- Student Security
- K-9 and Special Event Security
- Records and Property
- Committees and Councils

UNLV Police Services also has a student security unit, and they are noncommissioned/non-sworn civilians. This student security unit is similar to how a university/college public safety department operates.

Corrections (Jail or Prison)

There is a vast distinction between a correction or detention center (i.e., jail) and a prison. A **local jail population** is defined as a correctional or detention facility operated by a sheriff's office or police department, generally incarcerating individuals for less than 1 year before sentencing for an alleged crime. For instance, in Las Vegas, Nevada, the sheriff's office, the Las Vegas Metropolitan Police Department (LVMPD) operated the Clark County Detention Center. The North Las Vegas Police Department (NLVPD), a city police agency, operated the NLV Detention Center (city jail). The Henderson Police Department (in the same county as LVMPD and NLVPD above) operated the Henderson Detention Center (city jail). Therefore, jurisdiction mattered. If a person were arrested in the city of North Las Vegas, the officer would transport that person to the NLV Detention Center, whereas if the person were arrested in the city of Las Vegas, the officer would transport that person to the Clark County Detention Center. Sometimes, jails will contract out for federal inmates as a way to support the costs of running the jail. According to the Bureau of Justice Statistics, as of December 31, 2016, there were 6,613,500 persons under some U.S. adult correctional supervision; 1 in 38 adults (2.6%) over 18 years of age were in some correctional facility (Daeble & Cowhig, 2018).

A **prison population** is defined as a long-term confinement facility operated by a state or federal government, incarcerating individuals after they have been sentenced for their crime(s). For instance, Pelican Bay State Prison is located in Crescent City, California. It is a supermax state prison operated by the state of California. There is also a **military prison population,** which is defined as service personnel confined in a facility operated under the jurisdiction of U.S. military correctional authorities. Different branches of the military (e.g., Army, Marine Corps, and the Navy) have their prisons. Figure 2.5 illustrates the total U.S. population under the supervision of a correctional system.

Careers in a jail are coveted positions. Many police departments used to, and some still do, require a future police officer work in the jail before applying as a patrol officer, because jail is a contained environment. A fellow back-up correctional officer is only seconds away, instead of minutes away on the street. Also, the jail is an excellent way to learn how to communicate with inmates and earn their respect. It is almost seen as a passageway to patrol; however, many end up liking the jail, and

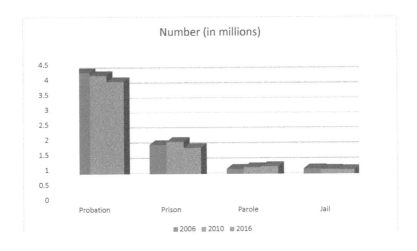

Kaeble, D. (n.d.). Probation and Parole in the United States, 2016. Retrieved February 22, 2019, from http://www.bjs.gov/index.cfm?ty=pbdetail&iid=6188

FIGURE 2.5 Total U.S. population in prison, jail, or on parole or probation 2000–2016 (Kaeble, 2018).

FIGURE 2.6 Jackson County Sheriff's Office Corrections, Sgt. DiCostanzo and Deputy Kolkemo.

all it has to offer, so much they stay. All too often, the pay difference between a correctional officer and a patrol officer is less than a dollar an hour, yet the safety level is much higher in the jail than on the street. Correctional officers are required to go through the same hiring process as any other police officer position; however, the academy is 6 to 13 weeks instead of 5 to 6 months for the police officer. Figure 2.6 illustrates a corrections deputy uniform.

Careers in the prison system are separate than those in the jails. Prisons house felony offenders sentenced longer than 1 year, whereas jails tend to be more of a short-term incarceration period for less violent crimes (including misdemeanors). Prison guards enjoy the same type of quick response from back-up officers as correctional officers do. Prison correctional officers used to be lower paid than jail correctional officers; however, this trend has been changing over the last 2 decades, and prison correctional officers are now on parody for their positions. Many jails and prisons have specialized details, which make them interesting and enjoyable for the officers. The following list identifies some of those details:

- Fugitive apprehension teams
- Emergency Operations Unit
- Gang Unit
- SWAT
- Detective Unit
- Regional Task Force
- Other various units/teams

Parole and Probation

Careers in parole and probation are all too often misunderstood, ignored, or unknown altogether. However, they offer some of the most independent, multifaceted, and new types of daily work when

The Top 10 States with the Highest Number of Adults on Probation 2016

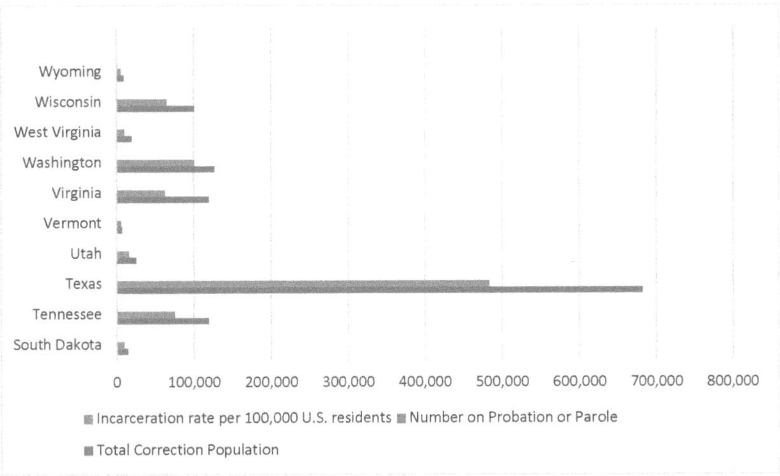

Kaeble, D. (n.d.). Probation and Parole in the United States, 2016. Retrieved February 22, 2019, from http://www.bjs.gov/index.cfm?ty=pbdetail&iid=6188

FIGURE 2.7 The top 10 states with the highest number of adults on probation, 2016 (Kaeble, 2018).

compared to the other law enforcement careers available. According to Kaeble (2018), in 2016, there were 4,537,100 adults in the United States under some court-ordered supervision, which is equivalent to one in every 55 adults. Figure 2.7 illustrates the U.S. population that was in prison, jail, or on parole or probation from 2000–2016.

According to the Bureau Justice of Statistics (BJS), **parole** is defined as a period when a person is released from prison and supervised per preset conditions. **Probation** is defined as court-ordered supervision where the person is released and allowed into the community under preset conditions. A **parolee** is a person who is either under the conditions of parole or probation. Federal parole is defined as a supervised release from prison, parole, special parole, and military parole.

> Since the Sentencing Reform Act of 1984 was enacted on November 1, 1987, offenders sentenced to federal prison are no longer eligible for parole but are required to serve a term of supervised release following release from prison. Those sentenced to prison prior to November 1, 1987, continue to be eligible for parole, as do persons violating laws of the District of Columbia, military offenders, and foreign treaty transfer offender. In 2008, the Annual Parole Survey included a new type of entry-to-patrol category-term of supervised release- to better classify the large majority of entries to parole reported by the federal system. (Kaeble, 2018, p. 8)

Because of the Sentencing Reform Act of 1984, the new term, ***community supervision***, was created and utilized in the parole/probation reporting field, in addition to parole and probation.

For example, in California, there are 58 counties with a probation department. The California Probation Department top cop is called the chief probation officer, which is an appointed position. The chief probation officer is appointed either by a county charter through the Board of Supervisors or by a judge in superior court. Probation officers are law enforcement officers who are given the powers of arrest by the state. The following list illustrates some of the duties and responsibilities of a parole and probation officer:

- Supervises released offenders
- Makes sentencing recommendations
- Enforces orders from the court
- Provides a variety of prevention and rehabilitation programs (criminal diversion programs)
- Fulfills community service aspect of parole and probation

Figure 2.7 illustrates the top 10 states with the highest number of adults on probation.

DECISION TIME 2.1

In 2009, the California the Department of Corrections faced the highest recidivism rates ever and prison overcrowding. After intensive reviews a prison reform act "Governor Schwarzenegger signed Senate Bill 678 (SB 678) on October 1, 2009, creating the California Community Corrections Performance Incentive Act of 2009" (Siskiyou County Public Safety Realignment and Release, 2013). The goal was to enhance probation recidivism and lower the number of criminals failing at probation and returning to prison.

If you were the chief probation officer for Doe County Probation Office (a make-believe probation office to be utilized for this exercise), and just like in the example your office faced alarming rates of recidivism (defined as the tendency for a criminal to reoffend), how would you begin to solve this situation? Look up the California courts, judicial branch of California website and research SB 678. Also, go to the County of Siskiyou California's (probation office) website and review the documentation on SB 678 and AB 109. Conduct other research on how probation efforts can be improved.

Answer the following questions:

1. What are the details of SB 678?
2. How is Siskiyou County Probation Office handling SB 678, and what is AB 109?
3. What else can be done to solve probation issues?

Conservation Police Officer and Game Warden (State or Federal)

Careers as game wardens can be found at both the state and federal level. The newly coined term for game wardens in the 21st century is **conservation law enforcement officers**. Game wardens face dangers that other law enforcement officers do not face because of the remoteness of the areas they serve. Game wardens also spend a significant amount of time in the field, which can be exciting on many levels, including the use of boats, horses, snowmobiles, various street vehicles. These luxuries also involve a certain level of danger, which can include humans, motor vehicles and other environmental factors.

Federal game wardens are law enforcement officers sworn to protect and serve through conservation and protection while working with the U.S. Fish and Wildlife Service. These protectors work for the U.S. Fish and Wildlife Service as ambassadors for wildlife. Federal game wardens' job responsibilities are under two main headings. The first is conservation and includes such things as protecting fish in Alaska and reptiles in Arizona. The second responsibility is service to wildlife.

From educated youth on the importance of wildlife, conducting surveys, and assisting with rescue operations, federal game wardens' work as guardians of wildlife never ends. Federal game wardens are commissioned/sworn officers and must have a bachelor's degree with a significant focus in the following:

- Natural resource management
- Natural sciences
- Park and recreation science
- Criminal justice
- Another related subject to management and protection of natural and cultural resources or
- be working on a 4-year course of study leading to a bachelor's degree

State game wardens are commissioned/sworn law enforcement officers sworn to protect and service through conservation and protection while working as a state police officer and in conjunction with the state fish and wildlife division. In Wyoming, the Game and Fish Department employees 82 game wardens of all types across the state (Johnston, 2019). Many game wardens enjoy a multitude of benefits including housing. For example, in Oregon, game wardens are troopers with the Oregon State Police. On top of all the regular law enforcement police academy work and training, the state game warden in Oregon must also attend game warden specific training, which can include the following:

- Boat operations
- Environmental crime investigation
- Federal wildlife laws
- Meat handling and inspection
- Restaurant and dealer inspection
- Horse packing
- Outdoor survival and navigation (Blue Mountain Community College, n.d.)

Division assignments for Oregon State Police (game wardens with the Oregon Department of Fish and Wildlife) include the following:

- 93 General Fish and Wildlife
- 12 Healthy Streams and Habitat
- 6 Commercial Fish
- 5 Special Investigation Unit (SIU)
- 4 aircraft pilots (GameWarden, n.d.)

Gaming Control Agent/Officer

Bright lights, slot machines jingling, and a city that never sleeps comes to mind when thinking of a gaming police officer. Any city in Nevada, especially Las Vegas, tops the list for gaming institutions. Many states allow casino-type gambling, especially those areas of American Indian reservations. Arizona also has many laws to cover state gaming. For instance, in Arizona, the Gaming Vendor Certification Unit (GVCU) makes decisions as to who can conduct business with the various gaming institutions. The GVCU employs special agents, investigators, intake officers, and auditors

(Johnston, 2019). These officers and agents conduct investigations and ensure compliance with state and federal laws to include the following:

- Reports
- Court testimony
- Audit of financial information
- Evidence
- Search warrants
- Undercover and surveillance work
- Interviews (Johnston, 2019)

In Nevada, the Nevada Gaming Control Board has an enforcement agent position. This position requires a bachelor's degree or equivalent combination of education and investigative experience. **Gaming control agents/officers** are required to go through a police academy and are given arresting powers in the state, thereby making them a commissioned/sworn employee.

School Police Officer and School Resource Officer

Even the career field of a school resource officer is diverse. There are school districts that have school police officers who fall under the direction of the principal of the school. For example, in Las Vegas, Nevada, there is the Clark County School District Police Department. These **school police officers** are commissioned/sworn employees who are given arrest powers by the state and work for a school district.

School resource officers (SRO) are commissioned/sworn law enforcement officers whose primary responsibility is the safety of the students as well as various crime prevention related activities. An SRO is employed and trained by the law enforcement agency to which the school is under their jurisdiction. The SRO works closely with school administration in always trying to create a safer environment for students and faculty. Many SROs also instruct various crime prevention–related programs such as DARE (Drug Abuse Resistance and Education) and GREAT (Gang Resistance Education and Training) classes. However, many local police departments offer such classes through their crime prevention division.

In today's society of active shooters and school violence, the push for more SROs has been apparent in some jurisdictions as one answer to save lives. One of the most significant barriers to this is the cost to staff the positions. It is not always apparent where the budget will cover this cost.

FACT BOX 2.2: SCHOOL RESOURCE OFFICERS SAVE THE DAY!

On Tuesday, March 20, 2018, a 17-year-old entered Maryland's Great Mills High School and fired a weapon. Blaine Gaskill, the school resource officer (SRO), acted quickly to ensure the safety of those he swore to protect. As the gunfire erupted, Gaskill did not waver; instead, he ran into the hail of bullets firing at the shooter. It was a real gun battle with bullets flying toward Gaskill and the shooter. Within seconds (not minutes or even hours) the incident was over. Two students were shot; one was a 16-year-old female student critically injured and the second was a 14-year-old male student in stable condition.

Then, 2 months later on May 16, 2018, an SRO ran toward the gunfire when a suspected gunman opened fire in Dixon, Illinois.

Is There Jurisdictional Overlap?

Since the United States does not have a national police force, the diversity of the law enforcement agencies in America can get overwhelmingly confusing. The array of agencies is not only a conundrum for citizens but the various agencies as well.

A college student who grew up in Sacramento, California, and then went away to college in Portland, Oregon, and now lives on campus could be under the jurisdiction of Sacramento Police Department (when visiting in Sacramento), under campus police (when living in the dorm), or Portland Police Bureau (when in the city), Oregon State Police (when on the highways), and a variety of federal agencies (if the student decided to engage in terrorist-related activities).

This confusion endures for law enforcement agencies as well. Other than safety or injuries, the next question every officer must ask when they arrive at a call for service is, "Whose jurisdiction?" Jurisdiction is paramount. Jurisdiction determines the following:

- Which agency investigates
- Which court handles the case
- All other resources

Historically, before GPS and online roadmap applications, police officers had reams of maps on paper they would have to review for those unique cases where jurisdiction was foggy. Luckily today the question of jurisdiction can be solved before a dispatcher in communications/911 even sends an officer to the call. No matter how easy it is to determine jurisdiction today, the case of whose jurisdiction is still of the utmost importance.

What Careers Are Available in the Civilian Policing Field?

What Is a Civilian Position?

Just as there are commissioned/sworn employees in law enforcement agencies, there are also non-commissioned/non-sworn or civilian employees. A **civilian or noncommissioned/non-sworn** person is an employee at a law enforcement agency who does not have state-given arresting powers. Any law enforcement agency needs a balance between commissioned/sworn officers and civilian/noncommissioned/non-sworn employees in order to make it all run correctly. It is a partnership between the two that keeps the wheels rolling smoothly in the right direction. Following are examples of different civilian positions at various law enforcement agencies across the United States.

Park Police Officer

A **park police officer** is ordinarily a civilian/noncommissioned/non-sworn employee who patrols identified parks for park violations. Often park police officers work under the direction of the police department that has jurisdiction over the parks that will be patrolled. Every so often, the park police fall under the jurisdiction of the parks department for the city or county. Park police officers often remain visible in the parks by walking or utilizing a motorized vehicle or a mounted unit. Some of the park rules that park police enforce are as follows:

- Respecting the natural scenery, plants, wildlife
- No firearms or hunting
- No fires (unless in a permitted area)
- No smoking
- No littering/dumping
- Keeping domestic animals under control (as per leash law)
- Disposing of pet waste properly
- Noise issues
- Allowing vehicles only in permitted areas
- Enforcing park hours

Community Service Officer (CSO)

Community service officers (CSO) are civilian/noncommissioned/non-sworn employees of a law enforcement agency. CSOs gained popularity during the financial crisis of 2007–2008 and as an answer to the ongoing hiring crisis in law enforcement. Since CSOs are civilians, they do not require the magnanimous amount of training as a commissioned officer, and they are paid much less and are generally part time, thereby not requiring benefits. CSOs also assist with calls for service, lightening the load of police officers by answering those non-emergency, nonviolent calls, freeing up the police officers to handle emergency calls immediately. A CSO uniform is different from that of a police officer for that department, and their vehicles are also different to identify their civilian status visibly. CSOs can respond to the following types of calls for service:

- Traffic control
- Crowd control at special events
- Assisting the public
- Writing various reports
- Visibility in high foot traffic areas

Figure 2.8 is a photograph of a community service officer vehicle.

Reserve/Auxiliary Officer

The term **reserve officer** varies depending on the law enforcement agency. Some agencies define a reserve officer as a retired police officer, who at some point in their career was a commissioned/sworn employee of a police department. This reserve officer is now employed either as a volunteer or part-time paid employee to assist with calls for service such as the following:

- Parking complaints/issues
- Traffic control
- Special event containment
- Informational or nonviolent police reports
- Various other community policing type of activities

FIGURE 2.8 Community service officer vehicle.

These types of reserve officers do not work full time and generally do not receive benefits. It is usually a way for the retired officer to stay busy and assist a local police department handle these types of calls for service.

The second type of **reserve officer** is similar to a CSO. This kind of reserve officer is generally between 18–21 years of age (but can be over 21 years of age as well) and is looking to enter the world of policing. This position offers the reserve officer a foot in the door to learn the duties and responsibilities of a police officer while proving one's dedication and passion for the career. For instance, the Las Vegas Metropolitan Police Department has just developed a new reserve officer program. This is a volunteer position, where the officers are required to volunteer a minimum of 20 hours each month, plus attend training. These reserve officers participate in a reserve police officer academy and upon successful completion will receive commissioned status and arresting powers in the state.

Cadet or Explorer

A **cadet or explorer** is a volunteer position as a law enforcement agency, where the focus is on education. Being a cadet or explorer is an opportunity for youth to learn more about law enforcement and the prospective agency. A cadet or explorer are generally interchangeable terms identifying a teenager from the ages of 14–17. Cadets/explorers volunteer to meet weekly at the police department to learn various aspects of policing. Cadets/explorers also assist with many volunteer opportunities at the police department such as the following:

- Special event crowd control
- Christmas events
- Thanksgiving events
- Shop with a cop event
- Senior appreciation day
- National night out event
- Representation of the department at various other events

A cadet/explorer program is a wonderful way for teenagers with interest in law enforcement to be an active participant with the agency and meet and interact with the various employees and different divisions. Many times, a cadet/explorer will end up working as a police officer for the police department once they are over 21 years of age and pass the hiring testing process.

What Is the Role of a Volunteer in Law Enforcement?

Volunteers play a vital role in local police departments. Many times, these unpaid volunteers assist with a citizen's academy program, with community outreach, or in various capacities at other special events. Volunteers also can sit on one of the various committees a multitude of agencies have, such as a use of force review board or a citizen's police and community committee.

POLICE STORY 2.1 **Dee Taylor Top Volunteer**

by Retired Lieutenant Tiffany L. Morey NLVPD

During my first few years a police officer, I was so busy learning the job that I had little time to pay attention to the vast world of volunteers around me. As I grew in my career, I soon branched out and began to meet some of the most amazing volunteers who were making huge differences in the lives of the cops at our department, specifically Dee Taylor. Dee was a volunteer with our police department and could be seen around our department often, offering assistance to the officers in any way she could. Dee was instrumental in her support with our citizens' academy. I was often in awe of the amount of time she volunteered to ensure that our citizens' academy ran smoothly, and she always ensured our citizens and officers were given everything they needed to be successful.

Whenever our department needed anything, they turned to Dee for help, and she was always there, giving 110%! Dee also assisted with our police unity tour. This is a cross-country bicycle tour where police officers ride bicycles across the country to the police memorial in Washington, DC. Dee assisted by driving a van that held much-needed water and protein and gave breaks where needed as well. Our department could not have participated in the level we did without her assistance. Dee also assisted with our Baker to Vegas run and even was a panel member on our entry-level police officer oral board interview and a board member for the crime prevention division hiring of a crime prevention specialist. Our department could not have participated in the level we did without her assistance.

I also distinctively remember many of our chiefs of police contacting her directly whenever they had a question or a specific need to be filled by a volunteer. No matter the request, Dee gave everything she could. Dee's charitable nature was never ending, and she often gave more of herself to our department as a volunteer than she gave to herself. Figure 2.9 is a photograph of Dee receiving an award at the North Las Vegas Police Department Citizens Academy.

I am sure our department was not the only one that had a fantastic volunteer; in fact I know some volunteers help make departments run more smoothly, and many would agree that without volunteers police departments could not operate.

FIGURE 2.9 Dee Taylor, volunteer at North Las Vegas Police Department.

What Careers Are Available in Social Services?

Social services are entities that ensure citizens are housed, fed, and job trained and have strong role models, thereby creating an active community. **Social services** are those careers in public service, generally provided by the government, nonprofit organizations, or other types of for-profit/private businesses. The main types of social services are in the areas of housing assistance/subsidies, food assistance/subsidies, health care, police and fire services, job training, and community management. Those who enter any law enforcement or criminal justice career field are entering a field of service and are looking to gain personal satisfaction from helping others. Compassion and dedication are required for these careers because of their critical role. Many careers in social services require a bachelor's degree while others require a graduate degree. Varying certificates and licenses can also be required in this multifaceted career.

Careers in social services are countless. Depending on the jurisdiction, the criminological factors present will determine the types of social services available to its residents. Social service careers are open to those with interest as health educators, mental health counselors and therapists, rehabilitation counselors, social and community service/health services, and social workers.

For instance, in Oregon, the following social services are available:

Victim Advocates

Domestic Violence Coalitions

Better Housing

Child Protective Services

Community Health Center	Maslow Project
Community Works	Mental Health
Rogue Valley Veterans and Community Outreach	Salvation Army (Hope House-Food Boxes-Store)
Disability Services Office (DSO)	DHS Self-Sufficiency Office
Hearts With a Mission	St. Vincent De Paul
Help Now	Living Opportunities
Housing Authority	Vocational Rehabilitation Office
Job Council	YMCA
Legal Services	JCMH Crisis Respite (Mental Health)
Lions Club Sight and Hearing Center	

In order for communities to thrive, they must be threaded together in a variety of ways. Negative forces that threaten this base must be stopped and positive forces must be reinforced to withstand the needs of the community members. Some people are naturally resilient and can weather the many hurricanes that come their way. However, others can struggle when tragedy occurs, and therefore the community must be prepared through its social services to repair and build the pieces back up.

In 2004, the Crime Victims' Rights Act was passed and required many in the criminal justice system to offer social services, which created a new career designated as a victim advocate. This was because this new act required city and state governments to ensure a victim's rights were followed. Some of these rights include the right to notification, to not be excluded from proceedings, to speak at the proceeding, to restitution, to consult with a prosecutor, from unreasonable delay, and to be treated with fairness. There were also many changes in the domestic violence laws, and there needed to be a voice for the victims of these crimes. In order to ensure a victim's rights are honored, many law enforcement agencies began employing victim advocates. In order to offset the cost for this new position, many agencies received funding under the Victims of Crime Act (VOCA) and continue funding through state and federal grants.

What Careers Are Available in Criminal Rehabilitation?

Careers in criminal rehabilitation that are most well known are in corrections/prisons and parole and probation; however, those positions are generally commissioned/sworn and require the employee to carry a handgun and go through an academy. There are many careers in the noncommissioned/non-sworn civilian world of criminal rehabilitation. Such civilian careers are in the government arena as well as the nonprofit world, and there are also others in the private business section. Many of the careers with governmental agencies focus on providing rehabilitative programming to the jail or prison population and those on parole or probation. Those working in this field of rehabilitation focus on changing criminal thinking patterns, educating through prosocial behaviors and cognitive behavior treatment, as well as future career technical training and transitional reentry programs.

The world of criminal rehabilitation is always evolving depending on the needs of those involved and what is new and innovative in the field and research that is being conducted. For example, at the California Department of Corrections and Rehabilitation, rehabilitative programs are being offered to all offenders to ensure success upon release. These different programs are offered at various stages of incarceration. The road to rehabilitation outlines the timeline of when these programs are offered. Figure 2.10 illustrates this road.

The Roadmap to Rehabilitation

The diagram below illustrates the steps to the rehabilitation program at the California Department of Corrections and Rehabilitation:

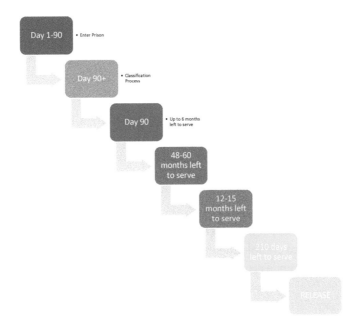

The Step-By-Step Process:
Offender Enters Prison
Step 1: Offender Enters Reception Area
Step 2: Begin Classification Process
Step 3: Programming: Day 90- Up to 60 Months Left to Serve
Step 4: Programming: 48-60 Months Left to Serve
Step 5: Programming 12-15 Months Left to Serve
Step 6: Programming: 210 Days Left to Serve
Step 7: Parole/Back into the Community

Force, W. T. (n.d.). Gavin Newsom. Retrieved February 25, 2019, from https://www.cdcr.ca.gov/Rehabilitation/Process.html

FIGURE 2.10 The road to rehabilitation (Force, n.d.).

What Is the Nonprofit World of Rehabilitation?

As the drug problem in America continues to grow, so do the rehabilitation efforts put forward. Many programs are funded through state and federal grants, and these are operated under nonprofit status. These organizations do incredible work and offer many opportunities for careers. In Oregon, the following organizations offer rehabilitation assistance to those in need:

Addictions Recovery Center (ARC)

Allied Health Services (Methadone Clinic)

The Medford Drop

Moore Center (Sobering)

Ontrack Recovery

What Careers Are Available in Crime Analysis, Records or Property Clerk, 911 Dispatch/Communications?

Crime Analysis

Before the late 1990s, careers in the field of crime analysis were all but sparse. With technology came at first supercomputers, and then by the millennium computers were at every desktop in every police department across the country. Crime stats were taken; however, it was only in the areas reported to the federal government, and they were not readily available. As the handwritten reports became obsolete, computer reports thankfully replaced everything and crime analysis was reborn. Smaller departments cannot always afford to employ a full-time crime analysis employee (or crime statistician). Larger departments (those with over 100 employees) generally will have at least one employee assigned to completing crime analysis, and they work hard for their paycheck. These employees regularly compile crime data in varying ways. The data is utilized during CompStat managerial meetings to determine problem areas in a jurisdiction. Alternatively, maybe an officer wants to know how many times they have responded to a particular part of town for burglaries? Is there a crime trend occurring? This data allows officers to be more proactive and begin to look ahead to see what trends are developing and how to respond to them.

Records or Property Clerk

Careers in records or as a property clerk are very hidden careers. All too often, a person happens to stumble on the job, knows someone who recommends the job, or is involved in some manner with the police department. A Records Division houses all the records at the police department. Police reports are the most often housed requested record. Whether a report is requested from a prosecutor, defense attorney, or a victim of a crime, the Records Division is responsible for not only all the requests but the dissemination of all the reports as well. Police reports list confidential information, not only about a victim of a crime (such as their address, work address, phone numbers, date of birth, and Social Security number), but the narrative portion of the reports can contain sensitive information as well. The Records Division employees are responsible for ensuring the confidentiality of this information.

Careers in records can be gratifying and prevalent as well, since every police department no matter the size will at least have one person (or many, many more) responsible for the records of the department. Employees must go through an intense hiring process, including a background check, due to the sensitive information the employee is exposed to daily.

Careers as a property clerk involve handling all the evidence for the police department. When an officer is on a call, if the officer finds evidence, the officer will book the evidence into the property room Such evidence could be a found bicycle, or blood evidence in a DUII case, a found wallet, drugs, weapons, anything that is booked into property as evidence, found evidence, or safekeeping. The property clerk is then responsible for taking the evidence the officer or detective or crime scene investigator booked into the property room and keeping the chain of custody as the property is either sent to be processed, returned to the owner, or stored long term. Property clerks deal with money, drugs, and other valuable items, so they must be honest and trustworthy. The hiring process is similar to the Records Division. Figure 2.11 illustrates the booking of evidence.

911 Dispatch/Communications

The official designator for those in dispatch is communications, yet most know them as 911 operators or the hero on the other end of the line. Many perspective police candidates always ask to go on a police ride-along; however, the candidate should also request to do a sit-along in communications. It is a fast-paced whirlwind of a place to learn a plethora of things. It is the central hub for any police

FIGURE 2.11 Property clerks are responsible for evidence once it is booked into evidence at a police department.

FIGURE 2.12 A 911 dispatcher in communications has to be able to multitask.

department, and one could learn more in one day in communications about how a department works than 1 week of ride-alongs on the street.

911 dispatchers are very smart. Testing has shown that, overall, dispatchers have the highest IQ around. Why is that? Does the profession attract those with a higher aptitude? Actually, yes! The job of a 911 dispatcher is tough. The dispatcher must be able to multitask at the highest level. Think about it. A 911 dispatcher is responsible for answering 911 telephone calls, dealing with all types of emergencies over the telephone, answering normal telephone calls that come into the police department and transferring them correctly, answering police officers over the radio and documenting their location and activities in CAD (computer-aided dispatch), dispatching officers to calls for service, running wants and warrants checks for officers, conducting report reviews for officers, researching jurisdictional issues, and much more. Moreover, all of this can be occurring at the same time. Also, it must be entered into the computer; therefore, fast typing skills are required.

Careers in communications can be awesome and inspiring. They can also be tough because the dispatcher handles stressful calls, yet once the officer arrives at the scene, the dispatcher never really gets a video review of what occurred (only in some instances). The hiring process has many different parts, ranging from a job application, oral board interview, practical testing (answering stressful phone calls and recording typing speed), background check, and a dispatcher academy. Figure 2.12 illustrates how dispatchers must be able to multitask.

What Careers Are Available in the Crime Scene Investigation Field?

What Is the Difference Between a Civilian CSI and a Commissioned/Sworn CSI?

Before the popular television series *CSI*, those in law enforcement worked tirelessly without much glamour. However, once the show became an overnight success, the interest in crime scene investigation developed a life of its own. It created an instant list of interested candidates. Television is not always fact; therefore, the lackluster comparisons left the glittery-eyed candidate ignorant of the real job.

Before 2007–2008, a vast majority of crime scene investigators (CSI) were commissioned/sworn police officers. These officers were required to work patrol (work patrolling the jurisdiction, responding to calls for service) for a certain amount of years (2–5 years) until they could apply for the position. Testing for the coveted position included a written and/or oral board interview and sometimes even attendance at an autopsy, since it is a significant part of the job and difficult for some to stomach (just because one dons the police uniform does not always mean they can handle the more vulgar parts of the job). Once chosen, the training begins. Even though the newly appointed CSI had already attended a police academy, and passed probation does not mean the CSI knows how to process a crime scene. Generally, a CSI academy is attended, which lasts approximately 2–4 months. This academy trains the new CSI in the basics of processing a crime scene. In order for the CSI to become an expert, many future years of training must be conducted. It can take upward of more than a decade to grow a properly trained CSI, and even then that CSI will only be an expert in a few technical areas. A decent CSI is always training, honing the required skills and keeping updated on current new technological advances.

After the financial crisis of 2007–2008, many law enforcement agencies across the United States experienced hiring freezes for patrol officers due to budget cuts. Therefore, when there was an opening in the Crime Scene Investigation Division, many chiefs and sheriffs did not allow a police officer to be taken from patrol. Agencies were facing shortages in patrol, and preciously trained police officers could not be sacrificed to a Crime Scene Investigation Division. However, these divisions still needed investigators; how were these agencies to answer this conundrum? The answer came in one word: *civilians*. Instead of requiring CSIs to be commissioned/sworn officers (knowing this can take upward of 2 years to grow an officer), agencies civilianized the Crime Scene Investigation Division, requiring the candidates to have an educational background in some forensic science. This placed the onus and cost of training on the individual instead of on the agency and did not take precious police officers from patrol.

See the following police departments and how they currently staff their Crime Scene Investigation Divisions:

- North Las Vegas Police Department: Staffed by civilian CSIs
- Las Vegas Metropolitan Police Department: Staffed by civilian crime scene analysts
- Henderson Police Department (Las Vegas area): Staffed by civilian crime scene technicians
- Medford Police Department (Oregon): Staffed by a civilian forensic unit
- Portland Police Bureau (Oregon): Staffed by commissioned/sworn officer as forensic science technician (FST)

FIGURE 2.13 Crime scene investigators process a crime scene.

There are both positive and negative issues with having a civilian work as a CSI. To begin, it is positive that civilian CSIs are required to have some college science education. Some departments dealt with issues of having a civilian process a crime scene in a violent neighborhood, whereas if the CSI was a commissioned/sworn officer first, that CSI would carry a firearm and be trained how to react during various situations that a civilian may not be equipped or prepared to handle. Agencies are dealing with the many strengths and weaknesses of commissioned/sworn and civilian CSIs; either way, the more important topic of new technology in the CSI arena is far more reaching.

CSIs process crime scenes using a variety of tools, including a photograph camera and a video camera, GPS tools, chemicals, and light source enhancement, and they analyze tool marks, shoe prints, tire prints; take fingerprints of live and deceased humans; and complete detailed crime scene sketches. After processing a crime scene, a CSI will prepare detailed investigative and supplemental case reports and work with detectives to process additional evidence. Figure 2.13 illustrates how crime scene investigators must be able to process all types of crime scenes.

What Careers Are Available in the Field of Forensics?

The field of forensics is very different from the world of crime scene investigations. A CSI responds to a crime scene and works with a detective in processing the crime scene. For example, a CSI responds to a homicide scene of a shooting and collects blood evidence. The field of forensics is the processing of the blood evidence found at the scene. A forensic technician, in a lab, would then take the blood evidence and test it to determine the DNA and blood type. DNA (deoxyribonucleic acid) technology has developed to the point that it is now one of the most useful tools used to convict suspects of certain crimes. A good analogy is the television show *CSI*, which shows how a crime scene investigator responds to a crime scene and collects evidence, such as a skeleton. The television show *Bones* shows how evidence found at the crime scene is then processed in a lab, which is the field of forensics. Compound microscopes, comparison microscopes, stereoscopic microscopes, polarizing microscopes, microspectrophotometers, and scanning electron microscopes are all tools utilized by a forensic technician.

Forensic technicians are often required to have a bachelor's or even a graduate degree in the sciences to include chemistry, math, English, and biology, along with classes heavy in forensics. The stereotypical lab coat is seen more in the field of forensics since the job is completed in a lab instead of in the field.

Other career options in the field of forensics are as follows:

- Criminalist
- Pathologist
- Biologist

FIGURE 2·14 Forensic technicians process DNA evidence.

- Computer forensic reconstructionist
- Anthropologist
- Psychiatrist

If a person is interested in the field of forensics, the first step would be higher education. Through a college or university, the student would participate in an internship program in one of these fields. Figure 2.14 illustrates how forensic technicians process evidence.

I Have Identified My Law Enforcement Career Path, Now What?

How Do I Locate Open Positions?

The first step to locating a career in law enforcement is to begin as a volunteer or as a student intern. Most positions in the law enforcement realm require some experience. The employer needs to see some work history in this field. The perfect answer is through volunteer or intern work. This is the way to get a foot in the door and prove one's work ethic and passion.

The workload of a college or university student can be daunting, and the thought of adding in one more thing to do can be overwhelming. It really can be the answer to getting hired down the line, especially after graduation. A career in law enforcement is a career in the service industry, and volunteering is a crucial component; therefore, the time must be etched out to ensure success in future endeavors.

How Do I Prepare for the Application Process?

The first step to the application process is *not* locating an opening and filling out an application. Many behind-the-scenes steps must be painstakingly practiced and worked through before beginning the application process. If the goal is to be hired as soon as possible, the worst course of action would be to find the nearest law enforcement agency testing for officers and apply without any preparation. As soon as the candidate walks through the door of a law enforcement agency asking for an application (or visits a website), that candidate is evaluated. Therefore, the candidate must ensure that preparation is conducted for every portion of the hiring process.

The candidate must start by creating a resume and portfolio. Once they have been created, the candidate can then look for holes where they need to improve. **Portfolios** contain useful documents a candidate has collected to enhance a resume. Items such as recommendation letters, thank-you letters, transcripts, certificates, and a sample research paper can be included. Some of the most often forgotten experiences are the actual classes a student completed at a college or university. If a specific class pertained to law enforcement was taken, and skills or certificates were earned, then by all means do not forget to list it in the resume and portfolio. Do not make the mistake of only listing college or university degrees on a resume. Additional skills can be added to any resume and certificates can be added to a portfolio. For example, at Southern Oregon University in the Introduction to Law Enforcement class, students go through a practical testing scenario of a "shoot/don't shoot" incident. The students then write a discussion and review their actions. This practical experience can be added to a resume under the skills and training heading.

Candidates can also help themselves by gaining online education and certificates. One great way to do this is through the Federal Emergency Management Agency (FEMA) Independent Study program, where students can gain valuable online training in the National Incident Management System (NIMS). The NIMS online classes prepare students for response to a catastrophic event (FEMA, 2017).

FACT BOX 2.3: BOOST YOUR RESUME AND GET A CERTIFICATE FROM THE FEDERAL GOVERNMENT TODAY!

Get prepared and at the same time boost your resume by getting a certification from the Federal Government in emergency management. NIMS was started in 2004 by the U.S. Department of Homeland Security. It developed standard procedures for emergencies by those in law enforcement. NIMS ensures, through online training, that those who respond to an emergency situation communicate effectively and work more efficiently as a team.

NIMS is just not for those already in law enforcement, but for anyone who wants to learn and become more educated in emergency management. Therefore, anyone can take their online classes and receive a certificate of completion.

Instructions:

1. Obtain a FEMA student identification (SID) number by registering at https://cdp.dhs.gov/femasid and click REGISTER.
2. Complete the application for your SID number.
3. Once you receive your SID number, go to https://training.fema.gov/nims.
4. Click on the many NIMS online training classes and complete the training.

Emergency Management Institute

FEMA

This Certificate of Achievement is to acknowledge that

has reaffirmed a dedication to serve in times of crisis through continued
professional development and completion of the independent study course:

IS-00100.c
Introduction to Incident Command System, ICS-100

Steven P. Heidecker

Steven P. Heidecker
Acting Deputy Superintendent
Emergency Management Institute

FIGURE 2.15 FEMA certificate.

5. After the training, you will take a quiz, and once you pass a link for the certificate will be e-mailed to you.
6. Do not forget to utilize this training and certificate(s) in your resume/portfolio.

Figure 2.15 shows a FEMA certificate.

What Is the Application Process?

The application process is the step in the hiring process where the applicant notifies the testing agency that they are interested in participating in the hiring process and the hiring agency determines if the candidate meets the minimum qualifications. The applicant should first obtain the job announcement for the position. A **job announcement** will list the required duties, responsibilities, educational requirements, and anything else the agency is requiring for the specified position. Most agencies list job announcements on their website. The following list illustrates the general requirements for most law enforcement agencies:

1. *Age:* Most police departments require the applicant be 21 years of age by the date of the application. However, others, such as the Los Angeles Police Department, allow an application to be filled out by a person who is 20 years of age when the candidate graduates

the police academy. Other positions such as cadet or reserve officers may have different age requirements.

2. *Citizenship*: Most police departments require U.S. citizenship or permanent resident alien who has applied for citizenship, either by the time the application is filled out or upon the conditional offer of employment (part of the hiring process). Many police departments have police officers, deputies, troopers, and federal agents who are born in other countries yet have American citizenship. Applicants do not have to live in the jurisdiction they are applying for; however, many agencies require that the applicant, once hired (generally within a certain number of days), live within a certain number of miles from the agency.

3. *Eyesight*: Most police departments allow visual acuity to be corrected and the norms are trending toward 20/30 corrected in each eye and not worse than 20/100 uncorrected in either eye (Department of Public Standards and Safety, 2016). According to the Los Angeles Police Department (LAPD) website, vision can be corrected in each eye to 20/30, uncorrected distance vision must not exceed 20/70 in either eye, and the better eye must be at least 20/40. Soft contact lenses must have been worn for at least 3 months. If LASIK refractive surgery/procedure has been completed, vision must be at least 20/30 in each eye. In relation to color vision, Oregon Department of Public Standards and Safety requires applicants to distinguish red, green, blue, and yellow. Red or green deficiencies may be accepted, as long as the applicant can read nine of the first thirteen plates of the Ishihara Test. For more information see the 24 Ishihara plates (https://www.colour-blindness.com/colour-blindness-tests/ishihara-colour-test-plates/). LAPD requires the applicant to accurately and quickly name colors and be free from other visual impairments that could possibly restrict the applicant from performing law enforcement duties.

4. *Driver's license*: Required as a part of the application process. Most departments do not require the driver's license to be in the state the applicant is applying for until the applicant is hired.

5. *Physical agility test or physical fitness test*: Applicants are required to either pass a physical agility test prior to being hired or during the police academy.

6. *Education*: The most common level of education for most agencies is a high school diploma or GED; however, many agencies have started to raise the bar and require either an associate's degree or at least 1 to 2 years (approximately 60 credits) of college work from an accredited institution with a minimum GPA (approximately 2.0).

7. *Character*: Honesty, integrity, personal ethics, intelligent, healthy, physically strong and agile, emotionally stable, self-confident, interpersonal skills, sets and achieves goals, sensitivity, respect for others, positive decision making and judgment, concern for feelings and others perspectives, impartiality in dealing with issues of race, sexual orientation, age, gender, ethnicity, religion, cultural diversity, ability to be a member of a team, recognizing achievements of others, be able to critically analyze and determine appropriate action, act assertively without overreacting, maturity, discipline, accepts responsibility for actions and mistakes, avoid unnecessarily risky behavior, use constructive criticism to improve, work well with minimal supervision, and tactful.

Disqualifiers are issues that an applicant may have that would cause the application to be denied. The following list illustrates some of the issues that could cause disqualification at the application stage of the hiring process. The issues in bold are generally found in the application portion of the hiring process. The other disqualifying factors could occur at other points in the hiring process, specifically the background check (the list is not comprehensive).

1. **Conviction of a felony**
2. **Conviction of domestic violence**
3. **Dishonorably discharged from the military**
4. **Abuse of illegal drugs, alcohol, or prescribed medications**
5. Purposefully withholding/omitting information or falsifying information or statements
6. Minimizing past mistakes or errors
7. Blaming others for mistakes
8. Inducing others to give false information
9. Condoning the unethical behavior of others through silence
10. Theft
11. Fraud
12. History of disrespect for the law
13. Failure to meet commitments to work, school, family, volunteer, or community activities
14. Tendency toward violence
15. Failure to follow all laws and common rules of conduct
16. Associations with individuals who break the law
17. Termination from a job or poor behavior (this is extremely variable and does not always cause disqualification)
18. Poor response to discipline during employment
19. Verbal or physical abuse or violence toward others (which indicates a lack of self-control)
20. Inability to get along with others in work or personal life
21. Failure to listen effectively
22. Use of derogatory stereotypes in daily life and daily language (jokes)
23. Rude or condescending remarks to or about others
24. Using physical force to resolve disputes
25. Overreaction to criticism (demonstrated)
26. Inability to work as a team player
27. Challenging or disruptive behavior toward authority
28. Using harassment, intimidation, or threats
29. Making poor choices given known circumstances
30. Indecision when options are not clear-cut
31. Failure to learn from past mistakes
32. Unwillingness to modify a position
33. Rigid adherence to rules without other consideration
34. Succumbing to peer pressure
35. Being argumentative, defensive, or blaming others for mistakes
36. Resorting to force to gain objectives

37. Unnecessarily confrontational
38. Unnecessarily taking personal risks or placing others at risk through actions

The application process is very serious. Candidates should research the job announcement for the position of interest and thoroughly prepare prior to filling out and submitting such application. Careers in the law enforcement arena are amazing and thoroughly awe inspiring and interesting; however, they are also first-responder jobs that are high risk and must be thoroughly explored before one commits completely.

What Are the Duties of an Officer?
The duties of a police officer, deputy, trooper, and federal agent can vary greatly depending on the type of jurisdiction. The main duties of a law enforcement officer are to preserve the safety of the public, find and arrest suspects, preserve peace, enforce laws, and be proactive to crime. There are basic aspects of the job of an officer that are universal, and the following list illustrates some of those duties:

- Arrest and apprehension of criminals
- Understanding use of force
- Understanding current laws applying to the Fourth Amendment of search and seizure
- Handcuffing
- Defensive tactics
- Understanding current laws applying to the Fifth Amendment
- Seizing contraband and evidence
- Understanding deadly force
- Arrest and search warrant
- Investigations
- Securing crime scenes
- Interviewing and interrogation
- Processing of crime scenes
- Chain of custody
- Search of missing persons
- Patrol procedures
- Problem solving
- Emotional intelligence
- Stress first aid
- Enforcing of criminal laws
- Emergency vehicle operation
- Issuing citations
- Property checks
- Foot patrol
- Traffic control and enforcement
- Directing traffic
- Standardized field sobriety tests

- Obtaining evidence for under-the-influence investigations
- Removing hazards from roadway
- Less lethal options
- Communication
- Providing descriptions
- Interacting with the public
- Mediating domestic disputes
- Comforting emotionally upset persons
- Advising offenders, witnesses, and victims on criminal procedures/law
- Referring and understanding local social services available
- Court procedures
- Testifying in court
- Writing and reviewing reports
- Conferring with the many parts of the criminal justice system
- Physical tasks appropriate for the type of task
- Working in various working conditions

FIGURE 2.16 Deputy Hohl and K-9 partner train patrol procedures.

SUMMARY OF CHAPTER 2

1. Careers in law enforcement are vast and multifaceted.

2. The two major different categories of careers in law enforcement agencies are commissioned or sworn positions and noncommissioned/non-sworn or civilian positions.

3. Depending on the law enforcement agency, the size of the agency, and jurisdiction, the careers offered can vary greatly. A candidate should take the time to research not only local agencies but also other communities and states to understand the variety of opportunities available.

4. It is crucial that a person interested in a career in law enforcement have goals to volunteer or participate in a college or university internship in order to not only gain a more thorough understanding of the profession but also to establish roots in the field.

5. Prior to starting the application process, future candidates must research and understand the job responsibilities and job announcements to look for those required skills and possible disqualifiers.

DISCUSSION QUESTIONS

1. What are the significant differences between local, county, and state law enforcement agencies?

2. Are there many career opportunities in the federal law enforcement field? Yes or No? Give some examples.

3. Why are civilian or noncommissioned/non-sworn law enforcement careers so important?

4. How much thought and preparation should a candidate put into the application process?

INTERNET EXERCISES

1. Using your preferred search engine, search "police department organizational chart," look through the results, and click on three different police department organizational charts.

    - What different divisions (such as patrol, K-9, detective/investigations/and so forth) do the different police departments have?
    - What else did you learn about a police department by its organizational chart?
    - Why is it important to look at a police department organizational chart before applying for that particular police department?

2. Go to the following website: https://www.discoverpolicing.org/explore-the-field/search-the-agency-directory/#/.

    - Enter the state you are most interested in finding a career in the "state" field.
    - Look how many law enforcement agencies are in that state. Are you surprised by the number? Is it higher or lower than you expected?

- Now click on a police department that interests you. How many officers work for that police department? What are the specialized units? Patrol types? Any other interesting information?
- Go back and search two additional police departments in the same state or chose another state and click on two additional police departments. Answer the previous questions.

3. Go to the following website for the FBI career paths: https://www.fbijobs.gov/career-paths.

   - Click on each of the five different career paths in operations and intelligence, special agents, intelligence analysts, surveillance, forensic accounting, and foreign languages, and review the facts.
   - Click on each of the seven different career paths in operations and intelligence, STEM, arts and communications, business and administration, facilities and logistics, legal, medical and counseling, police and security, and review the facts.

4. Which career path with the FBI is the most interesting to you and why?

See Active Learning for the Following:

- Practice quizzes
- eFlashcards
- Video links
- Cognella journal articles
- Answers to "Decision Time"
- News clips

SELF-ASSESSMENT TEST A-1: 16PF Answers

Primary Factor	Low	High	You Are (Low or high and list specific characteristics):	Officers Are Seen Showing
Warmth	Reserved, impersonal, distant, cool, reserved, impersonal, detached, formal, aloof	Warm, outgoing, attentive to others, kind, easygoing, participates, likes people	See your answers from Chapter 2	Tend to be HIGH in warmth
Reasoning	Concrete thinking, lower general mental capacity, less intelligent, unable to handle abstract problems	Abstract thinking, more intelligent, bright, higher general mental capacity, fast learner		Can be either LOW or HIGH or in between

Primary Factor	Low	High	You Are (Low or high and list specific characteristics):	Officers Are Seen Showing
Emotional stability	Reactive, emotionally changeable, affected by feelings, emotionally less stable, easily upset	Emotionally stable, adaptive, mature, faces reality, calm		Tend to be closer to HIGH in emotional stability, calm and resilient and low anxiety and emotionally stable
Dominance	Deferential, co-operative, avoids conflict, submissive, humble, obedient, easily led, docile, accommodating	Dominant, forceful, assertive, aggressive, competitive, stubborn, bossy		Tend to be LOW or average in dominance
Liveliness	Serious, restrained, prudent, taciturn, introspective, silent	Lively, animated, spontaneous, enthusiastic, happy-go-lucky, cheerful, expressive, impulsive		Can be either LOW or HIGH or in between and are serious
Rule consciousness	Expedient, nonconforming, disregards rules, self-indulgent	Rule conscious, dutiful, conscientious, conforming, moralistic, staid, rule bound		Tend to be closer to HIGH in rule consciousness, has high self-control
Social boldness	Shy, threat sensitive, timid, hesitant, intimidated	Socially bold, venturesome, thick-skinned, uninhibited, can take stress		Tend to be closer to HIGH in social boldness, also is bold and fearless
Sensitivity	Utilitarian, objective, unsentimental, tough minded, self-reliant, no nonsense, rough	Sensitive, aesthetic, sentimental, tender minded, intuitive, refined		Tend to be closer to LOW in sensitivity, also tough, pragmatic, and unsentimental
Vigilance	Trusting, unsuspecting, accepting, unconditional, easy	Vigilant, suspicious, skeptical, wary, distrustful, oppositional		Tend to be closer to LOW in vigilance, also trusting
Abstractedness	Grounded, practical, prosaic, solution oriented, steady, conventional	Abstracted, imaginative, absent-minded, impractical, absorbed in ideas		Tend to be closer to LOW in abstractedness, also practical
Private	Forthright, genuine, artless, open, guileless, naïve, unpretentious, involved	Private, discreet, non-disclosing, shrewd, polished, worldly, astute, diplomatic		Can be either LOW or HIGH or in between

Primary Factor	Low	High	You Are (Low or high and list specific characteristics):	Officers Are Seen Showing
Apprehension	Self-assured, un-worried, complacent, secure, free of guilt, confident, self-satisfied	Apprehensive, self-doubting, worried, guilt prone, insecure, worrying, self-blaming		Tend to be closer to LOW in apprehension, also self-assured
Openness to change	Traditional, attached to familiar, conservative, respects traditional ideas	Open to change, experimenting, liberal, analytical, critical, free thinking, flexibility		Can be either LOW or HIGH or in between and is also traditional
Self-reliance	Group oriented, affiliative, a joiner and follower, dependent	Self-reliant, solitary, resourceful, individualistic, self-sufficient		Tend to be closer to HIGH in self-reliance
Perfectionism	Tolerates disorder, unexacting, flexible, undisciplined, lax, self-conflictive, impulsive, careless of social rules, uncontrolled	Perfectionist, organized, compulsive, self-disciplined, socially precise, exacting will power, control, self-sentimental		Tend to be closer to HIGH in perfectionism, also self-disciplined, high self-control, and perfectionistic
Tension	Relaxed, placid, tranquil, torpid, patient, composed, low drive	Tense, high energy, impatient, driven, frustrated, overwrought, has high drive, time driven		Can be either LOW or HIGH or in between

Source: Changing Minds (n.d.).

References

16 Personalities. (n.d.). *Personality types.* https://www.16personalities.com/personality-types

Bureau of Justice Statistics. (2008). *Tribal law enforcement.* www.bjs.ojp.usdoj.gov

Cattell, H. E., & Mead, A. D. (2008). The sixteen personality factor questionnaire (16PF). In G. J. Boyle, G. Matthews, & D. H. Saklofske (Eds.), *The SAGE handbook of personality theory and assessment: Volume 2—Personality measurement and testing* (pp. 135–159). SAGE. https://doi.org/10.4135/9781849200479.n7

Changing Minds. (n.d.). *16PF factors.* http://changingminds.org/explanations/preferences/16pf.htm

Daeble, D., & Cowhig, M. (2018, April). Bulletin. Bureau of Justice Statistics.

DEPARTMENT OF PUBLIC SAFETY STANDARDS AND SAFETY (Rep.). (2016). Salem, OR. doi:https://www.google.com/search?client=firefox-b-1-d&ei=Yal8XMvqJtK6-gTfmJCQAg&q=dpsst medical examination &oq=dpsst medical examination &gs_l=psy-ab.3..35i39.4047.7842..9846...0.0..0.164.2843.9j17......0....1..gws-wiz.......0i71j0i67j0j0i20i263j0i22i30.8qXk0AdX-FM

Force, W. T. (n.d.). *Gavin Newsom.* https://www.cdcr.ca.gov/Rehabilitation/Process.html

GameWarden. (n.d.). *How to become a game warden in Oregon.* https://www.gamewarden.org/state/oregon

Hultman, M. (n.d.). *Labor market information* center. South Dakota Department of Labor and Regulation. https://dlr.sd.gov/lmic/menu_sdcis.aspx

Johnston, C. H. (2019). *Careers in criminal justice.* SAGE.

Kaeble, D. (2018, April 26). *Probation and parole in the United States, 2016.* Bureau of Justice Statistics. http://www.bjs.gov/index.cfm?ty=pbdetail&iid=6188

Federal Emergency Management Agency. (n.d.). *2017 national preparedness report.* https://www.fema.gov/media-library/assets/documents/134253

State of Oregon. (n.d.). *What we do.* Fish and Wildlife Division. https://www.oregon.gov/osp/programs/fw/Pages/about.aspx

Reaves, B. A. (2015). *Local police departments, 2013: Personnel, policies, and practices.* Bureau of Justice Statistics. https://www.bjs.gov/content/pub/pdf/lpd13ppp.pdf

Tribal Court Clearing House. (n.d.). *Tribal law enforcement.* https://www.tribal-institute.org/lists/enforcement.htm

Twersky-Glasner, A. (2005). Police personality: What is it and why are they like that? *Journal of Police and Criminal Psychology, 20*(1), 56–67. https://doi.org/10.1007/bf02806707

University of Nevada, Las Vegas. (n.d.). *About university police services.* https://www.unlv.edu/police/about

U.S. Department of the Interior. (2018, September 23). *How many countries are there in the United States?* https://www.usgs.gov/faqs/how-many-counties-are-there-united-states

Image Credits

Tbl. 2.1: Adapted from http://changingminds.org/explanations/preferences/16pf.htm.
Tbl. 2.2: Adapted from https://www.16personalities.com/personality-types.
Fig. 2.3: Copyright © 1999 by Mark Gandolfo. Reprinted with permission.
Fig. 2.4: Source: https://www.tribal-institute.org/lists/enforcement.htm.
Fig. 2.5: Source: http://www.bjs.gov/index.cfm?ty=pbdetail&iid=6188.
Fig. 2.7: Source: http://www.bjs.gov/index.cfm?ty=pbdetail&iid=6188.
Fig. 2.10: Adapted from https://www.cdcr.ca.gov/rehabilitation/about/process/.
Fig. 2.11: Copyright © 2012 by West Midlands Police, (CC BY-SA 2.0) at https://www.flickr.com/photos/westmidlandspolice/8211635324.
Fig. 2.12: Source: https://www.tinker.af.mil/News/Photos/igphoto/2000674461/.
Fig. 2.13: Source: https://www.scott.af.mil/News/Photos/igphoto/2000151178/.
Fig. 2.14: Source: https://archive.defense.gov/news/newsarticle.aspx?id=51342.
Fig. 2.15: Source: FEMA.

UNIT 3

The Tests

What Is the Written Exam?

3

"Everything you want is out there waiting for you to ask. Everything you want also wants you. But you have to take action to get it."

—Jack Canfield

KEY TERMS

Eight common errors in writing: (1) apostrophes, (2) commas, (3) directions, (4) double negatives, (5) homophones, (6) parallelism, (7) pronouns, and (8) spelling.

Four math rules: (1) analyze the information, (2) identify information, (3) solve strategically, and (4) double check the answer.

NIDO, the five memorization rules: (1) notes, (2) identifiers, (3) details, (4) direction, and (5) order facts logically.

Nine police report writing rules: (1) first person, (2) active not passive voice, (3) assumptions, (4) avoid using police jargon, (5) details, (6) opinions, (7) past tense and chronological order, (8) unnecessary words, and (9) vague.

POLIS, the five basic patrol procedure roles: (1) professionalism, (2) officer, (3) law, (4) integrity, and (5) service.

Six categories of questions on the written exam: (1) judgment and reasoning, (2) mathematics, (3) memorization and observation, (4) reading comprehension, (5) traffic maps, and (6) writing.

Superhero state of mind: A way to think positively before the written exam in order to succeed.

Three C's of reading comprehension: concentration, complete, and comprehension.

CHAPTER LEARNING OBJECTIVES

After reading the chapter, you should have a good understanding of the following:

- Who sets the requirements for the written exam
- Why specific questions are prohibited on the written exam
- The purpose of the written exam portion of the hiring process
- The different written exams on the market
- The most common six categories on the written exam and what each category looks like
- The four-math rules
- NIDO
- POLIS
- The nine police report writing rules
- The eight common writing rules
- The three C's of reading comprehension
- The superhero state of mind
- Why candidates need to study for the written exam
- The different study plans and how each works

What Is the Written Exam?

The written exam portion of the testing process is generally one of the most failed portions. Why? One reason is lack of preparation. Most candidates cannot just by happenstance take the written exam on a whim in hopes of obtaining a passing score. Not only is such a thing impractical, it is highly illogical. Days or weeks will not suffice for preparation. Little to no preparation *can* secure a passing score; however, it is not the best first impression a candidate wants to leave on an agency. A low exam score can also be the primary determining factor of seniority placement. Seniority in a law enforcement agency can determine things such as the shift worked. Therefore, candidates must intimately learn and understand the written exam and give it the time required for a rewarding and passing score.

The written exam that is administered across the country by various law enforcement agencies has been significantly modified in the last decade. Supreme Court decisions set requirements for the types of questions test writers are no longer permitted to utilize. Questions that required the candidate to have prior knowledge of the law, law enforcement procedures, or even the duties or responsibilities of a police officer can no longer be asked. Detailed information that is taught in a police academy cannot be asked on the written exam, especially if it requires a comprehensive answer. This type of knowledge is part of the training in a police academy, and an untrained candidate should not be required to know such answers. For example, the steps an officer goes through when responding to a burglary call is not a legal question to ask, since this is something that a non-police officer would have difficulty answering.

Why Is There a Written Exam?

After the candidate fills out an application with the hiring agency, the next step in the law enforcement hiring process is the written exam. The written exam helps ensure the candidate can read, understand,

and make sound decisions in a variety of categories. These skills are required for a police officer not only during police academy training, but during the field training process, continuing through probation, and finally for annual re-certification of abilities, such as defensive tactics, and various qualifications, such as firearms tests, that every officer must be able to pass. If a candidate is unable to study, prepare, and pass the written exam, then it would be easy to deduce that the candidate would not be able to study, prepare, and pass police officer's many daily requirements.

POLICE STORY 3.1 If You Don't Use It, You Lose It!

by Detective Jillian Winston, Jackson County (Oregon) Sheriff's Office

The written exam is one of the first hurdles to jump when applying to any law enforcement agency. Although the written exam is not extremely difficult, it seems to be a hurdle many can't clear. The first time I took the written exam, I failed it and rightly so. I didn't study because I believed I could easily pass, considering I was college educated. There were math questions on the written exam that I had not seen since high school. There were misspelled words on the grammar portion that I never worried about spelling correctly due to auto correct in the writing programs I used. The written exam is also timed, and that seems to be the most stressful and challenging part. A helpful piece of advice someone shared with me that I'd like to share is simple: study. Go to a bookstore, walk to the children's section, and locate a basic math workbook (addition, subtraction, division, multiplication, and fractions) and a basic grammar workbook. Swallow your pride and purchase the workbooks. Getting reacquainted with your basic math and grammar skills will help you answer some of the questions that before absorbed a lot of your valuable test-taking time. It's surprising how much knowledge can be lost when one doesn't practice a certain skill set for an extended period. Do yourself a favor and set yourself up to succeed by studying.

Do I Need to Study for the Written Exam?

I am a college graduate; therefore, I do not need to study for the written exam, right? *WRONG!* This could not be further from the truth. No matter the candidate's background, the written exam *must* be studied for, and a plan must be formulated in order to secure success. Many of the topics on the written exam will be familiar to the candidate; however, unless the information is current and the candidate has prepared and studied tirelessly for the questions, failure, or a low score, should be expected.

Although a candidate can cram study for the written exam, it is not the preferred method and often results in a low score. The human brain takes in data and recalls it at a higher rate when the information is added at a slower consistent rate over time. Therefore, it would stand to reason that if the candidate slowly studies the various categories a little bit at a time, over a more extended period, the intelligence retained will be superior. However, sometimes candidates do not have the luxury to spend weeks or months preparing and thereby must be aware of the various options for studying for the written exam. The needs and different situations diverse candidates may be faced with allow for the diverse types of study plans (for more information see the various study plans offered later in this chapter).

CASE STUDY 3.1 Share a Failed Written Exam Story

If you have ever taken a police officer written exam and failed it, you are not alone. The written exam is a tough test. Many candidates who have not passed the exam have either failed to study correctly or failed to study enough and the result was a failing score. This is a blow to one's ego and also ensures the candidate will have to wait months to a year to retest for that particular law enforcement agency.

There are many forums across the Internet where candidates share stories about a failed police exam. One such place is on Reddit. The police exam forum gives future candidates a chance to share stories about their experiences and more importantly learn from them.

Go to the Internet and search for "Reddit, Failed My First Police Exam. Anyone Want to Share Their Stories?"

Read through shared stories and find three different pieces of advice on how to prepare for the written exam.

Are There Different Written Exams?

Since every law enforcement agency is different and has unique needs, many different companies have developed police officer written exams. Although all the written exams utilized have many common threads, there are minor differences. Candidates should find out the written exam utilized by the hiring agency and apply the following information first to study the common areas of testing and then to further delineate the differences depending on the company that designed the written exam.

The following list illustrates many of the different companies that offer the written exam and the agencies that utilize them:

State: California

Various departments utilize the following written exams: CPS-HR, DELPOE, Frontline (NTN), LAPD, LASD, NPST by FSPI, PELLETB, SDPD

State: Florida

Various departments utilize the following written exams: CJBAT by IOS (Criminal Justice Basic Abilities Test), CJBAT by Morris McDaniel (Criminal Justice Basic Abilities Test), FBAT (Florida Basic Abilities Test)

State: Georgia

Various departments utilize the following written exams: ASSET Plus COMPASS, GA POST (Georgia Peace Officer Standards and Training), or SAT/ACT/CPE/ACCU-PLACER, SHIELD (Morris and McDaniels ELP)

State: Idaho

Various departments utilize the following written exams: Frontline (NTN), IPMA-HR PO-EL, LST (by Public Safety Testing-PST an IOS affiliate)

State: Illinois

Various departments utilize the following written exams: CWH-NGLE (I/O Solutions), Frontline (NTN), LESI, LST, NCJOSI, NPOST, NPST by FSPI

State: Michigan

Various departments utilize the following written exams: EMPCO, Frontline (NTN), MCOLES (Michigan Commission on Law Enforcement Standards)

State: Montana

Various departments utilize the following written exams: NPOST (Stanards and Associates)

State: Nevada

Various departments utilize the following written exams: CWH-NGLE (I/O Solutions), DELPOE, Frontline (NTN)

State: New Jersey

Various departments utilize the following written exams: LEE (EB Jacobs), NCJOSI

State: New York

Various departments utilize the following written exams: NCJOSI, NYPD, NYS (Civil Service Police Exam based on the LEAB-II police exam)

State: Oregon

Various departments utilize the following written exams: Frontline (NTN), LESI and CPS-HR

State: Pennsylvania

Various departments utilize the following written exams: CWH-NGLE (I/O Solutions), LEAB (EB Jacobs), NCJOSI, NDRT (Nelson–Denny Reading Test), NPOST (Stanards and Associates)

State: Texas

Various departments utilize the following written exams: CPS-HR, DELPOE, Frontline (NTN), IPMA-HR PO-EL, LEVEL (recommended by Texas Commission on Law Enforcement), NCJOSI, NDRT, NPOST, NPST by FSPI

State: Utah

Various departments utilize the following written exams: NPOST (Stanards and Associates)

State: Washington

Various departments utilize the following written exams: Frontline (NTN), LST (by Public Safety Testing-PST an IOS affiliate)

FACT BOX 3.1: VARIOUS WRITTEN EXAM COMPANIES

Candidates should be informed and find out which written exam the hiring agency utilizes. Once this information is located, the candidate can then begin to streamline studying for the exact type of written exam. The following list illustrates links to most of the different companies that sell written exams to various law enforcement agencies across the United States. Many of the links offer the candidate suggestions and even opportunities to take or purchase study guides for the particular assessment company. The more opportunities a candidate has to prepare for a particular exam, the better the score on the written exam.

CJBAT-LEO developed by Industrial Organizational Solutions (IOS) (https://iosolutions.com/product/cjbat-leo-interactive-online-practice-test-version-2/)

and

CJBAT developed by Morris and McDaniel (www.morrisandmcdaniel.com/pages/fdle.htm)

The CJBAT is comprised of two parts. For the first part the information is provided to the candidate. The study information is then taken away and the second part is the actual multiple-choice exam.

There are 100 multiple-choice questions that access the following:

1. Deductive reasoning: The ability to apply rules to problems and come up with answers
2. Information ordering: The ability to correctly follow a set of rules in a specific order
3. Inductive reasoning: The ability to combine separate pieces of information
4. Memorization: The ability to memorize information seen in a picture
5. Problem sensitivity: The ability to combine separate pieces of information
6. Spatial orientation: The ability to tell where you are in relation to another object
7. Written comprehension: The ability to understand written words and sentences
8. Written expression: The ability to write and understand words and sentences
9. Flexibility of closure: The ability to find a hidden object

The CJBAT-LEO (version 2) has 120 questions that provide insight to how a candidate will perform on the cognitive portions of the CJBAT (math, reading, and writing portions).

The FL CJBAT-LEO Practice Test (version 2) contains 120 questions that are designed to provide insight as to how the candidate will perform on the cognitive (i.e., reading, writing, and math) portion of the CJBAT.

CPS-HR developed by CPS HR Consulting (www.cpshr.us/services/testing/)

The CPS-HR is comprised of the following four content areas:

1. Observation and memory
2. Written communication
3. Reading comprehension
4. Analytical ability

CWH-NGLE developed by Industrial Organizational Solutions (IOS) (https://iosolutions.com/entry-level-exams/#entrylaws)

The CWH-NGL aims to assess those skills found in law enforcement officers. The exam is comprised of the following parts:

1. Cognitive ability: Reading comprehension, writing, grammar, and math
2. Situational judgment: Practical judgment, interpersonal skills, handling of stress, responsibility, emotional skills, and attitude

DELPOE (Darany Entry Level Police Officer Selection Test) developed by Darany and Associates

The exam has 169 multiple-choice questions with a time limit of 2 hours.

DELPOE is comprised of the following:

Cognitive abilities:

1. Observation: 40 questions
2. Reading comprehension: 35 questions

Written communication: 40 questions
Non-cognitive abilities:

1. Biodata: 54 questions

EMPCO developed by EMPCO Incorporated (www.empco.net/testing/information.php)

The EMPCO entry-level exam assesses the candidate's ability to process information and succeed in the law enforcement career field.

Frontline developed by the National Testing Network (NTN) (https://nationaltestingnetwork.com/publicsafetyjobs/ntn-test-law-national.cfm)

The Frontline testing system is comprised of three parts and has a 2-hour and 20-minute time limit.

1. Human relations video-based exam: During the video-based exam segment the candidate watches a video and then chooses the best response from a series of multiple-choice options. This portion of the exam is timed, and the candidate has 10 seconds to answer the question. There are 46 scenarios with a time limit of 90-minutes.
2. Written exam: The Frontline writing exam requires the candidate to watch a brief video (twice) and then write one written report in 10 minutes. The candidate will be shown an example of how to do this prior to having to complete this portion of the exam. The second part of the writing exam is a multiple-choice exam where candidates answer questions about what law enforcement officers need to include in a police report.
3. Multiple-choice reading exam: During the reading exam, candidates read over questions and choose the best word to fill in the blank. There are 30 questions to complete in 15 minutes.

FBAT (Florida Basic Abilities Test) (http://www.mdc.edu/justice/fbat/test-details.aspx)

The FBAT has two parts and is comprised of the following eight sections:

1. Deductive and Inductive Reasoning
2. Flexibility
3. Information Ordering
4. Memorization
5. Reading Comprehension
6. Situational Judgment
7. Spatial Orientation
8. Writing

LAPD developed by the Los Angeles Police Department (www.lapdwrittentest.com/home)

The LAPD entrance exam is unique since it is developed specifically for the Los Angeles Police Department. LAPD candidates must first complete the personal qualification essays (PQE). The PQE has a time limit of 30 minutes for each essay. The graders are looking for the candidate's character, self-esteem, and ability to communicate.

LASD or LEJFT developed by Los Angeles County Sheriffs (https://apps.hr.lacounty.gov/olt/Test/2/Version)

The LASD (Los Angeles County Sheriffs) entrance exam, or the LEJFT (Los Angeles Law Enforcement Job Family Test), is utilized specifically in California. The exam consists of 60 questions that are comprised of the following cognitive skills:

1. Data interpretation: The ability to understand records and numbers
2. Deductive reasoning: The ability to conclude a specific point from a general principle
3. Inductive reasoning: The ability to conclude a general principle from a specific point
4. Reading comprehension: The ability to understand what is read
5. Writing (clarity, grammar, and spelling): The ability to write, spell, and utilize proper grammar

LEAB developed by EB Jacobs (http://docplayer.net/14700895-Law-enforcement-aptitude-battery-assessment-preparation-guide.html)

The LEAB is utilized in New Jersey since half of the police agencies fall under the jurisdiction of the New Jersey Civil Service Commission. The exam has three sections and has a time limit of 3 hours and 40 minutes. The sections of the exam are as follows:

1. Life experience survey: Behavioral assessment (recommended completion in 15 to 45-minutes)
2. Written abilities exam: 48 multiple-choice questions (recommended completion in 2 hours). Questions cover deductive and inductive reasoning, information ordering, problem sensitivity, written expression, and written comprehension
3. Work styles questionnaire: Behavioral personality assessment (recommended completion in 15 minutes)

LESI developed by LESI® (Law Enforcement Services, Inc.) (www.lesi.com/)

The LESI® exam is looking at a candidate's cognitive abilities and personality traits. The exam is comprised of the following three parts:

1. Mathematics
2. Reading comprehension
3. Report writing (grammar and spelling)

LEVEL (recommended by Texas Commission on Law Enforcement), developed by Bannon & Associates (www.bannonandassociates.com/level-information.php)

LEVEL (Law Enforcement Validated Entry Level) was developed in Texas and it utilized by Texas law enforcement agencies.

LST developed by Industrial Organizational Solutions (IOS) (https://iosolutions.com/entry-level-exams/#entrylaws)

LST is comprised of the following four parts:
Cognitive ability:

1. Deductive and inductive reasoning
2. Information gathering
3. Spatial orientation
4. Written comprehension and expression
5. Visualization

Non-cognitive personality constructs:

1. Conscientiousness
2. Emotional stability
3. Extraversion

Non-cognitive biodata:

1. Adaptability/flexibility
2. Dependability
3. Initiative
4. Leadership
5. Physical activity
6. Service orientation
7. Social engagement
8. Stress tolerance

Non-cognitive integrity:

1. Antisocial behaviors
2. Orderliness
3. Safety orientation
4. Socialization

NCJOSI developed by Industrial Organizational Solutions (IOS) (https://iosolutions.com/entry-level-exams/#entrylaws)

NCJOSI exam is comprised of the following parts:

Cognitive ability:

1. Deductive and inductive reasoning
2. Flexibility
3. Information gathering
4. Problem sensitivity
5. Selective attention
6. Spatial orientation
7. Verbal comprehension and expression
8. Visualization

Non-Cognitive integrity:

1. Antisocial behavior
2. Orderliness
3. Positive outlook
4. Socialization

NDRT (Nelson-Denny Reading Test) developed by Nelson-Denny

The NDRT is utilized by many different government and non-government agencies to ensure the candidate has basic reading skills. The exam has two parts:

1. Vocabulary: 80 multiple-choice questions with a time limit of 15-minutes
2. Comprehension: The candidate reads passages and then answers 38 multiple-choice questions with a time limit of 20-minutes

NPOST (National Police Officer Selection Test) developed by Stanard & Associates (www.applytoserve.com/study/)

The NPOST is utilized as an entrance exam for not only city/municipal, county, state and federal agencies, but also as a mandated exam for Iowa and Utah. It is comprised of four parts:

1. Mathematics: 20 questions with a time limit of 20 minutes
2. Reading comprehension: 25 questions with a time limit of 25 minutes
3. Grammar: 20 questions with a time limit of 15 minutes
4. Report writing: 10 questions with a time limit of 15 minutes

NPST by Fire & Police Selection, Inc. (FSPI) (www.fpsi.com/police-sheriff-applicant-test-preparation/)

The NPST (National Police Selection Test) measures a candidate's ability to work with others effectively and is comprised of the following five parts:

1. Human relations: Ability to work with others in stressful situations and make sound judgments
2. Mathematics
3. Reading comprehension: Multiple-choice questions
4. Reasoning and analyzing skills: Ability to problem solve and interpret information
5. Writing ability: Ability to utilize proper grammar, spelling, and punctuation

PELLETB (https://post.ca.gov/LE-Entry-Level-Test-Battery-Applicant-FAQs)

The PELLETB (POST Entry-Level Law Enforcement Test Battery) is designed to measure a candidate's reading and writing abilities. The candidate is given 2.5 hours to complete the following five parts:

1. Clarity: Multiple-choice questions on the ability to choose the clear writing passages
2. CLOZE: Ability to utilize contextual clues to fill in missing words
3. Reading comprehension: 25 questions asked in a 25-minute time limit looking for the candidate's ability to read a passage and answer questions
4. Spelling
5. Vocabulary

NYPD developed by the New York Police Department (www1.nyc.gov/site/nypd/careers/police-officers/po-exam.page)

The NYPD entrance exam has 85 questions and a time limit of 2.5 hours. The exam is comprised of the following 10 cognitive abilities:

1. Deductive reasoning
2. Inductive reasoning
3. Information ordering
4. Mathematics
5. Memorization
6. Problem sensitivity
7. Reading comprehension
8. Spatial orientation
9. Visualization
10. Written expression

PO-EL developed by IPMA-HR (www.ipma-hr.org/assessment-services/assessments/test-detail/po-el-101-tip-entry-level-police-officer-test)

The PO-EL exam looks at whether the candidate can learn to perform the duties of a law enforcement officer. There are 100 questions and a time limit of 1 hour and 45-minutes, plus an additional 25 minutes for the TIP portion. The exam is comprised of the following five sections:

1. Ability to Follow Directions: 20 questions
2. Ability to Learn and Apply Information: 25 questions
3. Ability to Observe and Remember Details: 12 questions
4. Ability to Use Judgment and Logic: 100 questions
5. Ability to Verbalize: 23 questions

SDPD developed by the San Diego Police Department (www.sandiego.gov/police/recruiting/join/recwrittentest)

The SDPD is utilized specifically for the San Diego Police Department as an entry-level police officer exam. The three sections of the exam consist of the following:

1. Reading comprehension: Ability to read and comprehend written passages
2. Checking ability: Ability to detect similarities and differences among groups of items, ability to follow directions on a map, and ability to make proper critical decisions
3. Written communication: Ability to utilize proper grammar, punctuation, and spelling

Where Is the Written Exam Administered?

Historically candidates took the written exam portion of the hiring process at a designated location set by the hiring law enforcement agency. Some agencies, especially larger ones, still administer the written exam this way. However, with technology came the advancement of new ways to administer the written exam. Smaller agencies gravitated toward these new techniques since the cost to run a written exam was high. Agencies must have a location big enough for the number of candidates taking the exam, or they must pay to rent a suitable location. Plus, employees with the Human Resources Department and officers must be paid, possibly overtime pay, to coordinate the exam. It is a considerable effort to bring in the candidates, methodically hand out the exams, time the various portions of the exam, and ensure no cheating occurs. Finally, the exams must be scored, and the candidates must be notified of the score. The law enforcement agencies were not the only ones feeling the money and time crunch. Candidates were also victims of the costly effort of the hiring process. Many candidates test for multiple agencies across multiple states. If the candidate has to fly or drive to an out-of-town location and stay in a hotel, the costs add up quickly. Candidates can spend hundreds to thousands of dollars to try and get hired. While not every portion of the law enforcement hiring process can be completed from afar, the written exam was open for this new type of testing.

Several companies saw this trend and began offering an online testing option. For instance, the National Testing Network (NTN) offers continuous testing opportunities for not only law enforcement candidates, but other public sector jobs across the country. This new process is effective and efficient for both the candidate and the hiring agency. Not only does NTN provide flexibility for the candidate in taking the written exam, but it also allows departments to reach a broader candidate population.

To take the written exam through NTN candidates sign up through the NTN website, find a nearby test location, and take the proctored entrance exam on a computer. The exam is scored immediately and then sent to the agencies to which the candidate is applying.

What Six Categories of Questions Are on the Written Exam?

As seen in Fact Box 3.1, many different entry-level written exams are utilized by various law enforcement agencies across the United States. An agency's decision to utilize one exam over another depends on a variety of factors. Some agencies are required to use an exam due to civil service regulations. Most agencies make their decision based on input from the Human Resources division along with other research and job requirements. No matter how the decision is made as to which exam to utilize for the written exam portion of the hiring test, the constant is the composition of the exam itself.

The written exam will have a variety of questions that cover the following **six categories:**

1. **Judgment and reasoning (deductive and inductive)**
2. **Memorization and observation**
3. **Mathematics**
4. **Reading comprehension (data interpretation)**
5. **Traffic maps (directional orientation)**
6. **Writing**

No matter what category a question falls in, the candidate should always remember to do the following:

- Read each question carefully
- Answer the easiest questions first

- Take notes (if allowed)
- Be cognizant of the time, since written exams are timed
- Focus on the written exam itself, not other people in the testing location
- Double-check your answers

Judgment and Reasoning

Remember the following:

- **POLIS** (**p**rofessionalism, **o**fficer, **l**aw, **i**ntegrity, **s**ervice)
- Logical answer
- Roleplay
- Best course of action
- Sound judgment

One of the most critical skills for future police officers is sound judgment. Written exam questions that cover the candidate's judgment ask questions that supply the facts and allow the candidate to display judgment by responding correctly. Candidates are not required to know the hiring agency's policies and procedures (P&P); however, test makers often assume that some of the P&P are common sense. In order to succeed on the judgment and reasoning questions, the candidate needs to have a good understanding of a police department's basic P&P, especially patrol procedures.

Patrol procedures are essential, and the candidate must always remember to apply the procedures to every question. After all, the candidate is testing for the position of a law enforcement officer, not a football player or cashier. When a question is asked where the candidate must apply judgment and reasoning, the candidate must first ask how the question would apply to an officer and how an officer would best answer the question. There are five basic patrol procedure roles that should be utilized. The following acronym **POLIS** can be utilized to remember the five roles.

1. **P**rofessionalism
2. **O**fficer
3. **L**aw
4. **I**ntegrity
5. **S**ervice

Professionalism: A real professional law enforcement officer places the customer (citizen) first, ensures expertise in all areas of law enforcement, goes above and beyond, follows through with promises, communicates effectively, follows policies and procedures, praises peers instead of focusing on self, mentors others, thanks others, and has the right attitude.

Officer: An officer keeps the peace, assists citizens, maintains order, protects life and limb, protects property, obeys orders, values hierarchy, and efficiently completes tasks.

Law: Officers know the law, stay up to date on court decisions that change or alter the law, utilize minimum necessary force, and engage in peace-keeping activities to maintain order and enforce the law.

Integrity: Honesty is paramount; officers must maintain the highest of all morals and ethics; not accept gifts, gratuities, or favors; and be impartial.

Service: Law enforcement careers are service oriented, and therefore officers must be prepared to offer a service to the public at all times.

"What would you do if . . ." is the format in which judgment and reasoning questions are written. The candidate should first read the question slowly, two or three times. The judgment question provides the situation, and the candidate must review all the facts given and make a judgment call as to how to respond.

What would you do if you saw a man standing in the middle of the street, yelling in the air, and jumping up and down?

Would you talk to him?

Call for an ambulance?

Arrest the man?

What would the charges be?

What questions would you ask him?

More often than not, the correct answer can be found by *drawing a logical conclusion*. Next, the candidate should role-play and think of how a law enforcement officer would answer the question. This is done by slowly and methodically applying the POLIS roles to each question. What would an officer choose as the *best course of action*? The answer should show *sound judgment*, ensuring that the public's best interest, and all the **POLIS** roles, were considered.

Practice Exam Questions in the Category of Judgment and Reasoning

1. An 80-year-old woman calls the police and tells the dispatcher that her husband has just passed away. The woman is distraught and makes several comments about wanting to join her husband since she is now all alone. Which of the following is the best for the police to do?

   a. The woman caller and her problems are not the problems of the police, and the police should not interfere in her life.
   b. The police should try to locate any other family members for assistance.
   c. The police should contact social services, family, neighbors, or friends to assist the woman through this challenging time in her life.
   d. The police should find a proper mortuary and take care of the funeral, so the wife does not have to deal with it.

2. You are on patrol in a park, and you hear a young girl cry. When you investigate you see that she has fallen into a hole in the ground. What would you do first?

    a. Yell for the nearest citizen to call 911.
    b. Go to the young girl and question her as to how she fell into the hole.
    c. Tell dispatch (over your radio) to send an ambulance immediately, and carefully try to pull the girl from the hole.
    d. Ask the nearest citizens to try and save the girl while you tell dispatch (over your radio) to send an ambulance.

3. You are patrolling an apartment complex at 2:00 a.m. when you see a female and male looking into a window of an apartment. The male then pushes on the window, trying to open it. You should do which of the following?

    a. Note the time and date of the event and continue patrolling the complex.
    b. Arrest both the female and male immediately.
    c. Try to contact the manager of the apartment complex to see who lives in the apartment.
    d. Contact the female and male to determine why they are trying to open the window.

4. You are driving by a local bar, and you see two men in the parking lot, fist fighting. You should do which of the following?

    a. Keep driving; it is none of your business.
    b. Be careful to only talk to the men, if you try to stop the fight you may get hurt and you do not want that to happen.
    c. Call the bar to see if they know the men and can try and stop the fight.
    d. Stop immediately and try to stop the fight.

5. You see a woman limping down a neighborhood sidewalk leaving a trail of blood. You should do which of the following?

    a. Let her keep walking; this is none of your business, and it is her First Amendment right to be left alone.
    b. Tell dispatch (via the radio) that you need an ambulance and contact the woman to investigate what happened.
    c. Stop and talk to the woman and see if she has a family member or friend who can pick her up.
    d. Stop and talk to the woman and give her a ride home.

6. At 3:00 a.m. a man contacts you and tells you that a young girl just collapsed inside a fast-food restaurant. You should do which of the following?

    a. Ask the man to describe the young girl and tell you what happened.
    b. Call the fast-food restaurant to find out if the young girl is all right.
    c. Go immediately to the fast-food restaurant to investigate and call for an ambulance to meet you there.
    d. Go immediately to the fast-food restaurant and begin to investigate and find out what happened.

7. Thirty percent of the inmates released from prison never re-offend. This means which of the following?

    a. 70 percent of inmates released do re-offend.
    b. 30 percent of inmates have not been caught breaking the law.
    c. All of the above.
    d. None of the above.

8. Your coworker tells you that her supervisor, Sergeant James, has asked her out on a date three times. She has turned him down, but she fears he will ask her out a fourth time. What would you recommend your coworker to do?

    a. Tell Sergeant James's immediate supervisor of the issue
    b. Tell the chief or sheriff about the issue.
    c. Just ignore it; hopefully, Sergeant James will stop.
    d. Ask Sergeant James to stop the behavior because it is offensive.

9. You are on your way to take a report of a stolen vehicle. A person flags you down and asks for directions to the nearest seafood restaurant. You should do which of the following?

    a. If you know of a seafood restaurant, give the citizens quick directions and apologize that you have to leave so quickly, but you were on your way to a call.
    b. Ignore the citizen and drive away quickly.
    c. Tell the citizen that you do not have time to give them directions since you are on your way to a more important call.
    d. Just point to the nearest restaurant, even if it is not a seafood restaurant, and drive away quickly.

10. As a police officer, you have an idea of a way to lower the auto burglaries in the area; you should do which of the following?

    a. Tell your immediate supervisor.
    b. Don't do anything; you are a new officer and do not want to rock the boat.
    c. Ask the opinions of other officers, consider all the options, research the options, then run it by your immediate supervisor.
    d. Write up your plan and e-mail it to your chief or sheriff.

Mathematics

Remember the following:

- **The four math rules**
- Shortcuts

The mathematics portion of the written exam requires that the candidate understand basic addition, subtraction, multiplication, and division and have the ability to determine percentages. Generally, calculators are not allowed during the exam; therefore, the candidate must utilize scratch paper to work out the correct answer and then chose from the multiple-choice answers provided. The following **four math rules** are important to remember during the math portion of the exam:

Math Rule 1: Analyze the information

Read the question carefully, slowly, and take notes. When dealing with numbers, information can be lost easily; therefore, it is important to go slow.

Math Rule 2: Identify information

Look at the entire question and answer and begin to identify what the question is asking.

Math Rule 3: Solve strategically

Once it is understood what the question is asking, the solution can begin to be worked.

Math Rule 4: Double-check Answer

After the question has been solved, double-check the answer. Numbers are confusing, and one misstep can result in the wrong answer.

Shortcuts (Back-solving)

Back-solving is a popular shortcut that can be utilized on some math problems. If a math question asks for the value of a single variable and the multiple-choice answers are numbers, back-solving can be tried. The answers are plugged into the math question one at a time until the correct answer is found.

Example back-solving question:

In March, Drake had _____ dollars in his checking account. He withdrew a one-fourth of the money in April, and a one-third of the remaining money in May. Drake made no further transactions. If $120.00 remained in Drake's account, how much money was in his checking account to begin with?

    a. *$326*
    b. *$268*
    c. *$240*
    d. *$126*
    e. *$114*

To back-solve this question, start with answer C first. If Drake started with $240, then he withdrew $60 and had $180. Then he withdrew another $60 and had $120. Sometimes the candidate will get lucky and get the correct answer on the first try!

Shortcuts (Strategic Guessing)

If a candidate utilizes strategic guessing, the candidate is guessing and checking or working backward to solve a question. Start by reading the question and then guess a solution. Plug in the *guess solution* into the problem to see if it is the correct answer. If the guess is incorrect, try guessing again to get closer to the goal of the right answer.

Example strategic guessing question:

Joah takes a piece of fabric that is 48 inches long and is cut into two pieces. One piece is three times longer than the other piece. How long is each piece?

    a. *12*
    b. *24*
    c. *36*
    d. *2*

Start by guessing two random numbers, with one of the numbers being three times larger than the other. First, guess 4 + 12 = 16; the number is too small. Second, guess 6 + 18 = 24; the number is still too small. Third guess is 12 + 36 = 48. That is the answer since the first piece of fabric is 12 inches and the second piece is 36 inches long, which equates to 36 = 3(12), or one piece is three times as long as the other.

Shortcuts (Estimation)

Since the written exam is timed, candidates must always be cognizant of the time when taking every portion of the exam. Math problems are tough, and sometimes there is no time to figure out the precise answer for every question. Moreover, candidates may run into a math question where the formula to use eludes them. Estimation can come in handy in these types of situations where the candidate can quickly solve various math problems.

    Compare this process to grocery shopping. If the budget for shopping is $200, the shopper does not need to use a calculator to avoid going over at the register. Estimation can be done whenever a new item is added to the basket, $10 + $5 + $15 + $20 + $50 = $100. The addition may not be exact; however, there will be enough money left over to cover the sales tax.

Example estimation question:

You went shopping for your friend's party, and you spent, $29.99, $3.19, $1.29, $5.59, and $31.88. What is the total?

    a. *$71.94*
    b. *$88.99*
    c. *$52.31*
    d. *$102.98*

    Since the exam is timed, there may not be enough time to write down all the numbers and add them up. Instead estimation can be utilized by quickly adding $30 (29.99 rounded up) + $3 (3.19 rounded down) + $1 (1.29 rounded down) + $6 (5.59 rounded up) + $32 (31.88 rounded up). The answer of $72 is quickly found. The answer closest is answer A. If the candidate were to add up every single number, the exact answer is $71.94; therefore, estimation not only gave the candidate the correct answer but saved a bunch of time.

Calculating Area and Perimeter

Candidates must understand how to calculate area and perimeter. The perimeter is the length of the outline of a shape. The area is the measurement of the surface of a shape. To find the perimeter of a square, add the lengths of the four sides.

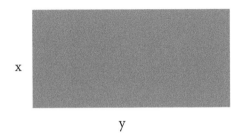

x

y

Perimeter = P

$P = x + x + y + y$

$P = 2x + 2y$

$P = 2(x + y)$

8

14

Perimeter = P

$P = 14 + 14 + 8 + 8$

$P = 2(14) + 2(8)$

$P = 2(14 + 8)$

$P = 2(22)$

Perimeter = 44 inches

To find the area of a square multiply the length and the width.

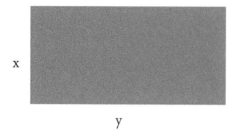

x

y

Area, A, is x times y.

10

10

$A = x(y)$

$A = x(y)$

$A = 10(10)$

$A = 100in^2$

Practice Exam Questions in the Category of Mathematics

1. Officer Miller works patrol with Officer Knudsen. Yesterday, Officer Miller purchased bagels for both officers for $2 each. Today, Officer Knudsen bought bagels for the two at another shop for $1.50 each. How much more did Officer Miller spend?

    a. $1
    b. $1.50
    c. $2
    d. $4

2.

12

22

Perimeter = _____inches

12

15

Area = _____in^2

3. 3x = 12

    a. 3
    b. 4
    c. 6
    d. 9

4. −31 − 8 + 31 =

    a. 8
    b. −8
    c. 0
    d. −39

5. In the United States, 13 out of every 20 cans are recycled. What percent of the cans are recycled?

    a. 5%
    b. 50%
    c. 65%
    d. 45%

6. Jake is a quarterback. This year, he completed 350 passes, which is 70% of all the passes he's attempted this year. How many passes has John attempted this year?

    a. 450
    b. 500
    c. 420
    d. 300

7. 219 + 391 + 500 =

    a. 1000
    b. 1115
    c. 2100
    d. 1110

8. $96.18 − $11.72 =

    a. $82.26
    b. $74.46
    c. $84.46
    d. $85.00

9. Joe had 87 marbles. He gave 18 to Jimmy and 6 to Sam. How many does he have left?

    a. 63
    b. 60
    c. 53
    d. 61

10. 22 × 5,843 =

    a. 126,543
    b. 128,546
    c. 109,887
    d. 131,051

11. 983 × 167 =

    a. 164,161
    b. 163,285
    c. 164,181
    d. 165,559

12. 122/2 =

    a. 60
    b. 51
    c. 61
    d. 70

13. 4321.4/82 =

    a. 51.2
    b. 57.2
    c. 48.63
    d. 52.7

Memorization

It is important to remember **NIDDO, the Five memorization rules:**

1. **N**otes
2. **I**dentifiers
3. **D**etails
4. **D**irection
5. **O**rdering facts logically

Law enforcement officers must have a keen memory in order to do their job correctly. Officers are constantly on alert for anything that occurs, and they must be able to remember what they see. The tough part of a memorization portion of a written exam is that it is timed. Anytime a candidate is timed, stress levels will rise, and mistakes will be made. In order to overcome these issues, the candidate must practice. One of the best ways to memorize a photo is through visualization. Candidates can practice this very quickly by walking around and observing. The candidate should practice always being prepared and paying attention to their surroundings. The environment is active and always ready to assist the candidate who wants to practice. The candidate can start by looking at a stranger for 1 minute. After the time limit, the candidate should look away and write down everything they remember of that person. If the candidate is at school, work, or another location, take 2 minutes while sitting in a new area to look around and memorize what is seen. After the 2 minutes, the candidate should look away and write down everything they remember seeing. This can be done anywhere and everywhere. The more the candidate does this, the better the candidate will become at memorization. Everyone is different and remembers in unique ways. The only way to learn the areas that need improvement is through practice. Various applications on a computer, smartphone, or tablet, such as Luminosity, can be utilized to assist the candidate in improving memory and memorization skills.

Memorization rule 1—Notes: If the candidate is allowed to take notes, the candidate must take notes! Often, notes are strictly forbidden on certain portions of exams because in real life officers find themselves in situations where they do not have time to get out a pen and paper and must utilize their memory only. Therefore, the candidate must practice holding notes in their memory. The only way to improve in this area is to practice.

Memorization rule 2—Identifiers: There are many types of identifiers that candidates should focus on. First, there are numbers such as a street address, license plate number, or the number of people and age of people, and the number of vehicles (or other object) in a photo. Next, there are signs such as business signs, names on buildings, or other landmarks.

Memorization rule 3—Details: What can be surmised from a photo? Is it a neighborhood? Is it an affluent or struggling neighborhood? Is it a business? What type of business? What are the people like? What are the people wearing? Are people happy, sad, or mad? Is it day or night? Is it cold or hot? Details can be remembered when the candidate visualizes telling a story with the photo. Think of a movie (or television show, novel, or a theatrical play) and try and make the details in the photo play like a movie.

Memorization rule 4—Direction: What is the direction that the people are facing? What direction are the vehicles are facing? Where are the businesses? Where is everything located concerning each other?

Memorization rule 5—Ordering facts logically: Now it is time to put it all together. There are many ways to do this. The easiest way is to tell a story. If the photo shows several people standing around a bus stop, the candidate could quickly develop a story like this:

"Two, tall, long brown haired, skinny, teenagers were laughing and standing, and five elderly, heavy adults were sitting and scared, all surrounded by three older cars and one new bus."

Practice Exam Questions in the Category of Memorization

FIGURE 3.1 Memorization photo 1.

Question 1: Look at the photo in Figure 3.1 for 1 minute and answer the following questions without looking at the photo:

1. How many people are in the photo?
2. How many men? How many women?
3. How many people are holding an object?

4. How many people are helping another person?
5. What are the people wearing? What color of clothing? Types of clothing?
6. What types of hairstyles do the people have?
7. How many windows are in the room?

FIGURE 3.2 Memorization photo 2.

Question 2: Look at the photo in Figure 3.2 for 1 minute and answer the following questions without looking at the photo:

1. How many people are in the photograph?
2. How many men? How many women?
3. How many people are holding an object?
4. How many people are wearing a hat?
5. What are the people wearing? What color of clothing? Types of clothing?
6. What types of hairstyles do the people have?
7. How many doors are in the room?

Question 3: Look at the photo in Figure 3.3 for 1 minute and answer the following questions without looking at the photo:

1. How many people are in the photograph?
2. How many men? How many women?
3. Are there officers in the photograph?
4. What color are the officers' uniforms?
5. Is there a clock in the photograph?

FIGURE 3.3 Memorization photo 3.

6. Is the day sunny, cloudy, rainy?
7. What are the people wearing? What color of clothing? Types of clothing?
8. What types of hairstyles do the people have?
9. How many windows are in the room?

FIGURE 3.4 Memorization photo 4.

Question 4: Look at the photo in Figure 3.4 for 1 minute and answer the following questions without looking at the photo:

1. How many people are in the photograph?

2. Is there an animal in the photograph?
3. What is the animal doing in the photograph?
4. What type of animal is in the photograph?
5. Are there vehicles in the photograph?
6. Are there trees in the photograph?
7. Is the day sunny, cloudy, rainy?
8. What are the people wearing? What color of clothing? Types of clothing?
9. What types of hairstyles do the people have?
10. What are the people in the photograph doing with their hands?
11. Are there any signs in the photograph?

FIGURE 3.5 Group A memorization photo 1 of 5, suspect.

FIGURE 3.6 Group A memorization photo 2 of 5.

FIGURE 3.7 Group A memorization photo 3 of 5.

FIGURE 3.8 Group A memorization photo 4 of 5.

FIGURE 3.9 Group A memorization photo 5 of 5.

Look at the photos in Figures 3.5–3.9 for 2 minutes. Then cover the photos and answer questions 5–7.

Question 5: You are an officer on patrol. You responded to a bank that had just been robbed. The surveillance camera took a photograph of the suspect. Figure 3.5 is the suspect. Which figure, 3.6, 3.7, 3.8, or 3.9, looks like the suspect in Figure 3.5?

1. Figure 3.6
2. Figure 3.7
3. Figure 3.8
4. Figure 3.9
5. None of the figures
6. All of the figures

Question 6: Which figure(s) shows a person who has long hair *and* is (are) female?

1. Figure 3.6
2. Figure 3.7
3. Figure 3.8
4. Figure 3.9
5. Figures 3.6, 3.7, and 3.9
6. Figures 3.7, 3.8, and 3.9
7. All of the figures
8. None of the figures

Question 7: Which figure(s) shows a person who has short hair *and* is (are) male?

1. Figure 3.6
2. Figure 3.7
3. Figure 3.8
4. Figure 3.9
5. Figures 3.6, 3.7, and 3.9
6. Figures 3.7, 3.8, and 3.9
7. All of the figures
8. None of the figures

Look at the photos in Figures 3.10–3.14 for 2 minutes. Then cover the photos and answer questions 8 and 9.

FIGURE 3.10 Group B memorization photo 1 of 5, suspect.

FIGURE 3.11 Group B memorization photo 2 of 5.

FIGURE 3.12 Group B memorization photo 3 of 5.

FIGURE 3.13 Group B memorization photo 4 of 5.

FIGURE 3.14 Group B memorization photo 5 of 5.

Question 8: You are an officer on patrol. You responded to a house that had just been burglarized. The surveillance camera took a photograph of the suspect. In Figure 3.10, the male is the suspect. Which figure, 3.11, 3.12, 3.13, or 3.14, looks like the suspect in Figure 3.10?

1. Figure 3.11
2. Figure 3.12
3. Figure 3.13
4. Figure 3.14
5. None of the figures
6. All of the figures

Question 9: Which figure(s) shows a person(s) with a beard?

1. Figures 3.10, 3.11, and 3.12
2. Figure 3.13
3. Figure 3.10
4. Figures 3.12 and 3.13
5. All of the figures
6. None of the figures

Look at the photos in Figures 3.15–3.19, for 2 minutes. Then cover the photos and answer questions 10–13.

FIGURE 3.15 Group C memorization photo 1 of 5.

FIGURE 3.16 Group C memorization photo 2 of 5.

FIGURE 3.17 Group C memorization photo 3 of 5.

FIGURE 3.18 Group C memorization photo 4 of 5.

FIGURE 3.19 Group C memorization photo 5 of 5.

Question 10: You are an officer on patrol. You responded to a convenience store where a suspect stole a case of beer. The cashier described the suspect as a young adult female with long hair. Which figure(s), 3.15, 3.16, 3.17, 3.18, or 3.19, is (are) most likely the suspect(s)? Choose the best answer:

1. Figure 3.15
2. Figure 3.16
3. Figure 3.17
4. Figure 3.18
5. Figures 3.15, 3.17, 3.18, and 3.19
6. Figures 3.15, 3.17, and 3.18
7. None of the figures
8. All of the figures

Question 11: Which figure(s) shows a male?

1. Figure 3.15
2. Figure 3.16
3. Figure 3.17
4. Figure 3.18
5. Figures 3.16 and 3.19
6. Figures 3.15, 3.17, and 3.18
7. None of the figures
8. All of the figures

Question 12: Which figure(s) shows a person over 50 years of age?

1. Figure 3.15
2. Figure 3.16
3. Figure 3.17
4. Figure 3.18
5. Figures 3.16 and 3.19
6. Figures 3.15, 3.17, and 3.18
7. None of the figures
8. All of the figures

Question 13: Which figure(s) show a person with short hair?

1. Figure 3.15
2. Figure 3.16
3. Figure 3.17
4. Figure 3.18
5. Figures 3.16 and 3.19
6. Figures 3.15, 3.17, and 3.18
7. None of the figures
8. All of the figures

Look at the photo in Figure 3.20 and information for suspect A in Figure 3.21 for 2 minutes. Then cover the photos and answer questions 14–16.

Suspect A

Name: Janice Marie Kempy

Alias: Kick Girl

Date of Birth: January 07, 1994

Height: 5' 7"

Weight: 145 lbs.

Hair: Blonde

Eyes: Green

Sex: Female

Race: White

Scars/Marks/Tattoos: Vine on right wrist and flowers on left ankle

Social Security Number: 680-21-3211

Wanted For: Fraud and Forgery

NCIC Number: 23-12

FIGURE 3.20 Group D memorization photo 1 of 2.

FIGURE 3.21 Group D memorization photo 2 of 2.

Question 14: What is suspect A's date of birth?

1. 1/17/96
2. 1/7/94
3. 11/7/96
4. 7/1/94

Question 15: What is suspect A wanted for?

1. Theft and fraud
2. Forgery and theft
3. Murder and rape
4. Fraud and forgery

Question 16: What is suspect A's height and weight?

1. 5'7" and 145 lbs.
2. 5'2" and 154 lbs.
3. 5'10" and 144 lbs.
4. 5'1" and 145 lbs.

Look at the photo in Figure 3.22 and information for suspect B in Figure 3.23 for 2 minutes. Then cover the photos and answer questions 17–19.

FIGURE 3.22 Group E memorization photo 1 of 2.

Suspect B

Name: Mario Esperanzo Perez

Alias: Pico

Date of Birth: July 17, 1989

Height: 5' 6"

Weight: 187lbs.

Hair: Black

Eyes: Brown

Sex: Male

Race: Hispanic

Scars/Marks/Tattoos: Snake on chest and cross on back

Social Security Number: 554-12-3450

Wanted For: Robbery and Motor Vehicle Theft

NCIC Number: 12-54

FIGURE 3.23 Group E memorization photo 2 of 2.

Question 17: What is suspect B's name and alias?

1. Mario Esperanzo Perez; Pico
2. Perez Julie Mario; Gondo
3. Esperanzo Mario; Como
4. Julio Perez; Pico

Question 18: What is one of suspect B's tattoos?

1. Snake on chest
2. Cross on shoulder
3. Snake on ankle
4. Cross on thigh

Question 19: What is suspect B's Social Security number?

1. 340-54-1250
2. 554-12-3450
3. 554-12-3455
4. 554-10-3450

Look at the drawing in Figure 3.24 for 2 minutes. Then cover the drawing and answer questions 20–25.

FIGURE 3.24 Memorization drawing 1.

Question 20: How many flags are there?

1. Four
2. Five
3. Six
4. Seven

Question 21: The flags are not which color?

1. Red
2. Purple
3. Blue
4. Green

Question 22: How many birds are in the photo?

1. One
2. Two
3. Three
4. Four

Question 23: What color of dress is the female wearing?

1. Yellow
2. Brown
3. Blue
4. Red

Question 24: The male has _____ _____?

1. curly brown hair
2. straight brown hair
3. curly black hair
4. straight blonde hair

Question 25: The female has _____ _____?

1. long black hair
2. short black hair
3. long brown hair
4. short blonde hair

Look at the drawing in Figure 3.25 for 2 minutes. Then cover the drawing and answer questions 26–30.

FIGURE 3.25 Memorization drawing 2.

Question 26: What is the title of the drawing?

1. The Lucky Girl
2. The Lovely Lady
3. The Good Girl
4. The Lucky Lady

Question 27: How many dresses are red?

1. One
2. Two
3. Three
4. Four

Question 28: How many females are in the drawing?

1. Four
2. Five
3. Six
4. Seven

Question 29: How many hearts are in the drawing?

1. Three
2. Four
3. Five
4. Six

Question 30: How many of the females have curly hair?

1. Three
2. Four
3. Five
4. Six

Look at the drawing in Figure 3.26 for 2 minutes. Then cover the drawing and answer questions 31–32.

Question 31: What is flying in the drawing?

1. Bee
2. Bird
3. Airplane
4. Fly

Question 32: There are flowers in the drawings; how many different colors are the flowers?

1. One
2. Two
3. Three
4. Four

FIGURE 3.26 Memorization drawing 3.

Look at the drawing in Figure 3.27 for 2 minutes. Then cover the drawing and answer questions 33–34.

FIGURE 3.27 Memorization drawing 4.

Question 33: How many people are in the drawing?

1. Seven
2. Eight
3. Nine
4. Ten

Question 34: How many people are standing up in the drawing?

1. One
2. Two
3. Three
4. None

Look at the drawing in Figure 3.28 for 2 minutes. Then cover the drawing and answer questions 35–36.

Question 35: How many people in the drawing are wearing a hat?

1. One
2. Two
3. Three
4. None

FIGURE 3.28 Memorization drawing 5.

Question 36: How many people in the drawing have short hair?

1. One
2. Two
3. Three
4. None

Reading Comprehension

Important to remember the following:

- **Three C's: Concentration, complete, comprehension**
- Notes
- Summarization

Most reading comprehension written exam questions provide a passage for the candidate to read and then multiple-choice questions are asked about the passage and overall meaning. Candidates must be prepared to either learn or brush up on their reading skills. Candidates first need to understand what their basic reading skills are. What does the candidate read? Novels, newspapers, or magazines? Social media only? Nothing? Depending on the reading skill level of the candidate, the candidate will need to start reading consistently and, afterward, review the material read.

Three C's—Concentration, complete, comprehension: Daily reading will not only build concentration and comprehension skills but will also begin to develop vocabulary skills as well. The candidate should focus on a complete passage to read. Do not focus on just skimming a magazine article or the first few paragraphs of a news article. Begin by choosing an entire passage and read it thoroughly. Make sure to concentrate and focus on the material; do not daydream and think about what chores need to be accomplished or what is left to complete at school or work. Focus solely on reading the material.

Notes: Active reading strategies should be utilized. Mark up the book, magazine, or newspaper! Highlight and take notes on words or sentences that are important or may require further investigation. Key points must be identified, and statements must be analyzed. Why did the author write the material? What issues were discussed? What were the strengths and weaknesses of the material? Is there a logical argument? If the reading material is online, notes can be taken on a digital device. Either way, notes must be taken!

Summarization: After the reading material is completed, the candidate should try and write one or two sentences that summarize what was just read. Summarizing can be difficult at first. However, the candidate should not acquiesce to defeat. Try, try, and try again. The more passages that are read, the better the summary will be.

Practice Test Questions in the Category of Reading Comprehension

Passage 1:

Read the following passage. Use the information from the passage to choose the most appropriate answers to the questions that follow the passage.

The Morey Police Department is hiring. They are looking for candidates to be police officers in their new sub-station that will be opening soon. Candidates must be of a high moral character and have integrity and must meet all of the minimum standards established by law. In order to apply the candidate must fulfill the following requirements:

- Be 21 years of age
- Have a high school diploma or GED
- Be a U.S. citizen
- Have a driver's license

Candidates must also be dependable, be able to learn quickly, comprehend, retain, and apply information. The candidate must also be able to make sound and commonsense decisions under pressure. The candidate need not apply if the candidate has

- used illegal drugs,
- been convicted of domestic violence, or
- been convicted of a felony.

Candidates who meet the minimum qualifications may apply before Sunday at 5:00 p.m.

1. In order to apply for the position of police officer at the Morey Police Department, the candidate cannot _____ (which of the following was not listed):

   a. have used illegal drugs
   b. have been convicted of a domestic violence
   c. have bad credit
   d. have been convicted of a felony

2. Candidates applying for the police officer position at the Morey Police Department must have a(n) _____.

   a. driver's license
   b. Associate's degree
   c. Bachelor's degree
   d. 30 credit/hours toward a college degree

3. Candidates applying for the police officer position at the Morey Police Department must be _____.

   a. 16 years of age
   b. 20.5 years of age
   c. 21 years of age
   d. 18 years of age

4. Candidates applying for the police officer position at the Morey Police Department must meet all the minimum standards _____.

   a. established by the department
   b. established by the federal government

    c.   established by the chief of police

    d.   established by law

Passage 2:

You are a police officer, and the following information includes the personal information and identifiers of the person you stopped and arrested. Utilize the information to answer questions 1–4.

Benny R. Johnson

White male

Date of Birth: March 13, 1971

Social Security number: 512-43-9967

Address: 3284 E. 84th Street, Logansport, IN, 21568

Home phone: 767-219-3497

Work phone: 758-229-6248

Height: 5 feet, 5 inches

Weight: 195 pounds

Hair: Brown

For officer information, fill in your name, your ID number as 20375, and badge number 488. For transporting officer, fill in the name of James Smith, ID Number as 12342 and badge number 163. The arrest occurred on January 12, 2019, at 1:30 p.m.

Instructions for officer arrest report:

1. Arresting officer:	2. ID number:	3. Badge number:
4. Transporting officer:	5. ID number:	6. Badge number:

7. Arrestee:	8. DOB:	9. Age:	10. Address:	11. City:
12. Zip code:	13. SSN:	14. H. phone:	15. W. phone:	16. Height:
17. Weight:	18. Hair:	19. Race:	20. Sex:	21. Time of arrest:

Form Instructions

Space 1. Fill in the arresting officer's last name, first name, and middle initial.

Space 2. Fill in the arresting officer's identification number.

Space 3. Fill in arresting officer's badge number.

Space 4. Fill in the transporting officer's last name, first name, and middle initial.

Space 5. Fill in the transporting officer's identification number.

Space 6. Fill in the transporting officer's badge number.

Space 7. Fill in the arrested person's last name, first name, and middle initial.

Space 8. Fill in the arrested person's date of birth using the mm/dd/yyyy format.

Space 9. Fill in the arrested person's age.

Space 10. Fill in the arrested person's address.

Space 11. Fill in the arrested person's city.

Space 12. Fill in the arrested person's ZIP code.

Space 13. Fill in the arrested person's Social Security number using the XXX-XX-XXXX format.

Space 14. Fill in the arrested person's home phone number, area code first.

Space 15. Fill in the arrested person's work phone number, area code first.

Space 16. Fill in the arrested person's height using numbers only. (For example, 5 feet, 11 inches; use 5'11".)

Space 17. Fill in the arrested person's weight using numbers only. (For example, 190 pounds; use 190 lbs.)

Space 18. Fill in the arrested person's hair type.

Space 19. Fill in the arrested person's race using the following values: W for White, B for Black, I for Indian, H for Latino, O for other races.

Space 20. Fill in the arrested person's sex using the following values: M for male, F for female.

Space 21. Fill in the time of arrest in military time.

Based on the information given in scenario 2, answer the following questions:

1. Which one of the following dates of birth is correct?

    a. 03/13/71
    b. 13/03/1971
    c. 03/13/1971
    d. 13/03/71

2. Which of the following names is listed correctly?

    a. Johnson, Benny R.
    b. Benny R. Johnson
    c. R. Johnson Benny
    d. Benny, Johnson R.

3. Which of the following heights is listed correctly?

    a. 5 inches, 5 feet

    b. 5" 5'

    c. 5' 5"

    d. 5 feet, 5 inches

4. Which of the times is correctly listed?

    a. 1330 hours

    b. 1:30 PM

    c. 0130 hours

    d. 1330 PM

Passage 3:

1. Investigating officer: Walker, B	2. ID number: J-0112	3. Badge number: 488
4. Assisting officer: Brenny, D	5. ID number: L-3321	6. Badge number: 329

Location: 1215 W. Rainbow Street	Date: 2-4-04	Time: 1715 hours

Striking vehicle

7. Driver 1: Howard, Drake	8. DOB: 9-21-80	9. Age: 23
10. Address: 5512 W. 14th Street	11. City: Medford	12. Zip code: 97502
13. SSN: 555-22-1761	14. H. phone: 333-717-2281	15. W. phone: 333-958-2356
16. Vehicle 1: Silver	17. Make: Honda	18. Model: Civic
19. License: 147AWR	Blank	Blank
20. Driver 2: Smith, Jim	21. DOB: 12-12-79	22. Age: 24
23. Address: 36 E. 14th Ave	24. City: Medford	25. Zip code: 97504
26. SSN: 323-79-2291	27. H. phone: 333-656-7894	28. W. phone: 333-525-4465
29. Vehicle: Blue	30. Make: Toyota	31. Model: Camry
32. License: 325YTR	Blank	Blank

Based on the information given in scenario 3, answer the following questions:

1. What is the location where this accident occurred?

    a. 1215 W. Rainbow Street

    b. 1512 W. Rainbow Street

    c. 1215 S. Rainbow Street

    d. 1512 E. Rainbow Street

2. What time did this accident occur?

    a. 5:15 PM
    b. 1715 hours
    c. 5:15 AM
    d. 1515 hours

3. Who was the assisting officer?

    a. Officer Smith
    b. Officer Walker
    c. Officer Howard
    d. Officer Brenny

4. What is the color, make, model, and license number of the striking vehicle?

    a. Silver Honda Civic 147AWR
    b. Blue Toyota Camry 325YTR
    c. Blue Toyota Camry 147AWR
    d. Silver Honda Civic 325AWR

Traffic Maps

It is important to remember the following:

- Review
- Laws
- Practice

Map reading and understanding how to get from place A to place B is an essential task for all law enforcement officers. Even with all the digital maps and programs available, there will still come situations where the officer must know how to read a map and understand spatial orientation. Written exam questions on traffic maps do not require any memorization; however, the candidate must understand how to get from place A to place B lawfully, in the quickest, shortest, and most efficient manner possible, all while being timed. All of these factors together create a stressful environment where mistakes can be made. In order to ensure the correct answer is chosen, candidates should remember the following information.

Review: The first step in correctly choosing the right answer in a traffic map question is to read the question and slowly review the directions and map elements carefully. Maps have directions, streets, locations and other various elements and must be studied thoroughly. Small mistakes or a location or direction overlooked or misunderstood can cause the candidate to choose the wrong answer.

Laws: Remember to apply and obey all traffic laws. Once the candidate reviews the map, traffic laws must be applied and not overlooked. For instance, when trying to calculate the quickest route from point A to point B, do not travel the wrong way on a one-way street.

Practice: Utilize maps often. Even if the driving directions to place A and place B are known, utilize a map to get there. Get used to using a compass and look at various locations and streets. Understand a compass fully. Most compasses only point north; therefore, the candidate should practice writing in south, east, and west on the compass. Candidates should also remember to look for the quickest route.

Practice Test Questions in the Category of Traffic Maps

Utilize the traffic map in Figure 3.29 to answer questions 1–5.

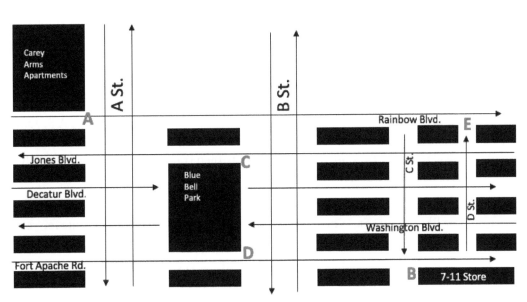

FIGURE 3.29 Traffic map 1.

1. If you are located at Carey Arms Apartments and travel east on Rainbow Blvd. to C St., then travel south on C St. to Washington Blvd., then travel west on Washington Blvd. past B St., you are closest to _____.

   a. A
   b. B
   c. C
   d. D
   e. E

2. If you are located at Blue Bell Park and travel east on A St. to Fort Apache Rd., then travel east on Fort Apache Rd. to D St., and then travel north on D St. to Rainbow Blvd., you will be closest to point _____.

    a. A
    b. B
    c. C
    d. D
    e. E

3. If you are located at point A and you travel east on Rainbow Blvd. to B St., then south on B St. to Jones Blvd., you will be closest to point _____.

    a. A
    b. B
    c. C
    d. D
    e. E

4. You are located at the 7-11 Store. You receive a call of a robbery in progress at the Carey Arms Apartments. Which of the following is the most direct route for you to take in your patrol car, ensuring you obey all traffic laws?

    a. Travel west on Fort Apache Rd. then north on A St.
    b. Travel north on C St. to Rainbow Blvd. then travel west on Rainbow Blvd.
    c. Travel north on D St. to Jones Blvd., then travel west on Jones Blvd. to A St., and then travel north on A St.
    d. Travel north on D St. to Washington Blvd., then travel west on Washington Blvd. to A St., and then travel north on A St.

5. You are located at Blue Bell Park near point C and must respond to a noise complaint at Rainbow Blvd. and D St. Which one of the following is the most direct route for you to take in your patrol car, ensuring you obey all traffic laws?

    a. Travel east on Jones Blvd. to D St. and north on D St. to Rainbow Blvd.
    b. Travel south on B St. to Decatur Blvd., then travel east on Decatur Blvd. to D St., then travel north on D St. to Rainbow Blvd.
    c. Travel north on B St. to Rainbow Blvd. then travel east on Rainbow Blvd.
    d. Travel south on B St. to Fort Apache Rd., then travel east on Fort Apache Rd. to D. St., and then travel north on D. St. to Rainbow Blvd.

Writing

One of the biggest obstacles for new police officers is police report writing. What about police officer-worn body cameras? They record everything, so the officer does not have to write a report, correct? *No!* Body cameras only record one point of view, and it is a limited view. Until technology allows several for flying drones to hover over every police officer, recording a continuous 360-degree view, the police report will continue to exist.

Writing is not an easy task. Most candidates cannot start writing correctly from the start; therefore, practice is essential. While the police academy and the hiring agency will train the candidate on how to write a basic police report, they do require the candidate to have basic writing skills such as grammar, punctuation, and spelling. Candidates must begin preparing for the rigors of writing. There are basic rules in police report writing that candidates can begin preparing for.

The following illustrate the **nine police report writing rules** candidates can study:

1. First person

Proper writing ensures that every sentence has a subject and verb that must match and agree. What does match and agree mean? It means that there must be consistency in the person and number. The person indicates whom the writer is talking about. There are three *persons* the writer can talk about:

1. First person: The writer is referring to himself or herself: *I* saw the photo on the ground.
2. Second person: The sentence is describing the audience: You should always take photos.
3. Third person: The sentence describes something that is neither the speaker nor the audience: *It is* something that should be done.

Police reports are always written in *first* person. When an officer responds to a crime scene, the officer will utilize various senses. The officer will hear, see, touch, and smell things at the crime scene. The officer could interview victims, witnesses, and even suspects. All of these things will be written in the police report from the officer's point of view.

Incorrect: You told me to tell you how the suspect stole my purse.

Correct: I asked Mrs. James what happened, and she told me that the suspect stole her purse.

Incorrect: I told Mr. Jones to tell me what happened. You said that the suspect entered his home after 7 o'clock in the morning.

Correct: Mr. Jones told me that the suspect entered his home after 7 o'clock in the morning.

Incorrect: The driver was told to step out of the vehicle.

Correct: I told the driver to step out of the vehicle

2. Active not passive voice

Do not use passive voice because it omits relevant and required information. Writing in active voice clearly states who did what. A police report needs to be as clear as possible since many times it details a crime.

Incorrect: The suspect was read his Miranda rights and handcuffed.

Correct: I read the suspect his Miranda rights, and Officer Brandlin handcuffed him.

3.   Assumptions

Do not make assumptions or stereotype. A police report should only contain the facts, not assumptions.

Incorrect: I could tell he was angry and wanted to hurt someone.

Correct: I asked the witness what he saw, and he yelled, "I do not have to talk to you!"

4.   Avoid using police jargon

Police reports are read by not only other police officers, but also by prosecutors and defense attorneys, jury members, and citizens. People outside of a law enforcement agency may not understand police abbreviations or codes. Avoid using police jargon or complicated words.

Incorrect: Mr. Dunlap advised me what happened.

Correct: Mr. Dunlap told me what happened.

Incorrect: I told dispatch I was code 4.

Correct: I told dispatch I was safe.

Incorrect: I observed the suspect breaking the car window.

Correct: I saw the suspect breaking the car window.

Incorrect: I hooked and booked the suspect.

Correct: I placed the suspect under arrest, placed handcuffs on him, and transported him to the correctional facility.

Incorrect: I was dispatched to back-up Officer Joply; however, he said he was code 4, so I remained in service.

Correct: The dispatcher sent me to back up Officer Joply; however, he said he was okay and did not need assistance, so I remained in service.

Incorrect: The driver was deuce, so I pulled her over.

Correct: The driver was swerving in and out of the travel lanes, so I pulled him over because I suspected he was under the influence of alcohol.

5.   Details

Do not forget the details. The details of the event are necessary and essential parts of a police report. Not being detailed enough or omitting parts of an investigation is sloppy and can lead a defense attorney to accuse the officer writing the report of intentionally leaving out information or even lying. Do not confuse writing an essay or book with a police report. A literary novel is a place to analyze and think of sentences as sophisticated patterns whereas a police report is an official document of the detailed facts. Police reports must stand the test of time to be used in court decades after they were written. Years after a crime, the police report may be the only official document left; therefore, it must be detailed to describe what occurred accurately. A police report must be able to stand alone and through details it should describe what happened first, second, third and so on.

Incorrect: I looked for the knife.

Correct: I looked for the knife in the master bedroom.

6. Opinions

A police report should contain only the facts, not opinions or hunches. It is not an officer's job to investigate and have an opinion about a situation. The police report should be a written record of the facts only and should contain objective, impartial facts, not subjective opinions.

Incorrect: I did not like the way she kept her house.

Correct: I saw that the kitchen had dirty dishes in the sink and the floor was dirty.

Incorrect: The suspect had a large scratch on his face that looked painful.

Correct: The suspect had a scratch on the right side of his face that started just below his right eye and ended just above his chine line.

Incorrect: The house was a mess; therefore, the suspect was a pig.

Correct: The house had various clothing items, toys, and papers laying on the carpet.

7. Past tense and chronological order

Write in past tense and chronological order from the officer's perspective. It is crucial to understand verb tense. One of the most common mistakes made in writing is utilizing several different verb tenses throughout the same passage. There are three main verb tenses:

1. Present tense: Describes action occurring in the present: I read the newspaper every day.
2. Past tense: Describes an action that took place in the past and is over: Last night I read the newspaper.
3. Future tense: Describes intended actions to occur in the future: I will read the newspaper tomorrow morning.

Police report writing is always past tense since the officer writing about the incident is writing a report after the incident occurred. The report is also written in chronological order from the officer's viewpoint.

Incorrect: I arrested the driver after I saw him swerving in and out of the travel lanes and completed three field sobriety tests.

Correct: I saw the driver swerving in and out of the travel lanes, so after completing three field sobriety tests, I arrested him.

Incorrect: You told me to tell you how the suspect stole my purse.

Correct: I asked Mrs. James what happened, and she told me that the suspect stole her purse.

Incorrect: The victim pointed to her husband. I arrived at the house.

Correct: When I arrived at the house the victim contacted me and pointed to her husband.

8. Unnecessary words

Even though police reports should be detailed, they should not be overly wordy. Do not include superfluous information because it makes the police report harder to read; it wastes time and is unprofessional.

Incorrect: I could not locate any further suspects at this time.

Correct: I could not locate any further suspects.

9. Vague

Remember to be detailed when writing a police report. Being vague can cause the reader of the report to infer the wrong information. It can also cause a defense attorney to accuse the officer who wrote the report of intentionally leaving out information or lying.

Incorrect: When I opened the front door to the house, I saw a mess.

Correct: When I opened the front door to the house, I saw the coffee table was turned upside down, the lamp was broken, and magazines and books were lying all over the carpet.

Candidates are not required to know how to write a police report; however, they are required to understand the rules of writing (grammar, punctuation, and spelling). In respect to writing the candidate should focus on the **eight common errors in writing**:

1. Apostrophes

An apostrophe tells the reader possession or contraction. In a singular use, for instance, the sentence *The book is Johnny's* tells the reader the book belongs to Johnny. To describe a plural possessive, where there were four boys named Johnny, the apostrophe would be added after the *s*: *All four of the Johnnys' dates were named Sasha.*

If the possessive ends in an s, such as the word *princes*, to show ownership, the apostrophe is added after the *s*: *The princes' guards were all on duty.* There are some words where an apostrophe is used to show possession, whereas another apostrophe usage is a shortened version of two words.

- *Your (possessive) book* versus *you're (you are) going to the store.*
- *Their horse* versus *they're (they are) going to the mall.*
- *Whose (possessive) car is this* versus *who's (who is) going to the party.*
- *The house has its (possessive) issues* versus *It's (it is) going to be a great vacation.*

2. Commas

The use of commas is often abused and misused. There are many rules regarding comma usage, and the rules are confusing. A comma is not unlike a period, except it indicates a smaller break. Think of a comma as a soft pause to separate words, clauses, or ideas in a sentence. Commas generally should not separate a subject from its verb.

Incorrect: My friend Marshall, is a great piano player.

Correct: My friend Marshall is a great piano player.

Incorrect: The things that are fun, may also be boring.

Correct: The things that are fun may also be boring.

Do not separate two nouns that are written as a compound subject or object.

Incorrect: Marshall, and her friends will be shopping at the mall today.

Correct: Marshall and her friends will be shopping at the mall today.

Incorrect: Sage will wear a blue jacket, and pants.

Correct: Sage will wear a blue jacket and pants.

A compound predicate is formed when the subject of a sentence does two or more things. Do not place a comma between two verbs in a compound predicate.

Incorrect: Austin wanted to buy another pair of shoes, but ran out of money.

Correct: Austin wanted to buy another pair of shoes but ran out of money.

When a writer uses multiple adjectives to modify a noun, there should be a comma to separate them. One distinct way to tell whether an adjective is coordinating is to try and switch the sentence order.

Incorrect: The sweet, little girl was playing with dolls.

Correct: The sweet little girl was playing with dolls.

Use of a comma before a conjunction should be utilized to separate independent clauses.

Incorrect: Austin is a good violin player but he's an even better singer.

Correct: Austin is a good violin player, but he's an even better singer.

Incorrect: My doctor is nice, but thorough.

Correct: My doctor is nice but thorough.

Incorrect: My sugar glider Huckleberry is tiny, and cute.

Correct: My sugar glider Huckleberry is tiny and cute.

The following are examples of the use of commas when writing a sentence with a list:

Incorrect: Finn likes cats dogs and movies.

Correct: Finn likes cats, dogs, and movies.

Comma usage with quotation marks is often incorrect.

Incorrect: "You have lipstick on your cheek", I said.

Correct: "You have lipstick on your cheek," I said.

3.   Directions

When writing directions, use lowercase letters for north, south, east, and west. If the information is a region or location, the direction can be capitalized.

Incorrect: I drove South on Rainbow Boulevard.

Correct: I drove south on Rainbow Boulevard.

Incorrect: I drove to interview the victim, who lives on west 3rd Street.

Correct: I drove to interview the victim, who lives West 3rd Street.

4.   Double negatives

When writing a passage, the author must ensure that the sentence does not contain two negatives, such as *not, without, hardly, barely, scarcely,* and *cannot,* because the words will cancel each other out.

Incorrect: The victim hasn't hardly any jewelry in her house.

Correct: The victim has hardly any jewelry in her house.

Incorrect: The suspect didn't take hardly any time to break down the door.

Correct: The suspect didn't take any time to break down the door.

5.   Homophones

Homophones are words that sound alike but are spelled differently, and they can be very confusing. The following list highlights common homophones:

accept/except

accept: a verb, to receive: The nonprofit center accepts donations.

Except: a preposition, to exclude: You can donate many items, except food.

affect/effect

affect: indicates influence: The Advil did not affect her headache.

Effect: a noun: The Advil did not have any negative side effects.

are/our

are: verb in present tense (to be): They *are* my sisters.

our: plural possessive pronoun (we): They will have *our* shoes.

here/hear

here: indicates location: Jerry please come back *here* and talk to me.

Hear: verb to indicate listening: Marshall, can you *hear* the mouse in the wall?

which/witch

which: starts an adjectival phrase: Zachery used his computer, *which* he received as a Christmas gift.

witch: scary or mean person: Josh dressed up as a *witch* for Halloween.

than/then

than: comparisons: Drake is much taller *than* his brother.

then: passage of time: Drake left the house and *then* went to the airport.

there/their/they're

there: different in various parts of speech: There will be a door charge to get into the bar.

their: a pronoun: The kids put their shoes by the front door.

they're: contraction for "they are": They're going to practice after school.

6.   Parallelism

Whenever expressing some ideas that are of equal importance in the same sentence, the writer should ensure they have the same grammatical form. Ideas should coordinate in pairs or a series, which are then linked by conjunctions such as *and, but, or,* and *nor.*

Incorrect: Once in the police academy, the recruit will take patrol procedures, defensive tactics, or study mental health issues.

Correct: Once in the police academy, the recruit will take patrol procedures, defensive tactics, or mental health issues.

Incorrect: A new employee should invest money in a 401K, in bonds, and in real estate.

Correct: A new employee should invest money in a 401K, in bonds, and real estate.

7.   Pronouns

A pronoun stands in for nouns in a sentence. Pronouns are often utilized to eliminate repetitiveness. The following list comprises some examples of personal, relative, and possessive pronouns that can be utilized in sentences.

I, me, you, he, she, him, her, it, we, us, they, them, one, who, whom, which, that, where, whose, mine, yours, his, hers, theirs, ours, its

For instance, the following sentence is repetitive:

The university offers a wide range of classes for the university students.

To reduce the redundancy, the following sentence is more appropriate:

The university offers a wide range of classes for its students.

8.   Spelling

Why should a candidate have to worry about spelling? Between Microsoft Word, Grammarly, or other programs that notify the writer of misspelled words, why is it a big deal? Although many writing programs do catch common spelling errors, they do not catch all spelling errors. Moreover, the candidate must be able to show writing ability, and spelling encompasses this requirement.

Spelling is one of the easiest errors to fix; however, it requires dedication to study the correct spelling of words. There are many lists on the Internet of the most commonly misspelled words. Fact Box 3.2 illustrates some of those words; however, the candidate should conduct Internet searches for commonly misspelled words as a part of a study plan in order to continuously practice spelling skills.

FACT BOX 3.2: COMMONLY MISSPELLED WORDS:

Correct/Incorrect

accommodate/accomodate	drunkenness/drunkeness
achieve/acheive	embarrass/embarass
acquire/aquire	exceed/excede
a lot/alot	existence/existance
apparent/apparant	fascinating/facinating
acquit/aquit	foreign/foriegn
argument/arguement	friend/freind
believe/beleive	gauge/guage
calendar/calender	harass/harrass
camouflage/camoflage	height/heighth
category/catagory	hierarchy/heirarchy
cemetery/cemetary	humorous/humerous
chief/cheif	hygiene/hygene
column/colum	ignorance/ignorence
consensus/concensus	imitate/immitate
deceive/decieve	immediately/imediately
definite/definate	independent/independant
desperate/desparate	indispensable/indispenseble
dilemma/dilema	intelligence/inteligance
disastrous/disasterous	jewelry/jewelery
	leisure/liesure

liaison/liason

maintenance/maintnance

millennium/millenium

necessary/necessery

niece/neice

neighbor/nieghbor

noticeable/noticable

occasion/occassion

occurrence/occurence

occurred/occured

original/orignal

perceive/percieve

personnel/personell

plagiarize/plagerize

possession/possesion

precede/preceed

privilege/priveledge

professor/professer

publicly/publically

readable/readible

receive/recieve

receipt/reciept

recommend/reccommend

relevant/relevent

seize/sieze

separate/seperate

sergeant/sargent

successful/successfull

vacuum/vaccum

willful/willfull

Practice Test Questions in the Category of Writing

1. The student's performance in class was _____.

    a. acceptable
    b. acceptible
    c. exceptable
    d. exceptible

2. The employee complained that his supervisor never _____ his above average performance.

    a. acknowledged
    b. aknowledged
    c. acnowledged
    d. acknowleged

3. Officer Brandt needed to purchase a new _____.

    a. calender
    b. calendar

   c. celendar

   d. kalendar

4. Janice moved out of her house because she was 20 years old and wanted to be more _____.

   a. independant

   b. indeependant

   c. independent

   d. indepandant

5. 5. Officer Jepidy was just promoted to a _____.

   a. lutenant

   b. lieutenant

   c. sargent

   d. sergeant

6. 6. Officer Samson forgot to include the _____ in the report, as one of the items that was stolen in the burglary.

   a. vacum

   b. vakum

   c. vakuum

   d. vacuum

7. Officer Satui wrote the following report which contained the following two sentences:

(1) The theft take place at the student union.

(2) The suspects took a number of different items.

Which of the following best describes the sentences?
   a. Only sentence 1 is grammatically correct.
   b. Only sentence 2 is grammatically correct.
   c. Both sentence 1 and 2 are grammatically correct.
   d. Neither sentence 1 nor sentence 2 are grammatically correct.

8. Read the following items and choose the sentence that contains the error.

(1) Most understand that one person cannot solve everything; however, one person can make a difference.

(2) By utilizing the following self-assessment tools a picture will begin to emerge of the type of person that the law enforcement world requires.

(3) When a person decides to take on the world of policing they first go through the arduous hiring process.

   a. Sentence 1 only
   b. Sentence 2 only

    c. Sentence 3 only

    d. All three sentences contain errors

    e. Only sentence 2 and sentence 3 contain errors

9. Read the following items and choose the sentence that contains the error.

(1) The diamond ring is Mr. and Mrs. Haas.

(2) He was last seen at the Ashland Skate Park

(3) The car is Mrs. And Mr. Smith's.

    a. Sentence 1 only

    b. Sentence 2 only

    c. Sentence 3 only

    d. All three sentences contain errors

    e. Only Sentence 2 and Sentence 3 contain errors

10. Read the following sentence and choose the correct answer.
When a police officer interviews a suspect, the officer must make a judgement as to whether or not the suspect is competant.

    a. The sentence is structurally incorrect.

    b. The sentence contains one misspelling.

    c. The sentence contains one or more misspellings.

    d. The sentence is structurally correct.

The Perfect Study Plan Takes 1 Year

One year! What?! Who has 1 year to prepare? All too often candidates have 1 or 2 weeks to prepare for the written exam, not 1 year. Some candidates can study for only 1 week and be successful on the written exam; however, this is rare. Instead most candidates find themselves in the following position. The candidate graduates with a degree and immediately begins searching for a job. A law enforcement officer position opens up at the nearest law enforcement agency, and the candidate fills out an application. Before the candidate knows it, they are taking the written exam. Then the dreaded results arrive, notifying the candidate of the failing grade. It is at this point that time slows, and the light bulb goes off in the candidate's head, like in a newspaper cartoon, and the candidate understands that a study plan is required.

It can take up to 1 year to go through the entire law enforcement hiring process. Agencies therefore only have openings once, and at most twice a year, unless it is a larger agency. If a candidate fails a written exam, the testing process comes to a halt, and the candidate must start all over again. Unless the candidate is willing to travel either throughout the state or to a new state, the candidate will have to wait months to have a try at the written exam again.

It is at this point that candidates realize how important the written exam is and how essential a timely study plan is. The most efficient type of study plan is the 1-year study plan. This type of study plan allows the candidate to identify areas of concern, slowly learn new material, and train the brain to identify the correct answer.

One-Year Study Plan

Length of Time	Amount of Time	Action
1 week (Week 1/52)	1 hour, 3 nights a week	Study and take practice exams in the category (time yourself): *Judgment and reasoning*. Copy the questions that you miss.
Remember to		Eat healthy and exercise.
1 week (Week 2/52)	1 hour, 3 nights a week	Study and take practice exams in the category (time yourself): *Memorization and observation*. Copy the questions that you miss.
1 week (Week 3/52)	1 hour, 3 nights a week	Study and take practice exams in the category (time yourself): *Mathematics*. Copy the questions that you miss.
1 week (Week 4/52)	Take off.	Take off.
1 week (Week 5/52)	1 hour, 3 nights a week	Study and take practice exams in the category (time yourself): *Writing* Copy the questions that you miss.
1 week (Week 6/52)	1 hour, 3 nights a week	Study and take practice exams in the category (time yourself): *Writing*. Copy the questions that you miss.
1 week (Week 7/52)	1 hour, 3 nights a week	Study and take practice exams in the category (time yourself): *Reading comprehension*. Copy the questions that you miss.
1 week (Week 8/52)	1 hour, 3 nights a week	Study and take practice exams in the category (time yourself): *Traffic map*. Copy the questions that you miss.
Remember to		Eat healthy and exercise.
1 week (Week 9/52)	Take off.	Take off.
1 week (Week 10/52)	2 hours anytime during the week	Compile all the questions that you missed in weeks 1–8 in one document.
1 week (Week 11/52)	2 hours anytime during the week	Retake the practice exam questions that you missed (and compiled in week 10)
1 week (Week 12/52)	2 hours anytime during the week	Copy all the questions from the retake exam (you took in week 11) and make a new list of questions that you have now missed a second time.
1 week (Week 13/52)	Take off.	Take off.
1 week (Week 14/52)	2 hours anytime during the week	Look over the new list of practice exam questions that you missed (from week 12), identify which categories they are, and make a new list of questions missed.

Length of Time	Amount of Time	Action
7 weeks (Weeks 15–21/52)	1 hour each week anytime during the week	Research the hiring agency you are going to be testing for: 1. Understand the overall test process for that agency and look up the type of written exam used. 2. Contact peers to see if they have gone through the testing process and meet with them to get ideas of how to study and to possibly study with them. 3. Take a university LET prep class. 4. Go to the hiring agency's informational session (if offered) and/or go on a ride-along or sit-along (in the communications/dispatch area). 5. Know your strengths and weaknesses by taking the self-assessment tests in this textbook. 6. Improve your strengths. 7. Improve your weaknesses. 8. Begin to study the hiring agency's vision and mission statements, values, and organizational chart. 9. Begin to study the hiring agency's policies and procedures.
Remember to		Eat healthy and exercise.
1 week (Week 22/52)	Take off.	Take off.
1 week (Week 23/52)	2 hours a week	Practice: *Reading comprehension* (time yourself): 1. Choose a passage to read in a newspaper, magazine, or book (or something similar). 2. Take notes. 3. Identify key points and summarize the passage. 4. If the one passage does not take 2 hours to complete, choose a second or third passage and complete steps 1–3.
7 weeks (Weeks 24–30/52)	1 hour each week anytime during the week	Practice: *Memorization and observation* (time yourself): Look around wherever you go Choose a person and study that person for 1 minute. After 1 minute, look away and write down what you remember about that person. Choose a location (such as a park or a mall) and focus on a large area with a lot going on (a lot of people and vehicles or other objects). After 2 minutes look away and write down what you remember about that large area.
Remember to		Eat healthy, exercise, and get a good night's sleep.

Length of Time	Amount of Time	Action
7 weeks (Weeks 31–37/52)	1 hour each week any time during the week	Practice: *Traffic maps* (time yourself): 1. At least 1 hour a week, utilize a map to go to a location (even if you do not actually go, choose point A and point B). 2. Pay attention to the landmarks, vehicles, and a compass, always knowing the directions north, south, east, and west.
1 week (Week 38/52)	Take off.	Take off.
7 weeks (Weeks 39–45/52)	1 hour each week anytime during the week	Practice: *Mathematics* (time yourself): 1. Using your favorite search engine, search for an appropriate math quiz and take the various ones you find. 2. Focus on addition (search math quiz addition). 3. Focus on subtraction (search math quiz subtraction). 4. Focus on multiplication (search math quiz multiplication). 5. Focus on division (search math quiz division). 6. Focus on percentages (search math quiz percentages). 7. Focus on integers (search math quiz integers). 8. Focus on fractions (search math quiz fractions). 9. Focus on area and perimeter (search math quiz area and perimeter).
Remember to		Eat healthy, exercise, and get a good night's sleep.
1 week (Week 46/52)	Take off.	Take off.
1 week (Week 47/52)	1 hour, 3 nights a week	Look over the new list of practice exam questions (you created in week 14) and retake this new test.
1 week (Week 48/52)	1 hour, 3 nights a week	Create a new list of the questions you missed from the exam in week 47 and retake this new exam.
2 weeks (Weeks 49–50/52)	2 hours a week each week	Practice: *Reading comprehension* (time yourself): 1. Choose a passage to read in a newspaper, magazine, or book (or something similar). 2. Take notes. 3. Identify key points and summarize the passage. If the one passage does not take 2 hours to complete, choose a second or third passage and complete steps 1–3.

Length of Time	Amount of Time	Action
1 week (Week 51/52)	1 hour, 6 nights a week	Start over by retaking practice exams in the following categories; spend 1 hour taking practice exams in each category: • *Judgment and reasoning* • *Memorization and observation* • *Reading comprehension* • *Police report writing* • *Traffic map* 1 hour: Create a new list of the questions you missed from these categories and retake this new exam.
Remember to		Eat healthy, exercise, and get a good night's sleep.
Week before the written test	1 hour, 4 nights a week	Retake the exam created in Week 51, composed of questions missed.
Night before the written test		Get at least 7–8 hours of good sleep, eat healthy, and review the important things to remember for the categories.

In order to ensure success, some tips to remember are the following:

- Schedule dates and times to study. If you miss a study day, do not forget to schedule a make-up day.
- Do not stress yourself out. Know yourself and when you need a day off.
- Be positive; think positive.
- Manage your time well. Make sure you time yourself whenever you take practice exams so that you can get used to being timed.
- Read each question four times before looking at the answer (this can help you determine the correct answer).
- Make sure to eat well, exercise, and get enough rest.

Six-Month Study Plan

Length of Time	Amount of Time	Action
1 week (Week 1/26)	1 hour, 3 nights a week	Study and take practice exams in the category (time yourself): *Judgment and reasoning*. Copy the questions that you miss.
Remember to		Eat healthy and exercise.
1 week (Week 2/26)	1 hour, 3 nights a week	Study and take practice exams in the category (time yourself): *Memorization and observation*. Copy the questions that you miss.
1 week (Week 3/26)	1 hour, 3 nights a week	Study and take practice exams in the category (time yourself): *Mathematics*. Copy the questions that you miss.

Length of Time	Amount of Time	Action
1 week (Week 4/26)	Take off.	Take off.
1 week (Week 5/26)	1 hour, 3 nights a week	Study and take practice exams in the category (time yourself): *Writing.* Copy the questions that you miss.
1 week (Week 6/26)	1 hour, 3 nights a week	Study and take practice exams in the category (time yourself): *Writing.* Copy the questions that you miss.
1 week (Week 7/26)	1 hour, 3 nights a week	Study and take practice exams in the category (time yourself): *Reading comprehension.* Copy the questions that you miss.
1 week (Week 8/26)	1 hour, 3 nights a week	Study and take practice exams in the category (time yourself): *Traffic maps.* Copy the questions that you miss.
Remember to		Eat healthy and exercise.
1 week (Week 9/26)	Take off.	Take off.
1 week (Week 10/26)	2 hours anytime during the week	Compile all the questions that you missed in the practice exams during the weeks 1–8 in one document and retake the exam questions you missed.
1 week (Week 11/26)	2 hours anytime during the week	Copy all the questions from the first retake exam (week 10) and make a new list of questions.
1 week (Week 12/26)	Take off.	Take off.
1 week (Week 13/26)	2 hours anytime during the week	Look over the new list of practice exam questions from week 11 and identify their categories.
1 week (Week 14/26)	3 hours anytime during the week	Research the hiring agency you are going to be testing for: 1. Understand the overall test process for that agency and look up the type of written exam used. 2. Contact peers to see if they have gone through the testing process and meet with them to get ideas of how to study and to possibly study with them. 3. Take a university LET prep class. 4. Go to the hiring agency's informational session (if offered) and/or go on a ride-along or sit-along (in the communications/dispatch area). 5. Know your strengths and weaknesses by taking the self-assessment tests in this textbook. 6. Improve your strengths. 7. Improve your weaknesses. 8. Begin to study the hiring agency's vision and mission statements, values, and organizational chart. 9. Begin to study the hiring agency's policies and procedures.

Length of Time	Amount of Time	Action
Remember to		Eat healthy and exercise.
1 week (Week 15/26)	3 hours anytime during the week	Practice: *Reading comprehension* (time yourself): 1. Choose a passage to read in a newspaper, magazine, or book (or something similar). 2. Take notes. 3. Identify key points and summarize the passage. If the one passage does not take 2 hours to complete, choose a second or third passage and complete steps 1–3.
1 week (Week 16/26)	3 hours anytime during the week	Practice: *Memorization and observation* (time yourself): Look around wherever you go Choose a person and study that person for 1 minute. After 1 minute, look away and write down what you remember about that person. Choose a location (such as a park or a mall) and focus on a large area with a lot going on (a lot of people and vehicles or other objects). After 2 minutes look away and write down what you remember about that large area.
Remember to		Eat healthy, exercise, and get a good night's sleep.
1 week (Week 17/26)	3 hours anytime during the week	Practice: *Traffic maps* (time yourself): 1. At least 1 hour a week, utilize a map to go to a location (even if you do not actually go, choose point A and point B). 2. Pay attention to the landmarks, vehicles, and a compass, always knowing the directions north, south, east, and west.
1 week (Week 18/26)	Take off.	Take off.
1 week (Week 19/26)	3 hours anytime during the week	Practice: *Mathematics* (time yourself): 1. Using your favorite search engine, search for an appropriate math quiz and take the various ones you find. 2. Focus on addition (search math quiz addition). 3. Focus on subtraction (search math quiz subtraction). 4. Focus on multiplication (search math quiz multiplication). 5. Focus on division (search math quiz division). 6. Focus on percentages (search math quiz percentages). 7. Focus on integers (search math quiz integers). 8. Focus on fractions (search math quiz fractions). 9. Focus on area and perimeter (search math quiz area and perimeter).

Length of Time	Amount of Time	Action
Remember to		Eat healthy, exercise, and get a good night's sleep.
1 week (Week 20/26)	Take off.	Take off.
1 week (Week 21/26)	1 hour, 3 nights a week	Look over the new list of practice exam questions (you created in week 11) and retake this exam.
1 week (Week 22/26)	1 hour, 3 nights a week	Create a new list of the questions you missed from week 21.
1 week (Week 23/26)	5 hours anytime during the week	Practice: *Reading comprehension* (time yourself): 1. Choose a passage to read in a newspaper, magazine, or book (or something similar). 2. Take notes. 3. Identify key points and summarize the passage. If the one passage does not take 5 hours to complete, choose a second or third passage and complete steps 1–3.
2 weeks (Weeks 24–25/26)	1 hour, 6 nights a week	Start over by retaking practice exams in the following categories; spend 1 hour taking practice exams in each category: • *Judgment and reasoning* • *Memorization and observation* • *Reading comprehension* • *Police report writing* • *Traffic map* Create a new list of the questions you missed from these categories and retake this new exam.
Remember to		Eat healthy, exercise, and get a good night's sleep.
Week before the written test	1 hour, 4 nights a week	Retake the exam created in Week 24, composed of questions missed.
Night before the written test		Get at least 7–8 hours of good sleep and eat healthy. Review the important things to remember for the categories.

In order to ensure success, some tips to remember are as follows:

- Schedule dates and times to study. If you miss a study day, do not forget to schedule a make-up day.
- Do not stress yourself out. Know yourself and when you need a day off.
- Be positive; think positive.
- Manage your time well. Make sure you time yourself whenever you take practice exams so that you can get used to being timed.
- Read each question four times before looking at the answer (this can help you determine the correct answer).
- Make sure to eat well, exercise, and get enough rest.

Three-Month Study Plan

Length of Time	Amount of Time	Action
1 week (Week 1/12)	1 hour, 3 nights a week	Study and take practice exams in the category (time yourself): *Judgment and reasoning.* Copy the questions that you miss.
Remember to		Eat healthy and exercise.
1 week (Week 2/12)	1 hour, 3 nights a week	Study and take practice exams in the category (time yourself): *Memorization and observation.* Copy the questions that you miss.
1 week (Week 3/12)	1 hour, 3 nights a week	Study and take practice exams in the category (time yourself): *Mathematics.* Copy the questions that you miss.
1 week (Week 4/12)	1 hour, 3 nights a week	Study and take practice exams in the category (time yourself): *Writing.* Copy the questions that you miss.
1 week (Week 5/12)	1 hour, 3 nights a week	Study and take practice exams in the category (time yourself): *Writing.* Copy the questions that you miss.
1 week (Week 6/12)	1 hour, 3 nights a week	Study and take practice exams in the category (time yourself): *Reading comprehension.* Copy the questions that you miss.
1 week (Week 7/12)	1 hour, 3 nights a week	Study and take practice exams in the category (time yourself): *Traffic maps.* Copy the questions that you miss.
Remember to		Eat healthy and exercise.
1 week (Week 8/12)	3 hours anytime during the week	Compile all the questions that you missed in the practice exams during weeks 1–7 in one document and retake the questions that you missed. Copy all the questions from the first retake exam and make a new list of questions that you have now missed a second time.
1 week (Week 9/12)	5 hours anytime during the week	Research the hiring agency you are going to be testing for: 1. Understand the overall test process for that agency and look up the type of written exam used. 2. Contact peers to see if they have gone through the testing process and meet with them to get ideas of how to study and to possibly study with them. 3. Take a university LET prep class. 4. Go to the hiring agency's informational session (if offered) and/or go on a ride-along or sit-along (in the communications/dispatch area).

Length of Time	Amount of Time	Action
		5. Know your strengths and weaknesses by taking the self-assessment tests in this textbook.
		6. Improve your strengths.
		7. Improve your weaknesses.
		8. Begin to study the hiring agency's vision and mission statements, values, and organizational chart.
		9. Begin to study the hiring agency's policies and procedures.
		And,
		Practice: *Reading comprehension* (time yourself):
		1. Choose a passage to read in a newspaper, magazine, or book (or something similar).
		2. Take notes.
		3. Identify key points and summarize the passage.
Remember to		Eat healthy and exercise.
1 week (Week 10/12)	5 hours anytime during the week	Practice: *Memorization and observation* (time yourself):
		Look around wherever you go
		Choose a person and study that person for 1 minute.
		After 1 minute, look away and write down what you remember about that person.
		Choose a location (such as a park or a mall) and focus on a large area with a lot going on (a lot of people and vehicles or other objects).
		After 2 minutes look away and write down what you remember about that large area.
		And,
		Practice: *Traffic maps* (time yourself):
		1. At least 1 hour a week, utilize a map to go to a location (even if you do not actually go, choose point A and point B).
		2. Pay attention to the landmarks, vehicles, and a compass, always knowing the directions north, south, east, and west.
Remember to		Eat healthy, exercise, and get a good night's sleep.
1 week (Week 11/12)	5 hours anytime during the week	Practice: *Mathematics* (time yourself):
		1. Using your favorite search engine, search for an appropriate math quiz and take the various ones you find.
		2. Focus on addition (search math quiz addition).
		3. Focus on subtraction (search math quiz subtraction).
		4. Focus on multiplication (search math quiz multiplication).

Length of Time	Amount of Time	Action
		5. Focus on division (search math quiz division).
		6. Focus on percentages (search math quiz percentages).
		7. Focus on integers (search math quiz integers).
		8. Focus on fractions (search math quiz fractions).
		9. Focus on area and perimeter (search math quiz area and perimeter).
		And, look over the new list of practice exam questions you created 3 weeks ago that you have now missed two times; retake this exam.
Remember to		Eat healthy, exercise, and get a good night's sleep.
Week before the written test	1 hour, 4 nights a week	Retake the exam created last week, composed of the questions missed.
Night before the written test		Get at least 7–8 hours of good sleep and eat healthy. Review the important things to remember for the categories.

In order to ensure success, some tips to remember are the following:

- Schedule dates and times to study. If you miss a study day, do not forget to schedule a make-up day.
- Do not stress yourself out. Know yourself and when you need a day off.
- Be positive; think positive.
- Manage your time well. Make sure you time yourself whenever you take practice exams so that you can get used to being timed.
- Read each question four times before looking at the answer (this can help you determine the correct answer).
- Make sure to eat well, exercise, and get enough rest.

Six-Week Cram Study Plan

Length of Time	Amount of Time	Action
1 week (Week 1/6)	3 hours each night, 3 nights a week	Study and take practice exams in the category (time yourself): *Judgment and reasoning.*
		Copy the questions that you miss.
		Study and take practice exams in the category (time yourself): *Memorization and observation.*
		Copy the questions that you miss.
		Study and take practice exams in the category (time yourself): *Mathematics.*
		Copy the questions that you miss.
		Study and take practice exams in the category (time yourself): *Writing.*
		Copy the questions that you miss.

Length of Time	Amount of Time	Action
Remember to		Eat healthy and exercise.
1 week (Week 2/6)	3 hours each night, 3 nights a week	Study and take practice exams in the category (time yourself): *Writing*.
		Copy the questions that you miss.
		Study and take practice exams in the category (time yourself): *Reading comprehension*.
		Copy the questions that you miss.
		Study and take practice exams in the category (time yourself): *Traffic maps*.
		Copy the questions that you miss.
Remember to		Eat healthy and exercise.
1 week (Week 3/6)	9 hours anytime during the week	Compile all the questions that you missed in the practice exams in one document and retake the questions that you missed.
		Copy all the questions from the first retake exam and make a new list of questions that you have now missed a second time.
		Research the hiring agency you are going to be testing for:
		1. Understand the overall test process for that agency and look up the type of written exam used.
		2. Contact peers to see if they have gone through the testing process and meet with them to get ideas of how to study and to possibly study with them.
		3. Take a university LET prep class.
		4. Go to the hiring agency's informational session (if offered) and/or go on a ride-along or sit-along (in the communications/dispatch area).
		5. Know your strengths and weaknesses by taking the self-assessment tests in this textbook.
		6. Improve your strengths.
		7. Improve your weaknesses.
		8. Begin to study the hiring agency's vision and mission statements, values, and organizational chart.
		9. Begin to study the hiring agency's policies and procedures.
		And,
		Practice: *Reading comprehension* (time yourself):
		1. Choose a passage to read in a newspaper, magazine, or book (or something similar).
		2. Take notes.
		3. Identify key points and summarize the passage.

Length of Time	Amount of Time	Action
Remember to		Eat healthy and exercise.
1 week (Week 4/6)	9 hours anytime during the week	Practice: *Memorization and observation* (time yourself): Look around wherever you go Choose a person and study that person for 1 minute. After 1 minute, look away and write down what you remember about that person. Choose a location (such as a park or a mall) and focus on a large area with a lot going on (a lot of people and vehicles or other objects). After 2 minutes look away and write down what you remember about that large area. *And,* Practice: *Traffic maps* (time yourself): 1. At least 1 hour a week, utilize a map to go to a location (even if you do not actually go, choose point A and point B). 2. Pay attention to the landmarks, vehicles, and a compass, always knowing the directions north, south, east, and west.
Remember to		Eat healthy, exercise, and get a good night's sleep.
1 week (Week 5/6)	9 hours anytime during the week.	Practice: *Mathematics* (time yourself): 1. Using your favorite search engine, search for an appropriate math quiz and take the various ones you find. 2. Focus on addition (search math quiz addition). 3. Focus on subtraction (search math quiz subtraction). 4. Focus on multiplication (search math quiz multiplication). 5. Focus on division (search math quiz division). 6. Focus on percentages (search math quiz percentages). 7. Focus on integers (search math quiz integers). 8. Focus on fractions (search math quiz fractions). 9. Focus on area and perimeter (search math quiz area and perimeter). And, look over the new list of practice exam questions you created 2 weeks ago that you have now missed two times; retake this exam.
Remember to		Eat healthy, exercise, and get a good night's sleep.

Length of Time	Amount of Time	Action
Week before the written test	1 hour, 4 nights a week	From the list created last week, composed of the questions missed from the categories studied last week- re-take this test
Night before the written test		Get at least 7–8 hours of good sleep and eat healthy. Review the important things to remember.

In order to ensure success, some tips to remember are the following:

- Schedule dates and times to study. If you miss a study day, do not forget to schedule a make-up day.
- Do not stress yourself out. Know yourself and when you need a day off.
- Be positive; think positive.
- Manage your time well. Make sure you time yourself whenever you take practice exams so that you can get used to being timed.
- Read each question four times before looking at the answer (this can help you determine the correct answer).
- Make sure to eat well, exercise, and get enough rest.

The Superhero Mind-Set Provides a Winning Solution for the Written Exam

Superhero? Should the candidate look to the skies for their nearest superhero to fly in and take the written exam for them? Alternatively, will the superhero be invisible and help the candidate choose the correct answer? Or does the superhero laser the correct answers to the candidate's mind? How does a superhero prepare a candidate for the written exam? Great questions. It is not a superhero but a **superhero state of mind** that the candidate needs to channel in order to succeed. Before entering the location where the written exam will be taken the candidate should follow the superhero state of mind instructions:

1. Stand up.
2. Place both hands on your hips.
3. Look up to the sky (causing your chin to be raised).
4. See yourself passing the written exam, flying through it with ease.

This is not a joke; it really does work. The superhero state of mind does not guarantee success. No magic pill or mind-set can do that; however, a positive and practiced minds-et can change the way a candidate reads the question and comes up with the correct answer.

Answers to Practice Tests

Judgment and Reasoning

1. C. The police should contact social services, family, neighbors, or friends to assist the woman through this difficult time in her life. Use the **POLIS** acronym, and choice C fits the best in providing service to the wife.

2. C. Tell dispatch (over your radio) to send an ambulance immediately and try to pull the girl from the pipe. You always want to get an ambulance headed to the scene since police officers are not paramedics; then you would try and save the young girl.

3. D. Contact the female and male to determine why they are trying to open the window. The female and male may live at the apartment and forgot their keys, or they may be trying to break into the apartment and burglarize it. You need to contact them immediately to investigate further.

4. D. Stop immediately and try to stop the fight. Police officers are required to keep the peace, and you do not know why the two men are fighting, so you need to stop the fight and investigate further.

5. B. Tell dispatch (via the radio) that you need an ambulance and contact the woman to investigate what happened. If a police officer sees a person who is injured, an ambulance needs to be called immediately. Then you need to investigate further to find out how the woman was injured.

6. C. Go immediately to the fast food restaurant to investigate, and call for an ambulance to meet you there. You do not know if the young girl needs medical attention, so you want to get an ambulance headed to the restaurant and then head to the restaurant to investigate further.

7. D. If 30% of the inmates released from prison never re-offend, does this mean that they have not committed a crime? Or does this mean that they have not been caught committing a crime? Since you do not know, the best answer is none of the above.

8. C. Ask Sergeant James, to stop the behavior because it is offensive. Then if Sergeant James does not stop, tell his supervisor.

9. A. If you know of a seafood restaurant, give the citizens quick directions, apologize that you have to leave so quickly, and explain you are on your way to a call. It is important that you get to the call to take a report of the stolen vehicle, so you should hurry; however, you do have time to be professional and give quick directions and kindly explain why you have to leave.

10. C. Ask the opinions of other officers, consider all the options, research the options, then run it by your immediate supervisor. Supervisors like to see tenacious and dedicated officers identify a problem, research the problem, come up with various solutions, take suggestions on how to solve the problem, and finally, after much consideration, run it by your supervisor.

Mathematics

1. A. Start by finding out how much money each officer spent. Officer Miller spent $2 \times \$2 = \$4$ and Officer Knudsen spent $2 \times \$1.50 = \$3$. Take $\$4 - \$3 = \$1$, so Officer Miller spent $1 more.
2. Perimeter = 68 inches, P = 22 + 22 + 12 + 12 or P = 2(22) + 2(12) or P = 2(22 + 12) or P = 2(34)
3. Area = $180in^2$; A = 15(12) or A = 15(12) or A = $180in^2$
4. B. Start by dividing each member of the equation by 3. 3x/3 = 12/3. The solution is 4.
5. B. Start with -31 and + 31 = 0, and you are left with -8.
6. C. Start by dividing 13/20 = 0.65 or 65%
7. C. Start by dividing 350 by 70% or 0.70 = 500
8. D. 219 + 391 + 500 = 1110
9. C. $96.18 − $11.72 = $84.46
10. A. 87 − 18 − 6 = 63
11. B. 22 × 5843 = 128,546
12. A. 983 × 167 = 164,161
13. C. 122/2 = 61
14. D. 4321.4/82 = 52.7

Memorization

Question 1:

1. 10.
2. Three men and 7 women
3. 2
4. 2
5. Green hoodie sweatshirt, white long-sleeved shirt, gray sweatshirt, red hoodie sweatshirt, gray long-sleeved shirt, pink sweatshirt, blue t-shirt and a black jacket, white striped t-shirt, t-shirt, and black sweatshirt
6. Three males with short hair, one woman with short hair, one woman with medium length hair, five women with long hair (one of the women with long hair has curly hair)
7. Four windows

Question 2:

1. 12 (five sitting at the table in the middle of the photograph, three standing in front of the table, one with only the bill of the hat seen and on the left side of the photo, one standing up on the right side of the photo wearing a hat, one sitting on the far right, and one is walking toward the person sitting on the far right)
2. Seven women (cannot tell the sex of the other people)

3. Six (five sitting in front of the table in the middle of the photograph, and one sitting in the far-right back side of the photograph)
4. Two (one is clearly visible on the right side of the photograph; the other is on the left side of the photo, but only the bill of the hat can be seen)
5. Six people are wearing the same long-sleeved black shirt, one has a pink long-sleeved shirt on with a black vest, one has on a yellow long-sleeved shirt, and one has on black pants
6. Three have hair in some type of a ponytail, and three have long straight hair
7. Two (one is open and one is closed)

Question 3:

1. 11 (nine civilians and two deputies)
2. Two men, six women; cannot tell on the rest
3. Two deputies
4. Dark green and light tan
5. Yes
6. Sunny
7. Two deputy uniforms, one blue long-sleeved jacket, one white/black striped long-sleeved shirt, one black long-sleeved shirt, one long-sleeved gray shirt, one black jacket with a gray hoodie, and one black jacket
8. Four have hair pulled back in some type of pon-tail, and four have long straight hair
9. Two

Question 4:

1. Two
2. K-9 patrol dog
3. Training and biting the decoy (person dressed in bite suit)
4. K-9 patrol dog
5. Five
6. Six
7. Cloudy
8. Deputy wearing dark green and black and a decoy wearing a bite suit
9. Short buzzed cut
10. One person is holding a dog leash and one person is hiding his hands
11. One blue sign and one sign that cannot be seen

Question 5: 3. Figure 3.8 is the same person as the suspect in Figure 3.5

Question 6: 5. Figures 3.6, 3.7, and 3.9 all have long hair and are females

Question 7: 3. Figure 3.8 has short hair and is a male

Question 8: 4. Figure 3.14 is the same person as the suspect in Figure 3.10

Question 9: 4. Figure 3.12 and 3.13 only. Figures 3.10 and 3.11 show one person with a beard and one person without, and Figure 3.14 does not have a beard.

Question 10: 6. Figures 3.15, 3.17, and 3.18

Question 11: 5. Figures 3.16 and 3.19

Question 12: 7. None of the figures

Question 13: 2. Figure 3.16

Question 14: 2. January 7, 1994

Question 15: 4. Fraud and forgery

Question 16: 1. 5'7" and 145 lbs.

Question 17: 1. Mario Esperanzo Perez; Pico

Question 18: 1. Snake on chest

Question 19: 2. 554-12-3450

Question 20: 2. Five

Question 21: 3. Blue

Question 22: 2. Two

Question 23: 4. Red

Question 24: 1. Brown curly hair

Question 25: 3. Long brown hair

Question 26: 4. The Lucky Lady

Question 27: 1. One

Question 28: 3. Six

Question 29: 3. Five

Question 30: 4. Six

Question 31: 1. Bee

Question 32: 3. Three

Question 33: 3. Nine

Question 34: 1. One

Question 35: 1. One

Question 36: 1. One

Reading Comprehension

Passage 1:

1. Have bad credit
2. Driver's license
3. 21 years of age
4. Established by law

Passage 2:

1. C. Answers A, B, and D are incorrect because dates should be written as xx/xx/xxxx; two numbers for the month, two numbers for the day, and four numbers for the year.
2. A. Answers B, C, and D are incorrect because the last name should precede the first name and the middle initial.
3. C. Answers A, B, and D are incorrect because feet are written with numbers, followed by an apostrophe; inches are written with numbers followed by quotation marks.
4. A. Answer B is not shown in military time, Answer C is 1:30 a.m. (not p.m.) and D uses both military and regular timed combined, which cannot be done (see Fact Box 3.1).

Passage 3:

1. A. Answers B, C, and D are incorrect because the numbers are in the wrong order and/or the direction of the street is wrong (E or S instead of W).
2. B. Answers A, C, and D are incorrect because they simply don't match the time noted in the description.
3. D. Answers A, B, and C are incorrect. The assisting officer is Officer Brenny; check the report again carefully.
4. A. Answers A, B, and D are incorrect. The striking vehicle is the silver Honda Civic. Check the report again carefully.

Traffic Maps

1. D
2. E
3. C
4. C. Answer A is incorrect because Fort Apache Rd. is a one-way street and only travels east. If you traveled west on Fort Apache Rd. you would be breaking a traffic law, driving the wrong way on a one-way street. Answer B is incorrect because C St. is a one-way street only going south and Rainbow Blvd. is a one-way street only going east. If you traveled north on C St. and west on Rainbow Blvd., you would be breaking two-traffic laws, going the wrong way on two one-way streets. Answer D is incorrect because Washington Blvd. stops at Blue Bell Park and does not go all the way through to A St.

5. C. Answer A is incorrect because Jones Blvd. is a one-way street and only goes west; you would be breaking a traffic law, driving the wrong way on a one-way street. Answers B and D are incorrect because they are not the fastest route.

Writing

1. A
2. A
3. B
4. C
5. D
6. D
7. B. Police reports are always written in the past tense, since the reports describe events that occurred in the past.
8. E.
9. A. The diamond ring belongs to Haas, so there should be an apostrophe to show possession.
10. C. The sentence contains one or more misspellings, *judgement* should be *judgment* and *competant* should be *competent*.

POLICE STORY 3.2 **Dress to Impress**

By Retired Lieutenant Tiffany L. Morey NLVPD

It is crucial for candidates to remember to *always* dress to impress. Throughout every portion of the hiring process, the candidate should remember always to dress professionally (in a suit or business attire). Even if the candidate is only picking up an application from the testing agency, the candidate should always dress professionally. Once, during the written exam portion of the testing process for one law enforcement agency, as the candidates had just passed 1 hour of testing, the chief of police for the hiring agency entered the testing location. He walked up to the front of the room and told all the candidates to put down their pencils. The chief then directed the candidates to stand up. The chief methodically walked up and down each aisle pointing to unknowing candidates as he passed them. As he rounded the last row, he told the candidates to whom he pointed out to grab their testing materials and leave the building. He said, "If you cannot take the time to dress professionally then we cannot take the time to continue the testing process with you."

Those candidates who had dressed professionally continued on in the process. Those who were asked to leave learned a harsh lesson. No matter the occasion (unless it is the physical agility test or physical fitness test) remember to dress to impress and dress professionally.

SUMMARY OF CHAPTER 3

1. The written exam is the most failed portion of the law enforcement hiring process because candidates do not practice, study, and prepare appropriately.

2. The written exam has been modified not to include questions that only police officers would know.

3. Written exams help ensure that candidates can read, understand, and make sound decisions in a wide variety of categories.

4. There are a variety of written exams on the market that law enforcement agencies use.

5. Written exams are either administered at the hiring agency or through an online company.

6. Candidates can prepare for all written exams by studying the six categories of questions.

7. Candidates should choose the 1-year study plan to prepare for the written exam properly. There are shorter cram study plans; however, they are not as successful.

8. The superhero mind-set allows the candidate to think positively before taking the written exam.

DISCUSSION QUESTIONS

1. Why is it essential for a candidate to prepare for the written exam?

2. What are the six categories of questions on the written exam?

3. There are many rules to help the candidate prepare for the written exam; what are those rules?

4. Why is the superhero state of mind so important?

INTERNET EXERCISE

The police officer written exam is a standard test. Candidates are fortunate to have many websites that offer free practice written exams to prepare. As candidates follow the study plans listed in this chapter, it is a good idea to take various practice exams.

1. Go to your favorite search engine and search for '"free practice police written exam questions."

2. Follow the study plan in this chapter to take the various free practice exams.

See Active Learning for the Following:

- Practice quizzes
- eFlashcards
- Video links
- Cognella journal articles
- News clips

Image Credits

What Is the Physical Agility Test or Physical Fitness Test?

"Physical fitness is not only one of the most important keys to a healthy body, it is the basis of dynamic and creative intellectual activity."

—John F. Kennedy

KEY TERMS

Physical agility test: A physical fitness test composed of various obstacles that must be performed in a specific amount of time.

Physical fitness test: A physical fitness test composed of various exercises that must be performed in a specific amount of time.

CHAPTER LEARNING OBJECTIVES

After reading the chapter, you should have a good understanding of the following:

- How agencies decide to use the physical agility test or the physical fitness test
- The difference between the physical agility test and the physical fitness test
- How to prepare for the physical agility test
- How to prepare for the physical fitness test
- How to do a proper push-up
- How to do a proper sit-up

What Is the Physical Agility Test or Physical Fitness Test?

The job of a police officer is challenging and demanding on many levels. Unlike many jobs in the 21st century that require the employee to sit at a computer all day long, the job of an officer requires sitting, standing, walking, jogging, running, squatting, crawling, lifting, and many other physical abilities. Officers guard crime scenes by standing in the same place for long periods. Officers direct traffic by standing and moving their arms to show drivers where to drive. Officers conduct surveillance, which requires sitting in a vehicle for long periods of time. Officers intervene in disputes where they have to control aggressive behavior by pushing or pulling. Officers engage in search and rescue operations by climbing, vaulting, crawling, and carrying. Officers chase suspects on foot, which requires them to either sprint short distances or run long distances. Many of these duties often place the officer's life at risk. For times like these, officers must be in excellent physical shape. Being physically fit is also the way to a healthier life and can reduce stress. Stress comes with the job of an officer; therefore, the ultimate goal should be to lower the job-related stress and lead a healthy life.

Hiring agencies have to ensure candidates can handle the daily rigors of being a police officer. Candidates must also show that they can handle the police academy by being physically fit. Police academies are not only mentally challenging, but they are physically demanding too. Between physical fitness tests, running, sprints, sit-ups, push-ups, defensive tactics (handcuffing, ASP baton training, ground-fighting, use of force techniques) and many other physical exercises, the academy recruit must be able to complete them all. Each state law enforcement training board sets the standards for a police recruit in the academy. The standards are based on validated research. The police recruit must always be prepared to perform these standards and pass them as well.

The job of a police officer is also stressful. One proven way to handle a stressful career is by being physically fit. Police officers who are physically fit are more apt to handle the various stressors of the job.

Why Talk to Your Doctor?

Candidates must ensure they are physically capable of going through the physical agility test or the physical fitness test and to prepare and train for either. Candidates should talk to a doctor before starting any new training program and before taking any physical test.

How Do Agencies Decide to Use the Physical Agility Test or the Physical Fitness Test?

Both the physical agility test and the physical fitness test provide the hiring agency a look at the physical fitness status of the candidate. The job of a police officer is multifaceted, active, and stressful. Officers who are physically fit are safer and are better prepared for the job. Decades ago, most law enforcement agencies utilized only the physical fitness test; however, with technology, research, and time came new developments in the way hiring agencies test candidates concerning physical fitness. It is not cheap for a hiring agency to put on a physical agility test or physical fitness test.

The testing requires proctors and staff to check in on the candidates and run the testing. In the end, it is up to the hiring agency to make the determination of which type of test to utilize for this portion of the hiring process.

What Is the Physical Agility Test?

Many companies offer variations of the physical agility test. In Oregon for example, there is the ORPAT, which is the Oregon Physical Agility Test. The ORPAT is a hybrid physical ability/job sample assessment meant to evaluate candidates on the essential physical capacities required to do the job. Developers of the ORPAT utilized scientifically accepted methods of multiple job task analysis to build the agility test. For instance, in one shift an officer might balance, stand, walk, jog, jump, run, crawl, bend, or lift. The agility test requires the candidate to perform all of these functions at one time to. The following list illustrates the physical abilities that these obstacles check:

1. Agility, ability to jump, ability to recover
2. Balance
3. Cardiovascular endurance
4. Coordination
5. Core body strength, core power
6. Depth perception
7. Flexibility
8. Lower and upper body strength
9. Mobility run
10. Muscular endurance
11. Speed
12. Visual acuity

The following list illustrates the various physical agility obstacles agencies utilize during the physical agility test:

1. Beam walk for 10–20 feet
2. Controlled falls
3. Crawling under a 30-inches high by 36-inches wide obstacle
4. Dummy drag (150–165 pounds)
5. Identification of a criminal suspect given at the beginning of the agility test (suspect was wearing a black jacket and a red baseball cap), and the candidate must identify the suspect at the end of the agility test
6. Jumping over 5 feet in length obstacle
7. Jumping over a 3-feet-high obstacle
8. Push/pull machine: PTM 1000 power training machine
9. Stair simulator
10. Wall or fence to climb or jump that is 4 or 6 feet
11. Window to climb

All of these physical agility obstacles most likely include some type of repetition. Not all agencies offer the same physical agility test; therefore, the candidate must research the type of obstacles the hiring agency utilizes.

POLICE STORY 4.1 **Physical Agility Debacle**

by Retired Lt. Tiffany L. Morey NLVPD

Instead of the normal 1.5–2-mile timed run, timed sit-ups, and timed push-ups, one police department decided to change things up and go with a new physical agility test. This new test was supposed to more appropriately gauge the candidate for the physical abilities related directly to the job of a police officer. The new physical agility test included a sprint for 300 meters, a window to climb through, a 4-foot cyclone fence to hop over, and dragging a 165-pound dummy. A female candidate was really worried when she found out about this new test because she had never done any kind of exercise other than slow-paced jogging. Her husband agreed to work with her three times a week at a local high school track to train for the new agility test. At the high school, her husband set up their own agility test. He had his wife practice 300-meter sprints on the track, jumping over a 4-foot cyclone fence, and finally, climbing a 6-foot wall, over and over again. After several weeks the candidate began to feel more confident in her abilities.

What the candidate could not predict was the second dummy. The candidate was so preoccupied with the different types of physical agility obstacles she would have to do that she failed to allow any other type of information into her brain. On the day of the test, she was stressed. Her heartbeat was racing, and she watched the other candidates run through the agility test with trepidation. An officer proctor finally called her name, and she sprinted to the start line. The proctor prepared the stopwatch, and before he pressed the magical go button, he began reading from a piece of paper. The proctor read, "You are a police officer on patrol, and you were just dispatched to a bank robbery. The suspect is described as a 6-foot tall male wearing a red hat, black shirt, and blue sweatpants." The female candidate did not listen to the proctor's description because she was too occupied with the agility course obstacles that seemed to stare back at her. The proctor finally yelled the word "Go!" and the candidate took off! She was fast, really fast. In fact, after she drug the dummy and sprinted the 300 meters, she found a second wind to sprint through the finish line. The proctor stopped the clock, and she screamed with joy when she saw that she ran the course in half the time! She started jumping up and down and even hugged the proctor. The proctor did not reciprocate and instead looked at his piece of paper and pointed to three additional dummies that were secretly positioned underneath the high school bleachers. The dummies were dressed in different types and colors of clothing. Each dummy had a piece of paper with the letter A, B, or C pinned to their shirt. The proctor looked at the candidate and asked her which dummy robbed the store. The candidate's face went white; she barely remembered the proctor's description of the suspect before the agility test began. She racked her brain, trying to recall a color of the hat, a type of shirt, anything. However, the candidate had been so stressed and then finally relieved after completing the agility test in under the prescribed time that she had washed out any other, what she had considered at the time, superfluous information. No matter how hard she tried, she could not remember that original description of the robbery suspect.

Ironically the candidate failed the physical agility test. Even though her physical abilities were above par, she did not pass because she failed to look at the big picture. Officers are placed under enormous amounts of stress at varying levels throughout their shifts. Each officer must be able to keep a cool head and take in all types of information and remember the information at a later time. The candidate failed to show she could do just that; therefore, she failed. It was a deep blow to her ego; however, it was a tremendous learning experience.

First, maybe you don't have a physical agility course in your backyard, but what you do have are local parks and schools, which have items that can double for the actual agility course and obstacles. Second, never give up. Enlist family members and friends to help and practice, practice, practice. Third, remember always pay attention and never take any amount of information, no matter how small, for granted.

The story does have a happy ending. One year later the candidate went on to pass a future physical fitness test along with all the other parts of the hiring process. She became a successful law enforcement officer and had a long career.

How to Prepare for the Physical Agility Test

Physical agility testing aims at placing the candidate through a variety of obstacles that simulate the actual job of a law enforcement officer. The best way to train for such agility tests is through powerful and short burst–type movements and exercise. Resistance training enables the candidate to sustain impact created by the obstacles. The various obstacles in the agility test require the candidate to walk, jog, run, jump, crawl, balance, and navigate through various items. One of the most important parts of training is always to time any obstacle performed. Since the physical agility test is timed, the candidate needs to get used to being timed when practicing. The following training ideas will assist the candidate in preparing for all types of physical agility tests.

There are videos available for exercises noted in "Active Learning."

Beam Walk

The balance beam utilized in most agility tests usually is 15 feet long, 6 inches wide, and 10 inches high. The balance beam walk must be completed in a controlled manner. Generally, if the candidate falls off the beam, the candidate must go back to the start of the beam walk to renegotiate the beam. Since agility tests are timed, this mistake could cost the candidate valuable seconds. The best way to prepare for this test is by walking along a raised item and getting familiarized with how balancing works. Candidates should time themselves, with the goal being to improve the amount of time it takes to walk across a prescribed practice beam. See Video 4.1 for the correct way to train for the beam walk.

Active Learning Video 4.1. Beam walk.

FIGURE 4.1 Balance beam 1.

FIGURE 4.2 Balance beam 2.

Figures 4.1 and 4.2 show the balance beam utilized during many physical agility tests.

Dummy Drag

Candidates are required to drag a 150–165-pound dummy a distance of 10–40 feet. Candidates utilize the under-the-arm technique in order to pull the dummy while walking backward. Candidates are required to perform this task in a continuous and controlled manner. Once the candidate begins dragging the dummy, the candidate cannot stop. Most tests allow the candidate two to three attempts to complete the test. The best way to train for this test is to nominate a friend or family member who is approximately 150–165 pounds to volunteer to practice how to perform the under-the-arm technique. See Figures 4.3, 4.4, and 4.5 for the correct way to perform the dummy drag.

Jumps

Candidates are required to jump over several obstacles. One obstacle is a rubber mat that is 5 feet × 3 feet. A second jump is required, and this is over a 3-foot or 4-foot portable vault and climbing rail. The candidate can jump over the vault or rail and do a controlled fall to the ground. The third jump is over a 3-foot cedar stick that has a 12-inch cone on each side. Video 4.2 shows how to train to jump over the rubber mat that is 5 feet × 3 feet.

Active Learning Video 4.2. Jump.

Figure 4.6 shows the jump over a rubber mat that is 5 feet × 3 feet.

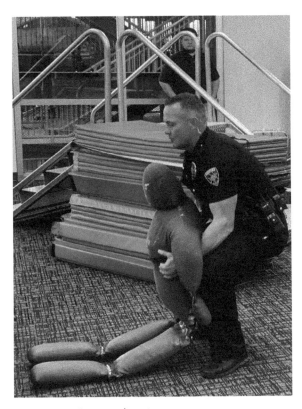

FIGURE 4.3 Dummy drag 1.

FIGURE 4.4 Dummy drag 2.

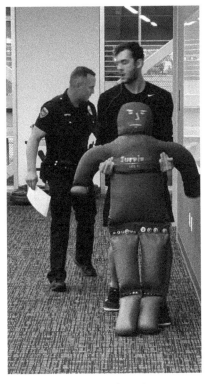

FIGURE 4.5 Dummy drag 3.

FIGURE 4.6 Jump.

FIGURE 4.7 Second jump 1.

Figures 4.7 and 4.8 show the second jump over a portable vault used during physical agility tests.

Figure 4.9 shows the third jump over a 3-foot cedar stick that has a 12-inch cone on each side, which is used during physical agility tests.

Box jumps are a great way to train for the various jumps in the agility test. Video 4.3 shows how to properly do a box jump.

Active Learning Video 4.3. Box jump.

Mobility Run

The mobility run is the entire physical agility Test. there is a start line and finish line and various obstacles along the way. The candidate has a time limit for completion. Candidates can shake up their workout by considering aerobic interval training. Interval training is a powerful tool that can assist the candidate in preparing for the mobility run portion of most agility courses. Although it has a fancy name, interval training is pretty simple and requires simply alternating short bursts of intense activity with longer intervals of less intense activity. For instance, if the candidate is training to meet a timed run, the candidate could interval train by training one set, three times a week, the following interval for 21 minutes each set:

1. Walking for 4 minutes
2. Fast walking for 30 seconds

3. Walking for 4 minutes
4. Jogging for 30 seconds
5. Fast walking for 3 minutes
6. Jogging for 30 seconds
7. Walking for 4 minutes
8. Sprinting for 30 seconds
9. Walking for 4 minutes
10. Sprinting for 30 seconds

Interval training makes the candidate more time efficient, improves aerobic activity, and does not require any special equipment. Another excellent training activity to help the candidate prepare for the entire physical agility process is the burpee.

FIGURE 4.8 Second jump 2.

Burpee
See Video 4.4 for the proper way to do a burpee.

Active Learning Video 4.4. Burpee.

FIGURE 4.9 Third jump 1.

FIGURE 4.10 Push/Pull machine 1.

FIGURE 4.11 Push/Pull machine 2.

FIGURE 4.12 Push/Pull machine 1.

Push/Pull Machine

Many physical agility tests, such as the ORPAT, utilize the PTM 1000 power training machine (push/pull machine). Figures 4.10–4.14 show the push/pull machine being utilized during the ORPAT.

Most candidates do not have a push/pull machine at home, nor can one be found easily at a local gym. The following training exercises can be done to prepare for the push/pull machine obstacle:

Bench Press

A bench press is a common skill that is tested and can also help the candidate prepare for the push/pull machine. Candidates can check the hiring agency to see how much weight is required to bench press. The candidate should then calculate 60% of that weight and begin lifting that amount. Each week five pounds can be added until the required lift is met. If the candidate cannot lift 60% of the weight required, the candidate should start at whatever weight is manageable and each week add five pounds until the required lift is met. See Video 4.5 for how to do a bench press properly.

Active Learning Video 4.5. Bench press.

Crunches

See Video 4.6 for how to do crunches properly.

Active Learning Video 4.6. Crunches.

Deadlift

See Video 4.7 for how to do a deadlift properly.

See Active Learning Video 4.7. Deadlift.

Plank

See Video 4.8 for how to do a plank properly.

See Active Learning Video 4.8. Plank.

Video 4.9 shows the incorrect way to do a plank.

See Active Learning Video 4.9.
Incorrect plank.

Russian Twist
See Video 4.10 for how to do a Russian twist properly.

See Active Learning Video 4.10.
Russian twist.

See Video 4.11 for how to do a complex Russian twist properly.

See Active Learning Video 4.11.
Complex Russian twist.

FIGURE 4.13 Push/Pull machine 2.

Stair Simulator

Many physical agility tests, such as the ORPAT have a type of stair simulator. A stair simulator is a moveable obstacle with a handrail and approximately five-to-ten-steps up to a platform and five-to-ten-steps down. Candidates are required to run up and down the stairs. Candidates can run up the stairs, one or two at a time. Most tests require the candidate to hit at least two steps on the way up and two steps on the way down for the stair portion of the test to count. No jumping is allowed on any portion of the stairs. The best way to train for the stair simulator is to practice on stairs, ensuring to run up and down during interval type training. See Video 4.12 for the correct way to train for the stairs portion of the agility test.

See Active Learning Video 4.12. Stairs.

FIGURE 4.14 Push/Pull machine 3.

Wall, Fence, or Window Climb

To train for the 4-foot or 6-foot wall or fence climb or the window climb, the candidate can engage in the following training activity:

Jump Split
See Video 4.13 for how to properly do a jump split.

See Active Learning Video 4.13. Jump split.

What Is the Physical Fitness Test?

Law enforcement agencies that utilize a physical fitness test generally use the chart of the U.S. Army Basic Training Physical Fitness Test standards as a guide. The following physical exercises comprise most physical fitness tests:

1. 1.5- or- 2-mile timed run
2. Push-ups
3. Sit-ups
4. 300-meter sprint
5. Vertical jump
6. Trigger pull
7. Flexibility test

How to Prepare for the Physical Fitness Test?

If a candidate does not work out, the candidate should consider making physical fitness a part of their lives moving forward. If the candidate is physically fit, the candidate should begin preparing for the rigors of the physical testing process. Do not wait until the last minute to start preparing. These tests are timed and are meant to test the candidate's physical capabilities. Candidates need to build up their level of fitness gradually. A good guide is to plan on 3–6 months for preparation.

Whatever physical training the candidate engages in, it is recommended that the candidate always time the activities. The physical fitness test is timed, so the candidate needs to get used to what it feels like to be under the constraint of a timed activity.

Aerobic Activities

It is a good idea to include aerobic activities such as walking, jogging, swimming, running on a treadmill, using a stair master or elliptical, or bicycle riding to get the heart pumping. The Mayo Clinic recommends at least 150 minutes of moderate aerobic activity or 75 minutes of vigorous aerobic activity each week. A good guide is to include aerobic activity:

Four times a week: 38 minutes for moderate activity or 19 minutes for vigorous activity

Three times a week: 50 minutes for moderate activity and 25 minutes for vigorous activity

Weight Training

Some agencies require some type of weight lifting as a part of the test. See *bench press* in this chapter for more information.

Timed Run

The toughest challenge for most candidates is the timed 1.5- or 2-mile run segment of the physical fitness test. In order to train for the timed run, the candidate must know how far to run. Candidates can get a program for their smartphone or another device to determine distance, or the candidate can utilize a track. Here are some measurements on a track:

- 100 meters: One straightaway
- 800 meters: Roughly half a mile or two laps around the track
- 1,600 meters: roughly 1 mile or four laps around the track

The Army Basic Training Physical Fitness Test minimum requirements along with other hiring agencies requirements are shown in Table 4.1:

Some agencies do have the same requirements for both men and women; therefore, the candidate needs to check the requirements for the hiring agency to ascertain the distance and timed requirements.

Training aids can be utilized to assist the candidate in preparing. An elevation training mask can assist the candidate by strengthening the diaphragm and allowing more forceful breathing to increase lung capacity. The mask forces the candidate to take deep breaths thereby increasing oxygen and blood flow. A training vest can be worn while running to increase stamina. Each week more weight can be added to the vest to build leg strength. The weight of the vest increases resistance in cardiovascular activities. In turn, the candidate uses more energy during workouts. When the vest is finally not worn, the candidate has more energy, feels a lightness, and can run faster and longer. The training vest also simulates the bullet-proof vest that officers wear; therefore, the candidate is preparing for their future career.

TABLE 1

Age Group	Gender	Push-Ups (2 minutes)	Sit-Ups (2 minutes)	2-Mile Run
17–21	Male	35–42	47–53	15:54–16:36
17–21	Female	13–19	47–53	18:54–19:42
22–26	Male	31–40	43–50	16:36–17:30
22–26	Female	11–17	43–50	19:36–20:36
27–31	Male	39	45	17:00
27–31	Female	17	45	20:30
32–36	Male	36	42	17:42
32–36	Female	15	42	21:42
37–41	Male	34	38	18:18
37–41	Female	13	38	22:42
42–46	Male	30	32	18:42
42–46	Female	12	32	23:42
47–51	Male	25	30	19:30
47–51	Female	10	30	24:00
52–56	Male	20	28	19:48
52–56	Female	9	28	24:24
57–61	Male	18	27	19:54
57–61	Female	8	27	24:48
62+	Male	16	26	20:00
62+	Female	7	26	25:00

Push-Ups

The candidate will have 2 minutes to complete the minimum number of push-ups required by the Army Basic Training requirements set forth for each age group and sex. There is a correct form for the push-up. A push-up is a total-body functional movement that increases strength and engages the core and lower body too. Push-ups can be done just about anywhere; however, the candidate must ensure they master the perfect push-up.

How to Do a Push-Up

1. Start in the up position, a high plank position. Focus on the ground. Place hands on the ground directly under the shoulders and push the toes into the ground. Engage all of the muscles from the core (tighten abs as if laughing), engage glutes and legs, and keep back straight.
2. Lower the body while keeping the back flat. Maintain focus on the ground. The chest will graze the ground. Do not let the butt pull in or out; ensure the entire body is in a straight line from head to toe. Keep elbows tucked close to the body.
3. Go back to position 1. Focus on driving hands into the ground.

Candidates can only rest in the up position, and only one attempt is allowed.
See Video 4.14 for how to properly do a push-up.

Active Learning Video 4.14. Push-up.

Common Push-Up Mistakes

1. It is not good if the lower back sags or arches. Focus on tightening everything from the core, glutes, and legs.
2. Don't forget to breathe. It is easy to concentrate so hard on doing the push-up correctly that breathing is ignored. Focus on inhaling on the way down and exhaling on the way up.
3. Don't let the arms flare out. It is tough on the shoulders if the arms flare out to 90 degrees. Keep the elbows tucked close to the upper body.
4. Try not to cheat. It is tempting to cheat and not do a correct push-up; however, cheating only hurts the candidate. Just put the time in; it will be surprising how fast improvement is made.
5. Don't let the head droop. Pick a point on the ground and stare at it. Doing this will force the head to remain up and not sag.

See Video 4.15 for common mistakes made while doing push-ups.

Active Learning Video 4.15. Push-up common mistakes.

Push-ups are difficult in the beginning; however, with persistence and consistency, the candidate will see significant gains soon after training begins. The candidate will need to train for a minimum of 10 weeks. Follow Table 4.2, which shows a 10-week push-up training program.

TABLE 2

Week	Jumping Jacks	Push-Ups	Notes
1 warm-up	10	10	Stretch triceps, chest, shoulders
1 timed workout		1 minute of push-ups Repeat 2 times 30 seconds of push-ups Repeat 3 times 15 seconds of push-ups Repeat 4 times	
2 warm-ups	10	10	Stretch triceps, chest, shoulders
2 timed workouts		1 minute of push-ups Repeat 2 times 30 seconds of push-ups Repeat 3 times 15 seconds of push-ups Repeat 4 times	
3 warm-ups	15	15	Stretch triceps, chest, shoulders
3 timed workouts		1.5 minutes of push-ups Repeat 2 times 45 seconds of push-ups Repeat 3 times 30 seconds of push-ups Repeat 4 times	
4 warm-ups	15	15	Stretch triceps, chest, shoulders
4 timed workouts		1.5 minutes of push-ups Repeat 2 times 45 seconds of push-ups Repeat 3 times 30 seconds of push-ups Repeat 4 times	
5 warm-ups	20	20	Stretch triceps, chest, shoulders
5 timed workouts		2 minutes of push-ups Repeat 2 times 45 seconds of push-ups Repeat 3 times 30 seconds of push-ups Repeat 4 times	
6 warm-ups	20	20	Stretch triceps, chest, shoulders
6 timed workouts		2 minutes of push-ups Repeat 2 times 45 seconds of push-ups Repeat 3 times 30 seconds of push-ups Repeat 4 times	
7 warm-ups	25	25	Stretch triceps, chest, shoulders

TABLE 2 *(Continue)*

Week	Jumping Jacks	Push-Ups	Notes
7 timed workouts		2 minutes of push-ups Repeat 2 times 1 minute of push-ups Repeat 3 times 45 seconds of push-ups Repeat 4 times	
8 warm-ups	25	25	Stretch triceps, chest, shoulders
8 timed workouts		2 minutes of push-ups Repeat 2 times 1 minute of push-ups Repeat 3 times 45 seconds of push-ups Repeat 4 times	
9 warm-ups	25	25	Stretch triceps, chest, shoulders
9 timed workouts		2 minutes of push-ups Repeat 2 times 1 minute of push-ups Repeat 3 times 45 seconds of push-ups Repeat 4 times	
10 warm-ups	30	30	Stretch triceps, chest, shoulders
10 timed workouts		2 minutes of push-ups Repeat 2 times 1.5 minutes of push-ups Repeat 3 times 1 minute of push-ups Repeat 4 times	

If the candidate needs a more active push-up workout the candidate can perform the following different types of push-ups:

Incline Push-Ups
These push-ups are performed by placing the hands on a stable platform that is higher than the ground. Step-up platforms utilized for step workouts are great tools to utilize for incline push-ups. Just make sure that the base under the platform is secure, so the platform does not slide, thereby injuring the candidate. The candidate starts by leaning on a bed, sturdy table, or wall and works down to the surface, at least six inches off the ground.

Diamond Push-Ups
These are done by placing hands on the floor, forming a diamond with the index fingers and thumbs.

Weighted Push-Ups
Can be done by wearing a weighted vest.

Wide-Inclined Push-Ups
Are done by placing the hands wider than shoulder width.

Sit-Ups

How to Do a Sit-Up

1. Lie on back.
2. Bend knees at approximately 90 degrees.
3. Keep feet flat on the mat.
4. Interlace fingers behind head with elbows out to the side.
5. Have a partner hold feet in place (not needed for training).
6. Keep buttocks on the ground at all times.
7. Move upper body forward, touching elbows to knees.
8. Return down, touching shoulder blades to the ground.

See Video 4.16 for how to do a sit-up properly.

Active Learning Video 4.16. Sit-up.

A sit-up is not counted if the hands separate or buttocks come off the ground, and resting is only allowed in the up position. Candidates are only allowed one attempt. Candidates must strengthen their abdominal muscles over time. It is essential in improving the sit-up technique as well as improving the number of sit-ups that can be done in a specific amount of time. Along with doing actual sit-ups, the candidate can strengthen the abdominal muscles by exercises like reverse crunches, planks, and Russian twists (see further explanation in this chapter).

How many sit-ups can you do in 1 minute? Try it. If that number is 30 sit-ups in, now multiply 30 by 0.75. The answer is now the new number of sit-ups that need to be done in each set.

Example:

30 sit-ups in 1 minute × 0.75 = 22.5 sit-ups

Complete four sets (1 minute each) of 22.5 sit-ups. Be sure to remember to time the sit-ups. It is good for the candidate to get used to being timed. Table 4.3 is a 10-week training example for sit-ups.

See Video 4.17 for common mistakes made while doing sit-ups.

Active Learning Video 4.17. Sit-up common mistakes.

300-Meter Sprint

Some agencies require the 300-meter sprint be done in 77–78 seconds or less. Candidates are only allowed one attempt at the 300-meter sprint.

How to Perform a 300-Meter Sprint

1. Begin at the starting line.
2. Once instructed to go, complete the 300-meter sprint as quickly as possible to the finish line.

See Video 4.18 for how to train for sprints.

Active Learning Video 4.18. Sprints.

Table 4.3.

Week	Set	Number of Sit-Ups (Utilizing the number in the example)	Rest
1	1	22.5	
1	Rest		1 minute
1	2	22.5	
1	Rest		1 minute
1	3	22.5	
1	Rest		1 minute
1	4	22.5	
2	1	24.5	
2	Rest		1 minute
2	2	24.5	
2	Rest		1 minute
2	3	24.5	
2	Rest		1 minute
2	4	24.5	
3	1	26.5	
3	Rest		1 minute
3	2	26.5	
3	Rest		1 minute
3	3	26.5	
3	Rest		1 minute
3	4	26.5	
4	1	28.5	
4	Rest		1 minute
4	2	28.5	
4	Rest		1 minute
4	3	28.5	
4	4	28.5	
5	1	30.5	
5	Rest		1 minute
5	2	30.5	
5	Rest		1 minute
5	3	30.5	
5	Rest		1 minute
5	4	30.5	
6		32.5	
6	Rest		1 minute
6	2	32.5	
6	Rest		1 minute

Week	Set	Number of Sit-Ups (Utilizing the number in the example)	Rest
6	3	32.5	
6	Rest		1 minute
6	4	32.5	
7	1	34.5	
7	Rest		1 minute
7	2	34.5	
7	Rest		1 minute
7	3	34.5	
7	Rest		1 minute
7	4	34.5	
8	1	36.5	
8	Rest		1 minute
8	2	36.5	
8	Rest		1 minute
8	3	36.5	1 minute
8	Rest		1 minute
8	4	36.5	
9	1	38.5	
9	Rest		1 minute
9	2	38.5	
9	Rest		1 minute
9	3	38.5	
9	Rest		1 minute
9	4	38.5	
10	1	40.5	
10	Rest		1 minute
10	2	40.5	
10	Rest		1 minute
10	3	40.5	
10	Rest		1 minute
10	4	40.5	

One excellent way to prepare for this timed test is to do interval and sprint training. Sprints are an excellent way for a candidate to train. Interval sprints require the candidate to focus on breathing, posture, and taking small strides. First, the candidate should go to a high school or university running track or measure out 110 yards (a good starting spring length) at another location. The candidate will then sprint the 110 yards while timed. Take that time and multiply it by .80, to determine the required training time.

Table 4.4.

Weeks	Yards	Number of Reps	Training Time (Utilizing the number in the example)
1	110	10	40 seconds
2	110	10	40 seconds
3	110	10	38 seconds
4	110	10	37 seconds
5	110	10	36 seconds
6	110	10	35 seconds
7	220	8	80 seconds
8	220	8	79 seconds
9	220	8	78 seconds
10	220	8	77 seconds

Example:

The candidate sprints the 110 yards in 50 seconds.

50 × .80 = 40 seconds

The candidate will need to train for a minimum of 10 weeks. Follow Table 4.4, which shows a 10-week sprint training program.

Vertical Jump

Many hiring agencies require the candidates to perform a vertical jump of 14–16.5 inches over the height of the candidate. Candidates are required to do the following:

1. Place chalk on fingers.
2. Start with one-body side toward a fence (or another object).
3. Keep heels together.
4. Reach upward as high as possible.
5. Place a mark (with fingers) on the chalkboard.
6. Step backward with one foot.
7. With a rocking motion bring the rear foot back together with the front jumping upward.
8. Reach as high with chalked fingers, again marking the chalkboard.

Candidates are allowed up to three attempts. There must be at least 14–16.5 inches between the two marks for a passing score.

One of the best ways to prepare for the vertical jump test is to build elastic energy through compression and stretching (see flexibility test) the muscles. Practice jump exercises are valuable as well.

1. Jumping on and off a box (or platform type object)
2. Jump squats (explosive movements)
3. Bulgarian bench split squats
4. Deadlifts
5. Hip flexor stretches

See Video 4.19 for how to do a vertical jump

Active Learning Video 4.19. Vertical jump.

Trigger Pull

One of the easiest tests hiring agencies utilize is pulling the trigger of a firearm with both hands. To practice for this test, the candidate can perform the following exercises:

1. Ball squeeze
2. Dumbbell hold
3. Handgrip device

Flexibility Test

In order to prepare for the flexibility test, the candidate needs to understand how the test is conducted:

1. The candidate sits on the floor.
2. Candidate removes shoes and with legs extended in front of the candidate.
3. The backs of the knees are on the ground, and the feet are flexed with the toes pointed up in the air.
4. The candidate sits straight up and slowly begins to lean forward.
5. Candidate reaches toward their toes with both hands until candidate can no longer stretch any further.
6. A second person measures (in centimeters) from the candidate's toes to the tips of the fingers.

There are a variety of stretches the candidate can do to gain flexibility.
See Video 4.20 for how to do the flexibility test.

Active Learning Video 4.20. Flexibility test.

See Videos 4.21–4.29 for different stretching exercises to assist the candidate in preparing for the flexibility test.

Active Learning Video 4.21. Stretching exercise 1.

Active Learning Video 4.22. Stretching exercise 2.

Active Learning Video 4.23. Stretching exercise 3.

Active Learning Video 4.24. Stretching exercise 4.

Active Learning Video 4.25. Stretching exercise 5.

Active Learning Video 4.26. Stretching exercise 6.

Active Learning Video 4.27. Stretching exercise 7.

Active Learning Video 4.28. Stretching exercise 8.

Active Learning Video 4.29. Stretching exercise 9.

SUMMARY OF CHAPTER 4

1. Hiring agencies can utilize a physical agility test or a physical fitness test to ascertain the physical abilities of a candidate.

2. There are various ways to prepare for the physical agility test or the physical fitness test.

DISCUSSION QUESTIONS

1. How does a candidate prepare for the physical agility test?

2. How does the candidate prepare for the physical fitness test?

INTERNET EXERCISE

The police officer hiring physical agility test, or the physical fitness test is different for each law enforcement agency.

1. Go to the Internet and search for three police departments you are interested in possibly working for someday.

2. For each police department search for the hiring process for new police officers.

3. For each police department search for the type of physical fitness test given during the hiring process.

4. For each police department list the type of obstacles or exercises the candidate is required to complete (as a part of the physical agility test or physical fitness test) and the time the candidate has to complete them.

See Active Learning for the Following:

- Practice quizzes
- eFlashcards

- Video links
- Cognella journal articles
- News clips

REFERENCE

The Oregon Physical Abilities Test Description. (n.d.). *The Oregon Physical Fitness Abilities Test.* https://www.oregon.gov/dpsst/at/pages/orpat.aspx

Why Is the Oral Board Interview So Important?

> "One important key to success is self-confidence. An important key to self-confidence is preparation."
>
> —Arthur Ashe

KEY TERMS

Three golden ticket tips: (1) The candidate includes a personal story in answers, (b) the candidate makes a complete circle with answers, and (3) if you do not say it or explain it you will fail it.

Eight steps to success: (1) understand the job duties, responsibilities, and qualities of a police officer, (2) research the hiring agency, (3) give detailed answers to oral board questions, (4) have a mock practical oral board, (5) study a plan, (6) practice aloud, (7) dress to impress, and (8) be professional.

Nine actions for perfect answers: (1) research, (2) write questions, (3) write bullet points, (4) write essays, (5) repeat, (6) type out, (7) acronyms, (8) memorize, and (9) practice aloud.

Role-playing: One way officers regularly prepare themselves for all types of calls by running different scenarios through in their mind while headed to a call for service.

Running resume: A document the candidate always adds to whenever something is accomplished, ensuring the resume always contains the most current information.

Superhero state of mind: The candidate needs to channel this positive state of mind prior to entering the location where the oral board interview will be taken. The candidate should stand up, place both hands on hips, look up into the sky (causing the chin to raise), and see oneself passing the oral board interview, flying through it with ease.

CHAPTER LEARNING OBJECTIVES

After reading the chapter, you should have a good understanding of the following:

- Why the oral board interview is so important
- How the oral board interview room can be configured and which agency members compose the interview panel
- How an oral board interview is scored
- Why oral board interviews are so intimidating
- How to prepare for the oral board interview, including the eight steps to success and the nine actions for perfect answers
- The job duties, responsibilities, and qualities of a police officer
- How to research a hiring agency and why it should be researched
- How the SARA problem-solving model can be utilized in an oral board interview answer
- Why practicing in front of a mirror, speaking the answers aloud, and running a mock practical oral board interview is essential
- The different study plans for oral board interview preparation
- Why a candidate's dress speaks volumes to the hiring agency
- Why a candidate should shake hands with the panel members when entering and exiting the interview
- Why it essential for the candidate to know the rank and last names of the panel members
- The three golden ticket tips and why are they valuable to success

Why Is the Oral Board Interview So Important?

The law enforcement oral board interview is where the candidate has the opportunity to show the hiring agency all that the candidate has to offer. All too often candidates miss out on this valuable opportunity. Make no mistake, it is either an opportunity to shine and move onward toward the goal of obtaining a career in law enforcement, or it can be a opportunity to fail. More often than not, candidates make the horrendous mistake of not preparing properly. It is easy for a candidate to conduct an Internet search for common questions asked during a law enforcement oral board interview. This type of search is quick, easy, and free. The most common questions that appear on a search are the following:

- "Tell us a little bit about yourself."
- "What have you done to prepare for the position of a law enforcement officer?"
- "What is your greatest weakness (or strength)?"
- "Why do you want to be a law enforcement officer?"

The questions asked might not be as difficult as once thought, and the next step is pondering how to study. Study? Why study? Between work, school, family, and friends, time is a rare commodity. Plus, the law enforcement testing process is tough. Preparing for the oral board interview is vital for success. No matter the background of the candidate, if the candidate does not adequately prepare for this portion of the hiring process, they can quickly watch their dreams circle the drain. Moreover, if the candidate takes the time to adapt and follow the guidelines in this chapter and prepares accordingly, they can breeze past this portion and move on to getting hired.

What Is an Oral Board Interview?

Whether the candidate is applying for a position as a cashier at McDonald's, as a top executive at Amazon, as a prosecutor for the county district attorney's office, as a victim's advocate, as a social worker, or as a police officer, the preparation for the oral board interview is the same. An oral board interview is a job interview. It is a platform where the hiring agency gets to hear from the candidate by means other than a written application. The interview allows the hiring agency to assess a candidate's attitude, motivation, oral communication skills, problem-solving skills, and understanding of police work.

Most hiring agencies require the candidate to fill out a job application, pass a written test, and possibly complete the physical agility or physical fitness test (and even maybe a personal history questionnaire) prior to being scheduled for an oral board interview. Once the applicant has passed the required portions of the testing process, the candidate will be notified when and where the oral board interview will be scheduled.

During the oral board interview there is a table in the room with three-five panel members on one side; the candidate either sits on the other side or, more often, the candidate is placed in the middle of the room in a single chair. See Figures 5.1 and 5.2 for possible variations of how the oral board interview room and table will be set up.

FIGURE 5.1 Oral board configuration 1.

FIGURE 5.2 Oral board configuration 2.

The three–five interview panel members could be composed of the following:

- One-two uniformed police officer(s) (or other commensurate position that the candidate is testing for)
- Uniformed sergeant (supervisor of the position the candidate is testing for)
- Uniformed lieutenant (not as common but can be utilized)
- Civilian volunteer or civilian employee

Since it is up to each hiring agency to determine who sits on the panel of the oral board interview, the panel members can also include human resource employees, psychologists, or other members deemed appropriate. The goal of the panel is to ensure that the candidate is evaluated by a person who holds the position tested for, the supervisor of the position, and a civilian employee (such as a civilian crime analysis employee, a victim's advocate, or a records clerk) or a civilian law enforcement volunteer. By building the panel with distinctive members, the panel is able to evaluate the candidate's answers to the questions on a variety of levels. The interview can also be monitored by the agency's Human Resource Department. Human Resources can record the interview to ensure every interview is fair and standardized so that every candidate is given the same opportunity.

How Is an Oral Board Interview Scored?

It is up to each hiring agency to determine the proper way to score the oral board interview. The most common way an interview is scored is by having each panel member place a numeric score next to each answer. Although the candidate may be numerically scored on each question asked, the most common ending score on an oral board interview is a pass/fail. For instance, there may be 10 questions on the oral board interview. The panel members may grade five dimensions for each answer. For each dimension, there may be a 1–5 score given by each panel member. If the hiring agency decides that 70% is a passing score, the panel members will add up the scores for each dimension on each question and then give a total score for all 10 questions. If the candidate receives 70% or higher, the candidate will be told they passed. If the candidate receives 69% or lower, the candidate will be told they failed and will not continue in the testing process. Figure 5.3 shows possible grading dimensions for an oral board interview. Figure 5.4 illustrates an oral board interview panel member rating sheet. Each panel member sitting in on a candidate's oral board interview would be required to fill out Figure 5.4. The total possible points for an interview utilizing Figure 5.4 would be 25 points. If the hiring agency utilizes a pass/fail scoring where 70% is passing,

Candidate will be graded on the following areas:

Oral communication skills: Speaks clearly, logically and intelligently. Ability to listen to others and organize thoughts and express them. Is prepared to answer the entire question in a logical and informative way and utilizes personal history to assist with the understanding of the answer to each question. Speaks correct volume and organizes thoughts well, has a start/middle/and conclusion to each question asked.

Interpersonal skills: Displays empathy, sympathy, and understanding of different values, beliefs and viewpoints. Maintain a cooperative working relationship with those who have differing viewpoints. Makes eye contact with the panel members and does not stare down or at only one or two panel members. Shakes hands with the panel members and remembers and utilizes their correct last name and positions with their respective departments.

Attitude and motivation: Attitude and motivation toward police and desire and focus to serve the public/customer service. Has a positive attitude and shows a passion and motivation for the position and shows self confidence in answering the questions.

Understanding the position: Demonstration of the familiarity of the pros and cons of police work. Firm grasp of the duties and responsibilities of a sworn officer. Knows the department testing for (studied website and social media and understands current issues and how department is addressing them). Dressed appropriately for the interview.

Problem-solving skills/judgment: Ability to identify a problem presented and provide answers/solutions that are logical, reasonable and relevant. Ability to exercise sound judgment consistent with the police role in society. Can methodically solve problem posed to student in a calm and reasonable manner with thorough evaluations. Displays and understands integrity and proper ethics and morals.

FIGURE 5.3 Oral board interview grading dimensions.

Oral Board Interview Panel Rating Sheet

Candidate Name: _____   Date: _____

Panel Member: _____

Score:
1- Candidate clearly **lacks** the dimension at all levels, and shows **no** variables
2- Candidate has a **less than 'basic'** understanding of the dimension only hitting on **1-2 variables**
3- Candidate has a **'basic'** understanding of the dimension hitting on at least ½ **of the variables**
4- Candidate has a **moderate to high** understanding of the dimension with minor issues
5- Candidate has **mastered** the dimension

Dimension:	Variables/Examples:	Panel Member Notes for candidate:	Score: *(circle)*
Oral Communication	Speaks Cleary, logically, expresses thoughts clearly. Speaks correct volume, organizes thoughts well, has a start/middle/and conclusion to each question asked. Utilizes personal history to assist with understanding of the answer. *CLEAR-EASY TO UNDERSTAND* *No "ummms" or long silence*		1 LOWEST------5 HIGHEST 1 2 3 4 5
Interpersonal Skills	Displays empathy, sympathy, understands different values, beliefs and viewpoints and can interact w/differing viewpoints *Relates to board members and members of the public, shakes hands, remembers names of panel members, thanks panel members-GOOD EYE CONTACT WITH EVERY PANEL MEMBER*		1 LOWEST------5 HIGHEST 1 2 3 4 5
Attitude and Motivation	Positive and motivated through communication and actions. Understands the focus is to serve the public *Attitude is positive/upbeat and candidate is clearly motivated for the position through their words and actions*		1 LOWEST------5 HIGHEST 1 2 3 4 5
Understands the Position	Demonstration A STRONG KNOWLEDGE OF THE DEPARTMENT TESTING FOR AND of the familiarity, pros/cons of police work. Firm grasp of the duties/responsibilities and current issues dept. is facing. *Lists the duties/responsibilities and relates* *actual stories*		1 LOWEST------5 HIGHEST 1 2 3 4 5
Problem Solving Skills/Judgment	Ability to identify a problem and provide answers/solutions, which are logical, reasonable, and relevant. Exercises sound judgment consistent with police role *Can methodically solve problem posed to student in a calm and reasonable manner w/thorough explanations-Displays integrity & high ethics/morals*		1 LOWEST------5 HIGHEST 1 2 3 4 5

FIGURE 5.4 Oral board interview panel rating sheet.

then the candidate would need to get at least 18 points to pass ($18/25 \times 100 = 72\%$). If the candidate received 17 points, the candidate would fail ($17/25 \times 100 = 68\%$).

Could one hiring agency like the answers given by one candidate and another not? Yes. Every law enforcement agency across America is different and has different issues and needs depending on the community they serve, along with a variety of other factors. While most hiring agencies are looking for the same set of values, ethics, morals, and integrity in every candidate, these agencies could invariably be looking for a few different characteristics in their candidates. For instance, there are police departments that understand there will be candidates who want to be a police officer, no matter the agency, and therefore these candidates will be testing for any open police officer positions available. However, there are police departments that want the candidate to understand the differences between agencies in America, understand what their specific department is like, and want the candidate to *only* test for their department. It is a legal reason for a candidate to fail an interview; therefore, if a candidate tells an oral board panel that they are testing for all departments, that agency could, in turn, *fail the candidate on that one answer.* The only way to know this information is for the candidate to understand and research the department they are testing for thoroughly (for more information see the section on how to research the hiring agency in this chapter).

Panel members receive training and instruction on how to score the answers given by each candidate. However, candidates should remember that the panel members are human beings, and unlike the written test where there is a correct answer, oral board interviews are somewhat subjective. The panel members will be given examples or representative answers they should expect to see (e.g., see Figure 5.4). However, there will always be subjectivity in an interview process even though there are objective directions given to the panel members. During an interview, panel members may differ in their reactions to answers given by a candidate. Once the candidate is finished with the interview and leaves the room, it is normal for the panel members to discuss the candidate. This may not always occur, although it can happen. The discussion ensures the panel members do not miss important information about a particular candidate. The scores are then combined and averaged to give the candidate a final score.

Why Are Oral Board Interviews Intimidating?

The oral board interview is most likely going to be one of the most stressful parts of the hiring process. First, the candidate is placed on the spot, literally in the middle of the room, where all of the focus is on the candidate. Even for the most seasoned candidates, this is intimidating and stressful. Many hiring agencies record the oral board interview, so now the candidate has a red blinking light aimed right at them recording everything that is said. Now add in three–five uniformed officers, which can make any sane person terrified. Finally, the candidate has most likely been preparing for this process for months to years. Everything is on the line. What is said in that room will either end the process or send the candidate to the next step. Either way, a lot is riding on this one interview. How could the oral board interview not be intimidating? It is intimidating, and the best way to lower the stress of the candidate is through practice and preparation, and lots of it!

The panel members understand that this is a stressful process; however, they are also looking to see how the candidate overcomes their nerves and fears. The job of a law enforcement officer is inherently dangerous. Officers are often placed in uncomfortable and nerve-racking situations. Although the officers are trained how to handle various types of calls, it all starts with being able to control nerves and stress during a basic oral board interview where the questions are relatively easy so long as the candidate prepares.

How to Prepare for the Oral Board Interview?

Preparation is vital for success in an oral board interview. Oral board interviews are intimidating and hold a tremendous amount of weight by foretelling a number of crucial factors to the hiring agency about the candidate. However, the candidate can tackle and conquer the oral board interview. The following **eight steps to success** are the beginning keys to success on the oral board interview:

1. Understand the job duties, responsibilities, and qualities of a police officer
2. Research the hiring agency
3. Give detailed answers to oral board questions (nine actions for perfect answers)
4. Practice aloud
5. Dress to impress
6. Practice a mock practical oral board

7. Be professional
8. Have a study plan

Step 1: Why Understand the Job Duties, Responsibilities, and Qualities of a Police Officer?

Candidates must have an understanding of the job duties, responsibilities, and qualities of a police officer for the hiring agency. Once a candidate knows what is expected they can first identify if they have the skills and experience necessary to meet certain qualities on the list and second prepare for meeting as many of the other qualities as possible. The following list illustrates common job expectations, duties, responsibilities, and qualities for police officers. The list is not all inclusive, so the candidate must check the hiring agency to confirm the exact list. Candidates can then identify the items on the list they share and ensure they include those keywords in their different answers during the oral board interview. For instance, one of the keywords identified as a police officer job responsibility is *administrative procedures*. If a candidate works in any career field and conducts administrative procedures, the candidate could say "I have been refining my skills as a supervisor in my current position as a cashier manager. I have various procedures I am responsible for conducting when I open the store. I even created a checklist to ensure the administrative procedures for opening and closing the store are followed by all employees. Administrative procedures are also adhered to by police officers. By already engaging in these same types of processes, I am preparing for a future career as a police officer."

- Actively engage in community and problem-oriented policing
- Administrative procedures
- Arrests and processes criminals
- Comprehend and understand legal documents
- Conducts interviews
- Conducts preliminary and follow-up criminal and traffic investigations
- Courage
- Correctional facility duties and responsibilities as required
- Deals with uncertainty
- Decision-making skills
- Dependability
- Direct traffic and maintains safe traffic conditions
- Emotional control
- Follows policies and procedures
- Fulfills court orders
- Gather evidence to ensure successful prosecutions
- Judgment
- Handles pressure
- Humanity
- Identify, pursue, and arrest suspects
- Inform citizens of community services or recommend long-term resolution
- Integrity
- Issue citations

- Legal compliance
- Lifting
- Keep updated on legal decisions
- Maintains order
- Mediation
- Meet training requirements
- Objectivity
- Observe various situations and emergencies
- Operate law enforcement emergency vehicle
- Operates as a team with coworkers to accomplish needed results
- Patrol work
- Photograph crime scenes
- Physically fit
- Prepares written reports
- Proactive in preventing crime and enforcing applicable federal, state, and local laws and ordinances
- Promotes positive community relations
- Professionalism
- Protects life and property through enforcement of laws and regulations
- Record facts
- Rescue work; render aid
- Review facts of incidents to determine if criminal act has occurred
- Sound judgment
- Testify in court
- Training in applicable topics

Step 2: How to Research the Hiring Agency?

Research the hiring agency? What does that mean? It means that the candidate must do their due diligence in learning everything they can about the hiring agency they might, someday, have a 20–30-year (or longer) career with. An candidate's investigation is two-fold in that it will answer questions about the agency the candidate may not know and it will significantly assist the candidate during the oral interview process.

1. Review the agency's website and memorize the following:
   a. Vision, mission, and values
   b. Command staff (chief or sheriff, assistant chief/sheriff, deputy chief/sheriff, captains, and so on)
   c. Organizational chart (how the agency is organized)
   d. Department policies and procedures
   e. CALEA accreditation (Commission on Accreditation for Law Enforcement Agencies)
2. Go on a ride-along
   a. Ask questions of the police officers
      i. Why they wanted to be a police officer
      ii. Why they like working for their police department

      iii. What they recommend a candidate do and know about the hiring process

      iv. Current issues with the police department

      v. Community policing or problem-oriented policing procedures

3. Review the agency's social media

    a. Follow the hiring agency's social media

      i. Be familiar with the current status of the hiring agency

4. SARA

    a. Understand how to apply the SARA problem-solving model to the crimes occurring at the hiring agency:

      i. Scanning

      ii. Analysis

      iii. Response

      iv. Assessment

         1. Study how different crimes, such as theft or burglary, are solved. Know and understand these theories, and if the hiring agency is having a current crime issue of bicycle thefts, for example, the candidate can not only bring this fact up during one answer to a particular oral board interview question, but the candidate can show how to apply the SARA model to the crime.

Once the candidate completes the four steps in researching the hiring agency, the candidate should create a document that contains *key words*. These key words should be utilized during the creation of detailed answers to commonly asked oral board questions.

Step 3: How to Develop Detailed Answers to Oral Board Questions?

One of the biggest mistakes many candidates make in preparing for the oral board interview is in the preparation of answers. It is easy to locate possible questions that may be asked during any law enforcement oral board interview. The issues that begin to pop up are often found when the candidate prepares to answer questions asked. For instance, one common question that is asked on a law enforcement oral board interview is "What have you done to prepare for the position of police officer?"

Candidates see this question and automatically think, "I know the answer to this question! The answer is easy! I live my life, therefore; I know what I have done to prepare!" The candidate may even go the extra step (in their mind) of thinking of all they have done to prepare:

- I went on a ride-along with the hiring agency.
- I almost have my associate degree (or bachelor's degree), or I have taken several college classes.
- I have a family member or friend who is in law enforcement.
- I have watched a ton of television shows and movies about cops, so I know and understand what the job is all about.

Fast forward to the oral board interview where the candidate is placed in a single chair in the middle of a room, sitting across from a table where two uniformed police officers, one uniformed sergeant, and one civilian employee. The candidate read about this set-up; however, the candidate had not thought about the interview process thoroughly enough to consider how stressful and intimidating it would be. As one panel member prepares to ask the candidate the first question, the candidate's heart starts fluttering out of control, hands begin shaking, lips quiver, and as soon as the candidate begins to speak, their voice cracks and most of the words that were only a thought of an answer are now lost. The candidate had gone on several police ride-alongs and was almost finished with a college degree, all in an attempt to become a police officer; however, in the midst of the chaotic moment of the actual interview, the words would not make a coherent sentence. So instead of the celebrated memoir the candidate had planned on explaining, the candidate bombed and only said "I went on a ride-along, and the officer did a lot because it was busy that night. I will graduate with my college degree in June and my uncle, who is a cop too, told me I would be good at this job."

This answer is all too familiar. More often than not, candidates fall prey to lack of preparation, and at the moment, fear consumes all. The panel members are excited during each new interview because it is a chance to meet someone new and learn many exciting things about that person and how they will make the hiring agency a better place. *However, the only way the panel can learn these things is if the candidate thoroughly explains and paints a vivid picture.* In this example, the candidate was not prepared, which resulted in a choppy, short, lackluster answer that provided no new information on the candidate. Panel members expect candidates to be nervous; but, the nerves should begin to wane if the candidate is prepared and continues to describe their detailed answer, bringing to life all the uniqueness the candidate has to offer the agency. The goal of an oral board interview is to find candidates who fit the position; the goal is not to fail all the candidates. The interview process takes a ton of coordination and costs the hiring agency thousands of dollars. The more qualified candidates found, the better the agency becomes. If an oral board interview process only produces failed candidates, everyone loses.

The following nine actions are winning solutions on how a candidate prepares answers for the oral board interview questions. The actions are tried and true and work!

- Action 1: Research and find 20–30 questions commonly asked on law enforcement oral board interviews.
- Action 2: Write one question on top of one piece of paper. Do this for 20–30 questions (the candidate will have 20–30 sheets of paper, each with one oral board interview question on the top of each piece of paper).
- Action 3: Take the first piece of paper, containing one oral board interview question on the top of the paper, and come up with 10–20 minimum answer bullet points for each question (do this for the 20–30 oral board interview questions, creating answer bullet points for each question on each sheet of paper).
  - Try to include key words from the research conducted on the hiring agency.
  - Try to include key words from the job duties, responsibilities, and qualities of a police officer.
  - Review Chapter 2, Figure 2.19, which details characteristics police officers commonly show. These characteristics could be used as key words to describe a candidate's personality.
  - Take Self-Assessment 2.1 in Chapter 2 to will assist the candidate in understanding their strengths and weaknesses and in creating key words for answers to interview questions.
- Action 4: Take the first piece of paper containing one oral board interview question on the top, with 10–20 answer bullet points below the question, and write out the answer to the question (utilizing the answer bullet points) in essay form. This essay will now morph into the answer the candidate will give when asked this question during an oral board interview.

- Action 5: Complete Action 4 for all 20–30 oral board interview questions and answers.
- Action 6: Take the handwritten answers from Actions 5 and 6 and on a computer type out the full essay answers. Do this for all 20–30 oral board interview questions and answers.
- Action 7: Take the sheet of paper created in Action 4 with the oral board question and answer bullet points and create an acronym of the answer. Repeat this for all 20–30 questions and answer bullet points.
- Action 8: Memorize the acronyms (and what each letter stands for) for all 20–30 questions.
- Action 9: Read aloud the typed-out answers for all 20–30 questions. Repeat, repeat, and repeat.

The nine actions for developing detailed answers to oral board questions look a lot different than the first example given in this section where the candidate briefly *thought* about the answer to a particular interview question instead of adequately preparing. Preparation is the key. If the candidate prepares properly and studies as detailed in this chapter, when stress and nerves take over (during the interview), the candidate will remember their training and preparation. Training is critical and law enforcement officers do it daily. Therefore, by properly preparing for the oral board interview, the candidate is practicing for having a career as a police officer. For instance, a police officer must qualify with their duty handgun. If the police officer only *thought* about shooting their handgun, they probably would not do well during qualification time. Yet, if the police officer studies, prepares, and constantly trains with their handgun, the result will be a masterful qualification. Then, if the police officer ever had to utilize deadly force with their handgun, the outcome could save their life or the life of their partner or innocent citizen. The hiring process for law enforcement officers is not unlike the job of an officer. The similarities are not by chance; they are meant to not only see how the candidate does during each test but to predict how the candidate will do in the job as well.

Step 4: Practice Aloud

Candidates must prepare for the oral board interview by practicing the answers aloud. Once the candidate follows the nine actions for creating detailed answers for the most common oral board interview questions, they must focus on preparation. Since an oral board interview requires the candidate to answer questions aloud, it is essential they prepare by reading the prepared answers to each question aloud. When a person is nervous or experiences stress the behaviors displays vary; however, some commonalities do exist. One typical response is for the candidate to become tongue-tied and forgetful. An oral board interview places the candidate in an uncomfortable and intimidating situation with a lot on the line. A candidate who is placed in such a situation almost immediately begins to exhibit these key characteristics. Through practice and memorization, a candidate can learn predetermined answers to common questions prior to the interview. Moreover, a candidate can ensure success by practicing the answers to the questions aloud. Since the interview will require the candidate to speak the answers aloud, it stands to reason that the more the candidate speaks the answers aloud the better prepared the candidate will be.

Candidates can also easily practice answering questions aloud in front of a mirror. While practicing in front of a mirror, the candidate should look for issues (such as found in the section on what *not* to do in an interview in this chapter) and practice correcting the issues identified.

One last area the candidate should focus on while practicing aloud is timing. Oral board interviews are timed. A useful guide is for the candidate to allow 1–3 minutes for each answer. If the candidate is answering a question in under 30 seconds or takes over 3 minutes, the candidate will need to work on either slowing down and adding information to the answer or visa-versa. Candidates could also practice raising their heartbeat prior to practicing answering a question aloud. This will allow the candidate to simulate stress while answering a question. A candidate can raise their heartbeat by doing jumping jacks or other vigorous activity such as push-ups, sit-ups, or running and then after the heart is pumping, the candidate should begin speaking aloud their answer to an oral board question. During this time, the candidate should practice remembering everything that needs to be said, try to relax, and breathe.

Step 5: Dress to Impress

The job of a law enforcement officer is professional and service oriented. Candidates should understand this by dressing to impress; this means dressing as a professional in an ironed (no wrinkles) business suit.

Male candidates:

A dark-colored business suit is recommended and should include a pair of slacks (pants), a jacket, and white (or other solid color, no bright colors) collared shirt and solid color tie. The solid-colored shirt can be short- or long-sleeved and should be tucked in. Dress shoes and a dress belt that match and are a solid color (black or brown recommended) should be worn.

Female candidates:

A dark-colored business suit is recommended and should include a pair of slacks (pants) and a solid-colored collared shirt (no bright colors). A jacket is optional, but if worn, the solid-colored shirt does not need to be collared. Dress shoes and a dress belt that match and are a solid color (black or brown recommended) should be worn.

Candidates should ensure that all pet hair or other fabric strings and debris are removed from their clothing/business suit prior to entering the interview location. A lint brush, roller, or even rolled-up tape can be utilized prior to entering the interview location and left in a vehicle or other safe location during the interview.

Candidates should also pay attention to the following (guidelines only):

1. Hair properly groomed
   a. Males: Be consistent with the hiring agency policy for male officers, generally off the collar (of a dress shirt) and out of the face, no facial hair other than a groomed mustache, and conservative in appearance.
   b. Females: Be consistent with the hiring agency policy for female officers; hair cannot extend past the eyebrows or ears or must be worn up and out of the face. Popular female officer long hairstyles include wearing hair in a bun or a type of French braid with the ends tucked up. Female candidates should remember officer safety is a key concern; therefore, ponytails (not worn in a bun) would not be recommended since

a suspect could easily grab the hair in a ponytail. Hairstyles must be balanced and conservative in appearance.

2. Make-up
   a. Conservative in nature and no bright colors, fake eyelashes, and heavy liners.
3. Facial hair
   a. Mustaches for male candidates are accepted; however, no rolled, twisted, or curled ends and no goatees or beards. Most hiring agencies follow these guidelines and may grant an exception to this policy if their officer is unable to shave due to pseudo folliculitis barbae (medical condition). It is recommended that candidates shave prior to the interview.
4. Fingernails
   a. Recommended no longer than 6 mm or one-fourth inch from tip of finger and only clear nail polish.
   b. Be trimmed and cleaned and neatly groomed.
5. Jewelry
   a. Male candidates should not wear earrings. Female candidates could wear one pair of earrings. The earrings must be conservative and must be no larger than 6 mm or one-fourth inch from the lobe of the ear. Necklaces and bracelets should be covered (or not worn). Only one ring per hand should be worn and must be either a wedding ring, law enforcement ring, or school or professional organization ring.
6. Clean and showered
   a. Candidates should be freshly cleaned and showered. Perfume or cologne can be worn; however, ensure that it is not too overpowering. A candidate can ask a family member or friend for advice if not sure.
7. Teeth
   a. Be sure to brush and floss teeth prior to the interview. Do *not* chew gum during the interview.
8. Tattoos
   a. Every hiring agency is different, and many agencies are updating their tattoo policies; therefore, the candidate should check the tattoo policy of the hiring agency. For instance, if the hiring agency tattoo policy states that any tattoos on the arms of police officers must be covered while on duty, the candidate should wear a long sleeve shirt that covers any arm tattoos.

It is recommended that items such as cellular telephones, wallets, and purses be left somewhere safe and not brought into the interview room.

FACT BOX 5.1: POLICE OFFICER PROFESSIONAL APPEARANCE STANDARDS

Law enforcement officers are bound by their department policies on their professional appearance while on duty. While every law enforcement agency is different and has its policy for professional appearance standards, there are consistent standards. For instance, the following standards are from the Baltimore Police Department (2017):

Hair: Must be neatly groomed and conform to the shape of the head. Only natural hair colors are permitted. Hair colors that are considered extreme, faddish, or artificial, such as purple, pink, or green, are prohibited. The bulk of the hair will not be excessive or present a ragged or unkempt appearance. A wig, track, or hairpiece shall present a natural appearance and conform to the same standards as natural hair. Extreme or fad hairstyles are prohibited, including, but not limited to, those that incorporate designs or sculptures using the hair and/or cut into the hair, and any style that presents an unprofessional or disheveled appearance.

Male members: Hair must be tapered in a conservative and professional manner. The length shall not extend beyond the top of the eyebrows or ears and the top of the uniform shirt collar. Sideburns shall be neatly trimmed. The mustache may be worn, but shall not be rolled, curled or excessively thick. Goatees, beards, and other styles of facial hair are prohibited. Makeup on male members is prohibited.

Female members: Hair will be styled such that the length does not extend beyond the top of the eyebrows or ears, below the lower edge of the uniform shirt collar. Braiding, twisting, and locking styles are permitted, provided they are conservative and professional in appearance. Hairstyles that are lopsided or distinctly unbalanced are prohibited. Female members may wear makeup that is subtle and professional in appearance. False eyelashes, heavy eyeliner, and bright colors are prohibited.

Fingernails: On all members shall not extend more than one-fourth inch from the tip of the finger nor interfere in any way in the performance of primary police tasks or with the safe drawing and firing of the service weapon. Fingernail polish shall be clear polish only.

Jewelry: Female members may only wear one earring per ear lobe, and earrings will not exceed 6 mm or one-fourth inch in diameter. Necklaces shall not be visible, and bracelets are prohibited. Exception: A medic alert tag on the wrist or around the neck is permitted. Rings may be worn but are limited to one ring per hand with none on the thumbs and are limited to wedding rings, law enforcement association rings, professional organization rings, or school rings.

Body art: Body mutilations and/or other body adornments shall not be visible. Tattoos shall not be offensive, obscene, or otherwise inappropriate. If the tattoo is deemed offensive, obscene, or otherwise inappropriate it shall be removed or concealed per department policy.

POLICE STORY 5.1 Recommendations for Women Candidates and Dressing to Impress

by Retired Lieutenant Tiffany L. Morey, NLVPD

As a retired female law enforcement officer, I often am asked by female candidates how to dress for the oral board interview. My recommendation has always been first to know and understand the uniform of the position applied for. Generally, a police officer, no matter the sex of the officer, is required to wear uniform pants, a uniform collared shirt (short- or long-sleeved), and a bulletproof vest (either worn under the uniform shirt or as the uniform shirt). There is, of course, additional equipment worn such as a duty belt (with various equipment) and uniform footwear (shoe or boot), and so on. However, the most crucial uniform element to understand is that the uniform is professional and unwrinkled. Therefore, my recommendation is that female candidates wear a business suit, to include either a collared shirt or a collared jacket and business *pants*. I do not recommend wearing a skirt. My reasoning has nothing to do with not trying to fit into the previous matronly duties of a female police officer, where female officers were required to wear skirts. However, my reasoning is more of comfort. The elusive movie *Basic Instinct*, where actress Sharon Stone, who is wearing a short skirt, is being interviewed by detectives, comes immediately to mind. Not that I am insinuating that a female candidate would wear a skirt that is too short and nothing else; however, why wear a skirt and then have to worry with all the issues that come with a skirt? Is it too short? Can I cross (or uncross) my legs during the interview? What can the panel members see? The oral board interview is nerve-racking enough; the last thing a female candidate should have to worry about is possible issues with the skirt worn. Pants ensure that the candidate is comfortable and is not showing something that should not be seen.

The next question is that what type of top should be worn. My recommendation is that the female candidate wears a button-up, collared top and to ensure the buttons are buttoned all the way up. The very top button does not have to be secured (the button under where a tie is worn); however, female candidates should be aware of not leaving several top buttons undone. A female candidate's cleavage should not be seen, and shirts should not be see-through. A female candidate could also wear a regular non-buttoned top (not too low cut) and wear a collared business suit jacket over the shirt top.

Should the candidate wear heels? My recommendation is no. A female candidate will not wear heels as a regular part of the police officer uniform; therefore, why wear them in an interview? Generally, flats (flat shoes with no heel) are more comfortable than a heeled shoe. Again, the answer falls in the realm of what is comfortable and professional (if the candidate feels most comfortable in heels, then wear heels). My recommendation is for the female candidate to wear a professional, comfortable, non-heeled-type shoe.

Finally, what color should the professional attire be? Again, I recommend being professional. The candidate wants to be remembered for the fantastic interview, not the bright orange suit worn. Therefore, I recommend wearing a black, dark or navy blue, dark gray, or dark tan solid-colored suit.

I have been a panel member on over 100 oral board interviews. These recommendations are just that, my recommendations. The female candidate is free to do whatever they please; however, I have found that the more comfortable candidates do better on their interviews.

Step 6: Mock Practical Oral Board Interview

After the candidate prepares the answers to 20–30 oral board interview questions by completing the nine actions for success process outlined in this chapter, the candidate should next participate in a mock practical oral board interview. The class that is offered in tandem with this textbook will culminate with a mock practical oral board interview. During this mock test, the student will be given a date, time, and location to respond to their interview. The instructor will utilize police officers from area police departments to be panel members. These panel members will be trained in the evaluation process and how to score each student. On the day of the interview the student will be called into the interview room, and each panel member will ask a different question, which the student will answer and be evaluated on.

The instructor will compile the scores and notes made by the panel members and provide this information to the student and future law enforcement officer candidate. The student can utilize this feedback to improve and continue to study.

If the candidate cannot attend a test preparation class, the candidate can conduct their own mock oral board interview. It is even suggested that students in the preparation class prepare for the classroom mock oral board interview in the same manner. The candidate or student should find one to four family members, friends, or fellow candidates/students to play the role of panel members. The oral board panel rating sheet in Figure 5.4 can be given to the role player panel member as a guide for what to look for and to make notations. Either way, any mock oral board interview where the candidate can practice aloud will allow the candidate to gain valuable skills.

Video Record

One of the best ways to prepare for a mock oral board interview is for the candidate to write out interview questions on a piece of paper, place a chair in the middle of any room, use a smartphone, tablet, or computer to video record answering the questions aloud. After answering five–ten questions aloud, the candidate can review the video recording. Although this process may seem silly, it is the exact opposite! First, it gives the candidate another opportunity to answer *aloud* one question at a time, remembering what to say and in what order. Second, it provides the candidate with a chance to review the recording and understand how the answers sound aloud. The candidate should look for the following:

- Were the answers thorough?
- Were the answers complete?
- Was anything forgotten?
- Were there nervous tendencies such as tapping a foot, or hand gestures that are too big?
- How long were the answers? A detailed answer should be between 1–3 minutes in length.

The more the candidate can practice by recording the answers spoken aloud, the better prepared the candidate will be for the actual oral board interview with the hiring agency.

Step 7: Professionalism

The candidate can do a variety of small things that speak loudly to the panel members. These items fall under the category of professionalism and cannot be overlooked. Candidates should do the following:

1. Shake the hands of each panel member when entering *and* exiting the room
   a. Handshakes should be firm (not a dead fish hand!).
2. Know the rank and last name of each panel member
   a. When shaking hands (at the entry and exit of the interview) with each panel member, ask for their last name. Example: "Hello, my name is Tiffany Morey. What is your last name? It is very nice to meet you, Officer Jones."
   b. At the end of the interview, shake each panel member's hand and thank the member for their time. Example: "Thank you Sergeant Smith for your time."
      i. Understand how to tell if a panel member is a police officer, sergeant, lieutenant, and so on (see Figures 5.5 and 5.6).

FIGURE 5.5 Tip 1: How to tell the rank of an officer.

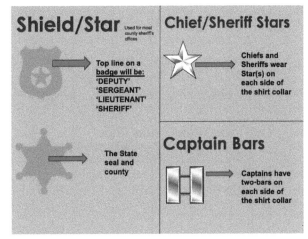

FIGURE 5.6 Tip 2: How to tell the rank of an officer.

1. If the candidate does not know the rank of the panel member, the candidate can either ask the panel member their rank or refer to the panel member by sir or ma'am.

See Video 5.1, which illustrates the proper way to enter an oral board interview room and make introductions professionally.

Active Learning Video 5.1. How to properly enter and make introductions for an oral board interview.

3. Eye-contact
   a. During the oral board, interview candidates should make eye contact with every panel member. It is not good for the candidate to look down all the time or look at a clock or the wall behind the panel members. Instead, the candidate should rotate eye contact with all panel members. Eye contact with the panel members should be made at random, not left to right and back again and again (in a circular motion); this would look strange. Video 5.2 illustrates the incorrect way to enter the oral board interview room without making eye contact (or without making introductions).

Active Learning Video 5.2. Incorrect way to enter an oral board interview without making eye contact.

Step 8: Study Plan

As with the written exam, the oral board interview answers must be prepared for and studied. The best way to prepare is through a scheduled study plan. The following study plans are examples that can be applied and changed depending on the candidate, the length of time a candidate has to prepare for the interview, and the specific requirements of the hiring agency.

Three-Month Study Plan

Length of Time	Amount of Time	Action
1 week (Week 1/12)	1 hour, 3 nights a week	Action 1: Research and find 20–30 questions commonly asked on law enforcement oral board interviews (see "Example Questions and Answers" section in this chapter). Action 2: Write one question on the top of one piece of paper. Do this for 20–30 questions (the candidate will have 20–30 sheets of paper, each with one oral board interview question on the top of each piece of paper).
Remember to		Eat healthy and exercise
1 week (Week 2/12)	1 hour, 3 nights a week	Action 3: Take the first piece of paper containing one oral board interview question on the top of the paper and come up with 10–20 minimum answer bullet points for each question (do this for the 20–30 oral board interview questions, creating answer bullet points for each question on each sheet of paper).
1 week (Week 3/12)	1 hour, 3 nights a week	Action 4: Take the first piece of paper containing one oral board interview question on the top, with 10–20 answer bullet points below the question, and write out the answer to the question (utilizing the answer bullet points) in essay form. This will turn into the essay answer the candidate will give when asked this question during an oral board interview. Action 5: Complete Action 4 for all 20–30 oral board interview questions and answers.
1 week (Week 4/12)	1 hour, 3 nights a week	Action 6: Type out the hand-written essay answer completed in Action 4 and 5 and print out the answer. Do this for all 20–30 oral board interview questions and answers.
1 week (Week 5/12)	1 hour, 3 nights a week	Action 7: Take the sheet of paper created in Action 4 with the oral board question, answer bullet points, and create an acronym of the answer to the question. Repeat this for all 20–30 questions and answer bullet points.
1 week (Week 6/12)	1 hour, 3 nights a week	Action 8: Memorize the acronyms (and what each letter stands for) for all 20–30 questions.
1 week (Week 7/12)	1 hour, 3 nights a week	Action 9: Read aloud the typed-out answers for all 20–30 questions. Repeat for 3 hours.
Remember to		Eat healthy and exercise

Length of Time	Amount of Time	Action
1 week (Week 8/12)	3 hours anytime during the week	Write out interview questions on a piece of paper; place a chair in the middle of any room; and use a smart-phone, tablet, or computer to video record the candidate as they ask a question and answer the question aloud. After answering five–ten questions aloud, the candidate can then review the video recording, noting any issues to correct. Ask and answer as many of the 20–30 questions as able in 3 hours.
1 week (Week 9/12)	5 hours anytime during the week	Write out interview questions on a piece of paper; place a chair in the middle of any room; and use a smart-phone, tablet, or computer to video record the candidate as they ask a question and answer the question aloud. After answering five–ten questions aloud, the candidate can then review the video recording, noting any issues to correct. Ask and answer the 20–30 questions the candidate did not ask/answer last week. If the candidate asked/answered all 20–30 questions last week, practice the questions/answers the candidate had issues with last week.
Remember to		Eat healthy and exercise
1 week (Week 10/12)	5 hours anytime during the week	Conduct your own mock practical oral board interview. Utilize family members or friends (one to four panel members), record your answers on video, and watch and note any issues.
Remember to		Eat healthy, exercise, and get a good night's sleep
1 week (Week 11/12)	5 hours anytime during the week	Conduct your own mock practical oral board interview. Utilize family members or friends (one to four panel members), record your answers on video, and watch and note any issues.
Remember to		Eat healthy, exercise, and get a good night's sleep
Week before the written test	1 hour, 4 nights a week	Action 8: Memorize the acronyms (and what each letter stands for) for all 20–30 questions. Action 9: Read aloud the typed-out answers for all 20–30 questions. Repeat for 4 hours.
Night before the written test		Get at least 7–8 hours of good sleep and eat healthy.

In order to ensure success, here are some tips to remember:

- Schedule dates and times to study. If you miss a study day, do not forget to schedule a make-up day.
- Do not stress yourself out; know yourself and when you need a day off.
- Be positive; think positive.
- Practice, practice, practice *aloud*, wherever you go, in a car, in a train or bus. Practice the acronyms aloud and practice your complete answers aloud; this is very important.
- Make sure to eat well, get exercise, and get enough rest.

6-Week CRAM Study Plan

Length of Time	Amount of Time	Action
1 week (Week 1/6)	3 hours each night, 3 nights a week	Action 1: Research and find 20–30 questions commonly asked on law enforcement oral board interviews (see "Example Questions and Answers" section in this chapter). Action 2: Write one question on the top of one piece of paper. Do this for 20–30 questions (the candidate will have 20–30 sheets of paper, each with one oral board interview question on the top of each piece of paper). Action 3: Take the first piece of paper containing one oral board interview question on the top of the paper and come up with 10–20 minimum answer bullet points for each question (do this for the 20–30 oral board interview questions, creating answer bullet points for each questions on each sheet of paper).
Remember to		Eat healthy and exercise
1 week (Week 2/6)	3 hours each night, 3 nights a week	Action 4: Take the first piece of paper containing one oral board interview question on the top, with 10–20 answer bullet points below the question, and write out the answer to the question (utilizing the answer bullet points) in essay form. This will turn into the answer the candidate will give when asked this question during an oral board interview. Action 5: Complete Action 4 for all 20–30 oral board interview questions and answers. Action 6: Type out the essay answer completed in Action 4 and 5 and print out the answer. Do this for all 20–30 oral board interview questions and answers.
Remember to		Eat healthy and exercise
1 week (Week 3/6)	9 hours anytime during the week	Action 7: Take the sheet of paper created in Action 4 with the oral board question, answer bullet points, and create an acronym of the answer to the question. Repeat this for all 20–30 questions and answer bullet points. Action 8: Memorize the acronyms (and what each letter stands for) for all 20–30 questions. Action 9: Read aloud the typed-out answers for all 20–30 questions. Repeat for 9 hours.
Remember to		Eat healthy and exercise
1 week (Week 4/6)	9 hours anytime during the week	Write out interview questions on a piece of paper; place a chair in the middle of any room; and use a smartphone, tablet, or computer to video record the candidate as they ask a question and answer the question aloud. After answering five–ten questions aloud, the candidate can then review the video recording, noting any issues to correct. Ask and answer as many of the 20–30 questions as the candidate can in 9 hours and/or repeat.
Remember to		Eat healthy, exercise, and get a good night's sleep
1 week (Week 5/6)	9 hours anytime during the week	Conduct your own mock practical oral board interview. Utilize family members or friends (one to four panel members), record your answers on video, and watch and note any issues.
Remember to		Eat healthy, exercise, and get a good night's sleep

Length of Time	Amount of Time	Action
Week before the written test	1 hour, 4 nights a week	Action 8: Memorize the acronyms (and what each letter stands for) for all 20–30 questions. Action 9: Read aloud the typed-out answers for all 20–30 questions. Repeat for 4 hours.
Night before the written test		Get at least 7–8 hours of good sleep and eat healthy. Review the important things to remember for the seven categories.

In order to ensure success, here are some tips to remember:

- Schedule dates and times to study. If you miss a study day, do not forget to schedule a make-up day.
- Do not stress yourself out; know yourself and when you need a day off.
- Be positive; think positive.
- Practice, practice, practice *aloud*, wherever you go, in a car, in a train or bus. Practice the acronyms aloud and practice your complete answers aloud; this is very important.
- Make sure to eat well, get exercise, and get enough rest.

The Superhero Mind-Set Provides a Winning Solution for the Oral Board Interview

Just like with the written exam, candidates must think like a superhero. Superhero? Should the candidate look to the skies for their nearest superhero to fly in and take the oral board interview for them? Alternatively, will the superhero be invisible and help the candidate during the interview to say just the perfect thing? Does the superhero laser the correct thing to say to the candidate's mind? How does a superhero prepare a candidate for the interview? Great questions! It is not a superhero but a **superhero state of mind** that the candidate needs to channel in order to succeed. Before entering the oral board interview location the candidate should follow the superhero state of mind instructions.

1. Stand up.
2. Place both hands on your hips.
3. Look up into the sky (causing your chin to be raised).
4. See yourself passing the oral board interview, flying through it with ease.

This is not a joke; it does work. The superhero state of mind does not guarantee success. No magic pill or mind-set can do that; however, a positive and practiced mind-set can change the way a candidate hears each question and answers it, saying just the right thing.

What Questions Are Asked?

Hiring agencies must ensure the questions on the oral board interview are written through consultation with a subject matter expert, or person who has knowledge of the position tested, to ensure the questions are applicable to the job applied for. If the position is for a police officer, then police officers are the subject matter experts and should be consulted for each question as to the appropriateness and possible correct answers.

Another essential component is to ensure that every question asked is the same for every candidate. To keep the oral board interview standardized, every candidate must be given the same chance to pass or fail. If during one interview the panel members were to ask follow-up questions to the first candidate that they did not ask of a second (or third and so on) candidate, the second candidate could have a legitimate concern, which could lead to litigation and the possibility of a second chance or even a monetary award. However, the initial oral board interview is not the same as the final chief/sheriff/command staff interview. During this final interview, a post-conditional job offer has been made, and the top command staff (chief, sheriff, assistant chief, assistant sheriff, majors, or captains) are conducting a final interview to get to know the candidate better.

If a candidate does not hear or understand a particular question, can the panel members repeat the question? Yes. The candidate can ask and should ask the panel members to repeat a question if the candidate did not hear it. However, the panel members cannot give further explanation or clarification of a particular question. Remember, every candidate must be treated fairly and the same. If the panel members were to clarify a particular question for one candidate further, then the panel members must do the same for every candidate after.

Are there specific questions that the panel members cannot ask a candidate? Yes. The hiring agency cannot ask candidates any questions regarding marital status, political beliefs, or religious affiliation.

For a more detailed list of the most commonly asked questions and suggested answers on a law enforcement oral board interview, see the section in this chapter on example questions and answers.

What to Expect the Day of the Interview?

The oral board interview generally occurs after the written test and physical agility or physical fitness test; however, every hiring agency is different, so the candidate should check with the hiring agency to understand the order of tests. The candidate will be notified of the date, time, and location of the interview.

Location

Know where the interview is located. Go to the location prior to the interview and understand where to park and how long it will take to drive, park, and walk. Candidates should not start the oral board interview off negatively by either arriving late or not arriving at all. Proper planning can ensure this does not occur.

Candidates should plan to arrive a minimum of 15–30 minutes early. Interviews can run on time or behind; one never knows. Therefore, the candidate must always arrive early to make a good impression. Once at the interview location, the candidate will need to check in and let someone know of their arrival.

Portfolio

Should candidates bring a portfolio to an oral board interview? The answer is yes. While most hiring agencies do not allow candidates to bring portfolios, every agency is different. Therefore, the candidate must always be prepared.

What goes into a portfolio? A portfolio should contain the candidate's detailed resume, letters of recommendation, plus a variety of other items. Candidates should remember to include pertinent information in their resume that shows how they have prepared for the position of a law enforcement officer. Candidates should maintain a **running resume,** which is a resume that the candidate always adds information to whenever something is accomplished. By keeping a running resume, the candidate ensures the most current information is included on the resume and nothing is forgotten. A candidate never knows when a current resume is needed; therefore, by keeping a running resume, the candidate always has a current resume ready to go. See the Internet Exercise at the end of this chapter to learn how to create a resume and portfolio.

While most hiring agencies do not allow candidates to leave portfolios during an oral board interview due to ensuring the process is equally fair for all candidates, there may be a time during the hiring process where agencies allow portfolios. For instance, the final interview may be the perfect time for a candidate to turn in a portfolio. For more information see the chapter in this textbook on the final interview.

Cover Letter

Every resume needs a cover letter. The cover letter represents a candidate's marketability by answering the all-important question of "Why should we hire you?" It is an opportunity for the candidate to market and sell themselves to the hiring agency. The candidate should detail what specific positive traits they bring to the table. First, review the resume to highlight the most interesting and marketable experience or qualifications listed. The candidate should then review the "Why Understand the Job Duties, Responsibilities, and Qualities of a Police Officer" section in this chapter for marketable key words. Finally, the candidate should take the self-assessments in Chapter 2 of this textbook. After learning the key attributes of oneself (through the self-assessments), the candidate can compare which are the same as those of a police officer and utilize the candidate's highlighted experience and qualifications and focus on all of those attributes in the cover letter.

The typical cover letter is two to three paragraphs in length and should focus on the candidate's most recent experience and qualifications. The candidate should focus on explaining why they are the best candidate for the position. After a rough draft is written, the candidate should read aloud their cover letter. It should take no longer than 60 seconds to read and should quickly and effortlessly paint a picture as to why the candidate is the best thing since sliced bread. The cover letter is an opening to begin a more in-depth conversation. Be careful not to make it too long and overly wordy. The candidate wants to set the stage but not complete an entire act. Instead, the candidate's cover letter should be the ice breaker that leaves the hiring agency wanting to learn more.

The cover letter also demonstrates the candidate's writing ability; therefore, the candidate must ensure the cover letter has an introduction, body, and conclusion and has no grammar, punctuation, or spelling errors. See Figure 5.7, which illustrates a sample cover letter.

Negative Panel Members

Be prepared for all different types of panel members who will sit and evaluate an oral board interview. Some panel members will make excellent eye contact, will nod their heads positively, and will even smile at the candidates. However, there are panel members who will do the exact opposite. Some will never smile or make eye contact since they are looking down at their evaluation sheets making notes. Candidates should not be discouraged by this type of negative behavior. In fact, candidates should be prepared for this type of displayed negative behavior. When candidates practice through the mock practical oral board interview, candidates can instruct a mock panel member to be negative through these types of behaviors. By not smiling, never making eye contact, and continually writing

Tiffany Smith
148 Highway 677
Ashlake, OR 97521
222-11-3455
TiffanySmith@gmail.com (**only include professional emails**)

January 01, 2020

Ashlake Police Department
111 Highway 678
Ashlake, OR 97521 (**Hiring agency contact information-the more detailed the better if you know who will be conducting your interview you can include their name below this contact information; however, it is alright to just document the hiring agency**)

To Whom it May Concern: (**if you know who will be overseeing your interview you can write their title or Rank and name here**)

I am interested in applying for the position of police officer with Ashlake Police Department. I recently volunteered for one-year at the Land Police Department in the victim's advocate office. During this time, I had numerous contacts with the Ashlake Police Department, and I was constantly amazed at their professionalism. I was then involved with the bike theft detail which Ashlake Police Department and Land Police Department worked on together. Through that detail I learned about community and problem-oriented policing. Each day as I learned more and more about the multi-faceted work of policing, I saw myself becoming interested in being a police officer one day too.
(**The first paragraph is an introductory paragraph where you introduce yourself and talk a little about the position you are applying for**)

I am qualified for the position of a police officer because I have excellent decision-making skills, I am dependable, and I have good judgement and common sense. Over the summer I worked at the County Transition Center. I began working at the Center as a part of my internship class at State Oregon University. I had only one quarter left until I graduated with my Bachelor's of Science Degree in Criminology and Criminal Justice and I was excited at the prospects of putting my education, experience, and training from many of my classes to work. I worked with parolees who were on parole and doing various work-related programs. One day while I was working the front desk, a parolee entered the building to sign-in for his daily program. It was apparent he was under the influence of something and his behavior was erratic. I immediately remember my training and the policy and procedure for dealing with parolees under the influence and I went to action. The parolee was taken into custody without incident and I was given the Employee of the Month award for my brave actions. I also did several guest presentations in the Introduction to Law Enforcement, and Introduction to the American Criminal Justice classes at our college about the incident.
(**The second paragraph is the body of the letter and provides the detailed information as to why you have the experience and qualifications for the position. Do not forget to include the key words identified**)

I want to thank you for taking the time to review my application and portfolio. I look forward to speaking with you further about the position of a police officer at the Ashlake Police Department.
(**The last paragraph is the conclusion of the letter where you thank the hiring agency and ask them to review your resume**)

Sincerely,
Tiffany Smith

FIGURE 5.7 Sample cover letter.

on the evaluation sheet in front of them, these mock panel members can prepare the candidate for what could occur during their actual interview. While it may never happen, the candidate must be prepared for the time it does happen. The candidate can overcome this panel member by continuing to make eye contact (just in case the panel member does look up once or twice) and not treating that panel member any different than the positive panel members who are not displaying such behaviors. Not all panel members are comfortable in an oral board interview situation and may overcompensate by doing these negative mannerisms. The behavior does not necessarily mean anything negative, and the candidate must overcome this type of panel member by moving on and not letting it affect them.

After the Interview
After the candidate completes the oral board interview, the candidate will leave the location. The candidate will be notified if they have passed and of the next step in the hiring process. If the candidate failed, this would end the testing process.

What NOT to do During the Interview?

Candidates must be familiar will negative mannerisms. One of the best ways to identify such key issues that could be detrimental to an oral board interview is to video record oneself while going through a mock practical oral board interview. Anytime a candidate is required to speak aloud answers in front of peers, stress and nerves can take over and negative mannerisms can begin to appear. The following list illustrates some of the mannerisms that candidates should be aware of and try to mitigate:

There are videos available where noted.

1. Negative body language
   a. Do not cross/fold your arms in front of your body; this is a negative sign that puts up a wall or barrier. Figure 5.8 illustrates how a candidate crossing their arms can appear negative to the panel members.

2. Improper volume of speech
   a. Either too low or too loud.

Active Learning Video 5.3. Improper volume of speech too high.

Active Learning Video 5.4. Improper volume of speech too low.

FIGURE 5.8 Do not cross arms.

3. Hand gestures
   a. Be careful they are not too big.

Active Learning Video 5.5. Improper hand gestures.

4. Inflect voice when appropriate
   a. Be careful not to inflect voice in the wrong place.

Active Learning Video 5.6. Candidate inflects voice improperly.

5. Lack of confidence
   a. Always looking at hands or always looking down (not making eye contact with panel members). Video 5.7 shows how a candidate can appear to lack confidence through not utilizing a firm handshake, not shaking the hand of every panel member, not making eye contact with panel members, and not engaging in proper introductions. See Video 5.1 for how to properly enter the oral board interview room with confidence and how to properly show professionalism by properly shaking the hands of all panel members, making proper eye contact, and utilizing the ranks and last names of the panel members in an introduction.

Active Learning Video 5.7. Candidate who lacks confidence.

6. Negative mannerisms
   a. Tapping foot

Active Learning Video 5.8. Candidate taps foot.

   b. Jostling keys, coins, or other material in pants pockets (do not place your hands in your pockets and make sure pockets are empty).

7. Do not ramble
   a. Be careful not to go off topic and ramble on about unrelated issues

8. Do not joke
   a. Oral board interviews are not the time to joke around. If during the interview, something is said that causes the panel members to laugh, that is all right; however, the candidate should not intentionally say something trying to initiate laughter. This could quickly backfire since not everyone has the same sense of humor.

Active Learning Video 5.9. Do not joke.

9. Do not use acronyms
   a. There used to be a time in society when acronyms were the new marketing tool; that is no longer the case since acronyms have been overused. If you use an acronym, the panel members will probably not understand what it means, and you will lose the effectiveness of what you were trying to do or show. If you do decide to use an acronym, make sure you define it clearly before you utilize it.

Active Learning Video 5.10. Do not use acronyms.

10. Do not bring your smartphone into the interview.
    a. Leave your smartphone in a safe location when going into an oral board interview. If the smartphone is left on the interview table or even inside a pocket, it can be distracting.

Active Learning Video 5.11. Do not bring smartphone.

POLICE STORY 5.2 Tap, Tap, Tap

by Retired Lieutenant Tiffany L. Morey, NLVPD

I sat on a number of oral board interview panels for the position of police officer. During one interview the candidate came in and sat in the provided chair. Three panel members were sitting at the table in front of the positioned chair. Two of us (panel members) were in full duty police uniform. I began with the first question: "Why do you want to be a police officer?" The candidate gave a very short answer, which included that it was something he wanted to do since he was young. While he was answering, he kept tapping his right foot, up and down and up and down. It was very distracting. The candidate's answers were very short, so within several minutes, we were almost done. I asked the final question, which was "Tell us anything you know about our police department." The candidate looked stunned. His mouth was wide open, and his eyes were just as round. All the while, he continued tapping his foot, never giving an answer. The silence that ensued was almost unbearable, so I put the candidate out of his misery and ended the interview. If the candidate had just gone on the Internet and looked up the department, he would have found tons of information that he could have related to us. He should have also reviewed our social media accounts. The candidate could have gained valuable information about us just from a few swipes on his smartphone. His surprise and lack of answer spoke volumes to the panel members. We knew that if he could not be bothered or if he did not care to learn anything about our department, that this was a look into the future of the type of officer he would be. Finally, if the candidate had practiced in front of a friend or video camera, he would have seen his nervous tendency to tap his foot. Obviously, the candidate failed this oral board interview. Had he just done those two easy steps he probably would have passed.

DECISION TIME 5.1

If you were a police officer for a local city police department and after 5 years you were asked to sit on an oral board interview as a panel member for new police officer candidates, think about the following situation:

As the candidates filed through the interview room, one female candidate entered and was dressed in shorts and a tank top. The female had light pink hair, and her make-up was very harsh with bright blue eye shadow and hot pink blush. She also had on long fake fingernails, a ring on every finger, and she was wearing at least five large necklaces. The candidate also had on numerous bracelets that jangled loudly as she moved her arms. The first question the female candidate was asked was to tell the panel members why she wanted to be a police officer. The candidate answered, "I have heard that this police department pays like $30.00 an hour! I only make minimum wage, so I figured, why not apply?" Her answers continued to be short and of the same quality and content.

What would you say to that female candidate? Would you want to move forward to hire her or would you recommend that she investigate the job duties, responsibilities, and qualities of a police officer? What about her casual dress? Would this be an issue? What would you tell her if she asked your opinion about her dress and answer to the first question?

CASE STUDY 5.1 Crime Reports

A candidate must have a thorough knowledge of the department testing for. Police officers are responsible for the crimes occurring in their jurisdiction. One of the best ways for a candidate to show an understanding of the department they are testing for is through complete knowledge of the crimes occurring in that jurisdiction. The following steps should be completed for the jurisdiction you will be testing for in order to gain a working knowledge of the current crimes occurring in the jurisdiction.

1. Find a law enforcement agency you are interested in applying to. Locate what city and state the agency is located in. Alternatively, you can use the city and state where you currently live.
2. Go to the following website: https://preview.crimereports.com/#!/dashboard?incident_types=Assault%252CAssault%2520with%2520Deadly%2520Weapon%252CBreaking%2520%2526%2520Entering%252CDisorder%252CDrugs%252CHomicide%252CKidnapping%252CLiquor%252COther%2520Sexual%2520Offense%252CProperty
3. In the search box, enter the name of the city and state (from question 1). For example, if you are interested in applying to the Los Angeles Police Department (LAPD), you would enter in the city Los Angeles, and state California in the search box.
4. Click the various crime icons to research the types of crimes are occurring in the searched area.
5. Take notes of the types of crimes occurring in the jurisdiction and memorize and utilize the information as part of your answer for the various questions you will be asked during your oral board interview. This knowledge will show the hiring agency you have researched and are current on the types of crimes occurring in the jurisdiction.
6. To go a step further, you can research more information on the crimes occurring by going on a ride-along and asking the officers about how they are working to solve these crimes or by following the agency on social media to see how they are working to solve these crimes.

Note: Not all agencies provide crime reports with information about current crimes. If you are looking for crime statistics on the hiring agency you are looking to apply to, you would need to either go on a ride-along and ask the officers about current crime in their jurisdiction, follow the hiring agency's social media postings, or contact the agency's crime analysis department and ask for an overall crime statistic map for the last 3–6 months (there may be a fee associated with this service).

The Three Golden Ticket Tips for the Interview

There are three golden ticket tips for the oral board interview. If the candidate follows the **nine actions for perfect answers** and adds in the three golden ticket tips, the candidate can guarantee success!

In order to understand how to succeed in an oral board interview, the candidate must understand what it is like sitting on the other side of the table. It is essential for candidates to understand what panel members are thinking and looking for in each candidate. For most hiring agencies, officers who are chosen to be a panel member for an oral board interview see it as an honor. These officers will have a direct hand in selecting future officers for the hiring agency. Panel member officers are excited to hear and learn about the candidates who will sit before them on interview day. However, if the candidate fails to prepare, as outlined in this chapter, failure is the only choice for panel members, and this is no fun. When a candidate prepares properly and includes the three golden ticket tips for each appropriate answer, the panel member is in awe and has respect for the candidate. Figures 5.9 and 5.10 illustrate two of the tips.

Tip 1: The candidate includes a personal story in answers.

Tip 2: The candidate makes a complete circle in answers.

Tip 3: If you don't say it or explain it you will fail.

FIGURE 5.9 Golden ticket tip 1.

Tip 3 is essential for candidates to understand fully. Panel members are eagerly awaiting to hear all that a candidate has done to be a law enforcement officer. If the candidate does not say it correctly or explain it thoroughly, the candidate will fail the oral board interview. What other choice do the panel members have? Candidates should work through their answer to a question aloud. Let the panel members know what they are thinking and why they are thinking of responding a certain way. Panel members are looking at how the candidate is thinking through the answers, and if the candidate is quiet, then the panel members have nothing to grade. Countless numbers of qualified candidates fail the hiring process of many law enforcement

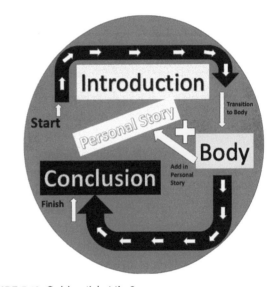

FIGURE 5.10 Golden ticket tip 2.

agencies across the United States because they fail to learn this one crucial tip.

It is that simple. For tip 1, a personal story is essential for the candidate to explain an answer. A personal story enables the candidate to go the extra mile in their answer to ensure the panel members understand fully. A personal story can help the panel understand why a candidate wanted to be a police officer or can explain what classes at college had the most impact. However, keep in mind that the personal story should not be inappropriate.

For tip 2, the candidate makes a complete circle with each answer. What does that mean? It is easier to understand than one may think. All too often, candidates do not prepare appropriately for their oral board interview. Then during the interview, the candidate gives very short and choppy answers. These types of answers lead the panel members to assume the candidate is not prepared and more importantly leave them wondering what the candidate has to offer. For each question asked the candidate must make a complete circle. The candidate must remember their English writing classes from high school and college. Or the candidate must review the basic parts of an essay. For every essay written there is an *introduction, body, and conclusion.* Answers to oral board interview questions are no different than a written essay. For a candidate to appear polished and prepared and to ensure the panel members fully comprehend their answer, candidates must look at each answer they give as containing everything that is in a short essay.

Sounds simple, doesn't it? Yes, it is very simple, yet it is all too often not done, and drones of candidates pass through the interview chair without sharing something so easy, yet so very important. Candidates need to take the time to develop and write out answers to various possible oral board interview questions and ensure they include an introduction, body, and conclusion.

Here is an example why the three golden ticket tips are key to success. Let us look at an answer to the following commonly asked oral board interview question:

"What have you done to prepare for a career in law enforcement?"

The following answer is common amongst candidates but does not include the golden ticket tips in the answer.

Example A: I have always wanted to be a police officer ever since I was a little girl and was taught DARE from Officer Janice. Since that day, I got a 3.8 GPA in high school, and I am about to graduate from college with a bachelor's degree in criminal justice.

The answer in Example A is given by many candidates. Although readers of this textbook will wonder how a candidate could give such a brief and broad answer, what is not expected during the interview are the nerves and stress. The oral board interview portion of the hiring process is generally very terrifying because it involves speaking aloud in front of others and the candidate will be sitting across from panel members dressed in full duty uniform. All of this is very nerve-racking and causes the candidate to forget! Public speaking is one of humans' greatest fears. To sit in front of respected law enforcement professionals and speak about oneself or relay information can be a daunting task. However, if the candidate prepares as instructed in this chapter, even when the stress of the interview begins, they will be able to work their way through it and remember their preparation.

Now let us look at an answer to the same question; however, the answer employs the use of the three golden ticket tips

Example B: I have looked at the preparation for a career in law enforcement as a career-long goal. I am going to outline to the board the steps I have taken to prepare for this career over the last 2 decades. (**THE INTRODUCTION PORTION OF THE ANSWER**) I have always wanted to be a police officer ever since I was a little girl and was taught DARE (Drug Abuse Resistance Education) in the fifth grade by Officer Janice of the Plainview Police Department. She was the first female police officer I ever met and who gave me the idea that I could be a police officer someday as well. I remember one day in class Officer Janice explained that while on patrol she saw a 4-year-old toddler walking in the street all by herself. The officer walked with the toddler until she was able to find where the child lived. The exhausted parents had fallen asleep, and the toddler had wandered out of the home's unlocked screened front door. Thanks to the efforts of Officer

Janice, the young child was returned to her parents unharmed. **(THE FIRST PART OF THE BODY PORTION OF THE ANSWER AND THE FIRST PERSONAL STORY)**

I remember wanting to help others the way Officer Janice had helped that toddler. Officer Janice's story followed me through high school, where I got my high school diploma with a 3.8 grade point average, and into college where I majored in criminal justice. One of my favorite classes was an introduction to law enforcement class, where the instructor believed strongly in the hands-on approach to learning. In this class, I participated in my first ever shoot/don't shoot practical scenario training. I will never forget how nervous I was when the instructor told me I was the on-duty police officer for the scenario and handed me a plastic laser handgun. The instructor read me the practical mock patrol scenario I was to respond to. I was shaking when I started the scenario and opened the door of the pretend business I was to respond to. My voice cracked as I contacted the role-player customer and asked what had occurred. Everything happened so fast during that 1–2-minute scenario. I had always respected those in law enforcement, thanks to Officer Janice; however, this scenario-based training truly opened my eyes to the difficult decisions that officers must make every day. I ended up shooting the suspect before the suspect was able to shoot me, and this ending to the scenario was a great relief! Through this college class and many others that followed, my decision to be a law enforcement officer was solidified. **(THE MIDDLE PART OF THE BODY PORTION OF THE ANSWER AND THE SECOND PERSONAL STORY)**

I have continued on this road to be a police officer by volunteering with the Plainview Police Department. Every week I volunteer 15 hours, and I have learned many valuable lessons that I will bring with me when I one day succeed in becoming an officer. I will never forget the one weekend where I met the Smith family. They were a family of four who had found themselves homeless. I was instrumental in working with social services to find them a temporary home and ensure they had food on their table. **(THE LAST PART OF THE BODY PORTION OF THE ANSWER AND THE LAST PERSONAL STORY)** This experience, along with the others I have just outlined, has allowed me to delve deeper into what it means to be a police officer. I have grown as a person, and I will graduate this June with my bachelor's degree. I know I am ready to take on the next chapter of my life as a police officer. **(THE CONCLUSION PORTION OF THE ANSWER)**

Videos 5.12 and 5.13 are examples of a candidate utilizing golden ticket tip 1 (personal story) as part of their answer for an oral board interview question.

Active Learning Video 5.12. Personal story example 1.

Active Learning Video 5.13. Personal story example 2.

The example answer given in Example B is truly the perfect answer. It is not perfect because of the stories told. It is perfect because it employs the personal story and makes a complete circle with the answer. The panel members sitting on an oral board will know that the candidate in example B does the following:

- Speaks clearly, logically, and intelligently
- Is able to organize thoughts and express them

- Is prepared to answer the entire question in a logical and informative way
- Utilizes personal history to assist with the understanding of the answer
- Has a start/middle/conclusion to each question asked
- Displays empathy, sympathy, and understanding of different values, beliefs, and viewpoints
- Has a good attitude and motivation toward police and desire and focus to serve the public
- Has a positive attitude, shows a passion and motivation for the position, and shows self-confidence in answering the questions
- Demonstrates the familiarity of the pros and cons of police work
- Is able to identify a problem presented and provide answers/solutions that are logical, reasonable, and relevant
- Does not ramble and does not vent inappropriately

Does this list look familiar? It should! The list is an example of what panel members sitting on an oral board interview panel are looking for. It highlights that the candidate fully understands the question asked and what the candidate has done to prepare and that the candidate can control their nerves and speak clearly and candidly.

Be careful! There is a fine line of applying the golden ticket tips appropriately and going overboard with superfluous information or rambling on and on. Candidates never want panel members to be checking their watches because the candidate has gone on and on and is not cognizant of the time. Be aware that many candidates are scheduled with starting times for their oral board interview on a given date; therefore, the panel does not have hours to listen to answers that are either not relevant or that give too much information. The goal is to tell a personal story that hooks the panel members and ensures they understand the answer; however, if the candidate crosses this line, the candidate can come off appearing egotistical and out of touch.

Remember, the panel members want to provide the candidate a passing score. The candidate holds the key to their success. If they prepare and learn to give a complete picture (with a personal story!), the candidate can all but guarantee success!

Example Questions and Answers

Here is a list of possible oral board interview questions and answers. The answers given are subjective, and the candidate must thoroughly investigate the hiring agency to determine if the suggested subjective answer given to a particular question is appropriate for the hiring agency. One crucial factor to remember is that this chapter recommends you prepare for 20–30 oral board interview questions. Some questions and answers are interchangeable. This can come in handy. For instance, the question "Why do you want to be a police officer?" is similar to "What have you done to prepare for a career in law enforcement?" and is also similar to "Tell us a little about yourself." The answers to all of these questions will be similar. Hopefully, hiring agencies will not ask candidates questions that are similar; instead, there will be a variety of questions. How this helps the candidate is through preparation. Candidates could invariably prepare answers for 50 questions; however, hiring agencies do not have hours to spend with candidates; therefore, the questions asked must be refined. By preparing for 20–30 questions, candidates have essentially prepared answers for 50 questions or more. The tricky part is for the candidate to be able to listen to the question asked, find the appropriate answer they prepared for, and apply the answer correctly. This is why this chapter suggests that candidates complete the nine actions for perfect answers for developing answers to various questions. Then as the candidate goes through the nine actions and creates the detailed answers, and finally acronyms for each answer, the candidate has a digital database they can quickly access in their mind. As panel members ask the candidate a question in the interview, the candidate can pull from the various (acronyms) answers and apply as needed.

Question list (possible answers are listed after the questions):

"Tell us a little about yourself."

"How would your family or friends describe you?"

"How would your last supervisor describe you?"

"Why do you want to be a police officer (or have a career in law enforcement)?"

"Describe the kind of work you expect to be doing as a law enforcement officer."

"What interests you most about a career in law enforcement?"

"What have you done to prepare for a career in law enforcement (or a career as a police officer)?"

"Can you tell us why you feel you are the best qualified applicant?"

"Why should we pick you over the other candidates?"

"Describe your background and experience as it relates to the job of a law enforcement officer."

"What have you learned from a previous job that will help you in a career as a police officer?"

"Why do you want to work at this agency?"

"Why do you want to work for this city?"

"What is your greatest strength or weakness?"

"If you responded to a convenience store for a possible person trespassing and after the call was handled you saw your partner go to the candy aisle in the store, pick up a candy bar, and place it in his pocket without paying for it, what would you do?"

"You are a police officer and you are sitting in the briefing room waiting for your shift to start. Another officer walks into the briefing room and sits down by you. You smell an odor of alcohol coming from his person. What would you do?"

"Describe a difficult problem you have had to overcome in your life."

"How do you handle stress?"

"The job of a police officer can often be stressful. Please describe a stressful situation in which you were involved and how you handled the stress."

"You are on patrol, parked, and running radar looking for drivers who are speeding. A red Honda goes past you and you clock the radar at 47 mph in a posted 35 mph speed zone. You conduct a traffic stop and contact the driver and see that the driver is your mother. What would you do?"

"Police officers are often faced with situations that change quickly. Please describe an experience where you needed to change and adapt your plans and how you handled the situation."

"Police officers are often required to make difficult decisions where they have to make a choice between different alternatives. If you had a doctor appointment at 2:00 p.m. to review important test results and while driving to your appointment you witnessed a traffic collision, what would you do?"

"Police officers serve a variety of diverse communities. What is diversity to you?"

"Are you prejudiced against any race, religion, or nationality?

"Being a police officer requires a commitment to ongoing personal development and training. Please tell us what you have done to prepare for a career in law enforcement through training and developing your skills."

"If you are a police officer on patrol and your supervisor tells you that there have been a lot of burglaries to garages in one particular neighborhood, how would you begin to be proactive in stopping the burglaries?"

"You are a police officer and you are eating lunch at a local restaurant during your lunch break. A woman approaches you with her 10-year-old son. She tells you that her son has been acting out at school by yelling at other students and not doing his homework. She wants you to scare her son so that he will start behaving. What would you do?

The previous questions with possible answers:

Question 1:
"Tell us a little about yourself."

Similar questions:
"How would your family or friends describe you?"
"How would your last supervisor describe you?"

Answers could include the following:

- Follow golden ticket tip 1 by having a personal story that tells the panel members about you (you can have more than one personal story, but be careful that your entire answer is 1–3 minutes in length).
- Follow golden ticket tip by having a complete story to your answer (introduction, body, and conclusion).
- Pick one to three of your greatest strengths and detail why they are a strength and how they have proven to be a strength (give an example or personal story).
- Pick one of your greatest accomplishments and detail why it is an accomplishment and how it makes you a better candidate (give an example or personal story). One example would be a college degree; however, do not just say "I have my bachelor's degree." Instead, include a personal story of how you overcame adversity by working full time and attending night and online classes and how this was tough to juggle and how you worked it all out. You can speak broadly; however, know when to delve deeper and tell the panel members a bit more about the topic at hand (this could be a personal story).
- From your research on the hiring agency, choose one to three of your favorite things about the agency and explain why these things made you want to work for the department (remember the panel members work for the hiring agency, so anytime you can show that you have researched the agency and know what they do, the better you will do on the interview).

- From your research on the hiring agency, know the job description and job responsibility of a police officer. Make sure to include key words from that list in your description of yourself. The panel members are looking for those key attributes. Know which key attributes you have and know when to include a story about a particular attribute. For instance, you could list five key attributes (honesty, integrity, responsible, hard-working, and works independently). Depending on your personal story, you would want to choose one to three of the key attributes to further explain. For example, "I am honest and very responsible. I also work independently, which can be shown through not only my current position as a cashier at Joe's Shack, but when I was a teaching assistant for my college professor. As a cashier, I am responsible for the daily transactions made in cash and on some type of credit or debit card. At the end of the shift I have to balance the transactions and am responsible for ensuring it is accurate. In the last 3 years I have never had a discrepancy. As a teaching assistant for Professor Jones, I was placed in charge of the editing the new open educational resource textbook. I worked for 3 months reviewing the entries made by six different professors. I made over 300 edits."

Question 2:
"Why do you want to be a police officer (or have a career in law enforcement)?"
Similar questions:
"Describe the kind of work you expect to be doing as a law enforcement officer."
"What interests you most about a career in law enforcement?"

Answers could include the following:

- Follow golden ticket tip 1 by having a personal story that tells the panel members about you.
- Follow golden ticket tip 2 by having a complete story to your answer (introduction, body, and conclusion).
- Your decision to have this career did not come lightly.
- List reasons why want to a police officer (it can be different for everyone).
  - I want to make a difference (go the extra step and tell them how you want to make a difference. Do you want to work with juveniles? Citizens with mental illness? Lower recidivism?)
  - I want to serve the community where I live (go the extra step and tell them how you want to serve the community; this is the perfect place to interject how you volunteer at the local [insert where you volunteer] and you want to now take the next step of having a career in law enforcement).
  - I am looking for a career, not just a job (explain that you got your bachelor's degree and you want to build your career on your passion for [insert your law enforcement focus] and the hiring agency will allow you to do this by [insert what the hiring agency offers that you are interested in]. You could also say that you are looking forward to the benefits offered at the hiring agency such as a future retirement plan, parity pay, health insurance, and so on).
  - I look forward to the exciting and rewarding work along with a career I can be proud of (go the extra step of tell them how this career will be exciting and rewarding for you. Have you seen a news story about a police officer who did something you hope to do

someday? This will show the panel members you understand the job and stay current with the news).

- ◦ I look forward to the advancement opportunities offered at your agency. Be careful with this response. Ensure the panel members that your number-one goal is to be a police officer. But once you have had years to learn the job of a police officer, you look forward to the many advancement opportunities (show you have researched the hiring agency by listing the advancement opportunities [insert what you are interested in such as investigations or crime scene investigator]).

- ◦ I look forward to having a career, not just a job, that I enjoy going to everyday. Be careful with this response. You do not want to appear as though the job you have now or have had in the past is awful; however, you do want to show you understand there are jobs that pay the bills and careers that not only pay the bills but fulfill many other human needs as well (explain the human needs that this new career will fill, such as helping your community).

- What did you learn through your research of the hiring agency that you like?

  - ◦ What shifts do the officers work? Do you like the different shifts? What different divisions does the agency have? Which do you like? Did you go on a ride-along? What did you learn from your ride-along or the officer you rode with? What did you learn from the hiring agency's website? Their social media? You can apply all that you learned from your research to answering this question. Being proactive by learning all you can about the hiring agency will show the panel members you are serious about your future career.

- What are the job duties, responsibilities, and qualities of a police officer at the hiring agency?

  - ◦ How are you qualified? Relate your skills and experience to those required of officers at the hiring agency.

Question 3:

"What have you done to prepare for a career in law enforcement (or a career as a police officer)?"

Similar questions:

"Can you tell us why you feel you are the best qualified applicant?"

"Describe your background and experience as it relates to the job of a law enforcement officer."

"What have you learned from a previous job that will help you in a career as a police officer?"

"Why should we pick you over the other candidates?"

Answers could include the following:

- Follow golden ticket tip 1 by having a personal story that tells the panel members about you.
- Follow golden ticket tip 2 by having a complete story to your answer (introduction, body, and conclusion).
- Schooling

  - ◦ The answer you give to explain your schooling can either ensure you succeed or can sink you. The best way to ensure you swim well is to place yourself in the position of one of the panel members listening to another candidate's explanation of their schooling. You choose which answer is more interesting. Answer A: "I went to a local high school in my hometown and I am about to graduate with a bachelor's degree from SOU." Or, Answer B: "I grew up in Portland, Oregon, where I attended Portland High School. My graduating high school class had 200 seniors and I gave the speech during graduation. My graduating G.P.A. was 3.2, and I always regretted not performing better. Yes, I have a type-A personality that drives me to do the best I can. I also graduated high school 1 year early, which required a lot of independent work and dedication. During my last year at high school I worked at Wal-Mart in the gardening department. I got paid minimum wage and quickly learned that I wanted things such as a 401K retirement account and health insurance out of my future career. I have to admit television shows and movies led me to wanting a career in criminal justice. While I understand the shows I watched were not always real and you cannot solve murders in 41 minutes, they did light a fire for me, figuratively speaking, and ensured I majored in criminal justice at Southern Oregon University (or SOU). While at SOU, I had the opportunity to take several classes that not only kept me interested in policing and always striving for more knowledge but taught me skills I can use once I am hired and trained as a police officer. For instance, in my Crime Control and Theories class, I learned about CPTED (crime prevention through environmental design) surveys. My professor not only instructed what a CPTED survey was, but I was trained how to conduct a survey. For the class I did a CPTED survey on a local apartment complex. My recommendations to the management of the complex were in the area of access control and territoriality. Thanks to the survey the complex added lighting and fencing in several locations, and crime statistics showed reduced crime in the area." Answer B is obviously the better answer and not because it is more detailed, but because it gives a better explanation of the schooling. The panel members do not know what SOU is. You should assume the panel members do not know the acronym. Next, panel members are interested in what you are learning. Assume that they do not know what classes you are taking or took in college. While you do not have to list every class, you should highlight the important classes that will allow them to understand how the classes you describe in the interview will help you in your future career as a police officer.

- Military backgrounds
  - The same applies as schooling. Do not just say *"I was in the military."* Instead, make sure you thoroughly explain how your past military experience will help you in your future career in law enforcement.
- Related law enforcement work experience
- No college education? No military background? No prior law enforcement related experience?
  - If you do not have any of this experience, do not fear. While many candidates will have at least taken some college classes, have military experience, or have some type of law enforcement related experience, not all do. Instead of focusing on this, you can focus on the job duties, responsibilities, and qualities of police officers. Look at the list in this chapter of common duties, responsibilities, and qualities of police officers, circle the qualities you have, and note how and why you have those specific qualities. For instance,

police officers must deal with a lot of people in a variety of different circumstances. If you worked in the service industry as a waiter or waitress, bartender, host or hostess, cashier, or in a department store, for example, you have worked in customer service. You just need to present your answer in a unique way to highlight your police officer–type qualities.

> Example: "I work in a busy restaurant as a bartender. I deal with many types of individuals on a daily basis. I often have to manage people who have had too much to drink or are fighting. I find I must constantly be aware of my surroundings and use my judgment as to the best decision to make in any given situation. One night, a boyfriend and girlfriend were celebrating their 1-month anniversary. After several drinks they began to argue. I could have just told them to leave the bar; instead, I saw a negative situation and tried to improve it. I began asking them how they met. As they told their story they agreed to order some food. While they were eating their salads, they told me their future plans to travel to London. Within the hour, they had made up and were laughing and happily planning they second-month anniversary. Not all situations end so merrily, and I have had my fair share of those as well. One time two men who were drinking shots and decided to start fist fighting. I immediately followed our company policy by calling 911 and notified the dispatcher of what was occurring. The police responded immediately, and the men were given the choice of leaving the bar separately or being arrested. They chose to leave the bar without further incident. My customer service background has given me the opportunity to learn patience and empathy in different situations. I know these qualities will help me be the become a good police officer."

- ○ You should consider enrolling in at least one criminal justice college class. While you do not have to immediately begin working on a college degree, one class can ensure you are staying current with your education, and you never know what one class could turn into. Police officers continually train on a variety of subjects. By enrolling, you are telling the panel members that you are taking your future in law enforcement seriously.

- Physical fitness is a top priority.
  - ○ For many reasons physical fitness should be important to police officer candidates, not only for safety but for health reasons as well. Candidates should readily explain their how they are physically fit. A short overview of how the candidate is working out weekly will ensure the panel members that the candidate is ready for the academy and a future physically demanding career in law enforcement. Candidates can also add that working out is a great way to lower stress, and since the job of a police officer is stressful, working out can be positive.

- Volunteer work or community service
  - ○ As described in many places in this chapter, those interested in a career in law enforcement should begin working as a volunteer or doing community service. Just as physical fitness is a lifelong choice for those in law enforcement, so should volunteer work or community service. The candidate can describe volunteer work or community service through a description of the work along with a personal story of something that happened

while volunteering or how your community service made a difference and how that made you feel.

- What did you learn through your research of the hiring?

  ◦ Did you go on a ride-along? Do not just say "I went on a ride-along"; instead, describe various portions of the ride-along that were interesting and related to the question. What did you learn from your ride-along or the officer who you rode with? What did you learn from the hiring agency's website? Their social media? You can apply all that you learned from your research to answering this question. Being proactive by learning all you can about the hiring agency will show the panel members you are serious about your future career.

- Have you read a law enforcement nonfiction book? Have you attended a law enforcement conference or class (even an online class)? Have you participated in a discussion forum?

  ◦ Relate these experiences to the job duties, responsibilities, and qualities required of a law enforcement officer in your detailed answer.

Question 4:
"Why do you want to work at this agency?"
Similar questions:
"Why do you want to work for this city?"

Answers could include the following:

- Follow golden ticket tip 1 by having a personal story that tells the panel members about why you want to work at this agency. This could be an interaction you had with members of the agency through a police contact or a ride-along, or it could be because of a news story or social media posting you saw about the agency.
- Follow golden ticket tip 2 by having a complete story to your answer (introduction, body, and conclusion).
- What did you learn through your research of the hiring agency?

  ◦ What is the vision, mission, and values of the agency? Do *not* just tell the panel members what these are (by reading them aloud verbatim); instead, tell the panel members about one of them (for instance, what the values of the agency are) and how you agree with the values and why or how you saw an officer with the agency apply these values. Remember, you want to show you have researched the hiring agency *and* relate the information through a story or through other research on the agency you have conducted. Make the information you found sound interesting. Think of what you would want to hear if you were an officer sitting on the panel.

  ◦ Identify the hiring agency's command staff (chief or sheriff, assistant chief/sheriff, deputy chief/sheriff, captain, major, and so on) *and* focus on one specific command staff member and what that person has done that is unique. You can find out this information through searching the Internet for an organizational chart and through research on the agency. Again, remember to apply all the information you have researched in a unique way when you explain it in your answer.

    ° Memorize the organizational chart (how the agency is organized) and the different divisions/departments. For instance, the hiring agency may have a chief of police and one deputy chief, one captain over one area command that houses patrol, and a second captain over a second area command that houses the detective bureau and all support services. Every agency is organized differently; therefore, it is essential that the candidate understand and recognize the specific organization and be able to answer questions about this organization.

    ° Study important department policies and procedures for the hiring agency and be able to discuss specific ones and how you understand them or have utilized them at your current or past employment or other experience.

    ° Is the hiring agency CALEA accredited (Commission on Accreditation for Law Enforcement Agencies)? If they are, make sure you understand what CALEA is, why it is so important, and what it says about the agency that is accredited.

    ° Did you go on a ride-along? What did you learn from your ride-along or the officer you rode with? What did you learn from the hiring agency's website? What divisions do they have? Which do you like and why? What did you learn about current issues from their social media?

    ° You can apply all that you learned from your research to answering this question. Your research will show the panel members that you are serious about your future career. Do not say "I went on a ride-along and learned a lot from Officer Smith." This short answer only tells the panel members you went on a ride-along, nothing more, and it is really not useful. Instead, say "I went on three ride-alongs. The first was with Officer Smith. I was very impressed with how professional and kind Officer Smith was on every call we went. I learned a lot about how officers respond to calls of domestic violence. When we were dispatched to a domestic violence call, Officer Smith parked several houses down from where we were dispatched. I did not know or understand why officers did that until Officer Smith explained it to me. Once he explained the officer safety reasons it was like a light bulb went off inside my head. On my second ride-along I asked Officer Jones if I could read the policy on officer safety. During lunch I read the policy and then asked several follow-up questions. More light bulbs went off inside my head! I am excited to continue learning and someday attend the police academy where I can learn more and apply the knowledge." This detailed answer shows the panel members how you have the qualities needed to make a good officer.

Question 5:

    "What is your greatest strength or weakness?"

Answers could include the following:

- Follow golden ticket tip 1 by having a personal story that tells the panel members about your greatest strength or weakness.
- Follow golden ticket tip 2 by having a complete story to your answer (introduction, body, and conclusion).

- Use the information you gleaned from Chapter 2 Self-Assessment 2.1 to identify your strengths and weaknesses.
- What are the duties, responsibilities, and qualities of officers at the hiring agency?
  - List and relate them to your strengths and how they will help you in your future career as a police officer, or with your weaknesses discuss that you need to improve in those areas and how you will do that.
- Do not use this as a weakness: "I care too much." That is a cop-out.
- Do not use this as a weakness: "I am bad at interviews and public speaking." Again, that is a cop-out.
- Do not use this as a weakness: "I get angry at stupid people really quickly." This would point out a fundamental flaw that would prevent you from being a good police officer.

Question 6:

"If you responded to a convenience store for a possible person trespassing and after the call was handled you saw your partner go to the candy aisle in the store, pick up a candy bar, and place it in his pocket without paying for it, what would you do?"

Similar questions:

"You are a police officer and you are sitting in the briefing room waiting for your shift to start. Another officer walks into the briefing room and sits down by you. You smell an odor of alcohol coming from his person. What would you do?"

Answers could include the following:

- Follow golden ticket tip 2 by having a complete story to your answer (introduction, body, and conclusion).
- Tell the truth. Remember, the panel members are evaluating you on your morals, ethics, and integrity.
- What is the hiring agency policy and procedure for theft by officers? Most policies and procedures are posted online, so research the hiring agency and know the policy. This will show the panel members you know how to do research and cared enough to do the research.
- Possible answers:
  - It is always good to first talk to your partner and find out if what you saw was really what happened. Could there be another reason your partner did not pay for the candy bar? Yes, maybe your partner overpaid for an item when last in the store or maybe your partner and the owner have another deal going on. Either way, you owe your partner the courtesy of explaining their side of the story. You are not your partner; therefore, cannot know all the reasons for your partner's actions. The only way to know is to ask and listen to the explanation.
  - Depending on your partner's explanation, you may have to confirm the explanation with the cashier or owner.
  - Depending on your partner's explanation (if your partner's explanation leads you to believe what you saw was in actuality theft), you will tell your partner that you will be

notifying the supervisor of what you saw occur. You will want to follow through to ensure your partner gets assistance. If your partner did steal the candy bar there could be other issues going on (problems at home, drug dependency, and so on). You will want to see what you can do to help your partner or ensure the supervisor is getting your partner the help needed (by finding out any underlying issues).

- Always keep the hiring agency's best interest in mind. Officers must be honest and have integrity. If an officer does not pay for an item, this is theft.
- Be careful to not come off too straight-laced; it can cast doubt on the validity of your answer.
- Remember to talk out your answer. It should never be easy to accuse another officer of a crime, and the panel members would like to see how you would work through this. The only way to do this is to talk it out and cover all the items listed in this section. Sometimes you can say too much; however, in this case your best course of action would be to talk aloud and work through the issue at hand.
  ◦ Example: "This is a serious issue. I would first want to speak with my partner about what I saw. I want to give my partner the benefit of the doubt since theft by an officer is not only against policy but is a very serious offense. If I ask my partner if they paid for the candy bar and my partner either ignores me or tells me it is none of my business, I would then tell my partner that they are giving me no other option than to notify the supervisor of what I saw. Since I have given my partner the benefit of the doubt by asking them first, I have to respect the requirement to my department and my own ethics, morals, and integrity. Further, I would try to find out if there were any underlying issues going on with my partner. I would ask my partner if everything is alright or if I can do anything to help out. However, if I was not very close with my partner, I may be overstepping our boundaries, so depending on our relationship, I may or may not delve deeper. No matter what occurs, this is a difficult situation. There are several key issues I must be aware of, and I cannot get stuck on any one of them. I must fully understand my duty and responsibility to my department, to the public I serve, and to ensure my partner has a voice as well."

Question 7:

"Describe a difficult problem you have had to overcome in your life."

Similar questions:

"The job of a police officer can often be stressful. Please describe a stressful situation in which you were involved and how you handled the stress."

Answers could include the following:
- Follow golden ticket tip 1 by having a personal story that tells the panel members about a difficult problem/situation you had to overcome in your life.
- Follow golden ticket tip 2 by having a complete story to your answer (introduction, body, and conclusion).
- What are the job duties, responsibilities, and qualities of a police officer at the hiring agency?
  ◦ Tell the panel members how you utilized those skills to overcome a difficult problem/situation in your life. Relate the skills and experience you used to those required of officers at the hiring agency.

- Detail how it is important to not be aggressive or hostile no matter the situation.
- Always remain calm and think rationally about the positive steps that will need to be taken to resolve the situation.
- You could also describe a problem/situation you went through and how you learned from it. Describe the various ways you could have solved the situation more appropriately, which became apparent after the situation played out and the situation could be re-played to find a more appropriate resolution. You can relate how this problem/situation helped you learn how to properly handle similar issues that occurred in the future. You can also relate this to what many officers do daily when responding to calls. **Role-playing** is one way officers regularly prepare themselves for all types of calls by running different scenarios in their mind while headed to a call for service. When officers receive a call for service, while they are driving (or walking) to the call, they practice role-playing the situation in their minds prior to arriving at a call. For instance, if an officer is sent to a bar where two citizens are fighting, the officer can role-play the various situations that could occur when the officer arrives and how to handle those situations. The officer could arrive and find the two citizens actively fighting, which would require the officer to break up the fight either through verbal commands (the officer would role-play in their mind what to actually say), going hands on (the officer would role-play in their mind utilizing various defensive tactics maneuvers), or utilizing another tool such as a taser (again the officer would role-play in their mind taking out their taser, making a verbal command to the citizens to stop fighting, and finally deploying the taser). The officer could also role-play a different scenario, such as if the officer arrived and the two citizens are actively yelling at each other. The officer could separate the citizens and the officer's partner could speak to one citizen and the officer could speak to the other. These are just various ways that officers prepare for calls they are responding to. You could discuss this, and not only will this show that you understand how officers mentally prepare for the calls they are responding to but how you utilize this as well after you have encountered a problem/situation in your life. By explaining this you are demonstrating to the panel members that you are familiar with this type of problem solving. Also, officers review calls they have already responded to by talking them out and reviewing various different ways they could have been handled so as to better respond the next time.

Question 8:

"You are on patrol, parked, and running radar looking for drivers who are speeding. A red Honda goes past you and you clock the radar at 47 mph in a posted 35 mph speed zone. You conduct a traffic stop, contact the driver, and see that the driver is your mother. What would you do?"

Answers could include the following:

- The answer to this question has two parts. The first part is the understanding of discretion. Police officers have discretion in certain parts of their job. If a police officer stops a vehicle for speeding and the driver was not reckless driving, was not involved in a traffic accident, and no drugs or alcohol are suspected, then the officer has the discretion to either warn the driver or write the driver a citation for a basic speed violation. In some jurisdictions the officer could also arrest the driver for speeding as a part of their available discretion. The second part of this question is honesty. Candidates must understand that this question is really a trick question. Many candidates do not think their answer to this question through (or have not prepared for it) and therefore immediately think the most appropriate answer is an undaunted "I would give my mother a citation"; however, candidates should remember how important honesty is when answering this trick question. It is very important to remember to be honest. Society expects law enforcement officers to be honest, and this does not mean only being honest in certain circumstances.

- Candidates should talk aloud as they work out this question because there could be several different answers and it is important that the panel members see that the candidate understands these options and is working through the options. Most importantly, the candidate must answer that their mother has placed them in a difficult position; however, officers must be honest, and the honest answer is that "I would not write my mother a speeding citation."

- If the candidate loves their mother, one possible answer would be for the candidate to say "I would be very torn in this situation. I love my mother and if I pulled a vehicle over and contacted the driver and saw that it was my mother, I would be very disappointed. My mother would be proud of me being a police officer and would understand the difficult position she placed me in by speeding. However, I also know my mother and know that if I explained how she not only placed me in this difficult position, but has also risked her life and the life of others on the road by speeding, she would understand my position and feel awful for breaking the law. Since I do have discretion to warn a driver for speeding and since my mother was speeding and not anything else such as reckless driving or driving under the influence, I would warn her for speeding and tell her that she can never speed again. I know my mother would take heed to my warning and it would not happen again."

  ◦ If a candidate does not have a mother (either because their mother has died or something else), the candidate should use this response as well, explaining that they do not have a mother who is alive; however, if their mother were alive they would proceed as described.

- There is a possibility that a candidate exists who does not love their mother. If this candidate did not care either way, the candidate could opt to use discretion and write their unloved mother a citation; however, the candidate must ensure that writing the citation is not retribution for past negative offenses the mother has done to the candidate. Either way, the candidate must talk out their answer to the panel members in an orderly and cognizant fashion (utilize golden ticket tip 2).

Question 9:

"Police officers are often faced with situations that change quickly. Please describe an experience where you needed to change and adapt your plans and how you handled the situation."

Answers could include the following:

- Follow golden ticket tip 1 by having a personal story that tells the panel members about an experience where you had to adapt.
- Follow golden ticket tip 2 by having a complete story to your answer (introduction, body, and conclusion).

- Explain how you always role-play what-ifs in your mind so that you are always prepared for possible outcomes and you have alternative plans ready for changing situations. See the answer to Question #7 and apply the role-playing suggestions.
- You could describe a situation where you had to adapt, although you did so with some resistance. You can talk about how you reviewed the situation and learned how to do something more appropriately in the future, thanks to this experience.

Question 10:

"Police officers are often required to make difficult decisions where they have to make a choice between different alternatives. If you had a doctor appointment at 2:00 p.m. to review important test results and, while driving to your appointment you witnessed a traffic collision, what would you do?"

Answers could include the following:
- What are the policies and procedures of the hiring agency in relation to off-duty conduct? They could assist the candidate in understanding and answering this question appropriately. For instance, some agencies leave the decision of off-duty conduct up to the officer. Other agencies require their officers be good witnesses only.
- What are the duties, responsibilities, and qualities of officers at the hiring agency?
  - Honesty, responsibility, traffic control, or investigation experience: These qualities and more describe a person who is willing to ensure the safety of those they protect and cannot be forgotten just because they are off duty. You should review the qualities and apply them to yourself through personal stories (using golden ticket tip 1).
- The correct answer would be to stop. You have witnessed a traffic collision. Just as when you are on duty there are policies and procedures you must follow. By ensuring you follow all policies and procedures you would immediately find out if there are any injuries and call 911 for assistance. You would then wait and be a good witness when on-duty officers arrived at the scene. You could tell the on-duty officers about your doctor appointment and *they* could decide whether they need your further assistance immediately or if they can get your name and number and you could fill out a witness statement at a later time.

Question 11:

"Police officers serve a variety of diverse communities. What is diversity to you?"

Similar questions:

"Are you prejudiced against any race, religion, or nationality?

Answers could include the following:
- Follow golden ticket tip 1 by having a personal story that tells the panel members about an experience where you either saw or learned about diversity.
- Follow golden ticket tip 2 by having a complete story to your answer (introduction, body, and conclusion).

- Culture is what shapes our identity and influences our behavior. Culturally diverse or multi-culturalism is "a system of beliefs and behaviors that recognizes and respects the presence of all diverse groups in an organization or society, acknowledges and values their socio-cultural differences, and encourages and enables their continued contribution within an inclusive cultural context which empowers all within the organization or society" (Dictionary.com, n.d.). It is important to understand what cultural diversity is.
- Understand the cultural diversity for the hiring agency jurisdiction you are testing for and be able to describe it along with the location of each culture in the jurisdiction and what the agency has done to ensure no issues arise. Or, you can describe issues that have arose and what the agency did (this shows an understanding of the hiring agency).
- Understand acceptance and validation of different languages and cultural heritage. For instance, if the agency you are testing for has a large Hispanic population, have you taken Spanish classes to ensure you can communicate more effectively? Or is there another culture you need to be aware of? Whatever the jurisdiction you must make sure you have researched and understand the unique cultural needs of the area. When you answer this question, you can show that you have researched the hiring agency and can relate what you know about it and what you are doing to improve the culture issues and make a difference yourself.
- Understand the importance of cultural exchange and communities that offer it (and understand the hiring agency and what they offer).
- Do not be afraid of people who have different backgrounds; instead, explain that you understand how to be friendly without judgment and be open to learning more about the different culture through mutual respect.
- Describe educational programs you have taken or plan to take that promote ethnic diversity.
- If you do not have a personal story of cultural diversity (golden ticket tip 1) you can utilize examples that have occurred in communities across the United States. For instance, in New York City, every year, two immigrant communities unite to celebrate diversity. "The annual Egg Rolls & Egg Creams Festival helps to introduce these two diverse communities (Jews from Eastern Europe and the Chinese) to each other and to audience members from other cultural groups. By increasing awareness through art, they believe they will create an opportunity for understanding and dialogue" (Community Toolbox, n.d.). This is just one example; however, it would be best to utilize an example that occurred in the jurisdiction in which you are testing. Therefore, you should conduct research both through the Internet and by asking officers questions while you are on a ride-along.

Question 12:

"Being a police officer requires a commitment to ongoing personal development and training. Please tell us what you have done to prepare for a career in law enforcement through training and developing your skills."

Answers could include the following:

- You could use a combination of your answers to questions 1, 2, and 3 (in this section) by focusing your answer on the personal development and training you have done.

- Follow golden ticket tip 1 by having a personal story that tells the panel members about how you have committed to your ongoing personal development and training to prepare yourself for a career in law enforcement.
- Follow golden ticket tip 2 by having a complete story to your answer (introduction, body, and conclusion).
- Understand the governing body in your state that will grant your powers as a law enforcement officer and those requirements. For example, In Nevada, POST (Peace Officers Standards and Training) is the governing body over law enforcement officers. How often does Nevada POST require firearms qualifications on an officer's primary duty handgun? What other training is required annually? Conduct research and know and understand the annual training that is required for all law enforcement officers. Then utilize this knowledge to show how you are currently meeting some of those standards (be specific in your answer) or how you plan on meeting them in the future. If you are not doing anything to meet any of the required training or qualifications, focus on how you can begin to so that you will be more prepared in your answer to this question.
- List what you have done to prepare. The list could include (and do not forget to thoroughly explain) being physically fit (do not just say "I work out"; instead, describe a weekly glance at your workout regimen).
- What law enforcement classes have you taken at college? Be sure to detail the classes where you learned relevant information. Do not just say "I took a lot of law enforcement related classes at college." Instead, describe a specific class and the detailed topic you learned that helped to prepare you for a career in law enforcement. Maybe you took a crime scene investigation class where you learned about the eight classifications of fingerprints and how to identify and classify them. You could offer to draw a plain whorl fingerprint or explain the difference between a radial loop and tented arch fingerprint. No matter the class you took, as long as you remember the three golden ticket tips, you will hook the panel members with your answer.

Question 13:

"If you are a police officer on patrol and your supervisor tells you there have been a lot of burglaries to garages in one particular neighborhood, how would you begin to be proactive in stopping the burglaries?"

Answers could include the following:

- Explain to the panel members that in one of your college classes (or if you did not learn this model in college, you could say through your research) you learned how to employ the SARA problem-solving model to solve crimes. You could tell the panel members that you would use the SARA model to proactively work your way through the garage burglary problem.
  - *Scanning:* You would start by scanning the problem area. Find out where the burglaries to the garages are occurring.
  - *Analysis:* Read the past burglary reports to find out if there are any mitigating circumstances or commonalities. Stop and talk to the homeowners and see if you can find out any additional information.

- *Response:* Develop an action plan for stopping the burglaries. One possible solution is to contact the media and do a public service announcement, notifying homeowners to shut their garage doors when they are not in their garage. You could also develop a door hanger to hang on the doors (notifying the homeowners to close and lock their garage doors) in the neighborhoods at risk.
- *Assessment:* Assessment is crucial since you do not want to continue with actions that have no effect. After 1 month of implementation, you would check the burglary statistics to see if the burglaries continued, were lower, or stopped. Depending on the results you could start the SARA process over again with a new response.

- Follow golden ticket tip 1 by having a personal story that tells the panel members about how you either read about, saw, or worked on a specific crime problem and how the specific crime was solved.
- Follow golden ticket tip 2 by having a complete story to your answer (introduction, body, and conclusion).

Question 14:

"You are a police officer and you are eating lunch at a local restaurant during your lunch break. A woman approaches you with her 10-year-old son. She tells you that her son has been acting out at school by yelling at other students and not doing his homework. She wants you to scare her son so that he will start behaving. What would you do?

Answers could include the following:

- Follow golden ticket tip 2 by having a complete story to your answer (introduction, body, and conclusion).
- You should talk your answer out to the panel members so that they understand how you are thinking. You should start with saying that this is an excellent chance for your department to engage in community policing; however, if handled incorrectly it could backfire. First, you need to find out more information. Ask the woman more about the history of her son's behavior. Did it just start? Has it been occurring for years? What exactly is her son doing? How big of a problem is this? Are there other issues at home occurring? Are there any issues with the father or siblings? After you find out further information you would want to tell the woman that even though you are there to assist her as a law enforcement officer for the community, and you will, if you were to scare her young son it could have several detrimental outcomes. One negativity could be her son's future view of police officers. Police officers are there to help the citizens of its community, not scare them. You do not want to risk scaring her son and hurting a future positive relationship. Therefore, you are looking at this as an opportunity for you to make a positive contact. Be careful not to just say, "I would tell the woman I will not scare her son!" You *are* going to tell the panel members that you are *not* going to scare the son, but that statement is harsh, so make sure you explain in detail to the panel members *why* you are not going to just simply scare the son. Explain your answer thoroughly. Second, there are many social services available to assist the woman. If the problems with her son are deep rooted, she will need long-term assistance from her community. You could be that connection that allows her and her son to get the needed assistance. A 10-year-old is

a young child and there could be many reasons he is acting out. You need to explain to the woman that scaring her son would not solve the issues that are causing him to act out and your hopes are to help her situation in the long term. You could volunteer to talk to her son in a positive way and have a basic conversation with him. Asking basic questions such as "How old are you? What grade are you in? Do you have a favorite class? What do you like to do outside of school? Do you have a favorite hobby?" Once you open up a dialogue with her son you could then offer to speak with him again in the future to continue the positive contact, if she would like. You would then end the conversation by offering social services in the community that could assist her with her son's behavior issues.

- Make sure you listen to the question asked. The details of the question could be different than the example given here, and the details could require a different answer or for you to ensure you deal with the details noted in the question. For instance, if the woman said that her son is 15 years old and she is worried that he might be violent at school, then you would want to address those specific issues. You would still want to not scare the child, and you would still offer social service assistance; however, you would go a step further and notify the school and the school counselor of the issue. You would also want to ask the mother if there are any weapons or guns in their home or if the son has access to weapons or guns. There are active-shooter situations that need to be understood, and this type of information could be the doorway to stopping an active-shooter situation. You need to make sure you tell the panel members this and verbally work through a question that brings up this type of situation.
- Anytime you can relate a personal story (golden ticket tip 1), or another recent story in the news, to the question ensures your answer is top notch. For instance, if the question has to do with a teenager's negative behavior and there is a possibility for that teenager to access a gun, then you would need to show you understand this connection and why it is important to take immediate action because of what happened in another city, and so on.

Do You Have Any Questions?

At the end of the oral board interview, the candidate will generally be asked, "This completes the oral board interview; do you have any questions?" At this point, the candidate is generally so excited that the interview is over that they quickly thank the panel members and run out of the room looking for the nearest oxygen tank. However, this is the time, yet again, for the candidate to shine. There are several options for a candidate who wishes to rise above the other candidates once this ending question is inevitably asked.

Option 1: The candidate can take this opportunity to ask the panel members a question. The question should be a real question, not a made-up question used only as a filler. An example of a made-up question could be, "Do you like working here?" This is a made-up question because the candidate should not expect a real and in-depth answer to this made-up question. Candidates would expect the panel members to say they like or love working for the department and nothing much more.

Real questions are questions that a candidate wants an answer to, and this authenticity shows through to the panel members. For instance, "What is your favorite part of the agency?" is a question that a candidate cannot easily find an answer for by doing a Google search on the Internet. It can only be answered by someone who has worked at the agency and has an opinion. Therefore, the panel members would know that the candidate wants to know the answer, instead of it being just another filler question. Another real question would be "If you could go anywhere in the department, where would it be: K-9, SWAT, gangs, supervision, or other areas?" Just make sure you know the different divisions the agency offers before asking this type of question. A candidate could do more damage than good if they ask about the K-9 division of the agency when the agency does not have a K-9 division. However, with proper research, such a question (ensuring the details are correct) could not only show the candidate has researched the hiring agency but also goes the extra mile to want to know a bit more of the intricate working details of the agency and the panel members. After all, the panel members are human beings too, and a real question asked of them is honorable.

Option 2: The candidate could take this time to promote themselves as a future police officer. The candidate should only utilize this second option if they did not promote themselves properly during the oral board interview. Most oral board interviews will begin with an ice breaker question such as "Tell us a little bit about yourself." If the candidate was nervous or too stressed to answer this question (or another related question) properly, the candidate can utilize this time in the end to inform the panel members why they would make an excellent police officer, or of any other relevant information they forgot to list.

Option 3: The candidate could ask both Option 1 and Option 2 questions. Depending on the oral board, this could be a great opportunity not only to ask the panel members a question but offer a final selling point for yourself as well.

See Video 5.14 by Lieutenant Hector Meletich of the Ashland Police Department for oral board interview recommendations.

Active Learning Video 5.14. Lieutenant Meletich oral board interview recommendations.

SUMMARY OF CHAPTER 5

1. Candidates must understand the job duties, responsibilities, and common qualities of police officers in order to relate them with their own skills and experience during an interview.

2. There are many recommendations for what *not* to do during an interview.

3. Eye contact during the interview must be practiced and perfected so that the candidate does not look down or only make eye contact with certain panel members.

4. Candidates must dress to impress during the interview.

5. The three golden ticket tips are key and can guarantee success on an oral board interview if utilized in conjunction with the steps and actions for success outlined in this chapter.

DISCUSSION QUESTIONS

1. What are actions that should not be done during an interview?

2. What are the three golden ticket tips and why are they important?

3. Why should women candidates not wear skirts or heels to an interview?

4. How and why do police officers role-play on their way to calls for service, and how can this behavior be utilized by a candidate during their oral board interview?

5. What key items show professionalism in a candidate?

INTERNET EXERCISE

1. Learn how to prepare your portfolio.

2. The first step is writing your resume. What type of resume is for you? That depends on a number of different factors. Resumes are advertisements for you. You must ensure you are using the correct type of resume. Here is a look at four different types of resumes:

   a. Chronological resume: The most commonly used resume format. Work history is listed in chronological order, with your most recent job first. This resume is preferred by most employers since it provides a quick look at work history.

      i. Who should use chronological resume? Those with a solid work history and no lapses between employment.

   b. Functional resume: Focuses on your experience and skills first. Employment history is listed under your skills; therefore, it is not as important.

      i. Who should use a functional resume? If you are changing careers or are a recent college graduate without a lot of work experience, this resume focuses on skills.

   c. Combination resume: Is exactly that, a combination of your experience and skills and also lists your work history. This resume is flexible and can be tailor fit to a specific job.

      i. Who should use a combination resume? If you are wanting the employer to see your detailed work experience, this resume will highlight who you are.

   d. Targeted resume: A resume that targets a specific job you are seeking. Everything in this resume will mirror the job requirements.

      i. Who should use a targeted resume? While these resumes take a lot of work, they can garner the best results. Therefore, if you have the time, choose this resume to show how you fit the job perfectly.

3. Now that you have chosen your resume, you need to find a job for your resume. Using your preferred search engine, search for a job title, your skills and knowledge sets, your preferred salary, and your zip code. Many criminal justice careers utilize the USAJOBS website: visit www.usajobs.gov/ for current employment opportunities. Following is a list of websites to further your search for a job. Remember jobs in the criminal justice field are everywhere! The following list is not comprehensive but will give you a good start of where to look:

   • https://nationaltestingnetwork.com/publicsafetyjobs/search.cfm?position=1#viewresults
   • https://www.discoverpolicing.org/careers/
   • https://post.ca.gov/Law-Enforcement-Jobs

- https://oag.ca.gov/careers/descriptions
- https://www.doj.state.or.us/oregon-department-of-justice/careers/careers-at-the-oregon-doj/

4. Develop a list of key words for your resume; you will need them to not only search for key positions but to prepare your resume.

    a. Here are some key words that will help you get started. You can circle the skills or experience you possess or want to learn.

        i. Professionalism, progressive, decision making, communication, empathetic, fair, respectful, trustworthy, controlled, shrewd, conservative, stable and mature, assertive and conscientious, dependable, self-assured, responsible, responds to disturbances, restrains, uses reasonable force, subdues resisting criminals, exercises sound judgment, protects personnel or others from the threatened use of deadly physical force, conducts searches, works with all members of the public to include the mentally ill, detects and collects evidence and substances that provide the basis of criminal offense or administrative violations, constantly pays attention, controls access to and from facilities, supervises various activities, conducts security or welfare checks, records activity, writes detailed reports, lifts, carries, or drags heavy objects, climbs elevated surfaces, pursue fleeing criminals, performs rescue operations, conducts video and audio surveillance for long periods of time, operates various technological equipment to include computers, plus many others.

5. Now develop your summary of qualifications for your job objective.

    a. Write about your experience, expertise, values, ethics, background, basically anything that qualifies you for the job you will be applying for.

        i. Example: "I am a committed and active volunteer and believe that to be in a service-related industry such as law enforcement you must always be aware of the needs in your community. For instance, I currently volunteer 10 hours a week at the local food bank."

        ii. Example: "I am an excellent writer. I am able to view a situation and write about it in a detailed, unbiased, and logical manner. In my criminal justice writing class in college I got an A. I understand the importance of being able to write about experiences."

        iii. Example: "I received the outstanding junior and senior award for our college criminal justice program."

        iv. Example: "I understand the importance of foreign languages and to that end I took 4 years of Spanish in high school and college. I am now fluent in English and Spanish."

6. Deal with work history problems.

    a. Unemployment: If you have been unemployed because you were laid off, fired, or you quit, or if you are returning to work after being in school or after parenting or an illness, you do not want to leave those years of unemployment blank in your work experience. Instead, this is the time to be creative. You will want to create a job title for the activity you were doing during the unemployed time. You do not want to leave blanks or let the employer fill in missing time with negative thoughts.

      i.   Example: Job title: "Student." Job skills: "Utilized various computer programs such as Microsoft Word, Microsoft Excel, and Microsoft PowerPoint on a regular basis. Completed complex assignments and research papers regularly."

7.   Finally, develop resume achievement statements.

    a.   You do not need drones of achievements to look appealing to employers. You just need to take your experiences and turn them into achievements. By doing this you are telling the employer you have the required skills and experience, you are good at using these skills, and you take pride in your work.

      i.   Think of projects you have done that support your job objective.

        1.   Example: "I worked as the team leader for my crime scene investigation class and we scored 100% on our mock practical crime scene work."

      ii.   Think of quantifiable results that show your abilities.

        1.   Example: "Through my work as a teacher assistant for my criminal justice professor, I was an assisting author in a new ground-breaking textbook."

        2.   Example: "While I worked as a teacher assistant for my criminal justice professor, I found a new way to assess student performance by utilizing a specific type of essay test question."

     iii.   Think of how you positively affected something.

        1.   Example: "In my Contemporary Issues in Policing class I worked on a project where I contacted local police departments to ascertain current issues. Through this police contact I found how our class could assist the department with notifying the public of the thefts that were occurring in the area. This one small project ended up being a 3-month long coordinated event that made a huge difference in the community."

8.   Where to place education on your resume?

    a.   Generally, the education is placed near the end of the resume; however, if the education is relevant to the job objective, then your education should be placed under "Summary of Qualifications" at the beginning of the resume.

9.   Don't forget about volunteer or community service. Careers in the criminal justice field are service-related careers. One huge component of such careers is the understanding of the importance of volunteer or community service. Find out the needs in your community and what you have to offer and get volunteering! To find a list of reputable organizations that are looking for volunteers you can go to www.volunteermatch.org.

10.   Professional affiliations are also important. Every career field will have at least one professional affiliation open to the candidate. Those interested in a career in criminal justice or law enforcement have a plethora of options. While most do charge a small annual membership fee, the return on your money is well worth the fee. Following is a list of possible professional affiliations in the criminal justice field. The list is not comprehensive.

    a.   American Criminal Justice Association: www.acjalae.org/
    b.   National Criminal Justice Honor Society, Alpha Phi Sigma: www.alphaphisigma.org/
    c.   Western Association of Criminal Justice: www.wacj.org/
    d.   National Criminal Justice Association: www.ncja.org/home

    e. International Association of Chiefs of Police: www.theiacp.org/

    f. National Sheriffs Association: www.sheriffs.org/

    g. International Association of Women Police: https://iawppublic.wildapricot.org/

    h. Federal Law Enforcement Officers Association: www.fleoa.org/

    i. Fraternal Order of Police: www.fop.net

    j. U.S. Deputy Sheriff's Association: www.usdsa.org/

    k. National Association of Police Organizations: www.napo.org/

    l. American Academy of Forensic Sciences: www.aafs.org/

    m. National Asian Peace Officers' Association: http://napoablue.org/

    n. National Black Police Association: www.blackpolice.org/

    o. National Latino Peace Officers Association: www.nlpoa.com

11. Additional or special skills should always be added.

    a. Do you type 100 words per minute? Do you have experience with Microsoft Excel and formulas? Whatever your skills, make sure to highlight them.

12. What else should be in a portfolio besides a resume?

    a. Letters of recommendation

        i. From professionals in the career field you are interested in

            1. Example: If you are applying for a cadet, you should have a letter of recommendation from a police officer or police supervisor.

        ii. From professors at a college or teacher at a high school

            1. This is why it is of the utmost importance to have good communication with your professors and always give 110% participation in your classes.

        iii. From professionals at organizations where you have volunteered or done community service.

        iv. Professionals who have known you for a long time (over 1 decade). This could be a family friend or neighbor.

    b. Certificates (certifications), training, or awards

        i. Relevant certificates, training, or awards should be included.

            1. Example: First-aid certification or FEMA certification (see Chapter 2 for example). If you do not have any certificates (or certifications), then take the time to get some. It is not that difficult.

            2. All relevant awards that highlight your relevant skills and experience. You should *not* include your fifth-grade award for "Student Who Wore the Most Color-Coordinated Clothing"; however, you should include college awards.

            3. Any other relevant certificate, training, or award that can show an employer you have the skills and experience required to perform the job.

    c. An introductory statement that introduces who you are. Make sure your contact information is readily visible as well.

        i. A professional photograph of yourself can be included on the introductory statement. This puts a face to your portfolio and helps the employer to remember who you are.

CLASSROOM EXERCISE

Practical Oral Board Interview Test

The professor could hold a practical oral board interview test.
The following are guidelines on how to set up the practical test:

1. Panel members: The professor can contact a local law enforcement agency and ask police officers to volunteer to sit on the oral board interview panel (two to five panel members are needed) as a panel member.

2. Oral board interviewi set-up: The professor can then set up a room with one large table and two to five chairs (for the panel members) on one side and one chair (for the student) on the opposite side of the table.

3. Questions to ask: There are a number of questions to ask during the oral board interview that are located in this chapter. The professor could also come up with their own questions. Depending on the questions asked it is a good guideline to ask four to five questions that should take each student 10–15 minutes each to answer. The professor could allow each student 2–3 minutes to answer each question asked.

4. Panel member rating sheet: The panel members could use the oral board panel rating sheet, as seen in Figure 5.4, and the students could be given the oral board interview grading dimensions to assist in studying.

5. Professor notes/grade: The professor can also take notes on the student's interview answers and give the students the panel members' rating sheets and professor's notes and grade after the interview is over.

6. Note: Resume/portfolio: The professor could also require students to bring a resume or portfolio to the interview, and it can be graded by the professor.

It is amazing how much the students get from the practical oral board interview test. It is much different to go through a practical test than to just study for one.

See Active Learning for the Following:

- Practice quizzes
- eFlashcards
- Video links
- Cognella journal articles
- Answers to Decision Time
- News clips

References

Baltimore Police Department. (2017, August 26). *Professional appearance standards.* https://www.google.com/url?sa=t&rct=j&q=&esrc=s&source=web&cd=1&ved=2ahUKEwi2u6CZqeLhAhUWup-4KHXvFBUMQFjAAegQIAhAC&url=https://www.powerdms.com/public/BALTIMOREMD/documents/61465&usg=AOvVaw0eYHq-ypcGnmlW0HP3owAn

Community Toolbox. (n.d.). *Understanding culture and diversity in building communities.* https://ctb.ku.edu/en/table-of-contents/culture/cultural-competence/culture-and-diversity/examples

Dictionary.com. (n.d.). https://www.dictionary.com/

c

Fig. 5.5c: Source: https://commons.wikimedia.org/wiki/File:US-O2_insignia.svg.

Fig. 5.6c: Source: https://commons.wikimedia.org/wiki/File:US-O7_insignia.svg.

Fig. 5.6d: Source: https://commons.wikimedia.org/wiki/File:US-O3_insignia.svg.

Fig. 5.9: Source: https://www.airforcemedicine.af.mil/News/Photos/igphoto/2000649850/.

What Is an Assessment Center?

"Every day, in every city and town across the country, police officers are performing vital services that help make their communities safer."

—Eric Schneiderman

KEY TERMS

CANTL: A quick way to remember how to pass an assessment center is with the acronym CANTL:

- **C:** Commitment and communication
- **A:** Act
- **N:** No negativity
- **T:** Team player, time management, and tools
- **L:** Leader

Citizen complaint assessment: The citizen complaint assessment is where the candidate will meet with a citizen who wants to file a citizen complaint on a police officer.

Critical incident assessment: The critical incident assessment is designed to place the candidate in a high-stress situation to see how the candidate responds.

Employee counseling assessment: The employee counseling assessment is where the candidate meets with a subordinate for a counseling session.

Group community issue assessment: The group community issue assessment is very similar to the GAC described in this chapter. Candidates are placed in the same room around the same table, and are given a community issue to solve in a prescribed amount of time. At the end of the assessment, the candidate writes an e-mail to their supervisor about the results of the meeting and the group's recommendations as to how to proceed with the community issue.

In-basket assessment center: The in-basket assessment center starts with the candidate being given many different types of paperwork. The goal is to see how the candidate organizes and delegates the paperwork.

Role-playing: Assessment centers are all about role-playing, and the candidate must become an actor for the role they are testing for and must play that role accordingly.

Group assessment center (GAC): The GAC format is where the candidate responds to a location designated by the hiring agency along with four–ten additional candidates. The GAC can be given after a candidate passes the written test, physical agility or physical fitness test, and oral board interview; however, it is up to the hiring agency to determine when and if a GAC is utilized. The candidates are placed in the same room and are seated at a table, and evaluators with the hiring agency sit at an adjacent table. Candidates are given some policing issue, and they must work through the issue as a group in a given amount of time.

Individual assessment center (IAC): The IAC format is sometimes utilized by hiring agencies who want an in-depth look at the candidate. The IAC is designed to place the candidate through a variety of different types of oral board interviews to gauge their answers, attitude, and thought process. The IAC is closer to an oral board interview format where the candidate is asked situational scenario questions and ethical-based questions.

Writing component (WC): The WC portion can be utilized in a variety of ways. One way is to utilize it as a part of the GAC. During the GAC candidates are told about a current issue and asked to come up with ways to solve the issue. During the GAC the candidates collaborate and discuss the best ways to solve to issue. After the GAC each candidate is asked to write an e-mail to their supervisor about the results and recommendations of how to handle the issue. The WC can also be part of the IAC process. The candidate will be told about a current issue, and the candidate will have to write an e-mail.

CHAPTER LEARNING OBJECTIVES

After reading the chapter, you should have a good understanding of the following:

- What an assessment center is
- The history of assessment centers
- How a group assessment center is different than an individual assessment center
- The writing component portion of an assessment center
- How to pass a group assessment center and an individual assessment center
- How to study for a group assessment center and an individual assessment center
- How assessment centers are used for promotions and the five types of promotional assessment centers

What Is an Assessment Center?

For decades the law enforcement hiring process for police officers was almost set in stone with a predetermined set of tests. Over the years, the process started to evolve to better meet the needs of hiring agencies. More and more thought and research were given to the various testing parts to ensure the best candidates were hired. One major complaint that continued to radiate throughout many agencies was that the hiring process had little relationship to the actual job the candidates would eventually do and had many inadequacies. Also, the hiring process was not particularly predictive in finding the best police officer. Just because a candidate was a good test taker did not always translate into being able to do the job of a police officer. As rotten apple officers, those officers who engage in some corruption, racial bias, excessive force, and so on, continued to be hired, agencies tried to meet the needs of everyone involved so that those candidates would not pass the extensive hiring process. One attempt to better predict the future performance of a candidate is through assessment centers.

An assessment center is a method of evaluating performance based on situational testing. The tests utilized during assessment centers are meant to elicit measurable types of behaviors. If the assessment center is developed correctly, it can relate directly to the specific position the candidate is testing for. As the candidate performs in an assessment center, evaluators compare each candidate and look for strengths and weaknesses.

The assessment center is generally given to those candidates who have already shown an aptitude for the position. For law enforcement, the assessment center is given to candidates who have already passed the entry written test, physical agility or physical fitness test, and the oral board interview. This ensures that those who are given the assessment center have the basic mechanics needed to understand and perform during the assessment.

The evaluators of the candidate's performance in an assessment center are looking for predetermined behaviors. Depending on the type of assessment and hiring agency, the evaluators generally note their observations and discuss their conclusions with the hiring agency.

Some hiring agencies also include a written component during the assessment center. During the writing component, the candidate is directed to write a report or e-mail to a supervisor about the results of the assessment center. The writing portion of the assessment center can be used to ascertain the writing ability of the candidate.

What Is the History of Assessment Centers?

"During World War II, agents of the Office of Strategic Command (OSS) came to realize that pure academic training and education were not adequately preparing their operatives for real-life situations in wartime" (Jetmore, 2017, para. 5). Even though the agents scored well on written tests, they did not perform well in the field. To answer this problem, the OSS created assessment center scenario-based tests to place the agents in high-stress situations to see how they performed. The OSS found that if the agents performed well in the field, they also performed well in the assessment center tests. The correlation led to the spread of assessment center testing not only in the government and public sector but in the private sectors as well.

What Types of Assessment Centers Will Candidates See?

Every hiring agency can utilize whichever police officer hiring tests they deem most appropriate for their agency and jurisdiction. While assessment centers are most commonly utilized for police officers who already work for a particular law enforcement agency and are preparing for a managerial/supervision promotional test to either the position of corporal, sergeant, lieutenant and so on, there are other agencies that utilize the assessment center for the initial hiring of law enforcement officers. Some hiring agencies do not utilize assessment centers at the initial police officer hiring level. Other agencies utilize a variety of different types of assessment centers. Therefore, it is up to the candidate to research the hiring agency to ascertain if the hiring agency utilizes an assessment center, and if they do which type.

Group Assessment Center

For the hiring process of police officers, there are generally two main types of assessment centers. The first is the **group assessment center (GAC).** The GAC format is where the candidate responds to a location designated by the hiring agency along with four–ten additional candidates. The GAC can be given after a candidate passes the written test, physical agility or physical fitness test, and oral board interview; however, it is up to the hiring agency to determine when and if a GAC is utilized. The candidates are placed in the same room and are seated at a table, and evaluators with the hiring agency sit at an adjacent table. The candidates are given some policing issue, and they must work through the issue as a group in a given amount of time. The goals of this type of the GAC are to see how the candidates work with other candidates and to identify candidate leaders and candidates with issues.

Individual Assessment Center

The **individual assessment center (IAC)** format is sometimes utilized by hiring agencies who want an in-depth look at the candidate. The IAC is designed to place the candidate through a variety of different types of oral board interviews to gauge their answers, attitude, and thought process. The IAC is closer to an oral board interview format where the candidate is asked situational scenario questions and ethical-based questions. Questions are asked that have to do with the following:

- Coworkers
- Ethics/morals
- Integrity
- Judgment
- Supervision
- Use of force

The candidate must respond to these types of questions by telling the panel members what they think they would do in the different situations given and why they would do it. The panel members look at how the candidate thinks and comes to a conclusion. The candidate's integrity, ethics, and morals are a top priority during the IAC.

Some hiring agencies utilize a combination of the IAC and the GAC. Candidates must research the hiring agency to find out if the agency gives an assessment center and the type of assessment center given in order to prepare properly.

Writing Component

The **writing component (WC)** portion can be utilized in a variety of ways. One way is to utilize it as a part of the GAC. During the GAC candidates are told about a current issue and asked to come up with ways to solve the issue. During the GAC the candidates collaborate and discuss the best ways to solve the issue. After the GAC each candidate is asked to write an e-mail to their supervisor about the results and recommendations of how to handle the issue.

The WC can also be part of the IAC process. The candidate will be told about a current issue, and the candidate will have to write an e-mail or another type of correspondence on how to handle the issue to their supervisor.

No matter the format of the WC, candidates should remember proper grammar, punctuation, and spelling and continue to keep in mind two of the three golden ticket tips when writing:

Tip #2: The candidate makes a complete circle in answers (introduction, body, conclusion).

Tip #3: If you do not say it or explain it you will fail it.

How Is an Assessment Center Conducted?

The candidate will be given a date, time, and location to respond to for the assessment center. The candidate should drive to the location prior to the assessment center to learn how long it takes to drive there, where to park, and what time the candidate needs to leave in order to arrive early. The candidate should arrive at the location at least 15–30 minutes early. The candidate should dress to impress by wearing a professional business suit.

For the GAC, the room where the assessment center will be conducted should have a large meeting table and chairs. The table will be where the candidates sit, and there will be an additional table or area where the panel members (evaluators for the hiring agency) will sit to watch and evaluate the candidates. Figure 6.1 illustrates the group assessment center configuration.

FIGURE 6.1 Group assessment center configuration.

For the IAC, it will be similar to the oral board interview set-up, where there is one table with the candidate on one side of the table and the three to five panel members are on the other side of the table.

How to Pass a Group Assessment Center?

The candidate must fully understand how the hiring agency is conducting the specific assessment center to best understand how to pass it; however, there are specific standards to remember for all assessment centers. Preparation for an assessment center is similar to the preparation for an oral board interview. Group assessment centers require that the candidate be able to communicate effectively and work with a team of other candidates as well. The hiring agency will determine either an issue for the group to discuss or the group could be given a controversial topic that requires open discussion and debate among the other candidates.

A quick way to remember how to pass an assessment center is with the acronym **CANTL**:

C: Commitment and communication

A: Act

N: No negativity

T: Team player, time management, and tools

L: Leader

1. Commitment and communication
   a. The candidate must communicate and be committed to the role given. If the candidate does not communicate what they are thinking (and do it positively), the evaluators will not have anything to evaluate the candidate on, and the candidate will fail.

2. Act
   a. ACTION! You are an actor! In order to pass an assessment center, the candidate must act. If the candidate does not take on the role that is assigned, the candidate will fail. For instance, if the candidate is told that they are a police officer who works for the hiring agency and there is an issue in the jurisdiction the agency patrols, and the group of officers are to meet and come up with suggestions on how to solve the issue, the candidate must take on the role of a police officer and act. The candidate must work with the other police officer candidates and work in those roles to come up with solutions to the issue at hand.
   b. The candidate should sit upright in their chair and be ready to participate in the discussion at all times. Do not slouch in the chair or display other various negative body language.

3. No negativity
   a. The evaluators are looking for negative behaviors from the candidates. For instance, if one candidate brings up a suggestion to fix the problem presented to the group and a second candidate either rolls their eyes or says, "That is an awful idea," this is seen as a negative behavior.
      i. Do not be argumentative, interrupt or be dismissive, talk over another candidate, or be confrontational.
      ii. Do be motivated, positive, and genuine; care about the topic; give a compliment if another candidate gives a good suggestion; and so on.

4. Team player
   a. Interaction with the other candidates must be positive. Police officers have to work with other police officers; in fact, they could save each other's lives one day. Therefore, a GAC is looking at how the candidates work with one another. If one candidate brings up an idea (even if it is not a great idea) say, "I like that idea; we could take your idea, and we could do this . . . as well." Alternatively, if there is a candidate who is not adding to the conversation, then say, "What do you think about this idea? Do you think that would work?" Identifying other candidates who have good ideas or assisting a candidate with participation in the group both show that the candidate is a team player.

5. Time management
   a. All assessment centers are timed, and the candidate must be aware of the time throughout the assessment. Most importantly, the candidate must remember to conduct a summation of what occurred during the assessment center prior to the ending of the assessment center. To do this properly, the candidate must know how much time has passed and when to begin the summation of what was done during the time prior and how it all should be surmised.
      i. Timekeeper: Should be chosen to utilize smartphone time clock or other timekeeping electronic to ensure the time is watched and to notify the group at specific intervals throughout the assessment. For instance, if the group is given 20 minutes for the assessment center, the timekeeper should inform the group after 10 minutes has passed and when there is 5 minutes remaining and 1 minute remaining.

6. Tools
   a. If there are tools in the room, make sure to utilize them. For instance, if there is a whiteboard with dry-erase markers in the room, the group should assign a person to write keywords about the meeting on the whiteboard.

7. Leader
   a. Police officers are leaders since they are expected to lead and direct on almost every situation they respond to or encounter. The assessment center is a time where the candidate must try and be identified as a leader.

How to Study for a Group Assessment Center?

Candidates should have thorough knowledge of the hiring agency, its organizational chart, and what issues the agency is experiencing in its jurisdiction. Many questions the group must answer center around current issues the hiring agency is experiencing; therefore, the more the candidate knows about the agency, the better prepared the candidate will be.

For instance, in one jurisdiction a current issue is that of bicycle thefts. One question that the GAC may be required to discuss is the following:

> You are the day shift police officers for a law enforcement agency. Over the last year, there has been a 50% increase in bicycle thefts, especially around the college. You have 20 minutes to meet with your other day shift officers and come up with solutions on how to decrease the bicycle thefts.

To work through this issue, candidates who have researched the hiring agency will have a leg up on the other more ignorant candidates. These candidates will have researched the hiring agency and know the organizational make-up, so they will understand the various divisions (K-9, Investigation Unit, Gang Unit, Bicycle Unit, and so on) that they can ask for assistance from. Candidates will also know what the hiring agency has done in the past for various crime sprees if they have researched the hiring agency. Maybe, the hiring agency conducted public service announcements to the citizens in the jurisdiction, notifying them to lock up their bicycles and never leave them unlocked and unattended. The hiring agency could also have tried a bicycle bait program in the past that was successful. If the candidate knew this information, the candidate could recommend doing this again and would appear a superhero to the evaluators for not only having background information about the hiring agency but being creative as well. The candidate should also employ the SARA problem-solving model for any criminal issues.

How Are Candidates Rated?

Candidates are rated by evaluators who are sitting in the same room but at a different table during the GAC. Figure 6.2 illustrates a group assessment center panel rating sheet that evaluators utilize GAC to evaluate the candidate's abilities in the various dimensions.

How to Pass an Individual Assessment Center

In order to properly prepare for the IAC, candidates can review the oral board interview chapter. While the questions asked during the IAC may be different than in a traditional oral board interview, the preparation for the questions is the same. Candidates are likely to see the following types of questions on an IAC:

- If you were offered money not to write a speeding citation, what would you do?
- If you were working in a correctional facility and an inmate asked you to use the telephone to call his wife during a no phone call time, what would you do?
- If you saw your police officer partner slap a suspect in handcuffs, what would you do?
- If you saw another police officer committing a crime, what would you do?
- If you had to arrest a family member, what would you do?
- You and your partners served a search warrant for suspected drug dealers, and during the search you found pounds of cocaine and a large amount of cash. While securing the cocaine and cash in the appropriate evidence bags, you saw one officer place an unknown amount of cash in his pocket. What would you do?
- Your squad supervisor has sent every officer on your squad to work a special detail for 1 week. When it was your turn to go, the supervisor sent a member of your squad for a second time. The following week, the supervisor sent another member of your squad for a second time. You have now been passed over two times. What would you do?
- It is a new year, and you have bid on a new shift. Six months into the shift you receive your evaluation, and it only notes negative things you have done. The evaluation does not list the many positive things you have done. What would you do?

Group Assessment Center Panel Rating Sheet

Candidate Name: _____   Date: _____

Panel Member: _____

Score:

1- Student clearly **lacks** the dimension at all levels, and shows **no** variables
2- Student has a **less than 'basic'** understanding of the dimension only hitting on **1-2 variables**
3- Student has a **'basic'** understanding of the dimension hitting on at least ½ **of the variables**
4- Student has a **moderate to high** understanding of the dimension with minor issues
5- Student has **mastered** the dimension

Dimension:	Examples:	Panel Member Notes for student:	Score: *(circle)*
Inclusiveness, to Have a Clear Understanding	Gets a clear overview of an issue; grasps information accurately; relates pieces of information; identifies causal relationships; gets to the heart of a problem; identifies the most productive lines of enquiry; appreciates all the variables affecting an issue; identifies limitations to information; adapts thinking in the light of new information; tolerates and handles conflicting ambiguous information and ideas.	11 points	1 2 3 4 5
Written Communication	Thoroughly and correctly writes what occurred; chronologically and in an easy to understand manner, covering all the facts with correct spelling and grammar.	20 points	1 2 3 4 5
Planning and Organization	Makes a plan of action; details what is needed; is organized in an easy to understand manner.	6 points	1 2 3 4 5

FIGURE 6.2 Group assessment center panel rating sheet.

- You work on a squad where two officers do not get along. It is obvious they do not like each other, and they are constantly arguing and bringing the morale of the squad down. What would you do?
- You are on patrol by yourself driving through a neighborhood at midnight. You see a man and woman standing in the driveway to a home, and the man punches the woman in the face. What would you do?
- You and your partner respond to a call of a domestic battery between two males. You walk up to the house, and one male opens the front door. You look up and see a second male on the second-floor stairs with a gun, and he begins shooting at you. What would you do?

No matter the question, the candidate must try to follow the three golden ticket tips:

Tip #1: The candidate includes a personal story in answers

Tip #2: The candidate makes a complete circle in answers (introduction, body, conclusion)

Tip #3: If you do not say it or explain it you will fail it

While not all answers to IAC questions will include a personal story (Tip #1), it is important that the candidate not forget Tips #2 and #3. Here is a question and example answer:

Example question: While you are driving a prisoner to jail, you see a traffic accident occur in front of you, what would you do?

Suggested answer: If I were a police officer, I would know and have a good understanding of my department's policies and procedures. I would first look at those to see how to respond. If the policies and procedures did not direct me, and there was no municipal, state, or federal law to direct me, I would then turn to common sense. (**The candidate should always refer to policy and procedure of the department, municipal, state, or federal laws for guidance. the evaluators will not expect the candidate to know any of those at length; however, it is important that the candidate understand they are what guide police officers.**)

Once when I worked at Wal-Mart, we had an emergency occur. It was a hectic afternoon, being the day before Thanksgiving. Many people go shopping the day before Thanksgiving for supplies for dinner; therefore, the store was very crowded. I was working as a clerk at one of the check-out registers when a fight broke out between two customers. They were fighting over who had arrived at the front of the line first. The two males were fist fighting, and everything was happening very fast. At the same time, a middle-aged woman collapsed and began having a seizure on the floor in front of my register. Luckily, I was prepared for such situations. I had read the Wal-Mart policy and procedure booklet many times, and I knew exactly how to handle these situations. While the booklet did not explain how to handle two intense situations occurring at once, it did outline how to handle each, and I used common sense for how to handle the situations at the same time. I first used our emergency phone to call 911 for the woman having the seizure. While they were directing me on how to keep her head safe, I told the clerk next to me to call our store security to handle the fight between the two males. (**While not all questions allow for the use of a personal story, the candidate must be prepared with different types of personal stories to fill in where appropriate.**

The personal story used here highlights that the candidate can handle the stress and pressure of the job of a police officer.) This event ended without anyone seriously injured and without further incident. Through past experiences like this one, I know I would be able to make the proper decisions as a police officer during stressful incidents.

In the situation outlined here, since I have a prisoner in my patrol vehicle and it would not be safe to leave the prisoner unattended, I would notify dispatch of the location of the traffic accident, the vehicles involved, and any other details about the traffic I had. If I could safely, without out getting out of my vehicle, find out if there are any injuries in the traffic accident, I would advise dispatch of further information. My priority is the safety of all; therefore, I could not leave the prisoner unattended, but by notifying dispatch of the incident, emergency services would be dispatched to the location to assist those who are injured and another officer could be dispatched to handle any traffic issues and the traffic accident report. I could then continue to take the prisoner to jail. **(Be sure to use golden ticket tip #2 and #3 and explain what you are doing and why you are doing it.)**

Here is another question and example answer:

Example question: You stop at the local convenience store at the beginning of your shift to get a bottle of water and a cup of coffee to go. As you go to pay for the drinks, the owner tells you that you do not have to pay. What would you do?

Suggested answer: If I were a police officer, I would know and have a good understanding of my department's policies and procedures. I would first look at those to see how to respond. If the policies and procedures did not direct me, and there was no municipal, state, or federal law to direct me, I would then turn to common sense. It is my understanding that most law enforcement agencies do not allow the taking of gratuities or the taking of any type of goods or services. **(The candidate should always refer to policy and procedure of the department, municipal, state, or federal laws for guidance. The evaluators will not expect the candidate to know any of those at length; however, it is important that the candidate understand they are what guide police officers.)** I understand this thinking because it is a slippery slope. If a police officer takes goods, or in this case bottled water and a cup of coffee, the owner of the convenience store might then expect something in return. That something could be an expectation of police services in the form of driving by the store regularly to deter criminals, or, if a crime occurred, the store might expect the officer to give the store owner a better level of police service to solve the crime. I realize that the owner may support the area police department and appreciate the service of the police officers and to show his thankfulness he wants to purchase the officer's water and coffee; however, this is where the slippery slope begins: a sort of quid pro quo, where the officer has been given something (the water and coffee) and therefore now owes the store owner something (police service). **(This is a great example of golden ticket tip #3 where the candidate explains fully the answer to the question; remember if you do not say it you will fail it.)** The best way to respond to this kind offer is to see it as just that, a kind offer of thanks from the owner. I would tell the owner, "Thank you for the offer. I truly appreciate the kind gesture and it means the world to me that you would take the time to recognize the hard work we do; however, our policy does not allow us to take any goods or services." I would then leave the amount due (for the water and coffee) in cash on the counter and thank the owner again and leave the store.

For more examples of how to answer these types of questions, see Example Questions and Answers" section in the chapter on oral board interviews in this textbook. Candidates should understand that some hiring agencies may ask similar questions during a regular oral board interview whereas other agencies will ask these questions during an IAC. It all depends on the hiring agency; therefore, it is of the utmost importance that the candidate research and understand the hiring agency and prepare accordingly.

How Are Assessment Centers Used for Promotion?

Many law enforcement agencies and even many corporations in the private sector utilize assessment centers for promotional testing. Assessment centers have proven to be one of the best predictors of future behavior. However, they are not the only answer to finding the best person for the job; therefore, many agencies will utilize an assessment center but will also employ the use of a written test and an oral board interview. The scores from all of the various tests will be combined for a final overall score. The hope is by utilizing a variety of different testing methods the top candidates will rise and the less effective candidates will not perform as effectively.

The most common types of promotional assessment centers generally include the following:

- In-basket assessment
- Group community issue assessment
- Critical incident assessment
- Employee counseling assessment
- Citizen complaint assessment

No matter the type of assessment center the candidate responds to, it is essential to remember golden ticket tip #3: If you do not say it or explain it you will fail it. Assessment centers are all about **role-playing**, and the candidate must become an actor for the role they are testing for and must play that role accordingly. Some candidates have a difficult time *role-playing*, and this can cause low scores and failed assessments. If a candidate knows role-playing will be difficult, then the candidate must *practice, practice, practice* by role-playing their answers to various types of assessments *aloud*.

The In-Basket Assessment

The **in-basket assessment center** starts with the candidate being given many different types of paperwork. The goal is to see how the candidate organizes and delegates the paperwork. For instance, the candidate may be given the following:

- A monthly calendar
- E-mail from the mayor that references a spike in burglaries
- E-mail from the chief of police that references attending a meeting at an apartment complex
- E-mail from a lieutenant about issues with an officer
- E-mail from the training department about the squad of officers needing training

The candidate will be expected to use the monthly calendar (which will have prior scheduled meetings on it) and then review the e-mails and number them from 1–4, with 1 being the most important that needs to be handled first and so on. Then the candidate will write on each e-mail as to how they would respond to the sender. These in-basket assessments are always timed, and sometimes at the end the candidate will sit in front of several evaluators and explain their reasoning. The evaluators can ask the candidate questions to understand their actions and handling of the e-mails further.

In an in-basket assessment, candidates must remember to look who the e-mail is from (an e-mail from the chief of police is going to be more important than an e-mail from another police officer). Then look if there are any conflicts in meeting dates or times. It is important to notify those involved in any meetings that need to be scheduled or canceled and re-scheduled. Also, remember to engage those in the department who have the expertise. If one e-mail is from the city manager asking the candidate to schedule a neighborhood watch meeting in a neighborhood that is having a lot of gang-related crime, the candidate should ensure a member of the Gang Division or a fellow police officer who has gang expertise either attends the meeting with the candidate or, if the candidate has a more important meeting to go to, the gang expert can go to the meeting for the candidate and report back. Finally, always remember to e-mail the person back and report what occurred at the meeting or another issue in the e-mail.

Sometimes there will be two equally important e-mails. The candidate must still number the e-mails according to importance. If the candidate checks for any conflicts on their calendar with meetings and the e-mails are still equal, the candidate will have to explain this. The most important factor in these types of issues is the explanation the candidate gives to the evaluators. The candidate would ensure to note they compared who sent the e-mail, what the issue was, and there were no conflicts to notify anyone about; therefore, either e-mail could have been handled first.

The Group Community Issue Assessment

The **group community issue assessment** is very similar to the GAC. The candidates are placed in the same room around the same table and are given a community issue to solve in a prescribed amount of time. At the end of the assessment, the candidate writes an e-mail to their supervisor about the results of the meeting and the group's recommendations as to how to proceed with the community issue. Some assessments differ in how they are administered. Some agencies may require the candidate to develop their solutions to the community issue on their own. Then the candidate must do a presentation to explain their solutions to the evaluators on their own. For more information see the GAC section in this chapter.

The Critical Incident Assessment

The **critical incident assessment** is designed to place the candidate in a high-stress situation to see how the candidate responds. Critical incidents could be the following:

- Call of a bank robbery in progress
- Call of a kidnapping and hostage situation
- Call of an active shooter

The candidates are on patrol, a call comes over the radio about a critical incident in progress, and the candidate is responsible for responding appropriately. Depending on the agency, the candidate will have to follow policy and procedure and will utilize all the tools available. The candidate could use patrol vehicle whiteboards by writing down where all the officers are located (or use the patrol vehicle itself as a whiteboard) and where more officers are needed. The candidate will need to call out emergency services such as a staging area for an ambulance and the media. SWAT and K-9 may need to be called out as well. The candidate's response will be different depending on the agency and how they respond to critical incidents.

The Employee Counseling Assessment

The **employee counseling assessment** is where the candidate meets with a subordinate for a counseling session. One example would be where the candidate role-plays the position of a supervisor (such as a sergeant), and a role-player (involved in the assessment) acts as the police officer under the sergeant's command to be counseled. Prior to entering a room, where there will be a desk or table, and the role-player for police officer will be waiting, the candidate will be given or told why the police officer is waiting for the candidate (role-playing as the sergeant of the police officer). Many times, the police officer has an attitude and has not been performing their duties as required. Depending on the scenario, the candidate could be told about specific past incidents where the police officer has either had a citizen complaint, violated department policy and procedure, been late to work, or engaged in some other type of negative behavior(s). The candidate will need to make a list of the issues and go into the meeting (assessment) with a plan.

One of the best ways to take on an employee counseling session is to employ the following five steps:

1. Explain to the *employee* what they did wrong.
   a. Ask the employee if anything is going on in their life that they need to know about. Do not pry too deep into the employee's personal life; however, the candidate should ask if everything is okay in their personal life. The candidate may have to ask a second time since it sometimes takes people being asked more than once to open up. However, be careful not to ask more than twice, because that can be seen as prying. If other issues are going on with the employee, the candidate should know what support the agency has to offer to the employee (such as an employee assistance program and so on).
2. Explain *why* it is wrong.
3. Explain *how* to fix it.
   a. If the employee needs training to help fix the issue, the candidate should recommend and detail the training required. For instance, if the employee was rude to a citizen, the candidate may require the employee to take a verbal judo training class to learn how to better communicate with citizens.
4. Explain to the employee *when* they have to fix the issue by (give an exact date).
5. Schedule a meeting in the future (1, 2, 3, or 4 weeks) to review the employee's performance and discuss any training classes taken and any other recommendations.

It is important to remember to do the five steps for *each* issue the employee is having. One of the biggest mistakes made in this type of assessment is not covering every issue in detail. The candidate should also remember not to get frustrated with the employee; however, they should not let the employee walk all over them.

- When the candidate walks in the room, if the employee is on their smartphone or otherwise engaged the candidate should ensure they have the employee's full attention, even if they have to ask the employee to put down the smartphone and pay attention to the meeting.
- If the employee displays negative behavior, such as rolling their eyes when the candidate says something, the candidate should tell the employee not to engage in such behavior.
- If the employee crosses their arms in front of their body, the candidate should ask the employee to uncross their arms, since this is a negative mannerism.

The candidate should show that they care about and want to mentor the employee and offer training where needed; however, there is a fine line where the candidate is role-playing the supervisor and must be able to control the meeting and not allow any negative behaviors from the employee.

The Citizen Complaint Assessment

The **citizen complaint assessment** is where the candidate will meet with a citizen who wants to file a citizen complaint on a police officer. One example would be where the candidate role-plays the position of a supervisor (such as a sergeant) and a role-player (involved in the assessment) acts as a citizen of the jurisdiction where the law enforcement agency is located. who wants to file a complaint on a police officer under the candidate's supervision. The role-player citizen will be waiting at a desk or table in a room where the candidate will enter. The candidate should introduce themselves, ask the citizen why they are there, and explain what occurred. The most important part of this process is to follow the following five steps:

1. *Listen* to the citizen.
2. *Repeat* back the main issues the citizen outlined and clarify any questions.
3. *Apologize* to the citizen for them having to go through the issue. Be careful *not* to take responsibility or admit any wrongdoing at this point. The candidate will still need to investigate the issue and contact the police officer and any witnesses involved before a determination can be made. However, the candidate can apologize to the citizen for having to go through the issue and having to take the time to come to the station to file a complaint.
4. *Explain* to the citizen that this complaint is very important, will be taken seriously, and will be investigated. Once the investigation is completed the citizen will be notified as outlined in the department policy and procedure for citizen complaints.
5. *Finish* with thanking the citizen for taking the time to come to the agency today and ask if the citizen has any final questions.

POLICE STORY 6.1 **Recommendations for the Assessment Center**

by Chief Pamela Ojeda (NLVPD)

First, let me start by saying please do not waste your time or anyone else's time by saying you are just taking the test to take it and see what it is like. You are not the type of leader any agency is looking for if you make such a big decision on a whim. Making well thought-out decisions is a key trait in a quality supervisor. Promoting to a supervisory role is a career goal and should be prepped and planned for appropriately.

The written portion of any test will be the easiest. It is usually comprised of state and local laws, policy and procedures, and possibly a leadership book. As a police officer, you work with these on a daily basis. Therefore, you should focus on the more important piece, the assessment center.

I have been a part of several assessment center processes, both as an assessor and as part of command staff selecting the scenarios to be used.

A good assessment center will create the scenarios based on current issues and/or trends that are occurring in that specific department. Be familiar with what the issues are in your department and community. It could be such things as the field training program, discipline issues, morale, accountability, high crime areas, community issues, and so on.

As you prepare yourself, you must start to think as a leader. When you walk into your first scenario of the assessment center, you need to step outside yourself as a police officer and now become the supervisor. Look at the bigger picture. You must think about how your decisions will affect not only your department, but also your community.

I always recommend wearing your uniform for the process. First impressions are important. A uniform shows command presence, and you want them to see you as a professional who can lead the department. Arrive early to your appointment so you have time to relax, collect your thoughts, and calm yourself.

As you participate in each scenario, be sure to say everything step by step, in detail. Don't assume they know what you are thinking or that they know your policy and procedures. The assessors will only have the instructions and checklist given to them. Remember, you're the supervisor, not the police officer. For example, don't say "I'm going to set up a perimeter." You're not an officer; you're the supervisor. You will say "I'm going to make sure a perimeter is set up." You will now be directing officers' actions and overseeing operations, not participating. The best example I have for this is when I was a newly promoted sergeant working in CSI. I was assisting with measurements for a diagram on a homicide scene. My lieutenant came up to me and told me to put my hands in my pockets, so I did. I stood there for a few minutes and then asked, "Now what?" He said, "Now you stand there." He was telling me if I am participating in a scene, I cannot properly supervise, and I could overlook something important.

Lastly, be sure to speak loudly, clearly, and with confidence. Remember at the end to sell yourself, because if you don't, no one else will.

SUMMARY OF CHAPTER 6

1. Candidates should understand what an assessment center is and how it works.

2. Candidates should be able to explain the differences between the group assessment center and the individual assessment center.

3. Candidates should be able to list the different ways to study for the group assessment center and the individual assessment center.

4. Candidates should fully understand the promotional assessment center for police officers who want to be promoted and the five different types of promotional assessment centers.

DISCUSSION QUESTIONS

1. What is the difference between a group assessment center and an individual assessment center?

2. How are hiring assessment centers different between promotional assessment centers?

3. Describe the five steps to the employee counseling assessment and the citizen complaint assessment.

INTERNET EXERCISE

1. Go to your favorite Internet search engine.

2. Search for police department assessment centers.

3. Review the different suggestions given on how to study and prepare for the different types of assessment centers.

CLASSROOM EXERCISE

Practical Group Assessment Center Test

The professor could hold a practical group assessment center test.

   The following are guidelines on how to set up the practical test:

1. Panel members: The professor can contact a local law enforcement agency and ask police officers to volunteer to sit on the assessment center panel (three to five panel members are needed).

2. Assessment set-up: The professor would then set up a room with one large table and 6–10 chairs around the table and a second table for the panel members to sit at and view the

main table. Six to ten students at a time would be told to meet at a particular time in the room. If a class has 30 students in it, the professor could have three groups of 10 students or five groups of 6 students, and so on. It is good to give a time limit of 10–20 minutes for the students to work through the community issue. It is also good to have a whiteboard or chalkboard in the room for the students to utilize.

3. Community issue: The students should be given a community issue to solve. It is recommended to use a current law enforcement issue where the college is located so that the students can research their area prior to the assessment center and so they are current on possible solutions. One example could be bicycle thefts. Many cities experience bicycle thefts, and the group of students could be given an assessment to come up with a plan on lowering the number of bicycle thefts. Once the students finish the group assessment center, they could be told to write a written component through an e-mail to their supervisor about the group's recommendations on how to solve the bicycle theft issue.

4. Panel member rating sheet: The panel members could use the group assessment center panel rating sheet in Figure 6.2.

5. Professor notes/grade: The professor would also take notes on the student's performances and writing component and give the students the panel members' rating sheets and professor's notes and grade after the assessment center is over.

It is incredible how much the students get from the practical group assessment center. It is much different to go through a practical test than to just study for one.

See Active Learning for the Following:

- Practice quizzes
- eFlashcards
- Video links
- Cognella journal articles
- News clips

Reference

Jetmore, L. F. (2010, June 17). *Assessment center promotional testing.* PoliceOne. https://www.policeone. com/police-jobs-and-careers/articles/2083870-Assessment-center-promotional-testing/

Why the Background Investigation Is Critical?

"Goodness is about character, integrity, honesty, kindness, generosity, moral courage, and the like. More than anything else, it is about how we treat other people."

—Dennis Prager

KEY TERMS

Background packet: A packet that the candidate must fill out that asks questions about the candidate's job history, school history, drug history, criminal history, and financial history and that requires the candidate provide official documents.

Official documents: The most commonly required official documents are a birth certificate, Social Security card, driver's license, proof of citizenship, marriage certificate(s), divorce decree(s), military service record form DD214, GED certificate or high school diploma, college diploma(s), and bankruptcy papers.

Past drug use guidelines: Many hiring agencies do not list their past drug use timeline openly. The federal government sets guidelines for past drug use for the hiring of agents, and many law enforcement agencies follow these guidelines.

CHAPTER LEARNING OBJECTIVES

After reading the chapter, you should have a good understanding of the following:

- Why the background investigation is critical
- Who conducts the background investigation
- One conviction that will stop a candidate from being hired as a police officer
- The background mistakes candidates should be concerned about
- Past drug use guidelines
- How to deal with issues in a candidate's past
- Why it is important to find official documents now

Why the Background Investigation Is Critical

Police officers are given a large amount of authority. This authority can be used to take a person's freedom away. It can be used to utilize necessary force, up to deadly force. It can be used to take possession of illegal evidence. Police officers are also entrusted to help those in need of help because they are being hurt or abused. The list goes on and on. Police officers are entrusted with the responsibility to keep citizens safe from crime; therefore, they must have a history of ethical and moral behavior. Police officers are expected to be beyond reproach, and since they are around a great deal of temptation, they must have the ability to rise above it all and not involve themselves in any corruption. One of the best predictors of future behavior is past behavior. Since the public must trust their police officers, hiring agencies must do everything in their power to ensure that the candidates they hire have extensive background checks to identify any possible problems.

Background checks for law enforcement officers are much more thorough because of the trust and authority officers are given. Every possible aspect of a candidate's life is accessed and investigated. Those who have been through the background investigation process have described it as being very frustrating and intrusive.

What Is the Background Check Packet?

To conduct a background investigation takes a lot of hard work, time, dedication, and money. Because of this, many hiring agencies only conduct background investigations on candidates who have passed the written test, the oral board interview, the physical agility or physical fitness test, and assessment center. Once a candidate passes the various tests, they are notified that they need to pick up and fill out a **background packet**. Candidates are generally given 1 week or less (depending on the hiring agency) to fill out the packet and provide with the required documents. The background packet can take hours to fill out and many times even longer if the candidate does not have the information or documents required handy.

One of the worst things a candidate can do is turn in an incomplete background packet. One of the many duties a police officer must do is fill out forms completely. A background packet is a form, and if the candidate fills it out *incompletely* the candidate is showing the background investigator that they cannot complete it, are hiding something, or do not care, and this sends a loud message to the hiring agency.

Figure 7.1 is an example background packet. Candidates should fill out this in the textbook or make a copy. While every hiring agency utilizes its background packet, the majority of the information requested is the same. The candidate needs to ensure that all blanks are filled in. *If there is a blank that the candidate has no answer fo,r the candidate should either write an N/A in the blank or draw a line across the blank. This tells the background investigator that the candidate addressed every question.* Many times, there is not enough room to answer a question completely. If this happens, the candidate must type out their answer to the question on a separate piece of paper. This is especially true for any questions where the candidate's answer could cause issues. For instance, if the question asked is "Have you ever stolen anything?" and if the candidate stole a piece of candy out of a bin at a supermarket when she was 10 years old, then the candidate would type out her statement on a separate piece of paper. The candidate would explain in the statement when it happened (be approximate as possible with dates and times), why it happened, take responsibility for it happening, and finally state it will never happen again. The candidate would then attach the statement to the back of the packet. The candidate would also label the top of the statement as "1" or "A" and write out "See attachment 1 or attachment A" as the answer for the question. This should be done for any statement that is typed out and further explained.

BACKGROUND PACKET EXAMPLE

Date:

PERSONAL INFORMATION

Full Name (Last, First, Middle):

Date of Birth:

Social Security Number:

AKA/Maiden Name:

Driver License (DL)Number: DL State Issued: DL Expiration:

Gender: Marital Status:

Height: Weight: Eye Color: Hair Color: Race:

Home Address:

Cellular Phone: Home Phone: Other Phone:

Email:

PERSONAL QUESTIONS:

1. List any other names you have gone by other than the one listed above:
2. List social security number(s) used other than the one listed above:
3. Have you applied for another law enforcement agency or criminal justice type of employment prior to this application? If yes, list the date(s) and companies/agencies you applied to below:
4. Have you taken a polygraph or voice stress analyzer before? If yes, list the date(s), companies or agencies, and outcome of each test below:
5. Have you committed a felony, (write in yes or no)? If yes, explain:
6. Have you driven a vehicle while under the influence of alcohol in the past three years and not been caught? (write in yes or no)? If yes, explain:
7. Have you ever not filed an IRS statement (write in yes or no)? If yes, list year(s) and explain:
8. Do you pay child support (or have you paid child support in the past)? Write in yes or no. If yes, explain the details and if you have ever been delinquent in your payments.
9. Are you prejudice against any group (write in yes or no)? If yes, explain:
10. Have you ever been in some type of physical confrontation with a person with whom you were in a romantic or intimate relationship with? Write in yes or no. If yes, list the date(s) and detail what occurred in detail:

11. Have you ever lied on a job application? Write in yes or no. If yes, explain:

12. Have you ever been rejected for any type of employment? Write in yes or no. If yes, list the date(s), employment name, employment location, and reason for rejection.

13. Have you ever been rejected for employment due to a background investigation? Write in yes or no. If yes, explain:

14. Have you ever been rejected for employment due to polygraph results? Write in yes or no. If yes, explain:

15. Have you ever been rejected for employment due to voice stress analyzer results? Write in yes or no. If yes, explain:

16. Have you ever been rejected for employment due to the oral board interview results? Write in yes or no. If yes, explain:

17. Have you ever been rejected for employment due to the physical agility or physical fitness test results? Write in yes or no. If yes, explain:

18. Have you ever been rejected for employment due to the assessment center results? Write in yes or no. If yes, explain:

19. Have you ever been rejected for employment due to the final interview? Write in yes or no. If yes, explain:

20. Have you ever been rejected for employment due to _____? Write in answer and explain:

21. Have you ever been employed and failed to pass the probationary period? Write in yes or no. If yes, explain:

RESIDENCES

List your residences for the past 10 years. Begin with your current residence. Include college, school, military, and personal residences. Do not leave any time unaccounted for.

From: Month/Year	To: Month/Year:	Street Number, City, State, County, Zip Code, & State	Landlord First and Last Name:	Contact Number:	Contact Email:

EMPLOYMENT

List your employment for the past 10 years. Start with the most recent and go backwards. Include college, school, military, and unemployment. Do not leave any time unaccounted for. Do not omit any employers.

From: Month/Year To: Month/Year	Name of Employer:	Job Title and Duties:	Supervisor:	Address (Street #, City, State, Zip):	Contact Number:	Email of Supervisor:	Website of Employer:	Reason for Leaving:	Ending Salary:

EMPLOYMENT QUESTIONS

1. Have you ever been terminated or asked to resign by any employment? Write in yes or no. If yes, explain and list employer information:

2. For your current employer, or if you are unemployed what would your employer say about your job performance? Is it exceptional? Above average? Average? Below average? And explain why:

3. Have you ever been late for work? Write in yes or no. If yes, list the date(s), employers, and explain:

4. Have you ever called in sick for employment when you were not sick? Write in yes or no. If yes, list the date(s), employers, and explain:

5. Have you gone two years or more of being unemployed? Write in yes or no. If yes, explain:

6. Have you ever been counseled or written up, or otherwise disciplined at any of your employers? Write in yes or no. If yes, explain:

7. Have you ever quit a job without giving notice required by the employer? Write in yes or no. If yes, explain:

8. Have you ever worked for an employer and not reported your earnings to the IRS? Write in yes or no. If yes, explain:

9. Have you ever worked while collecting unemployment, and you did not report the work to unemployment? Write in yes or no. If yes, explain:

10. At any of your employers have you ever taken any type of merchandise or supplies without authorization? Write in yes or no. If yes, explain:

11. At any of your employers have you ever taken money that you were not authorized to take? Write in yes or no. If yes, explain:

12. At any of your employers have you ever taken anything from a fellow employee that you were not authorized to take? Write in yes or no. If yes, explain:

13. Have you ever conspired with another person (or employee) to defraud an employer? Write in yes or no. If yes, explain:

14. Have you ever been accused of being dishonest? Write in yes or no. If yes, explain:

15. Have you ever been told you have no morals, no ethics, and/or no integrity by an employer? Write in yes or no. If yes, explain:

16. If you were ever bonded, was the bond ever canceled? Write in yes or no. If yes, explain:

17. Did you ever tell, give, or sell confidential information you knew while employed to another person for financial gain or another reason? Write in yes or no. If yes, explain:

18. Are you now, or have you in the past made payments to an employer (or paid an employer back) for money or merchandise stolen or lost? Write in yes or no. If yes, explain:

REFERENCES

List five (5) references who are adults and who know you well and who you have known for at least five (5) years minimum. Cannot list relatives.

Name (First and Last):	Relationship (how you know reference):	How long known (years):	Address (Street #, City, State, Zip):	Contact Number(s):	Email Address:	Occupation of Reference:

EDUCATION AND TRAINING

List schools (high school, college, trade school, university)- for each school list:

From: Month/Year	To: Month/Year	Name of School and Complete Address:	Credits:	Graduate (yes or no):	Major:	Minor:

PROFESSIONAL SOCIETIES, ORGANIZATIONS, LICENSES, REGISTRATIONS, SPECIAL SKILLS, KNOWLEDGE, OR ABILITIES

From: Month/Year To: Month/Year	Professional Society, Organization Name, License, Registration, Special Skill, Knowledge or Ability:	Website or Other Information:

Do you speak, read, and/or write any language other than English? Write in yes or no. If yes, explain:

Do you have any law enforcement training? Write in yes or no. If yes, explain:

CONVICTION RECORD

Have you ever been convicted, pled guilty, or no contest to any offense, domestic violence, or any other violation of any statute, ordinance, law, regulation by any civil or military authority, either in this country or other country (either as an adult or juvenile)? Write in yes or no. If yes, explain (even if expunged):

ARREST RECORD

1. Have you ever been arrested (convicted or not) for any offense or violation of any statute ordinance, law, regulation by any civil or military authority, either in this country or other country (either as an adult or juvenile)? Write in yes or no. If yes, explain (even if expunged):

2. Have you had contact with a police officer? Write in yes or no. If yes, explain:

3. Have you been warned about anything by a police officer? Write in yes or no. If yes, explain:

4. Have you been detained by a police officer? Write in yes or no. If yes, explain:

5. Have you been charged with a crime? Write in yes or no. If yes, explain:

6. Have you been arrested? Write in yes or no. If yes, explain:

7. Have any of your relatives been convicted or imprisoned? Write in yes or no. If yes, explain:

8. Have the police ever responded to your home? Write in yes or no. If yes, explain:

9. Have you ever been questioned as a suspect in a crime? Write in yes or no. If yes, explain:

10. Have you been connected with any criminal investigation? Write in yes or no. If yes, explain:

11. How many times have you been arrested? Write in yes or no. If yes, write in how many times:

12. Has a warrant ever been issued for your arrest? Write in yes or no. If yes, explain:

13. Have you ever not paid a parking or moving citation? Write in yes or no. If yes, explain:

14. Have you ever been on court-ordered probation? Write in yes or no. If yes, explain:

15. As a juvenile did you ever appear in juvenile court for an act that would have been a crime if you had been an adult? Write in yes or no. If yes, explain:

16. Have you ever applied to carry a concealed weapon? Write in yes or no. If yes, explain:

17. Have you ever stolen property without permission? Write in yes or no. If yes, explain:

18. Have you ever paid cash for something you thought may be stolen? Write in yes or no. If yes, explain:

19. Did you ever sell anything you knew was stolen? Write in yes or no. If yes, explain:

20. Are you now or have you ever been in possession of stolen property? Write in yes or no. If yes, explain:

21. Have you ever paid for or participated in any type of paid sexual activity? Write in yes or no. If yes, explain:

22. Have you ever viewed or looked for pornography? Write in yes or no. If yes, explain:

23. Have you ever been accused of, committed, arrested, tried in court, convicted, or been a victim of the following (circle all that apply and explain at the end):

ARSON   FORGERY   EMBEZZLEMENT   RAPE   ATTEMPTED RAPE   SEXUAL CHILD ABUSE

ASSAULT   RESISTING ARREST   HOMICIDE   MOLEST   BURGLARY   THEFT

BREAKING AND ENTERING   VANDALISM   GRAFFITI   ROBBERY   CHILD ABUSE

CHILD NEGLECT   SEXUAL CRIMES (SELF-EXPLOSRE, OBSCENE PHONE CALLS, PEEPING TOM, SEX IN A PUBLIC PLACE, BESTIALITY)

DRIVING UNDER THE INFLUENCE OF ALCOHOL OR DRUGS

24. Have you observed or participated in any crime? Write in yes or no. If yes, explain:

25. Have you ever been the subject of a court-order for the protection prohibiting harassment or staling? Write in yes or no. If yes, explain:

26. Have you ever been investigated by child protective services? Write in yes or no. If yes, explain:

27. List all criminal actions in which you were the defendant. List the following information for each incident:

Date:	Original Charge:	Charge Reduced to:	Location:	Court Disposition:	Police Agency:	Explain:

DRIVING HISTORY

1. Has your driver's license ever been canceled, refused, revoked, or suspended? Write in yes or no. If yes, explain:

2. If you answered yes to #1 above, how many times did you operate a motor vehicle after your license was canceled, refused, revoked, or suspended? Write in the number of times and explain:

3. Have you attended a driver school? Write in yes or no. If yes, explain:

4. What other states have you had driver's licenses in? And dates:

5. Have you been in a motor vehicle accident? Write in yes or no. If yes, explain date, injuries in accident, location, and if you got a citation:

6. Have you ever left the scene of an accident before the police arrived? Write in yes or no. If yes, explain:

7. Have you ever falsified information on an accident report or given police false information during a traffic stop or accident investigation? Write in yes or no. If yes, explain:

8. Have you ever been in a road rage situation? Write in yes or no. If yes, explain:

9. Do you have a motor vehicle currently? Write in yes or no. If yes, do you have the required state motor vehicle insurance? Write in yes or no. If no, explain:

10. Has your motor vehicle insurance ever been cancelled?

11. List your traffic citations for the last 10 years. List in chronological order with the most recent first.

Date	Charge:	Agency:	Details:

ALCOHOL AND DRUGS

1. Do you drink alcohol? Write in yes or no. If yes, type of alcohol and how much every week?

2. Did you ever drink more than you drink now? Write in yes or no. If yes, explain:

3. Has your alcohol drinking ever caused any issues in your family? Write in yes or no. If yes, explain:

4. Have you ever illegally had possession of marijuana (illegally possessed, used, purchased, or sold)? Write in yes or no. If yes, explain:

5. How many times have you used marijuana in the last year?

6. How many times have you used marijuana in the last two years?

7. How many times have you used marijuana in the last three years?

8. How many times have you used marijuana in the last four years?

9. How many times have you used marijuana in the last five years?

10. When was the last time you used marijuana (Month, Day, Year)?

11. Are you currently utilizing marijuana for any reason? Write in yes or no. If yes, explain:

12. Have you ever illegally had possession of cocaine (illegally possessed, used, purchased, or sold)? Write in yes or no. If yes, explain:

13. How many times in the last five years have you used cocaine?

14. How many times in the last ten years have you used cocaine?

15. When was the last time you used cocaine in any form (Month, Day, Year)?

16. Are you currently utilizing cocaine in any form?

17. Have you ever illegally had possession of prescription drugs (illegally possessed, used, purchased, or sold)? Write in yes or no. If yes, explain:

18. How many times did you have possession of illegal prescription drugs in your life?

19. When was the last time you used illegal prescription drugs in any form (Month, Day, Year)?

20. Are you currently using illegal prescription drugs in any form?

21. Have you ever illegally had possession of any hallucinogens such as LSD, mescaline, peyote, acid, mushrooms, angel dust, PCP, etc. (illegally possessed, used, purchased, or sold)? Write in yes or no. If yes, explain:

22. How many times did you have possession of hallucinogens in your life?

23. When was the last time you used hallucinogens in any form (Month, Day, Year)?

24. Are you currently using hallucinogens in any form?

25. Have you ever illegally had possession of opiates or dangerous drugs such as opium, morphine, heroin, Ecstasy, GHB, etc. (illegally possessed, used, purchased, or sold)? Write in yes or no. If yes, explain:

26. How many times have you had possession of opiates or dangerous drugs in your life?

27. When was the last time you used opiates or dangers drugs in any form (Month, Day, Year)?

28. Have you ever illegally had possession of amphetamines such as meth, Dexedrine, speed, crank, crystal meth, ice, glass, cross tops, etc. (illegally possessed, used, purchased, or sold)? Write in yes or no. If yes, explain:

29. How many times have you had possession of amphetamines in your life?

30. When was the last time you used amphetamines in any form (Month, Day, Year)?

31. Have you ever illegally had possession of illegal steroids (illegally possessed, used, purchased, or sold)? Write in yes or no. If yes, explain:

32. Explain how, why, and how many times in your life you used illegal steroids?

33. When was the last time you used illegal steroids (Month, Day, Year)?

34. Have you ever sniffed, inhaled, or huffed any type of inhalant such as glue, spray paint, etc. for the purpose of getting an effect (such as a high)? Write in yes or no. If yes, explain:

35. Have you ever illegally had possession of depressants or tranquilizers such as barbiturates, Valium, Quaaludes, etc. (illegally possessed, used, purchased, or sold)? Write in yes or no. If yes, explain:

36. How many times have you had possession of illegal depressants or tranquilizers in your life?

37. When was the last time you used illegal depressants or tranquilizers in any form (Month, Day, Year)?

38. Have you ever used any other person's prescription or given your prescription to another person? Write in yes or no. If yes, explain:

39. Have you ever illegally possessed or used any other controlled drug besides those already described? Write in yes or no. If yes, explain:

40. How many times in your life have you driven a vehicle after using any illegal or controlled drug: Write in the number of times:

41. When was the last time you provided illegal or controlled drugs to friends or other persons in exchange for money or other goods or services? Write in the last time (Month, Day, Year) and explain:

42. Have you ever manufactured, grown, or possessed a controlled substance? Write in yes or no. If yes, explain:

43. How many times have you used any illegal substance since the age of 21?

44. How many times have you used any illegal substance before the age of 21?

45. Do you know of any relatives or close friends that are currently using illegal drugs? Write in yes or no. If yes, explain:

46. Are you aware that the employment environment within this agency is a DRUG-FREE ENVIRONMENT, and any violation can lead to termination, (write in yes or no that you understand this statement):

MILITARY

1. Have you registered with the Selective Service for the draft? Write in yes or no. If yes, explain:

2. If you do not have military experience, write NO here and continue to the next section (if you have military experience continue with the questions in this section).

3. Have you ever served in any branch of the military (Air Force, Army, Coast Guard, Marine Corps, Navy, R.O.T.C, Other Military, Para-Military Organization, etc.)? Write in yes or no.

Branch of Military Service:	ID Number:	Date Started:	Date Ended:

4. Were you discharged from the military? Write in yes or no. If yes, explain type of discharge:

5. Have you failed to complete any term of enlistment? Write in yes or no. If yes, explain:

6. Have you ever been disciplined in the military (example: Article 15, Captain's Mast, Company Punishment, Court Martial, reduction in rank, other)? Write in yes or no. If yes, explain (in detail the type of discipline and result):

7. Have you ever gone AWOL or UA or did you go missing from formation or ship movement? Write in yes or no. If yes, explain:

8. Do you possess any military equipment that you are not authorized to have? Write in yes or no. If yes, explain:

9. Are you a member (or have you been a member) of the National Guard or U.S. Reserve? Write in yes or no. If yes, explain in detail the unit, name, number, and Commander's contact information:

ORGANIZATIONS

1. Have you ever been (or are you now) a member of any domestic or foreign organization or association or movement or combination of any which is communist, fascist, subversive, totalitarian, or advocates or approves the commission of acts of violence or force and denies any person their rights under the U.S. Constitution or the state? Write in yes or no. If yes, explain:

2. Have you ever been (or are you now) a member in a gang or other type of group that commits crimes? Write in yes or no. If yes, explain:

FINANCIAL STATUS

1. Do you currently pay all of your bills on time? Write in yes or no. If no, explain:

2. Have you ever filed bankruptcy? Write in yes or no. If yes, explain:

3. Have you ever had a check returned for insufficient funds? Write in yes or no. If yes, explain:

4. Have you ever been referred to a collection agency? Write in yes or no. If yes, explain:

5. Have you ever had your wages garnished? Write in yes or no. If yes, explain:

6. Has a landlord ever served you with eviction? Write in yes or no. If yes, explain:

7. Have you ever been the subject of a lawsuit by a landlord or property manager or someone you rented property from? Write in yes or no. If yes, explain:

8. Have you ever made a false claim to an insurance company (an insurance claim)? Write in yes or no. If yes, explain:

9. Have you ever had any issues or unresolved issues with the Internal Revenue Service? Write in yes or no. If yes, explain:

10. Have you ever had any issues or unresolved issues with the revenue department of any state? Write in yes or no. If yes, explain:

11. Have you ever had a bad credit rating? Write in yes or no. If yes, explain:

12. What is your current credit rating?

13. Have you ever had anything repossessed? Write in yes or no. If yes, explain:

14. Have you ever avoided any creditors? Write in yes or no. If yes, explain:

15. Have you ever been sued in court? Write in yes or no. If yes, explain:

16. List all your creditors:

Name of Creditor:	What is the credit for?	Amount Owed Today:	Minimum Monthly Payment:	Contact Information:

17. Does anyone owe you money? Write in yes or no. If yes, explain:

18. What monthly income do you have?

Name of Employer:	Position:	Monthly Salary:

19. Will the salary from this employment position pay your present financial obligations? Write in yes or no. If no, explain:

20. Do you gamble? Write in yes or no. If yes, explain:

21. Do you owe any debt due to gambling? Write in yes or no. If yes, explain:

SOCIAL NETWORK

1. List the social networking sites that you are affiliated with (or have been affiliated with in the past):

Name of Social Networking Site:	Username:	Password:

2. List all the email addresses you have ever used:

3. Have you ever posted any photographs or comments on any social networking site that may contain inappropriate material (based on age, disability, color, race, sex, religion, or national origin)? Write in yes or no. If yes, explain:

4. Have you ever posted any photographs or comments that may be embarrassing or sexually explicit? Write in yes or no. If yes, explain:

5. Have you ever posted any photographs or comments or viewed photographs of juveniles engaged in any activity that is unlawful? Write in yes or no. If yes, explain:

6. Did you erase, delete, clean, or amend any of your social networking sites in preparation for this employment or other similar recent employment? Write in yes or no. If yes, explain:

LAW ENFORCEMENT APPLICATIONS

1. List the agencies you have applied to in the last five years:

Name of Agency:	Date Applied:	Result:

LAW ENFORCEMENT EXPERIENCE

1. If you have never had any law enforcement experience, go to the next section. If you have had any law enforcement experience go to question #2.

2. What type of law enforcement experience have you had?

3. Did you have any citizen complaints? Write in yes or no. If yes, explain the complaint(s) and result of the complaint investigation(s):

4. Did you have any reprimands (demoted, dismissed, suspended, written-up)? Write in yes or no. If yes, explain the reprimands in detail:

5. Did you have any unsatisfactory personnel ratings? Write in yes or no. If yes, explain:

6. If you were a sworn (commissioned) police officer, did you ever violate any controlled substance laws? Write in yes or no. If yes, explain:

7. Did you ever use illegal drugs while on or off duty? Write in yes or no. If yes, explain:

8. Did you ever consume alcohol while on duty? Write in yes or no. If yes, explain:

9. Did you ever lie or distort the truth or facts in a police report? Write in yes or no. If yes, explain:

10. Did you ever lie or distort the truth during an investigation of any type? Write in yes or no. If yes, explain:

11. Did you ever cover for another officer who committed a violation or broke the law? Write in yes or no. If yes, explain:

12. Have you ever been terminated? Write in yes or no. If yes, explain:

13. Have you ever been involved in an internal affairs investigation? Write in yes or no. If yes, explain:

14. Have you ever damaged any type of police property? Write in yes or no. If yes, explain:

15. Have you ever used excessive force or more force than necessary for the situation? Write in yes or no. If yes, explain:

16. Have you ever been involved in a motor vehicle collision? Write in yes or no. If yes, explain:

17. Did you ever engage in any type of sexual activity while on duty? Write in yes or no. If yes, explain:

18. Have you ever accepted gratuity in violation of your agencies policy? Write in yes or no. If yes, explain:

19. Have you ever converted evidence or another person's property into your own personal use against your agencies policy? Write in yes or no. If yes, explain:

20. Did you know of any crimes committed by other officers that were not reported? Write in yes or no. If yes, explain:

MISCELLANEOUS

1. Have you ever inflicted pain on animals or humans and enjoyed it? Write in yes or no. If yes, explain:

2. Have you ever offered anyone a bribe? Write in yes or no. If yes, explain:

3. Have you omitted any information from this packet? Write in yes or no. If yes, explain:

4. Are any of your answers in this packet false? Write in yes or no. If yes, explain:

5. Are you concealing any information that you think may keep you from being employed by this agency? Write in yes or no. If yes, explain:

6. Are you applying to this agency because you have been requested to do so by any subversive organization? Write in yes or no. If yes, explain:

7. Have you ever committed a crime that has not been disclosed? Write in yes or no. If yes, explain:

8. Is there anything about your background, activities, character, employment, education, habits, home life, family, physical or mental condition, temperance, or anything thing else that was not asked in this packet that would be relevant directly or indirectly that could affect your eligibility for the position which you are applying? Write in yes or no. If yes, explain:

SIGNATURE

By signing below, you acknowledge that every answer in this packet is true.

_____

Signature

_____

Printed Name

_____

Date

Candidates make a bold statement by typing out detailed answers to any questions that might be an issue. The statement made is the type of police officer the candidate will make. Police officers are required to write detailed reports, fill out forms completely, and take responsibility for their actions. By typing out detailed responses to certain questions, the candidate is showing the hiring agency that they can write detailed reports, fill out forms completely, and take responsibility for their actions.

What Is a Background Investigator?

Once the hiring agency receives the completed background packet, the background investigation begins. Every hiring agency is different in how they conduct background investigations:

1. Some agencies are large enough and have an Internal Affairs division where its background investigators conduct the investigation.
2. Other agencies do not have a full-time Internal Affairs division and instead assign the background investigations to department detectives. These are the same detectives who are assigned all other criminal investigations.
3. Other agencies outsource the background investigation to an experienced investigator (generally a retired police officer who did background investigations) who is hired to conduct background investigations for an agency.

It is up to each hiring agency how in depth each background investigation is. Of course, the more comprehensive the investigation, the longer it takes and the more costly it is.

A good, in-depth background investigation involves the investigator not just sending out reference forms via e-mail and mail, but contacting the candidate's references, employers, landlords, professors, teachers, friends, and other contacts via the telephone or in person. Investigators could also visit the candidate at their home for an in-home interview. It is incredible how much an investigator can tell from the home of the candidate and how the candidate acts in their own home. Finally, the investigator will run a records check on the candidate to look at their criminal history as well their detailed financial and credit history. Background investigators have been known to fly all over the country to to investigate a candidate's background in person.

Depending on the agency and the state where the agency is located, the candidate could be required to take a polygraph test or voice stress analyzer (VSA) test. The results of this test would be compared with the background investigator's findings and could lead to further investigation. Finally, the background investigator might work with the psychologist conducting the psychological evaluation. The information gleaned from all of these tests must be reviewed by all involved to ensure the candidate, if recommended, will make a good police officer.

You Are Human—Mistakes Can Be Forgiven

If you made a mistake in your background, do not give up. While every law enforcement agency is different, there are many that understand what it is to be human and do forgive mistakes. The most significant factor is time. Many agencies want to see 2–3 years between the mistake and application date. For instance, if a candidate was cited for being in possession of alcohol as a minor when they were 18 years old, and they are now 21 years old and applying for a job as a police officer and have not been in trouble since, the agency is more likely than not to *not* use that one charge as a reason for not hiring the candidate. Some past mistakes cannot be overlooked in the hiring process; therefore, the candidate must check with the hiring agency prior to applying if there are any concerns.

What Mistakes Should Concern You

There are certain mistakes in a candidate's past that agencies do *not* overlook and can keep a candidate from being hired. Again, every hiring agency is different; however, there are some commonalities due to certain laws. Depending on the mistake, the candidate should be prepared to explain what occurred, take responsibility for the mistake, and state that it will not happen again; and, the longer the period between the mistake and application the better. The following list illustrates mistakes that candidates should be aware of and, depending on the agency, could be reasons agencies will not hire a candidate. Or, the candidate should be ready to explain in detail the issue by typing out a detailed statement that is attached to the background packet.

- Incidents of domestic violence, use of verbal or physical abuse or violence toward others indicating a lack of self-control. Candidates with domestic violence convictions will not be hired. The reason is that a candidate cannot carry a firearm if convicted of domestic violence per federal law 18 U.S.C. § 922.

- Conviction of a felony
- Associating with individuals who break the law
- Challenging authority
- Using force to resolve disputes
- Use of harassment, intimidation, or threats to gain advantage
- Associating with individuals who break the law
- Defensive and blaming others and not taking responsibility for actions
- Remaining silent or condoning others' improper actions
- Unnecessarily confrontational
- Overreaction to criticism
- Failure to learn from past mistakes
- False statements, misleading statements, or omitting information
- Minimizing past mistakes
- Unwillingness to modify position
- Inability to get along with others in work or in personal life
- Use of derogatory stereotypes in jokes or other daily language

Past Drug Use

Past drug use is the area that causes the most concern on the background check. Many hiring agencies do not list their past drug use timeline openly. This can be frustrating and confusing to many candidates. However, candidates must understand this can be a good thing. Many agencies do not have set **past drug use guidelines**; instead, they choose to look at the candidate's entire background and reasoning for past drug use and mistakes before making a decision. For instance, a candidate may have no prior issues in their background besides using mushrooms (psilocybin, or a hallucinogen) two times during their college career. If the use of mushrooms occurred 3 years ago, the hiring agency could make the decision, based on the totality of the candidate's background, to go ahead and hire the candidate. If the hiring agency had a public guideline for past drug use requirement of 10 years for hallucinogens, then the candidate would have to be cut at that point. Therefore, by not publicizing the past drug use requirements timeline, the hiring agency could choose to hire a candidate who had made a mistake 3 years ago by using mushrooms. When developing policy on past drug use, many law enforcement agencies look at the following:

- Drug used
- When drug was last used
- Frequency of drug usage
- Pattern of drug usage
- Involvement in the sale and distribution of drugs

The federal government sets guidelines for past drug use for the hiring of agents, and many law enforcement agencies follow these guidelines. According to the Federal Bureau of Investigation's website on past drug use, the following guidelines are used:

- Marijuana: 3 years since last use
- Illegal drugs: 10 years since last use

Therefore, if the candidate who used mushrooms twice in the previous 3 years applied for a job as an agent or a law enforcement agency that utilized the federal guidelines for past drug use, the candidate would have to wait 7 more years (to meet the 10 years since last year guideline).

Common Questions Asked and Answered:

Question: "What if marijuana is legal in my state?"

Answer: Most law enforcement hiring agencies follow federal guidelines for marijuana use, and it is still illegal at the federal level. However, some hiring agencies do not follow the 3 years since last use federal government rule. Some agencies require only a reasonable amount of time since the last use of marijuana. This reasonable amount of time could be as little as 1 year; it all depends on the hiring agency and what the chief or sheriff allows.

Question: "What if I had a prescription for marijuana?"

Answer: For most agencies, it does not matter whether the marijuana was prescribed, because this now raises the question as to why was it prescribed. If the candidate has a health issue, and this is the reason for needing the prescription for marijuana, the hiring agency will investigate this as well. They will ask and investigate if the candidate is mentally and physically healthy enough to do the job of a police officer.

Question: "What if I take Prozac for my moods or because I am bipolar?"

Answer: If you are taking Prozac with a prescription and you are under the care of a doctor (who prescribed you the Prozac), then this is generally a question for the psychologist who conducts your psychological evaluation and the medical doctor who conducts your medical evaluation. It will be up to them, working in conjunction with the background investigator to investigator, to make the determination if being on Prozac and the reasons you are on Prozac would cause you any issues in being able to perform the responsibilities and duties of a police officer.

Past Driving Practices

During a background investigation, a candidate's past driving record will be looked at. How many speeding tickets has the candidate had? Was the candidate ever convicted of reckless driving or driving under the influence of alcohol or drugs? Was the candidate at fault in a traffic accident and failed to pay the assessed fees? Did the candidate have their driver's license revoked, and if so, what was the reason? Past driving practices are tough to put a number on. Most agencies will not publicly list that if a candidate has two speeding tickets in 1 year, they will not be allowed to apply. Instead, the hiring agency will look at the totality of the candidate's driving record and time since the last issue and make a determination from that. The best advice for candidates is if there is a past driving issue, the candidate needs to write out a detailed statement of what occurred, take responsibility for the action, and state it will never happen again. The candidate should also get a copy of their driving record (usually obtained from their local Department of Motor Vehicles office) to understand their driving record and any issues.

Past Financial History

Issues such as late and missed payments for bills will cause concern. Bankruptcy, repossessions, not filing taxes, and missed child support payments are more serious and could cause the candidate issues depending on the hiring agency. No matter the past financial history issue, the candidate should prepare a typed statement of the circumstances that caused the candidate to have the issue. For instance, if a candidate was married and as a couple the candidate purchased a house with the hopes to fix it up and flip it and then the candidate went through a divorce and the house had to be sold before it could be fixed up and this caused a domino effect that caused bankruptcy, a hiring agency would understand. Therefore, no matter the financial issue, the candidate should prepare a written statement explaining the reason for the issue, take responsibility for the issue, and state that the issue will never happen again.

Past Employment

Issues in past employment can be concerning to not only the candidate but a background investigator as well. If a candidate had a personality issue with a past supervisor or if a candidate was fired from a past job, the candidate should be ready with a written statement to explain the situation. Candidates should be careful to not go on the offensive. Instead, the candidate should focus on what they should have done and what they will do in the future. Always keep the focus on the candidate and responsibility. Most hiring agencies will work with candidates who have issues in past employment as long as the candidate understands what occurred, takes responsibility, ensures it will never happen again, and there is some time between the issue and the application.

Careers in the criminal justice field are very different from other careers. Background investigators like to be able to investigate past employment to ascertain the candidate's work ethic, work behavior, customer service, judgment and decision background, how well the candidate works with other employees and supervisors, and many other factors. All too often, college students focus on schooling and forego work. This is a mistake on several levels. If the college student is working toward a career in the criminal justice field or law enforcement, the student needs to work to establish positive past employment. Even if the student volunteers 5 hours a week at the local shelter, that is considered working and allows the background investigator a place to contact to find out all kinds of information about the candidate.

What to Do About Issues in the Past

Whatever mistake the candidate made, the best thing the candidate can do is research the hiring agency for background requirements. Some agencies ask specific past drug use and past criminal history questions on a personal history questionnaire that is completed at the time of the application.

This is a great way to do things since the hiring agency and the candidate know right away whether there is something in the candidate's past that will keep them from being hired. However, this is not true for all agencies; therefore, the candidate could save a lot of time by researching the hiring agency to see the requirements, and if the candidate does not meet the requirements, they will not waste their time or the agency's time in testing.

However, do not get discouraged. Unless, the candidate has something in their past like a prior conviction of domestic violence, which means the candidate cannot carry a gun (i.e., the candidate cannot be a police officer) the candidate should not give up. Not all agencies have the same background requirements. While there are agencies that follow the strict background requirements of the federal government, many agencies look at the candidate as a person who made mistakes and, depending on when those mistakes occurred and the candidate's attitude about those mistakes, will overlook those mistakes. Do not let something you *think* is bad in your background keep you from a career in law enforcement. Know your background, ask questions, and find out if you have a chance. Call the hiring agency you want to test for and other agencies, ask your college professors, research, and ask professionals to find out if you can one day be a police officer.

Why It Is Essential to Find Needed Documents Now

Candidates should begin preparing for their background investigation *now*. During this portion of the hiring process, the hiring agency will require the candidate to provide a number of different types of documentation. If the candidate does not have these documents in hand, it can take days or weeks to get them, and it can be costly for the expedited processing of the documents as well. The following list represents the most commonly asked for documents:

- Birth certificate (original or stamped certified copy)
- Social Security card
- Driver's license
- Proof of citizenship
- Marriage certificate(s)
- Divorce decree(s)
- Military service record form DD214 (must be copy 4)
- GED certificate or high school diploma
- College diploma(s)
- Bankruptcy papers

The background investigation portion of the testing process is very stressful and invasive. However, it can be a foregone positive conclusion if the candidate knows what requirements the employer expects and knows their background.

POLICE STORY 7.1 **Turning on the Lights**

by Retired Trooper, now Background Investigator William A. Matson

Congratulations, you have made it to the background phase. In the past 13 years I have conducted over 125 backgrounds for state, county, city and other agencies, 15 in 2019. Here is what I have learned that can help you:

1. Give all information with as much detail as possible when filling out your packet. Pay attention to detail. Your penmanship, use of English, and detail will speak volumes.
2. The good, the bad, the ugly: There are no perfect applicants. Your investigator wants to see the real you. If you tell the investigator you can't remember your ex-girlfriend's phone number that is not good.
3. Prepare yourself to articulate any and every piece of information you include in your packet. For example, if the boss was a jerk and fired you, tell it like it is *and do not* try to explain away tough or embarrassing issues.
4. Expect the investigator to follow all leads you include in your personal history questionnaire (PHQ).
5. The investigator is looking for common sense, communication skills, the ability to multitask, the ability to function under pressure, integrity, organization, and passion, to name a few.

There are also some things that can sink your ship during a background investigation. These are actual happenings during my background investigations:

Applicant had sex with underage sister of the person he was married to. Applicant had been fired by the three most recent employers. Applicant had "forgot" to pay federal taxes 4 years in a row. Applicant stole keys to his place of employment and asked the office help for sexual favors before leaving. Applicant used and sold drugs. Applicant did not pay rent as a tenant. Applicant failed to disclose DUII and criminal activity while in the Army.

What the background investigation is all about is accountability. Think of it this way: I am applying for a career whose goal is to maintain a decent and orderly society. Should not the accountability I expect of others be the same accountability I expect for myself?

Hold your head high for you are embarking on a noble and honorable profession that has the respect of the vast majority.

FACT BOX 7.1: BACKGROUND INVESTIGATOR BILL MATSON'S RECOMMENDATIONS

Background Investigator Bill Matson conducts background investigations for a number of law enforcement agencies and has a lot of knowledge. Watch Video 7.1 to hear his recommendations to candidates on what to expect during the background investigation and how to prepare.

Active Learning Video 7.1. Background Investigator Bill Matson's recommendations.

SUMMARY OF CHAPTER 7

1. Candidates should understand why the background investigation is critical.
2. Candidates should fill out the example background packet in full, so when it is time to fill out the real background packet for a hiring agency, the candidate has all the information needed.
3. Candidates should research the hiring agency and know the guidelines on past drug use and whether the candidate meets those guidelines.
4. Candidates should be prepared with typed-out statements of explanation and take responsibility for any issues in their background.
5. Candidates should work on obtaining the official documents that are required for the background investigation.

DISCUSSION QUESTIONS

1. What is the background packet, and why is it important for the candidate to fill the example packet out prior to filling out the real one with a hiring agency?
2. What issues in a candidate's background could cause an issue, and what issues can be dealt with? Which issues would stop a candidate from being a law enforcement officer?
3. What is the best way to deal with issues in a candidate's background?
4. What official documents are required for the background investigation, and why is it important to obtain them prior to beginning the hiring process?

INTERNET EXERCISE

1. Go to your favorite Internet search engine.
2. Search for police department past drug use guidelines for police officers.
3. Review the different guidelines to get a good understanding of the parameters for past drug use.

See Active Learning for the Following:

- Practice quizzes
- eFlashcards
- Video links
- Cognella journal articles
- News clips

What Is a Lie Detector Test?

"Integrity is telling myself the truth. And honesty is telling
the truth to other people."

—Spencer Johnson

KEY TERMS

Lie detector test: The polygraph examination and voice stress analysis (VSA) are the most common tests utilized to detect if a candidate is lying. A lie detection or a truth verification exam would be a more appropriate description of the test.

Polygraph examination: The polygraph examination is a diagnostic instrument that

records the physiological variables in a subject due to stress.

Voice stress analysis (VSA): Voice stress analysis (VSA), sometimes called the CVSA, computer voice stress analysis, are computer programs that are written and designed to measure how stress and deceptive responses change voice patterns.

CHAPTER LEARNING OBJECTIVES

After reading the chapter, you should have a good understanding of the following:

- What a lie detector test is
- The more appropriate name for a lie detector test
- The history of lie detector tests
- What a polygraph examination and examiner are
- The three parts of the polygraph examination
- What a VSA is
- How to prepare for a lie detector test

What Is a Lie Detector Test?

Many law enforcement agencies utilize some **lie detector** test as a part of the police officer hiring process. The lie detector test is also utilized in the hiring process for those aspiring in the criminal justice field. The polygraph examination and voice stress analysis (VSA) are the most common tests utilized to detect if a candidate is lying. The lie detector test is another part of the law enforcement hiring process that causes considerable stress. However, understanding what the lie detector test is and knowing what to expect can ease the anxiety.

Not every state in the United States allows the use of a lie detector test for pre-employment testing. For instance, Oregon, New York, Pennsylvania, and Texas are four states that do not allow a lie detector to be utilized in pre-employment testing. However, if a person were to get a job as a federal agent with the Federal Bureau of Investigation (FBI) and that agent was posted in Oregon, the FBI would give that agent a lie detector test every 5 years as a part of their employment. Candidates should research their state and hiring agency to see if a lie detector test is given.

Why Is It Called a Lie Detector Test?

The term *lie detector* is a misnomer. *A lie detection* or *truth verification exam* would be a more appropriate description of the test since the polygraph examination "involves inferring deception through analysis of physiological responses to a structured, but unstandardized, series of questions" (American Psychological Assocation (APA), 2004). The subject taking a lie detector could be seen as having answers that were deceptive instead of outright lying. The difference between the two should be taken into account by the examiner reading the results. The background investigator should also want to conduct further investigation into why the subject showed deception. The hiring agency should want to understand the reasoning behind the deception completely, and the only way to properly do that is through a more in-depth background investigation.

According to Dr. David Corey, a police psychologist who conducts psychological evaluations, "Polygraph tests help detect deception, spur 'truth-telling' by applicants, and can be a useful tool when a background investigator finds discrepancies in an applicant's personal history" (Bernstein, 2007). Law enforcement agencies that utilize a polygraph examination or voice stress analysis as a tool in their toolbox find them to be useful. A lie detector test can be one tool to help determine the background of a candidate. For instance, if on a polygraph examination a candidate showed deception in a particular area, this should be the spark that notifies the background investigator to look deeper into the candidate's past. The hiring agency, through the background investigator, should want to find out the who, what, where, when, and why of the deception before making any final decisions.

What Is the History of Lie Detector Tests?

"William Moulton Marston is credited with being the father of the polygraph for his 1917 publication detailing the detector that he'd created two years earlier. Then came John Larson-a police officer and medical student in Berkley, California-with his own invention in 1921" (Roufa, 2019). Larson, who ironically was a police officer himself, believed that when a person lied, involuntary physiological changes occurred, and if they could record those changes, then the person could be caught in a lie.

What Is a Polygraph Examination and Examiner?

The **polygraph examination** is a diagnostic instrument that records the physiological variables in a subject due to stress. If a subject lies, it causes stress on the body, and in turn the body displays involuntary responses the polygraph diagnostic instrument measures. By using specialized instruments, the polygraph is able to collect physiological data from various sites on the human body at the same time. The digital polygraph system works by attaching to and measuring the following:

- Chest (thoracic): Respiratory activity is recorded by two pneumographs (convoluted rubber tubes or electronic sensors)
- Abdominal area: Respiratory activity is recorded by two pneumographs (convoluted rubber tubes or electronic sensors)
- Palms of hand: Electrodermal (sweat gland activity) is recorded by two sensors
- Fingers: Pulse blood volume change is monitored by infrared photoelectric plethysmograph
- Arm: Cardiovascular activity is recorded by blood pressure cuff
- Chair: Where the subject sits special movement and motion sensors detect countermeasure and body movements

"Together, these variables provide continual data regarding an individual's sympathetic and parasympathetic nervous system which are part of the autonomic division of the peripheral nervous system which controls physiological actions and reactions" (Central Polygraph Service, n.d.). Figure 8.1 illustrates the various locations the polygraph instruments are placed on the subject and chair during the polygraph examination.

To be certified as a polygraph examiner, the examiner must complete an accredited polygraph training program, and some states require the examiner to have a bachelor's degree and experience in psychology or law enforcement. Polygraph examiners must be trained in advanced interview and interrogation methods because the polygraph examination results must be interpreted once they are obtained. Polygraph examiners must conduct polygraph examinations according to the strict standards and methods accepted and approved by the American Polygraph Association and the U.S. Federal Government.

The Three Parts of the Polygraph Examination

There are generally three parts to the polygraph examination:

1. Pre-test
2. Polygraph examination
3. Post-test data analysis

During the first part, the pre-test period, the polygraph examiner speaks with the subject and completes required paperwork. The polygraph examiner then explains the polygraph equipment, how the process will work, and the questions that will be asked. During the second part, the polygraph examination, the examiner asks the questions, and as the subject answers the examiner collects a number of digital polygraph charts. The third and final part is where the examiner analyzes and

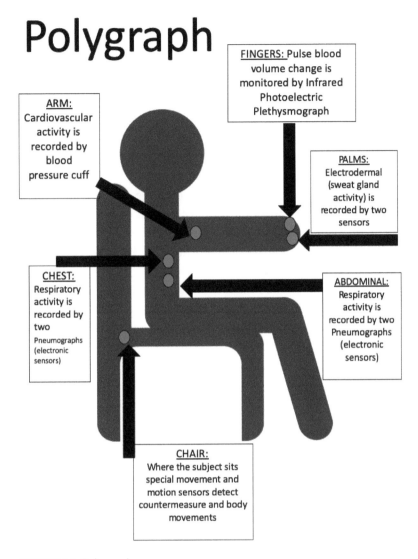

FIGURE 8-1 Polygraph.

interprets the digital polygraph charts and renders an opinion as to the truthfulness of the subject who took the examination (Central Polygraph Service, n.d.).

Each polygraph examination can be customized to the needs of the hiring agency. "Due to established laws, there is a strict limit of up to (4) pertinent test questions that may be established by the client for each polygraph examination (all other questions on the polygraph test are generic in nature and are established by the examiner for baseline purposes)" (Central Polygraph Service, n.d.).

The Employee Polygraph Protection Act of 1988 (EPPA)

The Employee Polygraph Protection Act of 1988 (EPPA) "prohibits most private employers from using polygraph testing to screen applicants for employment. It does not affect public employers such as police agencies or other governmental institutions" (American Polygraph Association, n.d.).

What Is a Voice Stress Analysis (VSA)?

Voice stress analysis (VSA), sometimes called the CVSA, computer voice stress analysis, is computer programs that are written and designed to measure how stress and deceptive responses change voices patterns. "VSA programs interpret changes in vocal patterns and indicate on a graph whether the subject is being deceptive or truthful" (Damphousse, 2008, p. 8). VSA are designed to "detect microtremors, which are caused by the stress of trying to conceal or deceive" (Damphousse, 2008, p. 8).

"The first scientific experiment on the road to development of CVSA was conducted in 1971 by Olaf Lippold, who discovered the muscle micro-tremor" (NITV, 2017). During the experiment, the subjects had involuntary vibrations of their arm muscles when relaxed; however, once the subject was stressed, the vibrations disappeared. VSA applies the same technology to detect micro tremors in the muscles of a subject's throat and larynx when the subject speaks but disappears when the subject experiences stress (NITV, 2017). "In 2002, over 1,300 state and local law enforcement agencies were using CVSA" (NITV, 2017).

VSA touts the polygraph examination as a more relaxed atmosphere since the subject is not hooked up to all the specialized equipment. For a VSA the subject simply wears a small microphone that is clipped to their clothing. The results can also easily be read by anyone, including the subject taking the VSA. To be certified as a VSA examiner, the person must first be employed by a law enforcement agency; then they must attend the standard VSA instruction process.

If I Am Honest Can I Fail a Lie Detector Test?

The polygraph and VSA do *not* measure truthfulness. Instead, both tests measure signs of physiological stress in the subject's body. Most candidates who take a lie detector test are terrified of the test. Whether it is ignorance of what the test is, being hooked up to all those cords, or having something in their past that they are worried about, there are numerous reasons a candidate could be stressed out. The simplest of questions could cause the best candidate to be anxious, and thereby the stress could cause the results to show as deceptive.

The information gained from the lie detector test should be seen as a tool of investigation that gives the hiring agency more information about the candidate. This information can then be used to investigate the candidate further. However, some agencies utilize the lie detector as a pass and fail test only and drop candidates because of the results of the lie detector test. Unfortunately, this policy creates a system that could be denying qualified candidates.

Example Questions Asked

The polygraph examination will ask relevant-irrelevant questions and comparison/control questions. An examiner will compare a subject's response to relevant-irrelevant questions. "A relevant question is one that deals with the real issue of concern to the investigation. An irrelevant question is one designed to provoke no emotion e.g., 'Is today Friday?'" (National Research Council, 2003). Examiners expect to see a similar reaction to both types of questions to someone who is not deceptive, and a deceptive subject will have a stronger reaction to the relevant questions.

Comparison or control questions compare responses to relevant questions. "The expectation is that innocent examinees will react more strongly to the comparison questions, and guilty examinees will react more strongly to the relevant questions" (National Research Council, 2003). The reason being is that the control question is designed to cause the subject to be concerned about their past truthfulness.

Questions asked during a lie detector test will generally cover theft from previous employers, falsification of information on job applications, criminal activities, and use of illegal drugs. There should be no trick questions; therefore, the candidate can review their background packet questions and answers to prepare for the types of questions that will be asked during the examination. According to Central Polygraph Service (n.d.), the following questions are sample polygraph pertinent test questions:

- "Have you used any type of illegal drug since (DATE)?"
- "Have you ever stolen anything from any place you have worked at?"
- "Have you ever committed a serious undetected crime?"
- "Have you ever sold or transferred any type of illegal drug?"
- "Have you ever engaged in domestic violence?"
- "Have you ever been a member of a street gang or terrorist organization?

Basic relevant-irrelevant questions and comparison/control questions include the following:

- "Is your name _____?"
- "Are you going to answer my questions truthfully today?"
- "Are you sitting down now?"
- "Is the year _____?"
- "Is the month _____?"

The following questions may also be seen on a lie detector test:

- "Have you stolen more than two hundred dollars in property or cash from a current or past employer?"
- "Would you ever steal cash or property from an employer?"
- "Would you ever lie to someone in a position of authority?"
- "Would you ever withhold information regarding your illegal drug use?"
- "Would you ever commit a serious crime and not disclose it?"
- "Would you ever physically harm someone during a domestic dispute?"
- "Would you ever commit a serious act against another person because of your personal bias?"
- "Would you ever deceive a family member?"
- "Would you ever not pay for an item of credit?"
- "Have you ever betrayed someone who trusted you?"
- "Have you ever lied to someone who trusted you?"
- "Have you ever filled out an official document with any false information?"
- "Have you ever done something that made you question your integrity?"
- "Have you ever cheated on a test?"

How to Prepare for the Lie Detector Test

Knowing what to expect during the polygraph examination or VSA will help the candidate have confidence in their answers during the actual examination. One goal should be to eliminate the physiological changes that occur when nerves set in. These physiological changes could cause a false failure on the lie detector test. There are a number of ways to prepare for the lie detector test to ensure to be as relaxed as possible about the examination. The first is to review the background investigation chapter in this textbook, fill out the example background packet, and be aware of any issues in the candidate's background that may be of concern. If a candidate is concerned something in their background is going to keep them from being employed in law enforcement, and the background qualifications are not publicly listed for the hiring agency, the candidate has several options. If the candidate is in college, and there is a professor with experience in law enforcement, the candidate could ask for a meeting with their professor and ask about the issues that are causing concern. The candidate could also call the hiring agency and ask to speak to someone in recruitment or someone who conducts the background investigations. The candidate should be honest and ask the employee at the hiring agency about the concerning background issues. Talking about issues in a candidate's background can be uncomfortable and embarrassing; however, it is better to find out now if the background issues will cause the candidate not to be hired or if they are nothing to worry about. Just think how more relaxed the candidate will be knowing that the issues in their background would not stop them from being hired as a police officer. Their responses during the lie detector test would be completely different and more relaxed. However, if the candidate is concerned about issues in their background and does not find out if they will be detrimental, their answers could be wrought with fear and stress, causing physiological changes and even a false failure.

Candidates can also prepare by knowing how to act before, during, and after the lie detector test. The following list illustrates some examples of what to focus on:

- Be on time
- Make a good first impression by dressing to impress
- Make good eye contact
- Make introductions by shaking hands
- Thank the examiner

While candidates cannot guarantee to fly through the lie detector examination, they can ensure it is a much quieter ride. By reading this chapter and following the advice given, candidates can know what to expect and how to mitigate the outcome.

SUMMARY OF CHAPTER 8

1. Candidates should understand what a lie detector test is and what the more appropriate name for the test is.

2. Candidates should understand and recognize the polygraph examination diagnostic instrument.

3. Candidates should know the difference between a polygraph examination and a voice stress analysis.

4. Candidates should understand how an honest person can fail a lie detector test.

5. Candidates should know how to prepare for the lie detector test.

DISCUSSION QUESTIONS

1. What are the parts of a polygraph examination diagnostic instrument?

2. How is a voice stress analysis conducted?

3. What are example questions asked during a lie detector test?

4. How does a candidate prepare for a lie detector test?

INTERNET EXERCISE

1. Go to YouTube

2. Enter the following search phrase: "What is a polygraph examination?"

3. Review the different videos.

4. Now enter the following search phrase: "What is a voice stress analysis?"

5. Review the different videos.

See Active Learning for the Following:

- Practice quizzes
- eFlashcards
- Video links
- Cognella journal articles
- News clips

References

American Polygraph Association. (n.d.). *Frequently asked questions.* https://www.polygraph.org/polygraph-frequently-asked-questions

American Psychological Association. (2004, August 5). *The truth about lie detectors (aka polygraph tests).* https://www.apa.org/research/action/polygraph

Bernstein, M. (2007, January 28). *Oregon police chiefs seek to overturn polygraph ban.* https://antipolygraph.org/blog/2007/01/28/oregon-police-chiefs-seek-to-overturn-polygraph-ban/

Central Polygraph Service. (n.d.). *How the polygraph works.* https://centralpolygraph.com/how-polygraph-works/

Damphousse, K. R. (2008, March 17). *Voice stress analysis: Only 15 percent of lies about drug use detected in field test*. National Institute of Justice. https://www.nij.gov/journals/259/pages/voice-stress-analysis.aspx

National Research Council. (2003). Appendix A. In *The Polygraph and Lie Detection*. National Academies Press. https://www.nap.edu/read/10420/chapter/12

NITV. (2017, July 13). What are the benefits of voice stress analysis for law enforcement? https://www.cvsa1.com/research-and-scientific-studies/what-are-the-benefits-of-voice-stress-analysis-for-law-enforcement/

Roufa, T. (2019, February 07). *Don't be nervous about taking a lie detector test*. https://www.thebalancecareers.com/polygraph-testing-criminal-justice-careers-974871

Image Credits

What Is the Psychological Evaluation?

"One of the truest signs of strength is accepting one's own weaknesses."

—Tadahiko Nagao

KEY TERMS

Three- or five-category rating system: A rating system utilized by psychologists to rate candidates after the psychological evaluation (psych eval) has been completed and evaluated.

Clinical interview: The psychologist administering the psych eval conducts a sit-down interview with the candidate to go over the self-reported history statement and any mental health treatment records reviewed during the interview.

MMPI-2: A screening instrument for certain high-risk professions that has approximately 567 questions and takes approximately 60 to 90 minutes to complete.

MMPI-2-RF PCIR: A screening instrument developed in 2008 specifically for those candidates in law enforcement because it provides a more interpretive report and is directly related to the essential duties of a police officer. It has 338 true-false questions and takes approximately 35 to 50 minutes to complete.

Personal history questionnaire: The part of the psych eval where the psychologist discusses the candidate with the background investigator in order to review the information garnered during the background investigation. This information can be utilized to help explain any concerns identified during the MMPI-2-RF written evaluation or clinical interview.

Post-conditional offer of employment: An employer tells the candidate, essentially, that the they have passed every part of the hiring process and depending on the results of the psych eval and medical examination, the candidate could be hired.

Three parts of the psych eval: An assessment tool such as the MMPI-2 or MMPI-2-RF, a clinical interview (including a self-reported history statement and any mental health treatment records), and finally the personal history (background) information provided by the hiring agency.

CHAPTER LEARNING OBJECTIVES

After reading the chapter, you should have a good understanding of the following:

- The psychological evaluation (psych eval)
- When a post-conditional job offer is required
- Why a psych eval is not a pass/fail type of assessment tool
- The different rating categories a psychologist can give a candidate
- Why psych evals are necessary
- What a candidate can expect during a psych eval
- Why there are so many unfamiliar questions on the written test portion of the psych eval
- How a candidate can get a copy of the results of their psych eval
- How a candidate can prepare for the psych eval

What Is the Psychological Evaluation?

Psychological evaluations have not always been a part of the process in the pre-employment selection process. In a study conducted by Oglesby in 1957, only 16% of the police agencies surveyed used any psychological screening of police candidates (Bartol, 1996). In 1967, the President's Commission on Law Enforcement and Administration of Justice recommended that all police candidates go through psychological screening. Then, in 1973, the National Advisory Commission on Criminal Justice Standards and Goals recommended the same. In 1980 and 1982 two court decisions held police agencies civilly liable for damages that arose from the failure to ensure psychological suitability of their officers (*Bonsignore v. City of New York*, 1982; *Hild v. Bruner*, 1980). After nearly 2 decades of recommendations, law enforcement agencies needed to recognize the need for psychological evaluations in the hiring process. So finally, in 2010, the Bureau of Justice Statistics reported that 98% of law enforcement agencies required a psychological evaluation as a part of the hiring process for police candidates (Corey & Ben-Porath, 2014). One organization in Atlanta, Overnight Transportation, saw the dramatic difference personality testing had on their hiring process. The extra test reduced on-the-job delinquency by 50–100% (Emmett, 2004).

Personality encompasses a person's feelings, ideas, behaviors, and thoughts and is unique to each person in diverse situations. Personality traits are very complicated to understand. To complicate matters more, it gets even trickier when professionals try to predict future behavior from personality traits. For example, if a person has an outgoing personality and seeks the approval of friends, does this mean that in their work environment they will display the same traits? The answer is yes and no. Confusing isn't it? During any employment, there are inevitable stringed expectations. These expectations can cause core personality traits to appear skewed. They can cause the sanest to alter their unique personality traits.

Candidates have always complained in frustration about how the psychological evaluation is a black hole of the unknown. Some have even expressed that the test must be flawed or just plain ineffective. Others who have tested for different employers have taken several psychological evaluations. Frustration inevitably sets in when one evaluation with one employer shows success whereas the evaluation with a different employer shows conflicting results. The following information in this chapter will help with the understanding of the psychological evaluation and how it works. The blindfolds will be taken off and the secrets will be revealed on how and why the psychological evaluation, or psych eval, is conducted.

A look back at the late 20th-century, job market mirrored what is occurring today. Back then the applicant had to be at the top of their game to succeed. No rock hiding clues on how to score higher could be left unturned. Jobs in areas such as the civil service field, police, corrections, firefighters, federal agents, and many other corporate and professional arenas were rare to find. It was not uncommon to meet a candidate who had been testing for such positions for 2, 3, even 4 years before being offered a job.

In the economic boom of the early 21st century, employers were hiring like never before. Thanks to the thriving housing market, cities saw the taxes roll in, allowing budgets to bulge, tearing the doors wide open for expansion, which, in the end, equaled hiring additional employees. Where jobs had once been scarce, they suddenly started flowing vigorously like a rampaging river. Unfortunately, some employers forgot to place due importance in the psychological evaluation. In the beginning it was almost effortless to hire those candidates who were at the top of the testing pool; however, soon after employers quickly realized the conundrum: a situation created by the economic boom and felt by every law enforcement agency around the country. For the first time in decades, employers found themselves having to search out qualified candidates actively. Candidate pools became depleted, and employers were forced to create new divisions whose sole purpose was to locate interested candidates. Employers found themselves actively searching for candidates and offering signing bonuses and attractive benefits packages, all in an attempt to hire the available candidate before the competing employer gave a more attractive offer. During this period, if the available candidate had a pulse, they could almost guarantee themselves a position of their choice because employers were more interested in hiring warm bodies to meet required numbers rather than ensuring that warm body could pass the psychological evaluation. A decade later employers would regret these relaxed and careless hiring practices. The inevitable occurred, and employers began picking candidates from the bottom of the barrel instead of from the crème at the top. In essence, all the top qualified applicants were immediately hired, leaving only the candidates with undesirable traits in the barrel. Instead of leaving those candidates and waiting for more viable candidates to emerge, as many psychologists recommended, employers decided to roll the dice, playing an almost Russian roulette–type game, taking a chance on the so-so candidate, with who knows what psychological issues hid away. Departments would soon learn that these candidates they hired who had possible personality issues had engaged in excessive use of force, conduct unbecoming an officer, or other behavior causing harm to the public and the department.

Psychological testing has been utilized as a testing tool by employers for 90 years and has grown dramatically during the last several decades. Computers, the Internet, and decades of testing and comparative analysis have given psychologists a faster, more streamlined avenue to predict highly desirable candidates as well as the ability to identify those candidates who display negative attributes. The future for psychological testing is bright thanks to all the technological advances and employers looking for every possible way to predict future behavior. These demands from employers to find the perfect employee have brought psychological testing to a new level as well. A playing field where employers can screen candidates, filtering through the square pegs trying to fit in the round holes, and invariably homing in on the top pegs with the perfect fit, albeit not flawless. Employers hate surprises, and psychological testing can reduce the surprises an employee can give them. All of these reasons have brought employers to not only look at psychological testing but to run to the nearest licensed psychologist to begin the process.

Is It Legal for an Employer to Require Me to Take a Psych Eval?

Great question! A psych eval is pretty invasive. The purpose of such an evaluation is to look for information about a candidate's mental health; therefore, it would appear to be a violation of privacy covered under the Americans With Disabilities Act. Wouldn't it? Well, the answer is yes and no. No, an employer cannot require anyone to take a psych eval and deny employment due to the results; however, there are situations in which it is legal to require such an evaluation.

The ADA statute has procedural requirements that do apply to all job candidates (*Buchanan v. City of San Antonio*, 1996; *Leonel v. American Airlines*, 2005). The statute allows an employer to require a candidate to submit to a medical exam or related testing only when

1. obtaining and analyzing non-medical information;
2. the candidate accepts a post-conditional offer of employment, dependent on the results of the examination; and
3. all candidates are required to take the same examination.

The psych eval is generally one of the last parts of the hiring process not only because it is costly to hire a psychologist to conduct the evaluation, but because of #2. The ADA requires an employer to make a post-conditional offer of employment to the candidate before requiring the candidate to submit to the psych eval. A **post-conditional offer of employment** is when an employer tells the candidate that they have passed every part of the hiring process up to this part and can be offered the job, depending on the results of the psych eval and medical examination (see Fact Box 9.1).

FACT BOX 9.1: POST-CONDITIONAL JOB OFFER

When a candidate is required to take a psych eval as a part of the hiring process, the candidate will be required to sign what is called a post-conditional job offer. The following illustrates what a candidate would be required to sign:

> I understand that I am participating in a psychological evaluation as a one part of the selection process for this position. I am aware that the purpose of this evaluation is to provide information to the department about my psychological status and suitability for working in a position for which I am applying. I understand that this assessment is not intended as counseling nor is it to obtain information for my use. I further understand that since the agency is the client of (psychologist information), all data and the report resulting from this evaluation belongs to the department. Accordingly, in consideration of professional services rendered, I waive any right I may have to know test results, interpretations made, and access to the original data from which final judgments have been made.

Signature of candidate _____   Date _____

Why Are Psych Evals Necessary?

Psych evals have gone through numerous revisions in trying to ascertain the best possible way to test one's personality. The evals are very good at predicting general trends and general behavior and are incredibly accurate. What the evals have not perfected is the ability to predict future actions. Instead, the predictions made by the psychologist administering the test are brought up through possible concerns or suspicions by what the testing results uncover.

There is a need for psych evals. The evals are not a complete answer for employers in finding the perfect candidate; however, they are a potent tool for employers to utilize in finding the most viable candidate for the job. What candidates must understand is that even though they may not get one job because of the results of their psych eval, they may get another job in a completely different field because of the results of their psych eval. It is all about personality traits and what the employer is looking for in the open position they are trying to fill.

Psych evals have been utilized as an evaluation tool by employers for 90 years, and the field has grown dramatically during the last several decades. Computers, the Internet, and decades of testing, along with comparative analysis, have given psychologists a faster, more streamlined avenue to predict highly desirable candidates as well as those candidates who display negative attributes. The future for the psych eval is bright, thanks to all the technological advances and employers looking for every possible way to predict future behavior. Various demands from employers to find the perfect employee have brought the psych eval process to a new level.

POLICE STORY 9.1 **Ignored the Warning Signs**

by Retired Lieutenant Tiffany L. Morey

After passing the written test, the physical fitness test, and the medical test, Candidate Smith arrived to take the psych eval for a local police department testing for entry-level police officers. When the psychologist reviewed the results of the test, he found that Candidate Smith displayed several potential risk factors (Category 2). The psychologist notified the hiring department of the concerns. The department decided to ignore the psychologist's concerns and hired Candidate Smith despite the potential risk factors. The department was between a rock and a hard place because they needed to hire a predetermined number of new police officers to cover new housing divisions and business districts. Candidate Smith passed the police academy and field training without any real problems; however, during the entire training process, he was closely supervised by department officers. The problems did begin to creep up once Candidate Smith was a solo officer out on the street alone, without any safeguards in place. Supervisors began receiving complaints about Candidate Smith. A commonality was found after reviewing three complaints that occurred one right after another: violence. Candidate Smith was a ticking bomb not needing much of a reason to be set off. Since Candidate Smith had not done anything too egregious up to this point, a supervisor recommended an employee development plan to assist Candidate Smith. This same supervisor found that two of the complaints against him were sustained (did occur). Then, one night soon after, Candidate Smith was dispatched to a large business about a drunk subject. What Candidate Smith did not realize was that he was video recorded by the business's security cameras. Candidate Smith began interviewing the drunk subject. When the subject did not respond precisely how Candidate Smith wanted him to, Candidate Smith proceeded to berate, curse, and throw the handcuffed subject face down to the ground. If the event had not been recorded, Candidate Smith would have undoubtedly denied the force, and it would have been the word of the drunk subject against Candidate Smith. The aftermath was that Candidate Smith was terminated—a very costly mistake for an innocent subject and the department that hired him against the potential risk factors discovered by the psychologist.

What Is on the Psych Eval?

There are **three parts of the psych eval**:

1. An assessment tool such as the MMPI-2-RF (written test)
2. A clinical interview (including a self-reported history statement and any mental health treatment records)
3. A personal history (background) provided by the hiring agency

Psych evals are generally looking to assess the following general personality traits:

- Problem-solving ability
- Intellectual ability
- Inter/intrapersonal ability
- Emotional maturity
- Depression susceptibility
- Decision-making skills
- Obsessions
- Impulse control
- Organizational skills
- Coping mechanisms
- Anger trigger points
- Social deviations
- Leadership ability
- Future aspirations
- Anger control
- Anxiety issues
- Susceptibility to stress

Psych evals are also tuned to be unique for the position the employer is looking to fill. The evaluation can be tailor fit to identify specific personality traits or characteristics. Most employers employ a two-part psych eval. The first portion of the eval is a written test, and the second portion is the oral interview with the psychologist administering the eval.

The Written Test: Why Are There So Many Unfamiliar Questions?

The questions on the written test portion of the psych eval may seem unfamiliar, but they are quantifiable in that they ascertain the most accurate answer. The test that was most often utilized for pre-employment testing was the Minnesota Multiphasic Personality Inventory (MMPI-2). The MMPI was developed in the 1930s by psychologist S. Hathaway and psychiatrist J.C. McKinley at the University of Minnesota. It has the title of being the most researched written psychological test in existence (Drayton, 2009).

The **MMPI-2** was often used as a screening instrument for certain high-risk professions and has approximately 567 questions on it and takes approximately 60 to 90 minutes to complete (Drayton, 2009). The questions have been described by those taking it as unfamiliar and repetitive. Because of the weirdness of the questions, those taking the test often wonder how one can interpret the results; however, there is some pretty fantastic sense to be made from all those questions. The sense comes from the 10 scales of the MMPI-2 and the validity scales of the MMPI-2, which a psychologist utilizes to interpret the results. After a candidate takes the MMPI-2 written test, a graph is produced, which contains information about the results and how they appear on the 10 scales and validity scales. These two scales are the two main ways a psychologist deciphers the results of the test. The 10 scales and the validity scales of the MMPI-2 help the psychologist determine the distinct personality traits of the candidate taking the test. Fact Boxes 9.2 and 9.3 illustrate the 10 scales and the validity scales of the MMPI-2.

FACT BOX 9.2: THE 10 SCALES OF THE MMPI-2

Scale 1 (Hs)—Hypochondriasis: Concern over physical well being

Scale 2 (D)—Depression: To identify depression

Scale 3 (Hy)—Hysteria: Stressful situations

Scale 4 (Pd)—Psychopathic deviate: Social deviation

Scale 5 (Mf)—Masculinity/femininity: Intelligence, socioeconomic status, and education

Scale 6 (Pa)—Paranoia: Rigid attitudes, self-concepts, and sensitivity

Scale 7 (Pt)—Psychasthenia: Obsessions, compulsions, doubts, and fears

Scale 8 (Sc)—Schizophrenia: Self-worth, self-identity, impulse control, and perceptions

Scale 9 (Ma)—Hypomania: Elevated mood, irritability, and speech

Scale 10 (Si)—Social introversion: Social contacts and responsibilities (Framingham, 2018)

FACT BOX 9.3: THE VALIDITY SCALES OF THE MMPI-2

The L scale: This is better known (and has a dubious reputation) as the lie scale, where candidates try to make themselves look better than they are.

The F scale: Referred to as faking good/bad, where candidates are trying to appear better or worse than they are.

The K scale: Referred to as defensiveness scale, where candidates try to present themselves in the best possible light.

The ? scale: Referred to as cannot say scale, where candidates leave many questions unanswered.

TRIN scale: The true response inconsistency scale, where candidates respond inconsistently.

VRIN scale: The variable response inconsistency scale, another way to detect inconsistent responses by candidates.

The Fb scale: A scale to detect if a candidate is still paying attention.

The Fp scale: Detects intentional overreporting.

The FBS scale: Symptom validity scale to establish the credibility of the test takers to determine personal injury or disability.

The S scale: Superlative self-presentation scale to look for underreporting and assess belief in human goodness (Cherry, 2020).

The validity scales represent the most critical reason candidates should respond openly and honestly to the questions. These validity scales give the psychologist an excellent basis for identifying if a candidate is trying to look psychologically healthier than they may indeed be.

One significant change to the MMPI-2 written test portion of the psych eval was regarding gender differences. The MMPI-2 specifically looked at differences by using gender-specific comparison groups and applying separate validations for men and women (Mason et al., 2017). Due to these notable exceptions, the MMPI-2-RF is now the most accepted psychological evaluation tool used in the law enforcement hiring process. The MMPI-2-RF utilizes non-gendered norms that were developed to be used in clinical decision making (Mason et al., 2017). These non-gendered norms meet civil service guidelines.

What Is the MMPI-2 RF?

The most widely accepted and researched clinical assessment tool used to be the MMPI-2; however, the MMPI-2 utilized gender-specific questions, and most psychologists no longer utilize it due to civil service guidelines. In 2008, police psychologist David M. Corey and expert Yossef S. Ben-Porath developed the Minnesota Multiphasic Personality Inventory-2 restructured form (MMPI-2-RF), police candidate interpretive report (PCIR). The **MMPI-2-RF PCIR** was explicitly developed for high-risk professions in law enforcement, utilizes non-gendered norms, has 338 true-false questions, and takes approximately 35–50 minutes to complete (Cherry, 2020).

The MMPI-2-RF PCIR assists psychologists in identifying high-risk candidates through evidence-based and legally defensible ways. Since the development of the MMPI-2-RF, many psychologists now utilize this new assessment tool for psych evals because it provides a more interpretive report and is directly related to the essential duties of a police officer.

- Compares the results to 2,276 men and women (1,138 of each gender between the ages of 18 and 80 and are non-gendered)
- Offers transparency through peer-reviewed research
- Provides guidance (Pearson, n.d.)

The MMPI-2-RF also identifies possible issues in the 10 job-relevant areas, which most police officers experience:

1. Emotions and stress
2. Task performance
3. Decision making and judgment
4. Acceptance of feedback
5. Assertiveness
6. Teamwork and social competence
7. Integrity

8. Dependability and conscientiousness
9. Drug use
10. Impulse control (Pearson, n.d.)

"The basic model for pre-employment psychological evaluations of police officer candidates consists of the administration of two broadband personality measures, one assessing abnormal behavior and functioning and the other assessing normal personality, followed by a clinical interview and consideration of personal history information" (Corey & Ben-Porath, 2014). Title I of the Americans With Disabilities Act of 1990 restricts an employer as to the types of inquiries that can be made during a hiring process. This model follows state and federal regulations for the hiring of police officers.

FACT BOX 9.4: THE MMPI-2-RF SCALES

According to Corey and Ben-Porath (2014), the following scales are utilized for the MMPI-2-RF:

Higher-order (H-O) scales:
  EID: Problems with mood/affect
  THD: Problems with thinking
  BXD: Problems with behavior

Restructured clinical (RC) scales:
  RCd: Unhappiness
  RC1: Physical health issues
  RC2: Low positive emotional response
  RC3: Low opinions of others
  RC4: Irresponsible behavior
  RC6: Concerns with others
  RC7: Anger and irritability
  RC8: Unusual thoughts
  RC9: Aggression and impulsion

Specific problems (SP) scales:
  MLS: Poor health
  GIC: Stomach issues
  HPC: Head/neck issues
  NUC: Dizziness/loss of balance
  COG: Memory issues

Internalizing scales:
  SUI: Suicide attempts
  HLP: Helplessness/issues solving problems
  SFD: Lack of confidence
  NFC: Indecisive

STW: Stress and worry
AXY: Anxiety
ANG: Anger issues
BRF: Unreasonable fears

Externalizing scales:
  JCP: Juvenile issues
  SUB: Substance abuse
  AGG: Physical aggression
  ACT: Overly excited

Interpersonal scales:
  FML: Family issues
  IPP: Submissive
  SAV: Social avoidance
  SHY: Shy and bashful
  DSF: Dislike being around people

Interest scales:
  AES: Aesthetic interests
  MEC: Mechanical interests

Personality psychopathology five (PSY-5) scales:
  AGGR-r: Aggressiveness
  PSYC-R: Psychoticism, disconnection from reality
  DISC-r: Under-controlled behavior
  NEGE-r: Negative emotion/anxiety/insecurity/fear
  INTR-r: Introversion/social disengagement

Candidates must realize is that there is no way to cheat the MMPI-2-RF. The validity scales are the precautions for such a cheating response. The candidate gives either a yes or no answer to each question asked. Candidates should not want to waste time trying to cheat the psych eval because all that will happen is that the results will show cheating and result in a negative evaluation. Instead, the candidate must learn to prepare for the MMPI-2-RF. Candidates should trust in the MMPI-2-RF and their personalities. If a candidate has desirable personality traits for the position applied for, then the results of the MMPI-2-RF will be positive. If the candidate does not have the personality traits deemed necessary, then the candidate should be thankful they have not wasted more time and should instead choose a better more fitting career.

What Questions Are on the Written Test?

All too often candidates have described the questions on the MMPI-2 and MMPI-2-RF as unfamiliar and mind-boggling. Unlike the entry written test taken in the law enforcement hiring process, which covers reading, vocabulary, memory, spelling, and so forth, this psych eval written test is different. Questions such as, "Find the sentence that is grammatically correct," will not be found. Instead, questions like, "I like crafty magazines," and "I can hear birds chirp," are asked. Answers are not as clear, and the candidate is confused as to the best answer. Candidates should not answer these questions the same way as the law enforcement written test, which asks questions on judgment, decision, memory, and vocabulary. The candidate should instead focus on being honest. Read each question and immediately come up with a response. For example, for a question that asks, "I would like to be a mechanic," if the candidate would like to be a mechanic then answer appropriately.

What Other Written Tests Are Utilized?

The MMPI-2-RF is the most utilized psychological inventory test by psychologists conducting the psych eval process as a part of the law enforcement hiring process. There are other tests on the market that psychologists can also utilize. The Personality Assessment Inventory (PAI), the Millon Clinical Multiaxial Inventory-III (MCMI-III), and the 16 PF (as covered in Chapter 2) are also utilized. These test instruments aid psychologists in identifying specific traits in behavior, attitude, beliefs, and suitability as a candidate. It is up to the individual psychologist to determine which psychological inventory test to utilize. All candidates are as different as fingerprints, so psychologists must utilize many tools to identify individual personality traits.

The Clinical Interview: What Types of Questions Are Asked?

The clinical interview is an essential component of the psych eval. The first portion of the psych eval is the written test. After the written, a sit-down oral clinical interview with the psychologist administering the test is given. During the **clinical interview**, the candidate will provide a self-reported history statement and any mental health treatment records. Valuable information is gained during this one-on-one clinical interview. During this clinical interview the candidate should try to relax and engage in conversation with the psychologist, because this period is a learning process for all involved. It is normal to be nervous; however, if the candidate is overly nervous, this can present negative signs to the psychologist.

The more the candidate prepares for this clinical interview, the more relaxed the interview will be, which in turn will allow the psychologist to see the real person behind the candidate on paper. The interview is critical and should be taken seriously. The psychologist may spend up to 60 minutes asking various questions about childhood experiences, background, school, and work history.

Candidates should be prepared for such questions, try to relax, not look at the time, and see this as an opportunity to show the psychologist a positive personality. However, be careful and do not try too hard to be someone else; it will inevitably come back to bite the candidate in the final evaluation process.

What Is the Personal History Questionnaire (Background Information)?

During the **personal history questionnaire** (statement) part of the psych eval, the psychologist discusses the candidate with the background investigator in order to review the information garnered during the background investigation. This information can be utilized to help explain any concerns identified during the MMPI-2-RF written evaluation or clinical interview. It is not only essential but a necessary part of the psych eval process. A person's personality is unique and complex, and an assessment tool, such as the MMPI-2-RF, can only delve so deep into a person's complexities. The personal history statement and the background investigation paints a complete picture when compiled with the assessment tool. Only after a thorough review is conducted, looking at all the evidence, can a recommendation be made. Surprisingly enough, it is not unlike an investigation that a police department completes during a criminal investigation. The psychologist will utilize every tool in order to get an honest, accurate account of the focus of the investigation. See Documents 9.1–9.3, for examples of personal history questionnaires that candidates are required to completed (Personal interview, Donald J. Johnson).

PUBLIC SAFETY POST-JOB OFFER RISK FACTOR QUESTIONNAIRE
PUBLIC SAFETY AGENCY: _____

Applicant Name:_____ Birth Date:_____ Age:_____
SS No.: XXX-XX-_____ Testing Date:_____ Interview Date:_____ Date of Report:_____
Background Investigator: _____ Position Applied For:_____

1. **Service Orientation:**
   Describe the reasons you want to eagerly serve, assist or help the public in a responsive, compassionate, respectful and enthusiastic manner by working in a career-oriented public safety position.

   _____
   _____
   _____
   _____
   _____

2. **Integrity/Ethics:**
   Name the ways you demonstrate and maintain high standards of ethical personal conduct, including attributes such as honesty, good character, integrity, impartiality and trustworthiness in following outlined laws, rules, regulations, and procedures as well as being able to interact with others without prejudicial attitudes regarding gender, sexual orientation, race, religion, national origin, disability, or social status.

   _____
   _____
   _____
   _____
   _____

DOCUMENT 9.1 Public safety post-conditional job offer questionnaire.

3. **Teamwork:**
   Give examples of what you do to establish and maintain effective, cooperative working relationships with coworkers to achieve organizational goals as well as subordinate personal interests for the good of the working group/agency.

   _____
   _____
   _____
   _____
   _____

4. **Conflict Resolution:**
   Detail what you do to communicate in a tactful and respectful manner, treat others with impartiality and identify and reduce interpersonal conflict in ways that show sensitivity to the feelings of others as well as establishing and maintaining rapport.

   _____
   _____
   _____
   _____
   _____

5. **Attention to Safety/Impulse Control:**
   Describe what you do to react appropriately, safely and decisively in a verbally confrontational or threatening situation that may involve high risk for sustaining physical harm while avoiding impulsive and/or unnecessarily risky behaviors.

   _____
   _____
   _____
   _____
   _____

6. **Decision Making & Judgement:**
   Describe the process you use to think, reason, problem solve and consider the consequences of your behavior in making judgments and decisions in a logical and rational fashion instead of impulsively doing the first thing that comes to mind.

   _____
   _____
   _____
   _____
   _____

7. **Flexibility/Adaptability:**
   Describe what you do to change your focus and adjust to the many different, sudden and sometimes competing demands inherent in your work and life activities. Discuss how you adjust to planned and unplanned work changes, the process you use to prioritize and effectively focus on several very different tasks/projects at the same time when required to work in unstructured situations with minimal supervision and/or differing supervisory styles.

   _____
   _____
   _____
   _____
   _____

DOCUMENT 9.1 _Continued._

8. **Conscientious/Dependability:**
Identify the ways you are able to be relied and depended on by members of your work group. Include in your answer how you are able to persevere in the face of long hours and other adverse working conditions, carefully attending to details like typos, missing or incorrect information, maintaining a punctual and reliable attendance record, being accountable for your work and analyzing and correcting prior mistakes or problems to improve performance.

_____
_____
_____
_____
_____

9. **Assertiveness/Persuasiveness:**
Describe the ways you are not intimidated and are able, without hesitation, to take control of situations in a calm and appropriately assertive manner, even under adverse or dangerous conditions, to communicate ideas and persuade others to adopt a desired course of action.

_____
_____
_____
_____
_____

10. **Emotional Regulation/Stress Tolerance:**
Describe how you are able to be composed, rational and in control particularly during time-critical and other stressful situations, maintain a positive self image under such adverse circumstances, accept personal limitations and mistakes all the while keeping an even-tempered composure and demeanor, exercising restraint and not over-reacting in emotionally-charged situations.

_____
_____
_____
_____
_____

DOCUMENT 9.1 _Continued._

PUBLIC SAFETY POST-JOB OFFER MENTAL HEALTH QUESTIONNAIRE
PUBLIC SAFETY AGENCY: _____

Name: _____   Today's Date: _____

Age: _____   Date of Birth: _____   Social Security Number:_____

DIRECTIONS: Answer the following questions honestly and completely. It does not matter if you make mistakes in spelling or grammar. Just try to express yourself as well as you can. IF THE QUESTION DOES NOT APPLY, LEAVE IT BLANK.

CURRENT MENTAL HEALTH ISSUES

1. Do you have current mental health issues? ☐ no ☐ yes. If yes, Describe the chief mental/emotional complaints or problems that currently bother you, like feelings of depression, anger, anxiety, auditory or visual hallucinations, etc., including symptoms: _____

_____
_____
_____

DOCUMENT 9.2 Public safety post-conditional job offer mental health questionnaire.

2. When did these problems start and how frequently do they occur?

STARTED: _____

_____

FREQUENCY: _____

_____

3. How do these problems interfere with you doing your daily life activities such as working, earning money, going to school, doing hobbies or recreating, engaging in love and social relationships with spouse, partner, family and friends, etc.? _____

_____

_____

4. What have you done to resolve or cope with these problems? _____

_____

_____

5. What more do you think needs to be done to resolve these problems? _____

_____

_____

6. Are you <u>currently</u> receiving mental health treatment? ☐ no ☐ yes. If yes, by whom? ☐ psychiatrist
☐ psychologist ☐ social worker ☐ MFT ☐ licensed professional counselor ☐ drug/alcohol abuse counselor
☐ clergy counseling ☐ other: _____
What is your diagnosis? _____
Where treated? _____ When? _____ How long? _____

<u>Past</u>: thoughts, intent, plan, means, attempt(s) to <u>injure yourself</u> (not suicide). ☐ no ☐ yes.
If yes, what: ☐ cutting ☐ deep body scratches drawing blood ☐ mutilating ☐ starving ☐ hair pulling
☐ head banging ☐ vomiting ☐ other:_____
Reason? _____
Started? _____ Stopped? _____ Where? _____
Treatment? ☐ no ☐ yes What? _____

History of Homicidal Violence

<u>Current</u>: thoughts, intent, plan, means, attempt(s) to <u>kill</u> someone? ☐ no ☐ yes.
If yes, who?_____
Reason? _____
Killed this person? ☐ no ☐ yes. If yes, what happened? _____

When? _____ Where? _____
<u>Past</u>: thoughts, intent, plan, means, attempt(s) to <u>kill</u> someone? ☐ no ☐ yes.
If yes, who?_____
Reason? _____
Killed this person? ☐ no ☐ yes. If yes, what happened? _____

When? _____ Where? _____

DOCUMENT 9.2 *Continued.*

History of Physical Violence/Assaulting Others

<u>Current</u>: thoughts, intent, plan, means, attempt(s) to <u>hurt</u> someone (exclude domestic violence)? ☐ no ☐ yes.

If yes, who?_____

Reason? _____

What did you do?_____

Started? _____ Stopped? _____ Where? _____

<u>Past</u>: thoughts, intent, plan, means, attempt(s) to <u>hurt</u> someone (exclude domestic violence)? ☐ no ☐ yes.

If yes, who?_____

Reason? _____

What did you do?_____

Started? _____ Stopped? _____ Where? _____

Child Abuse/Neglect/Abandonment

Did you ever abuse, neglect or abandon a child? ☐ no ☐ yes. If yes, describe: ☐ child physical abuse ☐ child sexual abuse ☐ child emotional abuse ☐ child neglect ☐ child abandonment

What happened: _____

Where did it happen: _____

When started: _____ When stopped: _____

How often did it happen: _____

Were you arrested/charged? ☐ no ☐ yes. If yes, what happened? Court action: ☐ jail ☐ probation ☐ prison ☐ dropped charges ☐ reduced charges other:_____

Spouse or Partner Violence

Did you physically abuse a spouse or domestic partner? ☐ no ☐ yes. If yes, answer the following:

What happened: _____

Where did it happen: _____

Who did it: _____ When started: _____ When stopped:_____

How often did it happen: _____

Who was arrested/charged: _____

Court action: ☐ jail ☐ probation ☐ prison ☐ dropped charges ☐ reduced charges

other:_____

Elder/Parent Abuse

Did you physically abuse an elder/parent? ☐ no ☐ yes. If yes, answer the following:

What happened: _____

Where did it happen: _____

Who did it: _____ When started: _____ When stopped:_____

How often did it happen: _____

Who was arrested/charged: _____

Court action: ☐ jail ☐ probation ☐ prison ☐ dropped charges ☐ reduced charges

other: _____

DOCUMENT 9.2 *Continued.*

Appetite Disturbance Disorder

Are you the proper weight for your height/body type? □ yes □ no. If no, are you: □ underweight □ overweight.

What do you currently weigh? _____ pounds. What is a healthy weight for you? _____ pounds.

Treatment for weight issues? □ No □ Yes. If yes, what type of treatment: _____

Started: _____ Ended: _____

Tobacco Use

Do you use tobacco products? □ No □ Yes. If yes, what : _____

Started: _____ How much: _____ How long: _____

Continued use: □ Yes □ No: When stopped: _____

Treatment: □ No □ Yes Describe: _____

Problematic Gambling

Do you have a problem with gambling and lose so much you cannot pay your bills? □ No □ Yes. If yes, describe:

_____

Type: _____

Age started: _____ How often: _____ How long: _____

Continued gambling: □ Yes □ No: When stopped:_____

Treatment: □ No □ Yes Describe: _____

GA: □ No □ Yes How long?: _____ Sponsor: □ No □ Yes How long?:_____

Alcohol/Use/Abuse

Use: □ no □ yes: □ current □ past Type used?_____

How much?_____ How often? _____ Age started? _____ Age stopped? _____

Treatment: □ no □ yes. Type?_____

How long?_____ Where?_____ When?_____

AA: □ no □ yes How long?_____ Sponsor? □ no □ yes: How long?_____

Relapsed? no □ yes How often?_____

Has use of alcohol caused problems in your life? □ No □ Yes. If yes, what problems? _____

_____

_____

Illegal Drugs/Inhalants

Use: □ no □ yes: □ current □ past Type used:_____

How much? _____ How often?_____ Age started? _____ Age stopped?_____

Treatment: □ no □ yes: Type?_____

How long?_____ Where?_____ When? _____

NA: □ no □ yes: How long?_____ Sponsor: □ no □ yes: How long?_____

Relapsed? no □ yes: How often?_____

Have you ever taken part in an illegal drug transaction (buying, selling, dealing, delivering, smuggling transportation)? □ No □ Yes. If yes, describe what happened: _____

_____

_____

DOCUMENT 9.2 *Continued.*

Has use of illegal drugs caused problems in your life? ☐ No ☐ Yes. If yes, what problems? _____

_____

_____

Prescription Medication Abuse

Prescription medication <u>abuse</u>? ☐ no ☐ yes. If yes: ☐ current ☐ past

Medication(s) abused: _____

How much? _____ How often? _____ Age started? _____ Age stopped? _____

Treatment: ☐ no ☐ yes: Type? _____

Where? _____ When? _____ How long? _____

Self-help group attendance? ☐ no ☐ yes. Type: _____ Time attended? _____

Relapsed? no ☐ yes How often? _____

Has abuse of prescription drugs caused problems in your life? ☐ No ☐ Yes. If yes, what problems? _____

_____

_____

_____

Sexual Addictions/Inappropriate Sexual Behavior

Describe the presence, if any, of a history of sexual addictions and/or inappropriate sexual behavior including use of internet porn, frequent use of the services of prostitutes or escorts, attendance at strip clubs, etc. _____

_____

_____

SPECIAL TOPICS

1. Sensitivity to Criticism/Rejection

Have you ever been concerned about, or do you worry about what other people are saying about you?

_____

How easily are your feelings hurt? _____

In what ways are you sensitive to criticism? _____

In what ways are you sensitive to being left out of things? _____

Everyone has experienced rejection. Describe how you responded to any rejection you may have experienced in the past: _____

_____

DOCUMENT 9.2 *Continued.*

2. Personal Behavior

Describe what you like about yourself (strengths): _____

_____

_____

_____

_____

Describe what you dislike about yourself (weaknesses): _____

_____

_____

_____

_____

Describe what particular behaviors you would like to change about yourself, such as:

- Do more of or start doing:_____

_____

_____

_____

- Do less of or quit doing: _____

_____

_____

_____

Give examples of the best things (successes/happiest times) that have happened to you: _____

_____

_____

_____

Outline the worst things (failures/regrets) that have happened to you: _____

_____

_____

_____

Describe your greatest fear or worry: _____

_____

_____

_____

What do you see as your biggest challenge in the years ahead? _____

_____

_____

_____

DOCUMENT 9.2 *Continued.*

Do you feel in control of your life or do you think other people and/or circumstances are controlling you?

_____

3. Anger/frustration Management

What kind of things really upset you? _____

_____

_____

What do you do to appropriately manage your anger and frustration? _____

_____

_____

How many times in the past have you slapped with an open hand, punched with your fist, pinched, grabbed or otherwise hurt someone else? _____

Describe what happened:_____

_____

_____

_____

4. Stress Coping

Explain what you do to cope physically and/or psychologically with stressful situations: _____

_____

_____

_____

_____

5. Life Goals or Ambitions

Describe your personal life goals or ambitions: _____

_____

_____

_____

_____

How do you think you have been doing so far in achieving your life goals? _____

_____

If you had to give yourself an overall rating on achieving your life goals on a scale of 1-10 where 1 = non-achievement, 5 = average achievement, and 10 = maximum achievement, what number would you use to rate yourself? _____

DOCUMENT 9.2 *Continued.*

PUBLIC SAFETY POST-JOB OFFER PSYCHOSOCIAL HISTORY QUESTIONNAIRE
PUBLIC SAFETY AGENCY: _____

DIRECTIONS
The purpose of this questionnaire is to obtain information about you that will help create an accurate description of your personal life. Therefore, answer the following questions as completely as you can. It does not matter if you make a mistake in spelling or grammar. Just try to express yourself as well as you can. IF THE QUESTION DOES NOT APPLY TO YOU, LEAVE IT BLANK.

GENERAL INFORMATION:

NAME: _____ DATE COMPLETED: _____

SOCIAL SECURITY NO.:LAST 4 DIGITS: _ _ _ _ AGE:____ Hand used for writing: ☐Left ☐Right ☐ Both

ETHNIC OR RACIAL BACKGROUND: ☐ Asian   ☐ Black/African-American   ☐ Hispanic

☐ Native American ☐ Native Hawaiian/Pacific Islander   ☐ White/Caucasian   SEX: ☐ Male ☐ Female

HEIGHT:____WEIGHT:_____ DESIRED WEIGHT:_____

HAIR COLOR: ☐ Auburn ☐ Black ☐ Blonde ☐ Brown ☐ Brunette ☐ Gray ☐ Red ☐ White

EYE COLOR: ☐ Black ☐ Blue ☐ Brown ☐ Gray ☐ Green ☐ Hazel

FAMILY OF BIRTH/ORIGIN
Birth Date/Birth Place
Date of Birth: _____ City/Country of Birth: _____

Where lived most of the time?_____ Time lived in Las Vegas: _____

Siblings
What number child, or your birth order, are you in your biological family?_____

How many brothers/sisters do you have?

Biological brother(s): _____   Half-brother(s): _____   Stepbrother(s): _____   Adopted brother(s): _____

Biological sister(s):_____   Half-sister(s): _____   Stepsister(s):_____   Adopted sister(s): _____

What was your past relationship with your brothers/sisters: _____

_____

What is current relationship with your brothers/sisters: _____

_____

Primary Parents
The **FATHER** who raised you or spent the most time with you: ☐ biological ☐ stepfather

☐ adoptive father ☐ grandfather ☐ uncle ☐ foster father ☐ other: _____

☐ Living ☐ Deceased. How did your father treat you while growing up? _____

_____

The **MOTHER** who raised you or spent the most time with you: ☐ biological ☐ stepmother ☐ adoptive mother

☐ grandmother ☐ aunt ☐ foster mother ☐ Other: _____

☐ Living ☐ Deceased. How did your mother treat you while growing up? _____

_____

_____

DOCUMENT 9.3 Public safety post-conditional job offer psychosocial history questionnaire.

Infancy, Childhood and Adolescence (birth to 18 years) History

Raised by both parents? ☐ yes ☐ no. If no, how old were you when your parents divorced or split up?_____

With whom did you live with most of the time while you were growing up? _____

At what age did you leave home and go out on your own? _____

Describe what is was like being a child in your family while growing up including any major problems you experienced during infancy, childhood or adolescence such as physical, sexual or emotional abuse, neglect, abandonment, etc., and by whom? _____

_____

_____

_____

_____

Rate your overall satisfaction with your home life while growing up:

☐ excellent ☐ above average ☐ average ☐ below average ☐ unsatisfactory

Family Relationship Issues

In the past, how did you get along with your family? ☐ close ☐ pleasant ☐ distant ☐ unhappy ☐ no relationship

☐ other: _____

How do you get along with your family now? ☐ close ☐ pleasant ☐ distant ☐ unhappy ☐ no relationship

☐ other: _____

FAMILY BY MARRIAGE

Marital Status

Describe your current marital status:

☐ Married (legally) ☐ Divorced ☐ Living with a partner ☐ Annulment

☐ Never married (single) ☐ Separated ☐ Widow/widower ☐ Other: _____

Number of times: married: ____ divorced: ____ widow: ____ widower: ____ Years since last divorce: _____

Number of times married and number of years married for each marriage:

Number of Marriages	1	2	3	4	5	6	7	8
Years Married								

Spouse/Partner:

Age: _____ Occupation: _____ Health: ☐ Healthy ☐ Ill or poor health

Do you have problems in your relationship with your spouse/partner? If yes, describe: _____

_____

_____

DOCUMENT 9.3 *Continued.*

Children

Name, age and sex of your biological children (BIO), stepchildren (S/C) and adopted children (A/C):

NAME	RELATIONSHIP	SEX	AGE	NAME	RELATIONSHIP	SEX	AGE

Children Relationships

Do you have children? ☐ no ☐ yes. If yes, describe your present relationship with your biological, step or adopted children.

Biological children: ☐ close   ☐ pleasant   ☐ distant   ☐ unhappy   ☐ no relationship
Stepchildren: ☐ close   ☐ pleasant   ☐ distant   ☐ unhappy   ☐ no relationship
Adopted children: ☐ close   ☐ pleasant   ☐ distant   ☐ unhappy   ☐ no relationship

Children's Health

How do you rate your children's health: ☐ healthy ☐ poor health
Describe health problems: _____
_____
_____

Family/Home Life Issues

Would you like to see changes in how you currently relate to your family by marriage? ☐ no ☐ yes. If yes, describe:
_____
_____
_____

LIVING ARRANGEMENTS

Current Living Arrangements

☐ Apartment   ☐ Condominium   ☐ House   ☐ Mobile home/trailer
☐ Hotel   ☐ On the street   ☐ Other: _____
Do you (check one):   ☐ rent ☐ own ☐ lease ☐ live for free ☐ other:_____   How long:_____
Live alone: ☐ yes ☐ no If no, how many people live with you: _____

Who are the people who live with you and what is your relationship with them: ☐ spouse ☐ partner ☐ children
☐ parent(s) ☐ roommate(s) ☐ friend(s) ☐ brother(s) ☐ sister(s) ☐ aunt(s) ☐ uncle(s) ☐grandparent(s)
☐ cousin(s) ☐ in-law(s) other:_____

Household problems

Do you have household problems? ☐ no ☐ yes. If yes, describe: ☐ problems with landlord   ☐ problems with
neighbors ☐ inadequate housing ☐ unsafe neighborhood ☐ Other: _____
_____
_____
_____

DOCUMENT 9.3 *Continued.*

EDUCATIONAL HISTORY

Schools Attended

On the chart below, describe your school history:

High School: 9 10 11 12 School Name: _____ Location: _____ Graduate: □ no □ yes year: _____ GED: □ no □ yes year: _____	Technical School: 1 2 3 4 5 School Name: _____ Location: _____ Graduate: □ no □ yes year: _____ Course of study: _____ _____
Post High School: 1 2 3 4 □ Community College □ University or College Graduate: □ no □ yes year: _____ Degree granted: _____ Course of study: _____	Apprenticeship: 1 2 3 4 School Name: _____ Location: _____ Graduate: □ yes □ no Year: _____ Course of study: _____ _____

School Grades

Average grades received: _____   Overall grade point average (GPA): _____

Relationships With Teachers

□ Got along well with: □ all teachers □ all but a few teachers □ poorly with all teachers

Academics

□ No academic problems □ Was a slow learner □ Had poor study habits □ Attended special education classes to remediate learning disability during grade(s): _____ □ Whole academic career was spent in special education classes □ Had to repeat ____ grade (s) □ Had tutoring in grade(s): _____

Problems with: □ Arithmetic □ Speech □ Concentration □ Grammar □ Memory □ Reading □ Paying attention □ Writing □ Spelling □ Other: _____

Discipline

□ No discipline problems   □ Had to be disciplined in school frequently □ Conflicts with other students
□ Was suspended from school in grade(s): _____   □ Was expelled from school in grade ____
□ Was a school dropout in grade _____

Graduation

□ Did you leave school without graduating? □ no □ yes. If yes, give the reason(s): _____
_____

School Attitude

□ No problems you remember □ Enjoyed school □ Was neutral about school □ Were anxious about going to school and did not want to attend classes □ Were sick and missed a lot of school □ Were afraid you would not do well academically □ Were afraid you would not fit in □ Boredom with school   □ Disliked school
□ victim of bullying by other students □ Other: _____

Participation in School Activities

□ None □ Team sports □ Football □ Basketball □ Baseball □ Track and field □ Wrestling
□ Intramural sports □ Choir □ Glee Club □ Cheerleading □ Student government □ Academic clubs
□ Hobby clubs □ Yearbook □ Student newspaper □ Band □ Other: _____
_____

DOCUMENT 9.3 *Continued.*

EMPLOYMENT HISTORY

Current Work Status

Currently working? ☐ yes ☐ no. If yes, ☐ employed full time _____ hours/week; ☐ employed part time ____
hours/week. You are employed: ☐ without ☐ with physical restrictions. If not currently employed, give the reason:

☐ fired: how long:_____   ☐ laid off: how long?_____

☐ resigned: how long:_____   ☐ permanently and totally disabled: how long: _____

☐ retired: how long:_____   ☐ student

☐ temporarily disabled: how long:_____   ☐ in the military

☐ other: _____

If not currently working, do you ever expect to return to work? ☐ no ☐ yes. If yes, when: _____

In what occupation? _____

Job History

Starting with your most recent employer first, outline your employment history for the past eight (8) jobs.

EMPLOYER	JOB TITLE	TIME EMPLOYED	
		FROM:	TO:
		FROM:	TO:
		FROM:	TO:
		FROM:	TO:
		FROM:	TO:
		FROM:	TO:
		FROM:	TO:
		FROM:	TO:

Describe what is, or has been, your primary occupation(s): _____

_____

Union membership? ☐ past and/or ☐ current Union name: _____ Years of membership:_____

Sick Days

Number of sick days taken the last 12 months when you were really sick: _____

Number of sick days taken in the last 12 months when you were not really ill: _____

Tardy or Late to Work

Number of times tardy or late to work in the last 12 months:_____

Work Issues

Job-related problems? ☐ no ☐ yes. If yes, describe:_____

_____

_____

FINANCIAL HISTORY

Financial Issues

Have you had financial problems such as: bankruptcy, history of making late payments, not paying your income
tax: ☐ no ☐ yes. If yes, describe: _____

_____

_____

Do you have enough monthly income to pay for basic necessities, such as shelter, utilities, food and clothing?

☐ no, not enough   ☐ yes, with: ☐ nothing ☐ a little ☐ a lot ☐ a great deal left over.

Household income the past 12 months has: ☐ stayed the same ☐ increased ☐ decreased

DOCUMENT 9.3 *Continued.*

Workers' Compensation

Have you ever filed a workers' compensation claim: ☐ no ☐ yes. If yes, was it accepted? ☐ no ☐ yes.
If yes: When? _____ For how long? _____ Claim still active? ☐ no ☐ yes. If yes, are you receiving
disability payments? ☐ no ☐yes. If yes, how much? $_____

Social Security

Have you ever filed a Social Security Disability Claim? ☐ no ☐ yes. If yes, was it accepted? ☐ no ☐ yes.
If yes: When? _____ For how long? _____ Claim still active? ☐ no ☐ yes. If yes, are you receiving
disability payments? ☐ no ☐yes. If yes, how much? $_____

Other Disability Insurance

Have you ever filed a Disability Insurance Claim? ☐ no ☐ yes. If yes, was it accepted? ☐ no ☐ yes.
If yes: When? _____ For how long? _____ Claim still active? ☐ no ☐ yes. If yes, are you still receiving

disability payments? ☐ no ☐ yes. If yes, how much? _____

TRANSPORTATION

Automobile/Accessibility

Own an automobile: ☐ yes ☐ no. If no, have access to an automobile: ☐ yes ☐ no. If no, how do you get around
town?_____
Car insurance: ☐ no ☐ yes   Vehicle is: ☐ safe ☐ unsafe ☐ dependable ☐ undependable

License/ID Card

Valid driver's license: ☐ yes ☐ no. If yes, issued by what state? _____
If no, do you have a state identification card? ☐ no ☐ yes. If yes, state of issue:_____

RECREATIONAL/LEISURE TIME ACTIVITIES

Current Activities

Describe what recreational/leisure time activities you like to do: ☐ art ☐ music ☐ sports ☐ movies ☐ watch tv
☐ computer ☐ video games ☐ other:_____

Time/Engagement

Number of hours per week engaged in these activities: _____
Reasons for not doing these activities: _____

_____

DOCUMENT 9.3 *Continued.*

PERSONAL RELATIONSHIPS

Current Relationships

Describe whether or not you currently have close/supportive or distant/unsupportive relationships/friendships with the following (Checkmark ✓ the appropriate column(s)).

Relationships with:	Close/Supportive	Distant/Unsupportive	No Relationship
Family members by birth:			
Family members by marriage:			
Relatives:			
Close friends:			
Acquaintances:			
Neighbors:			
Coworkers:			
Other: _____			

Relationship Issues

Describe activities you do with your family or friends?_____

_____

What social stressors do you experience?_____

_____

Have there been recent changes in social functioning/supports/stressors? □ no □ yes. If yes, describe:

_____

LEGAL REPRESENTATION/LAW ENFORCEMENT ENCOUNTERS

Complete the following if you have hired an attorney to represent you for current legal matters and/or have a past criminal history.

Pending Litigation

Are you involved in any active legal cases? □ no □ yes. If yes: □ civil □ criminal □ traffic □ other: _____
Name of law firm or attorney:_____
Describe the legal problem: _____

_____

Past Criminal History

Currently on: □ probation □ parole □ no □ yes. If yes, for what (offenses): _____
Number of misdemeanor arrest(s) _____ and/or conviction(s): _____ Outcome: spent: ____ months/years on
□ probation or in: □ jail □ prison
Explain:_____
Number of felony arrest(s): _____ and/or conviction(s): _____ Outcome: spent: _____ months/years on
□ probation or in □ jail □ prison
Explain:_____

_____

Number of traffic offenses/tickets: _____ Type of traffic offense(s): □ DUI □ speeding
□ driving without insurance □ license suspended/revoked □ driving without a license □ other:_____

DOCUMENT 9.3 *Continued.*

MILITARY SERVICE

Have you served in the military? ☐ no ☐ yes.   If yes, what branch:_____

How many years served?_____ What years did you serve? _____ Current service: ☐ active

military ☐ active reserves ☐ National Guard ☐ none

Have you served in the military the past 15 years? no ☐ yes. If yes, have you been deployed in a combat zone? no

☐ yes. If yes, how many times deployed? _____

Where? _____

When? _____

How long?_____

Post deployment, were you diagnosed with PTSD? no ☐ yes. If yes, describe treatment received: _____

_____

Where?_____ When? _____How long?_____

By whom? _____

Are you still experiencing the following symptoms? ☐ nightmares ☐ flashbacks ☐ increased startle response

☐ irritability ☐ other: _____

Service connected wounds/disability? ☐ no ☐ yes. If yes, describe:_____

Type of military training/duties (MOS):_____

Type of discharge: _____ Highest rank at discharge:_____

Early discharge: ☐ no ☐ yes.   If yes, the reason: _____

Did you attend and graduate from a military academy? ☐ no ☐ yes. If yes, what academy: ☐ Naval Academy

☐ Air Force Academy ☐ Coast Guard Academy ☐West Point ☐ other: _____

Any disciplinary action against you? ☐ no ☐ yes. If yes, describe:_____

_____

List any medals/citations awarded:_____

_____

_____

MEDICAL INFORMATION

List any major physical health problems for which you are currently receiving treatment:

☐ No major medical problems for which treatment is necessary.

_____

_____

_____

List the names of all prescriptions and non-prescription medication(s) you are currently taking, including the amount per day

and the name of the prescribing doctor to treat a medical condition.

☐ No use of medical and/or psychiatric medication.

_____

_____

_____

List all surgeries (for any reason), including the type of surgery, date performed, and the name of the doctor

performing the surgery:

☐ No surgeries.

_____

_____

_____

_____

DOCUMENT 9.3 *Continued.*

PREVIOUS PUBLIC SAFETY WORK EXPERIENCE

If you have previously worked in public safety, answer the following questions.

Describe your past law enforcement position.

Name of Public Safety Agency	Job Title	Years Employed	Reason for Leaving

Total number of **oral** or **written** reprimands received in the line of duty: _____

Total number of times suspended from duty/received a reduction in rank and/or salary: _____

Total number of citizen complaints filed against you and found to be false: _____

Total number of citizen complaints file against you and found to be true: _____

Total number of unsatisfactory personnel ratings received: _____

Total number of civil lawsuits filed against you as a result of your actions as a sworn public safety employee:

_____

Total number of criminal prosecutions filed against you as a result of your actions as a sworn public safety employed:

_____

Number of times you fired your weapon at someone (hitting them or not): _____

Number of work-related traffic accidents: _____

Number of times damaged department equipment and property: _____

_____

Answer the following questions that pertain to on-duty related incidents by reading the statement and, if it applies, place a checkmark (✓) in the ☐ next to the number.

1. ☐ Have been the subject of an internal investigation.
2. ☐ Have been a witness in an internal investigation.
3. ☐ Have lied or been untruthful in an internal investigation.
4. ☐ Have done things in your public safety career that you are not proud of.
5. ☐ Have been the subject of a criminal investigation.
6. ☐ Have been a witness in a criminal investigation.
7. ☐ Have committed a criminal act for which you could have been incarcerated.
8. ☐ Have lied or distorted facts in an official report.
9. ☐ Have been allowed to resign for "personal reasons" in lieu of termination.
10. ☐ Have been accused of misconduct that was racial or sexual in nature.
11. ☐ Have covered up for another public safety employee who committed a crime.
12. ☐ Have lied or been untruthful to a supervisor.
13. ☐ Have covered up for a fellow public safety employee who violated a department policy.
14. ☐ Have converted property obtained in the scope of your employment to personal use.
15. ☐ Have disseminated confidential information to anyone without a need to know outside of the public safety job environment.
16. ☐ Have intentionally extended your shift to receive unwarranted overtime.
17. ☐ Have witnessed another sworn public safety employee violate a department policy for which they could have been disciplined.
18. ☐ Have witnessed another sworn public safety employee commit a criminal act and did not report it.
19. ☐ Have witnessed another sworn public safety employee violate a person's civil rights.
20. ☐ Have been terminated or resigned your position.
21. ☐ Have mishandled or abused a person in your immediate control or under custody.
22. ☐ Have received official penalty days off.
23. ☐ Have used alcoholic beverages while on duty.
24. ☐ Have used illegal drugs while on duty.

DOCUMENT 9.3 *Continued.*

ADDITIONAL INFORMATION

Please add any other information about your life that you think may be of interest to disclose:

_____
_____
_____
_____
_____
_____
_____
_____
_____
_____
_____
_____
_____
_____
_____
_____
_____
_____
_____
_____
_____
_____
_____
_____
_____

I attest all of my answers on this questionnaire are accurate. That is, I have not willingly withheld information or distorted the facts of my past experiences. Willful distortion of the facts and/or lying is grounds for immediate disqualification.

_____   _____
APPLICANT SIGNATURE   DATE

DOCUMENT 9.3 _Continued._

POLICE STORY 9.2 **None of Your Business**

by Dr. Donald J. Johnson

Candidates should understand the importance of the personal history questionnaire, or any questions asked by the psychologist conducting the psych eval. I was sitting at my desk, reviewing a batch of candidates for one law enforcement agency. I had just started reading through one candidate's personal history questionnaire when I read the answer the candidate wrote for one specific question.

The first question was "How do you rate your children's health: _____ Healthy _____ Poor health? Describe health problems: _____."

The candidate answered the question and wrote in "they are fine, like you care."

The second question was "Describe your marital status: _____ Married (legally) _____ Never married (single) _____ Divorced _____ Living with a partner _____ Separated _____ Widow/widower."

The candidate answered the question by drawing a line above the listed answers and wrote in "none of your business."

This type of answer did raise some questions. When I am meeting with a candidate, I am looking at many personality traits. I look for traits such as flexibility, adaptability, assertiveness, emotional regulation, stress tolerance, anger and frustration management, stress coping, ability to follow directions or instructions, demeanor, and response style. If a candidate fails not only to answer questions that are clearly asked on a form but answers in such a way to demonstrate a particular type of demeanor, this behavior speaks volumes to me. In this case, the issue of attitude was of primary concern.

The learning lesson in this example is to be as open and candid as possible. Whenever answering questions during the psych eval, remember, you are always being evaluated on everything you do and say, and also everything you don't do or don't say (nonverbal behavior, aka "attitude"). The job of a law enforcement officer is a huge responsibility. Officers are entrusted with a person's safety and can take their freedom away as well. The job is in the service industry, and officers are there to serve the public. Therefore, candidates must be prepared to open the door to their lives and be okay with answering all types of questions, no matter how difficult.

What Happens After I Finish the Psych Eval?

According to Corey (n.d.), the developer of the MMPI-2-RF, the psychologist administering the psych eval goes through a six-step process in evaluating the data obtaining during the evaluation process.

Step 1: Assess protocol validity; look for deception (review clinical interview and background investigation)
Step 2: Assess substantive scales in the assessment tools
Step 3: Assess background findings
Step 4: Assess interview findings
Step 5: Complete mitigation analysis
Step 6: Reach a suitability determination

As the psychologist reviews the results of the MMPI-2-RF, notes will be made on possible issues. For example, during a demonstration of a review of a candidate's MMPI-2-RF, Corey (n.d.). noted the following:

> The test taker's responses indicate a level of overly assertive behavior that may be incompatible with public safety requirements for behavioral control. This level of domineering behavior is very uncommon among police officer candidates. Only 5.1% of comparison group members give evidence of this level over-assertive behavior.
>
> Compared with other police officer candidates, the test taker is more likely to become impatient with others over minor infractions.
>
> The test taker is more likely than most police officers or trainees to exhibit difficulties cooperating with peers and supervisors.

After reviewing the MMPI-2-RF, the personal history statement, the clinical interview, past mental health records, and the agency background investigation, the psychologist could note the following mitigation analysis: "Test findings indicating: 1) Overly assertive/domineering behavior, 2) Low interpersonal awareness and sensitivity, 3) Possible underreporting. Background and interview findings are convergent with these risk-related test findings: 1) Conflictual relationships in the military, 2) Marital altercations overheard by a neighbor, 3) PTSD with ongoing sleep impairment (Corey, n.d.).

The psychologist will then attend the chief or sheriff or top cop review of the candidates once all the psych evals have been completed. During this process, the psychologist will review the findings of the candidates and make a recommendation, sometimes to include categories 1–3 or categories 1–5 recommendations. In the end, it is up to the hiring agency to determine whether a candidate is hired; the psychologist only makes recommendations. See Document 9.4, which illustrates the public safety post-conditional job offer psychological screening rating sheets Dr. Johnson utilizes in ascertaining the results of the psych eval.

PUBLIC SAFETY POST CONDITIONAL JOB OFFER PSYCHOLOGICAL SCREENING RATING REPORT

Applicant Name:_____

Birth Date:_____ Age:_____ SS No.:XXX-XX-_____

Testing Date:_____ Interview Date: _____ Date of Report:_____

Gender: ☐ male ☐ female   Handedness: ☐ right ☐ left ☐ ambidextrous

Ethnicity: ☐ African-American ☐ Asian: _____   ☐ Caucasian

☐ Hispanic ☐ Pacific Islander: _____

☐ Native American: _____

DOCUMENT 9.4 Public safety post-conditional job offer psychological screening rating report.

Donald Johnson, "Public Safety Post Conditional Job Offer Psychological Screening Rating Report." Copyright © by Donald Johnson. Reprinted with permission.

☐ other: _____

Height: _____ Weight: _____

Hair Color: ☐ blonde ☐ brown ☐ black ☐ gray ☐ white ☐ red ☐ auburn ☐ brunette ☐ bald

Eye Color: ☐ blue ☐ brown ☐ gray ☐ hazel ☐ black ☐ green

Primary language spoken: _____ Secondary: _____

Public Safety Agency: _____

Position Applied For: _____

Reason For Assessment: The applicant is being referred for a post conditional job offer psychological evaluation to determine if there are present psychological contraindications to adequately perform the essential job functions of the applied for position.

BEHAVIORAL OBSERVATIONS

- **Attire/Dress:**
  ☐ appropriate ☐ not appropriate for ☐ age ☐ occasion ☐ weather
  ☐ casual ☐ formal ☐ matching ☐ mismatched ☐ stylish ☐ out of style
  ☐ conservative ☐ revealing ☐ stained ☐ unstained ☐ unwrinkled ☐ wrinkled

- **Personal Hygiene:**
  ☐ clean ☐ unclean ☐ healthy ☐ unhealthy ☐ unkempt ☐ neglected

- **Teeth:**
  ☐ normal ☐ decayed ☐ missing
  ☐ broken ☐ dentures ☐ implants

- **Skin:**
  ☐ normal ☐ cuts ☐ bruises ☐ acne ☐ abnormal coloring
  ☐ disfigurement ☐ piercings ☐ tattoos ☐ scars

- **Facial Hair (for men):**
  ☐ shaved ☐ unshaven ☐ full beard ☐ moustache ☐ goatee ☐ sideburns

- **Eye Contact:**
  ☐ makes ☐ does not make appropriate eye contact

- **Facial Expressions:**
  ☐ cheerful ☐ responsive ☐ calm ☐ smiling
  ☐ sad ☐ serious ☐ crying ☐ tearful

DOCUMENT 9.4 *Continued.*

☐ frightened ☐ apprehensive ☐ tense ☐ worried
☐ defiant ☐ angry ☐ embarrassed ☐ blushing
☐ suspicious ☐ frowning ☐ grimacing
☐ expressionless ☐ fixed ☐ bored
☐ other: _____

- **Standing Posture/Position:**
  ☐ normal ☐ relaxed
  ☐ tense/rigid ☐ slouching ☐ upright/erect ☐ stooped over
  ☐ other: _____

- **Sitting Posture/Position:**
  ☐ normal ☐ relaxed
  ☐ tense/rigid ☐ slouching ☐ upright/erect ☐ stooped over
  ☐ other: _____

- **Walking Gait/Pace:**
  ☐ normal pace ☐ fast paced ☐ slow pace
  ☐ does not need assistance ☐ needs assistance
  ☐ limping ☐ wide-based
  ☐ other: _____

- **Voluntary Motor Movements:**
  ☐ no restriction ☐ restriction in movements were observed
  ☐ mobile ☐ immobile
  ☐ normal ☐ fast ☐ slow speed of body movement
  ☐ coordinated ☐ uncoordinated
  ☐ no problems ☐ problems with swallowing
  ☐ other: _____

- **Involuntary Motor Movements:**
  ☐ does not manifest ☐ manifests repetitive or stereotyped involuntary muscle movements such
  as ☐ tremors ☐ twitches or ☐ tics of the: ☐ upper extremities ☐ face ☐ mouth ☐ eyes
  ☐ lower extremities
  ☐ other: _____

Body Balance & Spatial Orientation:
  ☐ no reported problems ☐ reported problems with body balance/equilibrium:
  ☐ lightheaded, floating, or rocking sensation (dizziness)
  ☐ spinning or whirling sensation or an illusion of movement of self or the world (vertigo)
  ☐ other: _____

DOCUMENT 9.4 *Continued.*

Following Directions/Instructions:
☐ able ☐ unable to understand and/or follow: ☐ simple instructions ☐ detailed instructions
☐ able ☐ unable to understand and/or follow: ☐ simple directions ☐ detailed directions
☐ other: _____

Awareness:
☐ No deficits in awareness was observed: ☐ focused ☐ attentive
☐ Deficits in awareness was observed: ☐ distractible ☐ disoriented
☐ other: _____

Demeanor:
☐ congenial ☐ friendly ☐ cooperative ☐ sociable
☐ argumentative ☐ hostile ☐ preoccupied ☐ suspicious ☐ evasive ☐ resistant ☐ tense
☐ shy/withdrawn ☐ uncongenial ☐ distrusting ☐ uncooperative ☐ mistrustful ☐ demanding
☐ other: _____

Response Style:
☐ responsive ☐ non-responsive ☐ credible ☐ non-credible response style
☐ non-defensive response style ☐ defensive response style
☐ other: _____

Rapport:
☐ readily established ☐ gradually established ☐ not established
☐ positive ☐ negative examiner-applicant interaction
☐ other: _____

Historian:
☐ detailed ☐ not a detailed historian
☐ reliable ☐ unreliable recitation of ☐ current and/or ☐ past life history
☐ other: _____

Validity/Reliability of Evaluation Results:
☐ valid/reliable ☐ invalid/unreliable evaluation results due to ☐ consistency ☐ inconsistency
across data sources
☐ other: _____

EVALUATION RESULTS

Minnesota Multiphasic Personality Inventory-2-RF

Protocol Validity
• Unscorable items: ☐ no ☐ yes • Over-Reporting: ☐ no ☐ yes • Under-Reporting: ☐ no ☐ yes

DOCUMENT 9.4 *Continued.*

<u>Substantive Scales</u>
- Somatic/Cognitive Dysfunction:
  ☐ not indicated ☐ indicated
- Thought Dysfunction:
  ☐ not indicated ☐ indicated
- Interpersonal Functioning:
  ☐ adequate ☐ inadequate
- Emotional Dysfunction:
  ☐ not indicated ☐ indicated
- Behavioral Dysfunction:
  ☐ not indicated ☐ indicated

Discussion:

_____

_____

_____

_____

_____

PERSONALITY BASED COMPETENCIES

Determined from answers given on the Risk Factor Questionnaire.

1. **Service Orientation:** Describes relevant reasons for wanting to serve, assist or help the public in a responsive, compassionate, respectful, and enthusiastic manner by working in a career-oriented public safety position.
   ☐ yes ☐ no. If no, explain: _____

2. **Integrity/Ethics:** Names ways to demonstrate and maintain high standards of ethical personal conduct, including attributes such as honesty, good character, integrity, impartiality, and trustworthiness in following outlined laws, rules, regulations, and procedures as well as being able to interact with others without prejudicial attitudes regarding gender, sexual orientation, race, religion, national origin, disability or social status.
   ☐ yes ☐ no. If no, explain: _____

3. **Team Work:** Gives examples of what is done to establish and maintain effective, cooperative working relationships with coworkers to achieve organizational goals as well as subordinate personal interests for the good of the working group/agency.
   ☐ yes ☐ no. If no, explain: _____

4. **Conflict Resolution:** Details what is done to communicate in a tactful and respectful manner, treat others with impartiality, and identify and reduce interpersonal conflict in ways that shows sensitivity to the feelings of others as well as establishing and maintaining rapport.
   ☐ yes ☐ no. If no, explain: _____

DOCUMENT 9.4 *Continued.*

5. **Attention to Safety/Impulse Control:** Describes what is done to react appropriately, safely, and decisively in a verbally confrontational or threatening situation that may involve high risk for sustaining physical harm while avoiding impulsive and/or un-necessarily dangerous behaviors.
☐ yes ☐ no. If no, explain: _____

_____

6. **Decision Making & Judgement:** Describes the process used to think, reason, problem solve, and consider the consequences of behavior in making judgments and decisions in a logical and rational fashion instead of impulsively doing the first thing that comes to mind.
☐ yes ☐ no. If no, explain: _____

_____

7. **Flexibility/Adaptability:** Communicates what is done to change focus and adjust to the many different sudden and sometimes competing demands inherent in work and life activities. Is able to describe how to adjust to planned and unplanned work changes, the process used to prioritize and effectively focus on several varied or different tasks/projects at the same time when required to work in an unstructured situation with minimal supervision and/or under differing supervisory styles.
☐ yes ☐ no. If no, explain: _____

_____

8. **Conscientiousness/Dependability:** Identifies the process used to be able to be relied and depended upon by members of the work group as well as being able to persevere in the face of long hours and other adverse working conditions, carefully attending to details like typos, missing or incorrect information, maintaining a punctual and reliable attendance record, being accountable for completing work tasks as well as analyzing and correcting prior mistakes or problems to improve performance.
☐ yes ☐ no. If no, explain: _____

_____

9. **Assertiveness/Persuasiveness:** Describes ways to avoid being intimated and be able, without hesitation, to take control of situations in a calm and appropriately assertive manner, even under adverse or dangerous conditions to communicate ideas and persuade others to adopt a desired course of action.
☐ yes ☐ no. If no, explain: _____

_____

10. **Emotional Regulation/Stress Tolerance:** Describes the process used to be able to be composed, rational, and in control, particularly during time-critical and other stressful situations, maintain a positive self-image under such adverse circumstances, accept personal limitations and mistakes all the while keeping an even-tempered composure and demeanor, exercising restraint and not over-reacting in emotionally-charged situations.
☐ yes ☐ no. If no, explain: _____

_____

DOCUMENT 9.4 *Continued.*

RISK CATEGORY RATINGS

Risk category ratings are based upon the analysis of written responses on clinical questionnaires, verbal answers to questions asked during the examination and clinical interview and behavioral observations.

☐ Category I: No significant risk factors are identified that would disqualify this applicant from successfully performing the work tasks contained in the public safety job description.

☐ Category II: Potential risk factors cannot be ruled out relevant to this applicant's ability to successfully perform the work tasks contained in the public safety job description due to:
☐ defensiveness or under-reporting of symptoms
☐ non-purposive random responding
☐ claims of being highly virtuous and responsible with few or no described personality weaknesses or flaws to which most people will admit
☐ other psychological factors identified as relevant risk factors.
☐ Other: _____
_____

A very careful scrutiny of all background information in relationship to personality based competencies is suggested in order to determine the presence of disqualifying factors.

☐ Category III: Significant disqualifying risk factors are identified regarding this applicant's ability to successfully perform the work tasks contained in the public safety job description.

DISCUSSION

DOCUMENT 9.4 *Continued.*

Is the Psych Eval a Pass/Fail Test?

Each person has their personality traits, limitations, and competencies, and these are evaluated through different methods. The psychologist is looking for a complete picture of the candidate and will report both strengths and weaknesses to the employer. A psych eval is not referred to as a test, because it is *not* a test; it is an evaluation. If a candidate has taken a psych eval in the past and failed, the candidate may be a pessimist on the subject. However, what the candidate might be failing to consider is the pass/fail concept. Psych evals cannot be compared to written tests. Written tests have a right and wrong answer and a candidate can pass or fail the test depending on how many questions they answer incorrectly. Psych evals do not work in this fashion. Therefore, it is a difficult concept to grasp how to figure out how to pass something that is not graded on a pass or fail scale. Criticism begins with psych evals during the grading process. If a candidate was not hired into a specific position due to the results of their psych eval, it could be difficult for the candidate to move on. Sometimes the candidate will never understand why they were not hired and how their psych eval played a role in their demise. Candidates generally brush it off as bad luck and end up hating the psych eval process altogether for how it hampered their life long goals. What the candidate failed to understand is the big picture of psych evals.

Psych evals begin with the employer and the position being filled. The psychologist administering the evaluation must look at the results in an objective, quantitative way so that each person is assessed in the same manner. The first order of business is for the psychologist to conduct a thorough investigation into the open position. Job demands, requirements, working conditions, stressors, culture, qualifications, and expectations are reviewed first. Key subject matter experts are interviewed. The psychologist will watch a successful employee performing various job-required tasks. The psychologist then speaks with key executives to identify what the employer is looking for in the perfect candidate. The psychologist will use relevant and reliable information to establish the principles and methods for the evaluation required. Finally, after all the data is analyzed, the psychologist can come up with essential personality traits that the impeccable candidate will need to fill the open position successfully.

How Does the Psychologist Rate the Psych Eval?

As the candidates go through the law enforcement hiring process step by step, information is gathered during each step. The beginning employment written test offers a look into how well the candidate knows and understands the hard data. The background investigation will delve into the candidate's history and open other drawers into the candidate's past. Finally, the psych eval will identify specific parts of the candidate's personality and critical traits that may or may not make the candidate perfect for the open position. Generally, the psychologist conducting the evaluation will meet with the employer after all the testing is completed. The purpose of this meeting is not to give a pass or fail result but to give an opinion of the data discovered. More often than not, a perfect candidate is never found; however, some candidates begin to swell above the rest, revealing the desirable personality traits. The APA has a policy that states that forensic psychologists should not use a pass or fail system of evaluating. Psychologists utilize a rating system instead. Not all psychologists rate the candidates in the same way; however, there is a consensus on the following system. The following list illustrates a **three-category rating system** utilized by Dr. Johnson:

- Category 1: No significant risk factors are identified that would disqualify this applicant from successfully performing the work tasks contained in the public safety description.
- Category 2: Potential risk factors cannot be ruled out as relevant to this applicant's ability to successfully perform the work tasks contained in the public safety job description due to (1) defensiveness or under-reporting of symptoms, (2) non-purposive random responding, (3) claims of being highly virtuous and responsible with few or no described personality weaknesses or flaws to which most people will admit, (4) issues with background that need further investigation (for example if a candidate has been deployed overseas the psychologist would want to identify possible PTSD symptoms), (5) other psychological factors identified as relevant factors. Meticulous scrutiny of all background information concerning personality-based competencies is suggested in order to determine the presence of disqualifying factors.

- Category 3: Significant disqualifying risk factors are identified regarding this applicant's ability to successfully perform the work tasks contained in the public safety job description.

Other psychologists utilize a **five-category rating system**. The following list illustrates a five-category rating system:

- Category 1 and Category 2: No significant risk factors are identified that would disqualify this applicant from successfully performing the work tasks contained in the public safety description.
- Category 3 and Category 4: Potential risk factors cannot be ruled out as relevant to this applicant's ability to successfully perform the work tasks contained in the public safety job description due to defensiveness or under-reporting of symptoms, non-purposive random responding, claims of being highly virtuous and responsible with few or no described personality weaknesses, issues with background that need further investigation (for example if a candidate worked for another law enforcement agency for only 11 months the psychologist would want further investigation as to what happened at that agency), flaws to which most people will admit, or other psychological factors identified as relevant. Meticulous scrutiny of all background information concerning personality-based competencies is suggested in order to determine the presence of disqualifying factors.
- Category 5: Significant disqualifying risk factors are identified regarding this applicant's ability to successfully perform the work tasks contained in the public safety job description.

POLICE STORY 9.3 **Legend in His Own Mind**

by Dr. Donald J. Johnson

I have worked for over 3 decades as a psychologist conducting psychological evaluations for many different law enforcement agencies and hotel/casinos in the Southern Nevada area. I have seen it all, and my recommendation to those candidates who will one day go through the psychological evaluation process, is to do the following:

1. Know the job and understand the qualifications required and acceptable background issues.
2. Know yourself and your personality and understand possible personality traits that may cause issues in #1.
3. Look at #1 and #2 and see if they can coexist to move forward to #4; if they cannot, then stop and look for a different career path.
4. Be honest; do not bend the truth to try and make yourself appear better than you are.

I have seen almost everything, and the one constant that keeps candidates from moving forward in the hiring process is #4. One such instance of this occurring was during an interview for a psych eval. I immediately noticed that the candidate was a legend in his mind. When I asked the candidate about prior drug use, the candidate told me he had never used drugs. When I asked the candidate about prior criminal violations, the candidate told me he had never broken the law. I remember thinking, "There is no way he could be that perfect." The MMPI-2 RF I gave him did not reveal anything concerning; therefore, I was prepared to give him a Level 1 psych eval but was waiting until the chief's review. During the chief's review for this agency, the following employees were present: chief of police, background investigators, and me. As we reviewed all the candidates, the specific candidate who was a legend in his mind was up for review. The background investigator opened his computer and clacked away on the keys. The investigator then turned the computer screen around for all of us to see. There was a photo on his computer, and the photo was of the candidate smoking marijuana from a bong.

The candidate was not hired. Moreover, by lying, the candidate has ensured he will never be hired by any other agency as well. Had the candidate told everyone involved the truth, then depending on when he had utilized marijuana, he would still have had a good chance of being hired. Unfortunately, because he lied to all involved, he ruined his chances.

Can I Find Out Why I Was Not Recommended for Employment Due to the Results of the Psych Eval?

What if a candidate is contacted by the hiring agency after the psych eval and is told they will not be continuing in the hiring process? What options are left for the candidate? If a candidate fails the written test, the answer is simple: Follow the instructions in this textbook and try again. The same goes with the oral board interview or the physical fitness or physical agility test. However, when a candidate is stopped from continuing with the hiring process due to the results from the psych eval, the candidate must keep their head up. The candidate will not know if they were stopped from continuing in the hiring process because of the psych eval. Typically, the hiring agency will send the candidate a rejection letter stating the candidate has failed to meet the standards required for continuing with the conditional job offer. The letter does not explicitly state which portion of the conditional job offer the candidate failed; therefore, the candidate is left to ponder what happened. Candidates are also required to sign a conditional offer of employment statement before they take the psych eval (see the conditional offer of employment in Fact Box 9.1). This statement notifies the candidate that they understand all the data from the psych eval belongs to the hiring agency and the candidate waives all rights to know the results. All too often candidates are faced with this exact conundrum, and the candidate is left with a few options: to hang one's head low, accept defeat, and chose a different career path, never really understanding why.

The American Psychological Association (APA) policy is to inform the applicant the results of the psych eval are the sole property of the hiring agency (who paid and ordered the psych eval). The candidate is directed to contact the hiring agency if they want a copy of the psych eval. However, most employers will not release the report, and neither will the testing agency.

What is a candidate to do at this point? Should failure be accepted? No! There is another option for this candidate. Do not accept failure! Every police department is different. Every hiring agency will contract different psychologists to conduct their psych eval, and the associated tools the psychologists utilize to conduct the psych eval are different as well. It is not uncommon for one candidate to receive the rejection letter ceasing the continuation of the testing under the conditional job offer yet test for a different department and get hired.

Confused yet? It is confusing and frustrating. The hiring process is a long, daunting, almost humiliating process to endure. The candidate is tested and tested over and over again. Backgrounds are explored, financial records are opened, past criminal history is investigated, and then, as if the candidate's personal life has not been scrutinized enough, the candidate must brave the psych eval. At this point, many candidates lose hope, and for a good reason. The best advice at this time is not to lose hope. If the candidate has the passion for this career, studied this textbook, taken the associated self-assessment tests, and does not see any glaring personality issues, then the candidate should endure. The proverb by Thomas H. Palmer, first coined in the 1700s, "If at first, you don't succeed, try, try, again," is at play at full speed in this context.

POLICE STORY 9.4 **Try, Try Again**

---

by Dr. Donald J. Johnson

I have conducted psych evals for 10 agencies in southern Nevada for over 3 decades, and I have conducted psych evals on candidates who have failed other psych evals for other police departments. I have gone on to recommend hiring after I conducted a psych eval, and for the life of me I cannot understand how some of these candidates failed other psych evals. However, this is the world of confidentiality, and just as I do not release the results of the psych evals I conduct on candidates, other psychologists do not release their evals; therefore, the conundrum of misunderstanding exists. I wish I could offer more substantial suggestions for candidates who may fail a psych eval. However, the only suggestions I have is to try, try, again. Do not accept failure if this career is your passion and you have no superseding reasons to suspect you would not make an excellent police officer.

How to Prepare for the Psych Eval

Preparation for the psych eval portion of the hiring process is not the same, nor as straightforward, as preparing for the written, oral board interview, or even the physical fitness or physical agility tests. To perform well on the psych eval, the candidate will need to develop emotional intelligence. Behavior modification is not something that can occur overnight; it requires a long-term commitment.

The following five steps to passing the psych eval are a guide to success:

1. The first step is the training of the mind to be strong. As issues in life pop up, deal with them head on and do not hide them away or let them escalate.
2. The second step is to tell the truth; do not lie! One of the surest ways to fail is to lie. The MMPI-2 and MMPI-2-RF have a built-in lie scale. Such questions as "I have never made anyone angry," or "I have always been honest," are meant to validate if the candidate is telling the truth. Therefore, be careful to read each question slowly and thoroughly and, moreover, never lie, no matter what.
3. The third step is not to overthink the questions. The questions on the MMPI-2 and MMPI-2-RF can be confusing and have a time limit. The best answer is always the first answer though. Once the candidate starts to overthink the question, not only will valuable time be lost, but chances are the wrong answer will be chosen. Wrong answers can

eliminate the candidate. Do not second guess the questions. The best way to do this is to practice a self-assessment test. There are many self-assessment tests in this textbook, along with links to websites with many more personality and mental health tests. Take the time to take these tests and understand how the questions are asked and how the results are formulated.

4. The fourth step is to be consistent. Consistency is checked; therefore, the answers must be consistent. The test is filled with questions that are the same yet asked in different ways. Therefore, the best way to succeed is to read the question thoroughly and fully understand the question before answering it, always knowing there is a time limit.

5. The fifth step is to prepare to answer test questions while being timed. Personality tests are timed. Although there is generally enough time to answer all the questions, the candidate will need to respond efficiently. The luxury of meticulously analyzing each question is no longer an option. It is a high-pressure experience, and the only way to lower the stress is to practice. Practice taking tests.

The psych eval requires the candidate to conduct preliminary self-assessment testing. These self-assessments should allow the candidate to understand their personality as well its strengths and weaknesses. Also, personalities can change over time; maybe when a candidate was younger they were controlling; however, through life experiences, the candidate has become more relaxed. As time goes on, personalities can become more organized and dependable. The change becomes visible when thinking of friends over time. It is very common for adults to become more emotionally stable between the ages of 20–40. Unfortunately, at the same time, these same adults start to become more closed-minded, and with each passing year, it becomes more challenging to get that same adult to try new things. What this data shows is that personality traits do change over time, albeit not always for the best. Therefore, the candidate should regularly conduct self-assessment personality testing in order to understand their changing personality and how it can affect their future career aspects and job performance.

Candidates should start with the self-assessments in Chapter 2. Then the candidate can move on to Self-Assessments 9.1–9.4. Once the candidate has completed all the self-assessment tests and personal history questionnaires, the candidate should have a better understanding of their personality and whether that personality would fit well with the required job responsibilities and tasks of those in law enforcement. If the tests show the candidate's personality fits the mold of those in law enforcement, the candidate should move on with the preparation for the hiring process. If the answer is no, that is all right. Completion of Self-Assessment 9.4 should give the candidate a head start to a new career path. Not everyone fits the mold for a career in law enforcement. It is tough on many levels and requires a drive, passion, and a type of personality that can handle all types of stress without aggression.

There are a variety of personality tests that a candidate can take online. One such website (https://psychcentral.com/quizzes/) offers free mental health tests. There are ADHD tests, anxiety and mood tests, autism tests, eating disorder tests, OCD and PTSD tests, sleep tests, and many other psychological tests. Candidates should take full advantage of such tests to ascertain not only personality issues but other mental health issues as well.

SELF-ASSESSMENT 9.1

The first part of understanding the psych eval is understanding the types of questions asked during it. The first part is the personal history questionnaire. See Documents 9.1, 9.2, and 9.3 and fill out the three separate questionnaires. After completing the three questionnaires, review the answers. Are there any answers that cause any concern? Is there anything that can be done about these concerns? If there is a solution, then begin working on it immediately. If there is no solution, then do not continue to stress over the issue. If nothing can be done to change the answer, then the worst course of action would be to continue stressing over it. Instead, understand what the issue is and be prepared to answer and explain it. Also, always be prepared to take responsibility for any issue. Responsibility is a massive part of being in law enforcement. If a candidate takes an issue and tries to explain their way out of it, the response to the answer is not always positive. However, if the candidate takes to the time to review the issue, take responsibility for the issue, and learn from the issue, there can be positive takes on a negative issue due to how the candidate handled it by taking responsibility.

For instance, if a candidate had a history at one place of employment of not getting along with the immediate supervisor, the worst course of action would be for the candidate to blame the supervisor and focus on all that the supervisor did to instigate issues with the candidate. The better course of action would be for the candidate to take responsibility and explain that the candidate now better understands the position of a supervisor and that no matter the personality conflict between the employee and supervisor, the supervisor must be respected for the position occupied. The candidate can further take responsibility by explaining how the candidate could have better handled the situation and that the candidate will work hard to have it never repeated.

The candidate must always remember how important responsibility is. All too often, candidates waste time trying to explain issues away. These actions only hurt the candidate in the long run. It is difficult to continue to find fault in a candidate who takes responsibility for an issue and promises it will never happen again. To clarify, this does not mean a candidate should lie or be less than honest in an explanation of an issue. It only means that if a candidate had any negative part in the issue, the candidate should immediately take the high road and take responsibility instead of playing the blame game.

SELF-ASSESSMENT 9.2: BIG FIVE PERSONALITY TRAITS

There are many personality tests on the market. The good thing is that many are free and do not cost the test taker; however, one must always be aware of the free personality test and ensure the organization offering the free test is providing a good look into the test taker's personality and not outputting garbage.

One such free personality test is online (https://www.123test.com/personality-test/). This personality test contains 120 statements. There is no time limit, and it takes approximately 15 minutes to complete. After the test is completed, click on the standard test only (which is free). The results are based on the big five personality test. This test offers a concise measure of the five major parts of a personality and the six facets that further delineate each part.

The big five personality traits are openness, conscientiousness, extraversion, agreeableness, and neuroticism (OCEAN). These five core personality traits have been growing since the beginning research in 1949 from D.W. Fiske to McCrae and Costa in 1987 (Cherry & Gans, 2019).

Openness

High:

Creative

Likes new challenges

Can think abstractly

Low:

Scared of change and new ideas

Not imaginative

Not abstract

Conscientiousness

High:

Prepares

Attention to detail

Likes a schedule

Low:

Messy

Does not return items

Procrastination

Does not make deadlines

Extraversion:

High:

Center of attention

Likes talking to new people

Highly social

Talks before thinking

Low:

Likes being alone instead of in social environments

Does not like being the center of attention

Carefully thinks before talking

Agreeableness

High:

Cares for people

Assists those in need

Low:

Insults and hurts people's feelings

Manipulates people

Neuroticism

High:

Worries and is under much stress

Mood swings

Low:

Handles stress well

Rarely depressed

Does not worry

SELF-ASSESSMENT 9.3: CAREER APTITUDE TEST

The next assessment is the career aptitude test. This is a useful test that can direct the candidate toward the best career for their personality. Do not be sidelined though, if the results show another area other than criminal justice. Instead, be excited! The results should not hamper the test taker; instead, they should be a recommendation and offer additional places to look for viable careers.

To take this career aptitude test, go to www.123test.com/career-test/ and follow the instructions. The test takes approximately 5–10 minutes and asks the test taker to choose from sets of photographs.

The results are based on the six personality types in the Holland model. Dr. Holland found that one person would not fit into just one of the six types. Instead, any one person could have interests in all six types. When the types were ranked, a specific Holland code emerged. Different people's personalities found different environments likable. Most people are attracted primarily to two or three areas, and these areas become the person's Holland code.

Realistic (R—Doers)

Athletic ability

Work with objects, tools, animals, plants

Practical, stable, reserved, concrete, independent, systematic

Investigative (I—Thinkers)

Think abstractly

Analytical

Scientific

Scholarly, cautious, logical, curious

Artistic (A—Creators)

Design anything

Creative

Imaginative, innovative, emotional, original

Social (S—Helpers)

Teacher

Mediator, friendly

Idealistic, responsible, forgiving

Enterprising (E—Persuaders)

Sell things

Organize, self-confident

Energetics, adventurous, ambitious

Conventional (C—Organizers)

Work well in a system

Well organized

Efficient, practical, thrifty

Polite, ambitious, obedient (University of Missouri, n.d.)

FACT BOX 9.5: DR. DONALD J. JOHNSON'S PSYCH EVAL RECOMMENDATIONS

Watch Video 9.1 to hear Dr. Johnson's recommendations to candidates on what to expect during the psych eval and how to prepare.

Active Learning Video 9.1. Dr. Donald J. Johnson psych eval recommendations.

SUMMARY OF CHAPTER 9

1. A post-conditional job offer is required before a psych eval can be completed.

2. Psychologists rate a candidate's psych eval results based on rating categories instead of pass or fail.

3. Candidates can expect to take the MMPI-2-RF or other related personality assessment test, along with a personal history questionnaire and an interview during the psych eval.

4. Candidates can prepare for the psych eval by taking the various self-assessments and understanding their own personality's strengths and weaknesses.

DISCUSSION QUESTIONS

1. Why are psych evals conducted?

2. What does the MMPI-2-RF measure, and why do psychologists utilize it as a part of the psych eval?

3. Do candidates pass or fail a psych eval?

4. Can a candidate get a copy of their psych eval?

See Active Learning for the Following:

- Practice quizzes
- eFlashcards
- Video links
- Cognella journal articles
- News clips

References

Americans With Disabilities Act of 1990, Pub. L. No. 101-336, 104 Stat. 328 (1990).

Bartol, C. R. (1996). Police psychology: Then, now, and beyond. *Criminal Justice and Behavior, 23*(1), 70–89. https://doi.org/10.1177/0093854896023001006

Bonsignore v. City of New York, 1982 (United States Court of Appeals, Second Circuit February 08, 1982).

Buchanan v. City of San Antonio (United States Court of Appeals, Fifth Circuit June 13, 1996).

Cherry, K. (2020). *What Is the Minnesota Multiphasic Personality Inventory (MMPI)?* VeryWellMind. https://www.verywellmind.com/what-is-the-minnesota-multiphasic-personality-inventory-2795582

Cherry, K., & Gans, S. (2019). *What are the big 5 personality traits?* VeryWellMind. https://www.verywellmind.com/the-big-five-personality-dimensions-2795422

Corey, D. A. (n.d.). Case demonstrations using the MMPI-2-RF police candidate interpretive report (PCIR). Lecture presented at Pearsons

Corey, D. M., & Ben-Porath, Y. S. (2014). *User's guide for the police candidate interpretive report* [Pamphlet]. Pearson.

Drayton, M. (2009). The Minnesota Multiphasic Personality Inventory-2 (MMPI-2). *Occupational Medicine, 59*(2), 135–136. https://doi.org/10.1093/occmed/kqn182

Emmett, A. (2004, October). Snake oil or science? That's the raging debate on personality testing. *Workforce Management, 83*(10), 90–92.

Framingham, J. (2018, October 13). *Minnesota Multiphasic Personality Inventory (MMPI)*. https://psychcentral.com/lib/minnesota-multiphasic-personality-inventory-mmpi/

Gale, S. F. (2002, April). Three companies cut turnover with tests. *Workforce, 81*(4), 66–69.

Hild v. Bruner (US District Court for the District of New Jersey July 28, 1980).

Leonel v. American Airlines (United States Court of Appeals, Ninth Circuit March 04, 2005).

Mason, S. N., Bubany, S., & Butcher, J. N. (2017, March 06). *Gender differences on personality tests.* https://www.google.com/url?sa=t&rct=j&q=&esrc=s&source=web&cd=1&ved=2ahUKE-wiApIf38aDhAhWKrlQKHW0eB7UQFjAAegQIBBAC&url=http://mmpi.umn.edu/documents/gender-differences-in-personality-faq-3-8-2017.pdf&usg=AOvVaw2JLRBWdcY49qGgnO1zWyl7

Pearson. (n.d.). *Minnesota Multiphasic Personality Inventory-2.* https://www.pearsonclinical.com/RelatedInfo/products/mmpi-2_rfpcir.html

University of Missouri. (n.d.). *Guide to Holland Code* [Brochure]. Author.

What Is the Medical Examination?

"A healthy diet is a solution to many of our health-care problems. It's the most important solution."

—John Mackey

KEY TERMS

Medical examination: The medical exam is generally required by state statute or administrative rule (in the state the hiring agency is located) that requires the candidate to go to a medical doctor's office for a variety of medical tests to check their ability to perform the physical demands of the job of a law enforcement officer.

Post-conditional offer of employment: The post-conditional offer of employment is when an employer tells the candidate they have passed every part of the hiring process and can be offered the job depending on the results of the psychological evaluation and medical examination.

CHAPTER LEARNING OBJECTIVES

After reading the chapter, you should have a good understanding of the following:

- The medical examination
- How a hiring agency can require a candidate to take a medical examination
- What types of tests will be done during the medical examination
- How a candidate's prescribed medications are evaluated
- How to prepare for a medical examination

What Is the Medical Examination?

The **medical examination** is generally required by state statute or administrative rule (in the state the hiring agency is located) that "requires all law enforcement officers and applicants demonstrate the physical abilities to perform the critical and essential tasks of a law enforcement officer" (Department of Public Safety Standards and Training (DPSST), 2016, p. 1). A licensed physician or surgeon is paid by the hiring agency to "ensure (candidates) meet the required minimum physical standards as established by the Board on Public Safety Standards and Training" (DPSST, 2016, p. 1).

In plain English, the candidate goes to a medical doctor's office and is given a variety of medical tests to check their ability to perform the physical demands of the job of a law enforcement officer.

Can a Hiring Agency Require I Take a Medical Examination?

Yes. A hiring agency can require candidates to take the medical examination as a part of the law enforcement hiring process. When a candidate is required to take the medical examination (just as with the psychological evaluation) as a part of the hiring process, the candidate will be required to sign a waiver. The waiver, otherwise known as a **post-conditional offer of employment**, is when an employer tells the candidate they have passed every part of the hiring process and can be offered the job depending on the results of the psychological evaluation and medical examination.

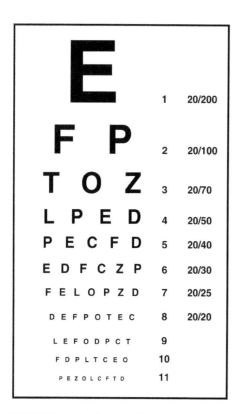

What Types of Tests Will Be Done During the Medical Examination?

While every hiring agency is different, most medical examination contains similar tests. The following list illustrates the most common tests candidates are evaluated on during the medical examination. Note that the individual standards listed may be different depending on the hiring agency; therefore, the candidate is advised to research the hiring agency to find out the specific requirements for that agency. The following list is just a guide, and the information was taken from the Department of Public Safety Standards and Training (2016) medical examination for police, corrections, parole and probation officers and liquor enforcement inspectors.

1. Eyes and vision: the Snellen eye chart helps to determine the clarity of distance vision, nearsightedness, blurry distance vision, and legal visual acuity requirement (Eye Tests, the Eye Chart and 20/20 Vision Explained, n.d.). Figure 10.1 is the Snellen eye chart.

FIGURE 10-1 Snellen eye chart.

a. Monocular vision (seeing with only one eye at a time) must be at least 20/30 correct in each eye not worse than 20/100 uncorrected in either eye.

b. Binocular vision (seeing with both eyes) must be at least 20/20 corrected.

c. Soft contact lenses: Candidates with uncorrected vision worse than 20/100 must wear soft contact lenses to meet the corrected vision requirement.

d. Color vision: the HRR (Hardy Rand and Rittler) standard pseudoisochromatic test is used to check the color vision of a candidate. "The HRR Pseudoisochromatic Plate Test 4th Edition supports very efficient color deficiency screening" (Lite Company, n.d.). Candidates are shown a variety of plates to screen for color deficiencies. Candidates must be able to distinguish blue, green, red, and yellow. Candidates who fail to meet the color vision standards may meet this standard by showing the ability to correctly discriminate colors via a field test approved by the hiring agency.

e. Depth perception: The random stereo test is given to candidates. "The Random Dot Stereogram E (RDE) has been shown to be a simple and effective test for the detection of binocular abnormalities and defective visual acuity in children" (Hope & Maslin, 1990, p. 319).

f. Peripheral vision: Visual field performance must be 140 degrees in the horizontal meridian combined.

Candidates can do their own self-vision checks by following the instructions in Self-Assessments 10.1 to 10.5.

SELF-ASSESSMENT 10.1: SELF-VISION TEST

You can check your own vision for free by following the instructions:

1. Go to https://visionsource.com/patients/free-eye-chart-download/.
2. Click on the eye chart and download it.
3. Print out the eye chart and tape it at eye level to any wall (no windows) in a room that is well lit.
4. Stand 10 feet from the wall/eye chart.
5. Cover one eye, read the letters aloud, and keep track of which letters you get correct (it is easier if you have a person assist you and point to the letters and keep track of the letters you get correct). Continue until you can no longer read the letters.
6. Document the smallest line where you identified most of the letters correctly (if you could read five out of the eight letters you would document 20/20).
7. Repeat steps 4–6 with the opposite eye covered.
8. Or, go to your favorite search engine and search for "free vision test."

SELF-ASSESSMENT 10.2: SELF-COLOR VISION TEST

You can check your own color vision for free by following the instructions:

1. Go to https://enchroma.com/pages/test.

2. Follow the instructions, and in less than 2 minutes, you will have the results of the test.
3. Or, go to your favorite search engine and search for "free color vision test."

SELF-ASSESSMENT 10.3: SELF-DEPTH PERCEPTION VISION TEST

You can check your own depth-perception vision for free by following the instructions:

1. Go to https://www.youtube.com/watch?v=uuoCREqckbU.
2. Follow the instructions on the video to check your depth-perception.
3. Or, go to your favorite search engine and search for "free depth perception vision test."

SELF-ASSESSMENT 10.4: SELF-PERIPHERAL VISION TEST

You can check your own peripheral vision for free by following the instructions:

1. Go to http://www.vutest.com/visual-fields/index.php.
2. Follow the instructions on the video to check your peripheral vision.
3. Or, go to your favorite search engine and search for "free peripheral vision test."

SELF-ASSESSMENT 10.5: SELF-MULTIPLE VISION TESTS 10.5

You can check your visual acuity, astigmatism, light sensitivity, near vision, color vision, and AMD for free by following the instructions:

1. Go to https://www.essilor.com/en/vision-tests/test-your-vision/.
2. Follow the instructions on the video to conduct various vision tests.

2. Ears and hearing
   a. Candidate's external canal, tympanic membrane, and so on will be checked.
   b. Hearing loss in candidates must be no greater than 25 (db) at the 500, 1,000, 2,000, and 3,000-Hertz levels in either ear. No single loss in excess of 40 db.
   c. Amplification devices can be used to meet the hearing requirements.

Candidates can do their own self-hearing check by following the instructions in Self-Assessment 10.6.

SELF-ASSESSMENT 10.6: SELF-HEARING TEST

You can check your own hearing for free by following the instructions:

1. Go to https://www.starkey.com/online-hearing-test#!/HearingTestLandingPrimary#HearingTestApp.

2. Follow the instructions on the video to check your hearing.
3. Or, go to your favorite search engine and search for "free hearing test."

---

3. Cardiovascular
   a. Resting blood pressure must be less or equal to 160 mmHg systolic and 100 mmHg diastolic.
   b. Candidates who have cardiovascular issues must be examined by a general practitioner to address the issue and conduct further medical evaluations.
4. Chest and lungs
   a. Candidates with obstructive or restrictive spirograms (FVC or FEB1 less than 80% or FVC/FEV1 ration of less than 70%) must be examined by a general practitioner to address the issue and conduct further medical evaluations.
   b. Pulmonary function test is conducted.
5. Abdominal
6. Head, neck, and throat
7. Musculoskeletal
   a. Candidates flexibility is checked: arms, fingers, head (motions), bending, squatting and stooping.
   b. Spine and extremities exams are conducted.
8. Neurological
   a. Candidate's cerebellar and cranial nerves and reflexes (including pathological) are checked.
9. Skin
10. Lab work
    a. Candidates provide a blood sample(s), and the following lab work is requested (list is not comprehensive):
       i. CBC
       ii. Chemistry panel
       iii. Tuberculosis
       iv. Urinalysis/drug screen
       v. Other

What About Prescribed Medications?

The candidate's current prescribed medication list must be reviewed, and the side effects must not interfere with the candidate's ability to perform the essential job duties and tasks of a law enforcement officer. The hiring agency will generally not make a decision about a candidate's prescription medication until the candidate has taken the psychological evaluation and the medical examination. Once those two evaluations are conducted, along with the background investigation, the hiring agency will have a better idea of who the candidate is and will understand the reasoning behind the prescription medication and the side effects of it as well. The most important factor is if the prescribed medication interferes or could interfere with the candidate's ability to perform the essential job duties and tasks.

If a candidate is seriously concerned about any prescription medication they are taking, and if it could interfere with their ability to perform as a law enforcement officer, the candidate can start by contacting their physician or psychiatrist who prescribed the medication. The candidate can tell them their future aspirations and ask if the physician or psychiatrist thinks the prescribed medication could cause issues. While their answer may not be exactly what the hiring agency may want, it will give the candidate a good start in understanding of the possible concerns that may be brought up.

Document 10.1 illustrates the critical and essential tasks for the following roles:

- Police officer
- Corrections officer
- Parole and probation officer
- Liquor enforcement inspector

The tasks listed are from the Department of Public Safety Standards and Training (DPSST, 2016, pp. 11–20).

Police Officer
Critical & Essential Tasks

Conduct Investigations

- Advise persons of their Constitutional rights as legally required.
- Comply with legal parameters.
- Conduct criminal surveillance.
- Conduct drive-by identification applying appropriate legal parameters.
- Conduct follow up investigations of violations of law.
- Investigate incidents, evaluate information and evidence to determine if there are sufficient grounds to believe a violation of law has occurred.
- Evaluate information, evidence and observations to determine if legal grounds exist to arrest persons without a warrant.
- Interview (talk with) people to obtain information.
- Listen closely to interviewee to ensure full understanding.
- Observe people to detect signs of deception, manipulation, etc.
- Observe the environment of a particular location (like a crime scene) to identify potential evidence.
- Perform Law Enforcement Data System (LEDS) or other criminal justice data base inquiry.
- Prepare and conduct photo line-up applying appropriate legal parameters.
- Read criminal investigation reports.
- Read statements.
- Review records and photographs to identify people (suspects, witnesses, etc.).
- Take written statements from people.
- Utilize drug test kit and interpret results.

Search and Seizure

- Legally conduct pat down of person.

- Legally search person, vehicle or premises.
- Prepare and serve search warrants applying appropriate legal parameters.

Report Writing

- Diagram crime scenes.
- Complete required report forms.
- Document actions, observations, interpretations, and/or conclusions.
- Proofread reports to identify and correct mistakes.
- Use word processor or word processing program to write report.
- Write descriptive, thorough narrative reports in a timely manner.
- Write reports documenting statements/confessions.
- Write reports using correct English for clear communication.
- Write reports using correct sentence structure for clear communication.
- Write reports using correct spelling and punctuation for clear communication.
- Write legibly.

Community Services

- Administer first aid.
- Comfort emotionally upset persons.
- Communicate effectively in the English language.
- Conduct a police officer mental hold.
- Conduct crime prevention.
- Conduct welfare check.
- Cooperate with other agencies.
- Deliver emergency messages (e.g. death notifications, etc.).
- Develop and implement problem solving strategies.
- Develop community partnerships.
- Interact with people who do not speak English as a primary language.
- Make lawful stops, detentions and arrests.
- Mediate and assist people in problem solving.
- Perform CPR/use AED.
- Provide mutual aid.
- Refer persons to other agencies that provide services.
- Take child into protective custody.
- Treat everyone equally and fairly with respect.
- Use proactive strategies.
- Use sensitivity when dealing with people.
- Understand the needs of people with disabilities.
- Understand strategies for dealing with people in extreme circumstances or in crisis.
- Understanding strategies for dealing with people who are impaired or under the influence of intoxicants or drugs.
- Serve subpoenas or civil processes.

Evidence Process

- Collect crime scene evidence.
- Collect DNA evidence.
- Collect latent prints.
- Document chain of custody of evidence.
- Obtain fingerprints from individuals.
- Photograph crime scene.
- Photograph evidence.
- Photograph suspects/victims.
- Preserve crime scene.
- Process evidence.
- Secure crime scene.
- Secure lost/stolen/seized property.

Patrol Services

- Arrest persons as authorized by arrest warrants.
- Conduct area search.
- Conduct bar checks.
- Conduct building searches.
- Conduct civil stand-by.
- Conduct crowd control.
- Conduct field interviews.
- Conduct patrol of assigned area.
- Coordinate response of other resources.
- Defuse hostile situations.
- Establish perimeters.
- Evaluate situations, applying legal standards and requirements to determine appropriate course of action (decision making).
- Investigate suspicious persons.
- Issue citation in lieu of an arrest.
- Knowledge of K-9 operations.
- Lodge persons in custody in jail.
- Mediate civil disputes.
- Operate a mobile data terminal or computer.
- Operate office equipment.
- Perform equipment inspection.
- Prepare for trials/hearings.
- Request additional resources (both police and non-police).
- Respond to call for police services.
- Testify in hearings/court.
- Transport persons in custody.
- Use fire extinguisher.
- Use information on crime occurrences to determine patrol patterns.

- Use police radio.
- Use pursuit intervention tools (e.g. spike strips).

Traffic Services

- Assist operators in exchanging information at crash scenes.
- Collect evidence at crash scenes.
- Conduct high-risk traffic stops.
- Conduct unknown-risk traffic stops.
- Diagram traffic crash scenes.
- Direct traffic.
- Explain legal procedures to traffic violators.
- Have vehicles towed.
- Investigate major traffic crimes.
- Investigate traffic crashes.
- Investigate violations of motor vehicle laws.
- Locate and verify vehicle identification number.
- Operate Intoxilyzer.
- Perform Field Sobriety Testing.
- Photograph crash scenes.
- Protect crash scenes and responders.
- Provide motorist assistance.
- Utilize speed measurement devices.
- Issue traffic citations and warnings.

Vehicle Operations

- Inspect vehicle equipment.
- Operate safety and emergency equipment in vehicle.
- Safely operate vehicle.
- Safely operate vehicle in emergency responses.
- Care for patrol vehicle.
- Operate a vehicle while in pursuit.

Use of Force

- Apply force within legal parameters using proper judgment and decision making.
- Articulate clear, verbal commands.
- Awareness and/or understanding of defensive tools commonly used by police officers.
- Utilize appropriate tools and tactics in response to use of force situations.

Maintain Professional Competence

- Complete and stay current on relevant training.
- Demonstrate competent performance.

- Maintain and secure equipment and weapons.
- Meet/maintain standards for certification.
- Meet standards in use of appropriate tools and tactics.
- Understand and apply case law.
- Understand and apply policies/procedures.
- Understand and apply laws, local codes/ordinances.
- Review legal and Legislative updates.
- Read and comprehend written material (e.g. legal decisions, policies and procedures, training materials, ORS, etc.).
- Demonstrate ability to adapt to evolving policing environment.

Maintain Professional Standards

- Adhere to Code of Ethics.
- Follow agency policies and procedures.
- Meet and maintain minimum ability to perform job tasks.
- Maintain a professional image.

Sitting, Standing, Walking, Running

- Maintain balance while walking on narrow or elevated surfaces.
- Run on flat surface.
- Run to assist another officer.
- Move in response to attacking person(s).
- Run up/down stairs.
- Run/chase after fleeing person.
- Sit continuously (car, desk, etc.).
- Stand continuously or for extended times.
- Walk continuously or for extended times.
- Walk or move backwards.
- Walk up/down stairs.
- Walk/run on irregular, potentially hazardous surfaces (slick, muddy, rocks, etc.).

Crawling, Climbing, Over/Under Obstacles

- Climb over railings or over other external features/obstacles.
- Crawl on hands and knees to search under vehicle/residence/structure, etc.
- Climb or pull oneself over a vertical obstacle (e.g. a fence).
- Crawl under an obstacle.
- Crawl through a physically confined area (crawl space, culvert, etc.).
- Climb up/down ladder.
- Climb through a window or other small opening.

Lifting, Carrying, Pushing

- Carry objects from one location to another.
- Carry/drag an unresisting person (with assistance).
- Carry/drag an unresisting person (without assistance).
- Lift objects (not people) up off the ground.
- Lift objects above head.
- Lift objects down from elevated surface (waist high or above) and place on ground or floor.
- Physically force open locked, or blocked door/gate.
- Pull-push resisting person through vehicle or structure window to remove person from vehicle or structure.
- Pull-push unresisting person through vehicle or structure window to remove person from vehicle or structure.
- Push/pull objects—other than vehicle.
- Pull oneself up to see over obstacles (such as high fences, window ledges, etc.) and/or to gain access to building or structure.

Jumping, Vaulting

- Jump over ditch, hole, or other depression.
- Jump over hazard such as water, broken glass, etc.
- Jump over raised barrier (e.g., low fence).
- Jump up/down from elevated surface.

Struggle, Fight, Defend

- Catch falling person to avoid injury.
- Dodge/evade blows, thrown objects.
- Draw and fire duty weapon at moving threat in all lighting conditions.
- Draw and fire duty weapon in a state of physical exhaustion.
- Defend oneself in a physical altercation on the ground.
- Extract a struggling person from a structure or motor vehicle.
- Fire shoulder weapon (rifle, shotgun, etc.).
- Grip and hold a person to maintain physical control (assisted and unassisted).
- Handcuff—mechanically restrain compliant subject.
- Handcuff—mechanically restrain non-compliant subject.
- Hold/restrain a struggling person.
- Physically defend against and control a single attacker.
- Physically defend against and control multiple attackers.
- Physically intervene to break up fights/physical confrontations between two or more persons.
- Place a struggling suspect in a structure or motor vehicle.
- Re-load duty weapon in combat conditions.
- Subdue a fleeing person to stop flight.

- Take down and subdue a resisting person or attacker.
- Use firearms in physical confrontation.
- Use defense tool(s) (baton, electrical control device, OC spray) to subdue person in physical confrontation.
- Use nerve pressure points to control/subdue resisting person.
- Use various holds to control/subdue resisting-combative suspects.

Combined Physical Activities

- Accurately use vision and hearing for threat assessment in use of force situations
- Being struck by, and/or striking person (physical altercations)
- Carrying object up/down stairs/steps
- Conduct area searches (walking, standing, kneeling, crawling, lifting, bending, etc.) looking for item or person
- Conduct physical person searches of individuals
- Draw, aim, fire and retain service weapon
- Drive agency vehicle in a wide range of routine and emergency conditions
- Falling/being knocked down in struggle or pursuit—recovering to feet—resuming struggle/pursuit
- Maintain visual contact in pursuit (car and foot) in unpredictable terrain and conditions
- Multi-task while operating a patrol car (radio communications, computer, weapons and tools, etc.)
- Participate in Defensive Tactics Training (DT's) and scenario-based training
- Physically struggling with multiple persons
- Pursue subject on foot, negotiating barriers and hazards (running, jumping, climbing, etc.)
- Rapidly exit vehicle (standing up from a seated position inside the car) and move away from the car
- Routine use of color computer monitor
- Struggle with and subdue subject after pursuit/evasion; place subject in vehicle for transport
- Subdue and physically/mechanically restrain; lift/carry/drag person from one area to another
- Transport person (resisting, not resisting) between locations, maintaining physical control, negotiating stairs, doorways, obstacles and other features
- Understand speech through electronic devices (telephone, radio, cell phone, etc.) in a wide range of environmental conditions
- Use breaching tools to break door, force through door
- K-9-unit activity (keep up with track)

Psychological Elements with Physical Effects

- Being exposed to hazardous substances (drugs, chemicals, infectious diseases, etc.)
- Continuing to function in a physical confrontation after being struck/injured
- Cope with the emotional and physical impact of being shot at.
- Cope with the emotional and physical impact of being subjected to verbal threats of violence

- Cope with the emotional and physical impact of constant exposure to personal legal liability
- Cope with the emotional and physical impact of constant scrutiny and criticism (management, attorneys, judges, the public, etc.)
- Cope with the emotional and physical impact of seeing, hearing, smelling and reading about horrific events/occurrences
- Cope with the emotional and physical impact of shift work
- Cope with the emotional and physical impact of witnessing the abuse, injury or death of a child
- Cope with the emotional and physical results of being struck by—exposed to bodily fluids
- Cope with the long-term emotional and physical impact of constant exposure to deviance (distorted world view)
- Cope with the physical effects of acute emotional stress (fear, anger) (self and family)
- Cope with the physical effects of chronic (cumulative) emotional stress (self and family)
- Maintaining a state of hypervigilance (highly concentrated mental and sensory attention) over protracted period of time
- Viewing, handling, exposure to human remains

General Physical Activities

- Balancing, while leaning, stretching or ducking around obstacles
- Bend down or kneel on knees to conduct search activities or to minimize exposure
- Bending over from waist (to pick up objects off ground, etc.)
- Cardio-vascular endurance (sudden onset, sustained, high-demand physical exertion for longer than three minutes)
- Getting into and out of a vehicle (sitting from standing position and standing from seated position)
- Reaching from various positions to grasp objects/persons
- Talking on phone, radio, while using computer
- Transition between sitting and standing
- Twisting at the waist
- Typing on keyboard
- Use computer mouse
- Using computer keyboard in vehicle
- Crawling on hands and knees

Sensory Acuity, Discrimination (under low stress or normal conditions)

- Accurately determine full-range colors (clothing, substances, skin tones) in varying light conditions.
- Detect and identify visual images in low-light conditions.
- Visually detect and identify images, facial and body features, and movement of persons and objects in varying light conditions.
- Visually detect and identify transitory and subtle changes in body language (pupil constriction/dilation, skin color and respiration changes, etc.).

- Detect and identify faint and/or odd odors.
- Detect and understand faint auditory signals (whispers, transients [clicks, pops, impacts], air movement, etc.).
- Detect and understand speech in the presence of a wide range of environmental sounds, including high levels of ambient background noise.
- Three-dimensional vision, sufficient for clear depth perception, image placement and location sufficient for complex visual tasks (driving a vehicle in emergency conditions, pursuit of persons over complex surfaces in unpredictable conditions, stairs, steps, obstacles, weapons use, etc.).

Corrections Officer
Critical & Essential Tasks

Booking, Receiving, Releasing Tasks

- Observe and document inmates' physical markings.
- Inventory, record, and secure inmates' personal property.
- Obtain information for the intake process from the transporting or arresting officer and from the inmate.
- Review intake forms and/or court documents for accuracy, completeness, and timeliness.
- Prepare necessary forms, files, etc., to initiate inmates' facility record.
- Ensure inmates are photographed and fingerprinted.
- Inspect inmates' documentation prior to release or transfer.
- Release or transfer inmates per established processes.

Communication, Crisis/Conflict Management Tasks

- Verbally resolve conflict between inmates and staff.
- Appropriately respond to inmates' questions.
- Verbally reprimand inmates for rules and regulations violations.
- Testify in court.
- Distribute, post, and/or explain inmates' guidelines, rules, and rights.
- Diffuse potentially hostile or difficult situations.
- Communicate effectively with inmates, staff, other professionals, etc.
- Verbally resolve conflict between inmates.

Escorting & Transporting Tasks

- Transport inmates (resisting, not resisting) within a facility, negotiating physical barriers.
- Maintain control of inmates while loading, unloading, and driving transport vehicles.
- When required, provide armed supervision and transport inmates outside the facility.
- Escort inmates within the facility.
- Escort inmates in a vehicle.

Facility Security & Emergency Tasks

- Patrol tiers, cell areas, corridors, and other security areas inside the facility to ensure security, and observe inmates' behaviors.
- Observe and report breaches of security or unsound security practices.
- Notify supervisors of potential emergencies and hazards.
- Move inmates to evacuate an area or facility.
- Respond to emergencies (including drills).
- Inspect and report any concerns (sanitation, maintenance, safety, and security) related to the physical structure of the facility.
- Verify the identity of individuals bringing inmates into the facility.
- Verify the identity of inmates entering and leaving the facility.
- Inspect inmates' mail or packages for unauthorized items.
- Issue facility keys to authorized personnel.
- Inspect and verify the identification of persons entering and leaving the facility.
- Inspect vehicles and/or containers entering and leaving the facility.

Medical & Psychological Assistance Tasks

- Identify inmates' stress factors.
- Report severe depression or unusual behavior that might indicate self-destructive behavior (suicide).
- Observe inmates to recognize symptoms of substance abuse.
- Observe incoming inmates' physical condition.
- Observe incoming inmates to identify mental health issues.
- Investigate and document inmates' injuries.
- Determine the need for emergency medical care.
- Request psychiatric/mental health treatment for inmates.
- Administer first aid, CPR, mouth-to-mouth resuscitation, and use of AED (Automated External Defibrillator).
- Use gloves, masks, gowns, etc., to prevent contact with infectious diseases.
- Ensure proper cleanup of bio hazards.
- Supervise inmates taking prescribed medications.
- Recognize and respond to inmates with special needs (juveniles, sex offenders, physically disabled inmates, etc.).
- Supervise inmates with mental health concerns.
- Medically screen inmates.
- Take emergency steps when inmate suicide is threatened or implied.

Other Job-Related Tasks

- Know and apply standards for Corrections in Oregon.
- Understand and apply laws pertaining to PREA (Prison Rape Elimination Act).

- Adhere to the Code of Ethics.
- Meet and maintain minimum standards for corrections officers.
- Treat everyone fairly and respectfully.
- Participate in training to maintain knowledge and/or skills.
- Evaluate situations; apply legal standards and requirements to determine the appropriate course of action.
- Follow orders and directions.

Required Physical or Sensory Perception Capabilities

- Bend over from the waist at or below waist level.
- Walk continuously.
- Stand continuously.
- Walk up and down stairs.
- Sit continuously (car, desk, etc.).
- Lift objects off the ground.
- Carry and place objects.
- Lift objects from an elevated surface and place on the ground or floor.
- Maintain a state of hypervigilance (increased awareness of the surrounding environment).
- Cope with the physical effects of acute emotional stress (self, others).
- Cope with the physical effects of chronic emotional stress (self, others).
- Cope with the chronic physical effects of shift work.
- Cope with the emotional and physical impact of verbal abuse and/or threats by inmates.
- Cope with the emotional impact of working with seriously mentally ill inmates.
- Kneel, squat and recover to feet.
- Perform repetitive hand movements (typing, mouse, bar code scanning, etc.).
- Bend over from the waist at or below waist level.
- Accurately resolve visual images in various conditions, up to 100 feet.
- Accurately determine a full range of colors.
- Resolve and understand faint auditory signals.
- Resolve and understand speech in a noisy environment.
- Detect and resolve odd odors.
- Accurately resolve visual images in low light conditions.
- Utilize three-dimensional vision sufficient for accurate depth perception in high-risk situations.
- Accurately visually detect and resolve transitory and subtle changes in "body language."

Search, Seizure & Investigation Tasks

- Search all areas for contraband.
- Pat search inmates.
- Perform unclothed searches of inmates.
- Search clothing and property left for inmates.
- Investigate inmates' criminal activity.
- Process evidence seized during searches of inmates and/or cells, rooms, etc.

- Document the chain of evidence.
- Seize contraband material.
- Confiscate inmates' possessions.
- Inspect and/or search inmates' clothing.
- Search inmates' personal property.
- Investigate and initiate remedial action on security breaches.
- Search inmates entering and leaving the facility and all other areas.
- Complete required documentation including narrative reports.

Supervise & Monitor Inmate Tasks

- Apply "progressive" inmate discipline (type of discipline based on the offense).
- Observe and investigate unusual traffic or movement.
- Investigate unusual odors or sounds.
- Identify, observe, and document the activity of agitators and aggressors.
- Respond to inmates' behavior and movement to prevent or stop a physical conflict between inmates.
- Facilitate inmates' access to legal and religious materials.
- Instruct inmates in housekeeping and sanitation procedures.
- Monitor and log inmates' behavior and activities in disciplinary or administrative segregation.
- Control access to and from all living areas.
- Monitor and control inmates' activities.
- Observe inmates to verify presence and determine physical condition.
- Document inmate movement.
- Direct inmates to enter and leave cells.
- Conduct head or facility count.

Use of Force & Physical Control Tasks

- Respond appropriately to fights or physical confrontations between inmates.
- Subdue, mechanically restrain, and remove an inmate to and from a holding area or cell.
- Recover from being knocked down or falling and resume struggle or pursuit.
- Use reasonable force to maintain order, protect self, others, and prevent escape.
- Qualify and/or engage in required training for firearms and other weapons.

Parole and Probation Officer
Critical & Essential Tasks

Sitting, Standing, Walking, Running

- Run to escape an attacking person.
- Walk up and down stairs.
- Sit continuously (car, desk, etc.).

- Walk and run on irregular, potentially hazardous surfaces (slick, muddy, rocks, etc.).
- Walk or move backwards.
- Run to assist another officer.
- Walk backwards.

Lifting, Carrying, Pushing

- Lift objects (not people) up off the ground.
- Push and pull objects, other than a vehicle.
- Carry objects from one location to another.
- Lift objects up to and down from an elevated surface (waist high or above) and place them on the ground or the floor.
- Lift objects above head.
- Carry duty gear (10 to 30 pounds).

Jumping, Vaulting

- Jump over a ditch, a hole, or other depression.

General Physical Activities

- Bend over from the waist to perform activities such as picking up objects from the ground, etc.
- Twist at the waist.
- Bend down or kneel to conduct search activities or to minimize exposure.
- Type on a keyboard.
- Use a computer mouse.
- Talk on the telephone or radio while using a computer.
- Balance while leaning, stretching or ducking around obstacles.
- Transition between sitting and standing.
- Reach from various positions to grasp objects and persons.
- Get into and out of a vehicle (sitting down from a standing position or standing up from seated position).
- Tolerate extreme environmental conditions such as rain, snow, heat, cold, wind, etc.
- Pull open heavy file drawers.

Struggle, Fight, Defend

- Grip and hold a person to maintain physical control (assisted).
- Grip and hold a person to maintain physical control (unassisted).
- Extract a struggling person from a structure or a vehicle.
- Place a struggling person in a structure or a vehicle.
- Use various holds to control (subdue) resisting or combative people.
- Hold (restrain) a struggling person.

- Physically defend against and control a single attacker.
- Physically defend against and control multiple attackers.
- Take down and subdue a resisting person.
- Draw and fire a duty weapon in a state of physical exhaustion, during or subsequent to a physical altercation.
- Reload a duty weapon in combat conditions.
- Draw and fire a duty weapon in self-defense or to defend another person.
- Handcuff (mechanically restrain) a compliant person.
- Handcuff (mechanically restrain) a non-compliant person.
- Catch a falling person to avoid injury.
- Tackle a fleeing person to stop flight.
- Engage in ground fighting with a person.
- Use hand weapons, such as a baton, taser, OC spray, etc., to subdue a person in physical confrontation.
- Use firearms in a physical confrontation.
- Use nerve pressure points to control (subdue) a resisting person.
- Physically intervene to break up physical confrontations between two or more people.
- Dodge (evade) blows and thrown objects.
- Block kicks, strikes, and punches.

Combined Physical Activities

- Drive a vehicle in a wide range of routine and emergency conditions.
- Rapidly exit a vehicle (standing up from a seated position inside the vehicle) and move away from the vehicle.
- Pursue a person on foot, negotiating barriers and hazards (running, jumping, climbing, etc.).
- Struggle with and subdue a person after a pursuit or evasion; place a person in a vehicle for transport.
- Multi-task while operating a vehicle (radio communications, computer, weapons, tools, etc.).
- Subdue and physically or mechanically restrain a person (lift, carry, or drag the person from one area to another).
- Understand speech through electronic devices (telephone, radio, cell phone, etc.) in a wide range of environmental conditions.
- Transport a resistant or non-resistant person within a detention facility or between locations, maintaining physical control, negotiating stairs, doorways, obstacles and other features.
- Accurately use vision and hearing for threat assessment in use of force situations.
- Routinely use a color computer monitor.
- Draw aim and fire a service pistol.
- Be struck by, and/or strike a person (physical altercations).
- Physically struggle with multiple persons.
- Fall or be knocked down in a struggle or pursuit and recover to feet to resume the struggle or pursuit.
- Carry an object up or down a staircase or steps.

- Participate in Defensive Tactics Training (DT's).
- Conduct person searches.
- Conduct area searches (walking, standing, kneeling, crawling, lifting, bending, etc.) looking for an item or a person.
- Bend over into a vehicle to secure a person's seat belt.
- Render various firearms safe.

Psychological Elements with Physical Effects

- Continue to function in a physical confrontation after being struck or injured.
- Cope with the physical effects of personal acute emotional stress such as fear, anger, etc.
- Cope with the physical effects of personal chronic (cumulative) emotional stress.
- Cope with the emotional and physical results of being struck by or exposed to bodily fluids.
- Cope with maintaining a state of hypervigilance (highly concentrated mental and sensory attention) over protracted periods of time.
- Cope with the emotional and physical impact of being subjected to verbal threats of violence.
- Cope with being exposed to hazardous substances, such as drugs, chemicals, infectious diseases, etc.
- Cope with the emotional and physical impact of seeing, hearing, smelling and reading about horrific events and occurrences.
- Cope with the emotional and physical impact of witnessing the abuse, injury or death of a child.
- Cope with the emotional and physical impact of constant scrutiny and criticism (management, attorneys, judges, the public, etc.).
- Cope with the long-term emotional and physical impact of constant exposure to deviance (distorted world view).
- Cope with the emotional and physical impact of constant exposure to personal legal liability.
- Cope with the emotional and physical impact of being shot at.
- Cope with the emotional and physical impact of constant exposure to high risk offenders.
- Cope with constant changes in laws, procedures, and policies.
- Cope with ambiguity in operating requirements and/or expectations.
- Cope with clients who are mentally ill.
- Cope with demands of being on call.
- Cope with job related stress (unrealistic expectations, lay-offs, etc.).

Sensory Acuity, Discrimination

- Accurately visually detect and resolve images, facial and body features, and movement of persons and objects in varying light conditions, at distances up to 100 feet.
- Accurately determine full-range colors (clothing, substances, skin tones, etc.) in varying light conditions.
- Resolve and understand faint auditory signals (whispers, transients [clicks, pops, impacts], air movement, etc.).
- Resolve and understand speech in the presence of a wide range of environmental sounds, including high levels of ambient background noise.

- Detect and resolve faint and/or odd odors.
- Accurately resolve visual images in low-light conditions.
- Utilize three-dimensional vision (clear depth perception, image placement and location) sufficient for complex visual tasks, such as driving a vehicle in emergency conditions or pursuing people over complex surfaces in unpredictable conditions (stairs, steps, obstacles, weapons use, etc.).
- Accurately visually detect and resolve transitory and subtle changes in body language, such as pupil constriction, pupil dilation, skin color, respiration changes, etc.
- View, read, and interpret messages on computer screen.

Create, Maintain, Access Offender Files & Documents

- Prepare an electronic warrant request.
- Conduct a release plan investigation to develop a supervision plan for the offender.
- Make computerized chronological entries.
- Write computerized reports.
- Enter treatment data electronically.
- Generate Compact papers via computer.
- Generate risk assessments via computer.
- Fill out various forms related to community supervision.
- Prepare basic business correspondence.
- Generate caseload management reports via computer.
- Assemble and file materials in the case file in a prescribed order.
- Maintain various department records such as logs, action plans, case plans, etc.
- Write reports consisting of several short descriptive phrases, sentence fragments or very short sentences.
- Write in-depth narrative reports containing complete sentences and paragraphs.
- Complete reports consisting primarily of check-off boxes or fill-in-blanks.
- Develop and maintain personal descriptive information on offenders.
- Develop and maintain various basic administrative systems to record report schedules, violations, etc.
- Assess various kinds of written and spoken information to formulate a specific recommendation for action by the adjudicating authority.
- Generate a 'to do' list via computer.

Supervise Offenders—Direct Client Activities

- Observe the offender to assess their mental and physical state.
- Observe behavior and language to assess the offender's commitment to the supervision plan.
- Provide counseling to the offender, their family, etc. to resolve domestic problems.
- Meet regularly with the offender to provide counseling, encouragement, and structure.
- Encourage and/or direct the offender to fulfill legal requirements such as support payments, fines, etc.
- Generate urinalysis information via a computer.

- Track the offender's address updates via computer.
- Generate and/or change legal data such as conditions, expiration dates, affidavits, etc. via computer.
- Check on the offender's supervisor fees via computer.
- Generate action plans.
- Use Risk/Needs Assessment to guide an interview with the offender.
- Discuss Parole Board/Supervising Authority's decision with the offender to explain and/or clarify special conditions, reasons for denial, appeal procedures, dates, etc.
- Observe and assess the offender to determine "criminogenic needs."
- Assess offender to determine "presenting problem."
- Discuss the offender with other parole or professional staff to determine approaches, solutions, etc.
- Discuss possible violation of parole or other accusations in order to allow offender to refute and/or explain findings.
- Provide social service referral information.
- Make referrals and appointments for the offender at service agencies.
- Reply to the offender's inquiries requesting assistance.
- Explain rules and regulations to the offender.
- Read aloud and explain documents, such as conditions of parole, to the offender to obtain the offender's signature.
- Explain legal terms and documents to the offender.
- Explain charges to the offender and serve pertinent documents.
- Conduct first interview with the offender to establish ground rules of supervision.
- Discuss supervision plan with the offender to develop an encouraging and supportive relationship.
- Answer technical questions concerning referrals.
- Establish a professional relationship and role with the offender.
- Interview the offender to obtain personal information.
- Hold the offender accountable if an interview or other information reveals the offender is doing something questionable, improper, etc.
- Discuss the offender's finances to establish a budget.
- Discuss offender's progress with referral personnel to assess the effectiveness of the program.
- Explain the offender's legal rights and restrictions, such as voting, gun possession, distance travel, etc.
- Develop a supervision plan based upon the individual offender's risk, needs, and responsivity.

Supervise Offenders—Indirect Activities

- Act as an advocate to help place the offender with a referral resource.
- Respond to and/or address domestic issues.
- Consider institution records, behavior, etc. to formulate and recommend special conditions for
- Review cases with other PO's to formulate problem solving strategies.
- Review special conditions to formulate and recommend modifications and/or additions to the adjudicating authority as appropriate.

- Investigate and/or challenge the offender's various claims to determine the truth.
- Review and/or monitor medical prescriptions.
- Discuss the suggested supervision plan with a senior officer and/or supervisor.
- Confer with senior officer/supervisor on an ongoing basis to assess the effectiveness of the offender's supervision plan.
- Conduct an orientation session (reach in) for new or transferred inmates to disseminate general information concerning the parole system and answer questions.
- Conduct an orientation/intake session for new or transferred offenders to disseminate general information concerning community supervision.
- Review the offender's finances to determine compliance.
- Request lab analysis of suspected narcotics.
- Complete a property/evidence receipt for seized or found property.
- Talk with the offender's family (advise, inform, notify).
- Explain community supervision to families and how they can contribute to the offender's success.
- Contact present or past employers to obtain employment information.
- Obtain medical and/or mental health records.
- Contact other states for their records.
- Conduct a complete investigation of dwelling units, families, jobs, etc., to approve the offender's "release plan."
- Request and provide rationale for evaluation of the offender's mental health.
- Read a "hit" notice to ascertain the offender's status.
- Read the offender's file to assess background and potential, such as work experience, criminal history, family, etc.
- Read and paraphrase psychological and medical reports.
- Communicate with the court and/or prosecutor to obtain information concerning a particular offender.
- Communicate with personnel at the offender's place of detention to learn the offender's status and/or location.
- Conduct community meetings and/or notifications.
- Attend neighborhood or community association meetings.

Monitor Probation Progress/Compliance

- Plan and carry out home, employment, and collateral visits to "contact" the offender, family, employer, neighbors, referral agencies, etc.
- Supervise taking urine sample and fill out appropriate forms.
- Examine offender's body for signs of drug use.
- Arrange for a urinalysis test with the appropriate agency.
- Administer sobriety and drug tests.
- Search the premises, grounds, vehicle, etc.
- Observe the offender's demeanor, clothing, speech, and physical mannerisms to assess mental and/or economic state.

- Review and respond to various kinds of written and oral information.
- Visit the proposed residence to assess suitability.
- Plan and execute surveillance (moving and/or stationary) of the offender.
- Plan a meeting with an offender to have greatest positive effect.
- Collect and collate confidential information and use the same to supervise individual offenders.
- Assess the offender's family and home to formulate the most effective supervision strategy.
- Identify potential problems with the offender and discusses options.
- Visit job sites.
- Inspect the offender's dwelling units and rooms.
- Assess the seriousness of a violation to determine whether an arrest is appropriate.
- Determine from data obtained from discussions, observations, review of case history, etc., whether there has been a violation or other unacceptable behavior.
- Consult with booking, courts personnel, police agencies, and holding facilities on offender's disposition.
- Review court orders and papers regarding offender's sentencing.
- Document violations.
- Comprehend and apply rules governing the conditions of supervision.
- Interview neighbors, law enforcement, etc. to evaluate the offender's community conduct.
- Discuss the basic facts of the case with a senior officer or supervisor to determine whether a warrant should be issued for a violation.
- Discuss the basic facts of the case with a senior officer or supervisor to determine the level and type of sanction to be imposed.
- Collect or arrange for collection of a DNA sample.
- Arrange for forensic analysis of electronic devices.
- Review various social media and other electronic information.
- Arrange for polygraph and/or plethysmograph examinations.
- Obtain relevant juvenile records.
- Obtain and/or review immigration records.

Prepare For/Monitor Hearings—Court Proceedings

- Monitor court proceedings to learn the offender's status.
- Offer testimony to adjudicating authority concerning a particular offender.
- Make presentations of facts at revocation hearings.
- Prepare case documentation for presentation.
- Formulate and offer a recommendation for disposition to hearing officers.
- Comprehend and apply rules concerning the hearings and/or violations process.
- Read, comprehend, and apply relevant Oregon Revised Statutes and Oregon Administrative Rules.
- Undergo cross examination by a defense attorney.
- Present allegations and testimony to the adjudicating authority in violations proceedings.
- Review reports and notes for court testimony.
- Testify credibly in hearings.
- Attend court to observe proceedings or plea.

- Explain hearing procedures to offenders, complainants, victims and witnesses.
- Read and comprehend subpoenas.
- Present and question witnesses at Morrissey hearings to establish violation facts.
- Discuss the case with the offender's attorney.
- Prepare and submit affidavits.
- Issue citations to appear in court.

Administer First Aid

- Administer basic first aid.

Arrest, Search, & Seizure

- Present the offender at the place of detention and provide necessary documentation.
- Plan and execute operations to apprehend an absconder.
- Obtain the offender's fingerprints.
- Transport the offender.
- Direct the actions of parole officer(s) arriving to assist.
- Advise person(s) of their constitutional rights.
- Arrest offender with a warrant.
- Arrest offender without a warrant.
- Search a person who has been arrested.
- Plan a strategy for conducting a search of a person, premises, vehicle, etc.
- Plan a strategy for making an arrest.

Inter-Agency or Intra-Agency Relationships

- Contact law enforcement personnel to collect information concerning offenders and/or charges.
- Use personal contacts to assist an offender.
- Ask local police to provide assistance.
- Develop relationships with employers, referral resources, etc.
- Discuss the offender with treatment staff to collect information for assessment and recommendations.
- Confer with a senior officer or supervisor to clarify procedures, policies, etc.
- Participate in community organizations to represent the Agency.
- Develop and maintain a liaison with other criminal justice personnel.
- Work with local police agencies to identify persons of interest.
- Notify law enforcement and other concerned agencies of the offender's presence in the community.

Foundational Knowledge and Skills

- Serve as a duty officer.
- Describe the offender to other parole officers (e.g. absconder, parolee).

- Access the Internet for information.
- Comfort emotionally upset person(s).
- Attend in-service training.
- Operate telephones, including cell phones.
- Use mobile and/or portable radio equipment.
- Use voice commands to control and direct person(s).
- Adjust communications to ensure understanding.
- Adjust to responsivity issues such as cultural, gender, etc.
- Use body language to project, control, and influence.
- Photograph offenders.
- Provide status to dispatch by radio and/or telephone.
- Observe a person's body language to assess their attitude, intentions, etc.
- Communicate with other officers or other officials during high risk situations.
- Read the Agency's procedural manuals to obtain directions, clarification, etc.
- Read and comprehend legal documents such as sentencing orders, opinions, etc.
- Receive and communicate by email.
- Access the Oregon Judicial Information Network (OJIN).
- Access local law enforcement databases.
- Provide informal on-the-job training to new officers.
- Effectively prioritize job tasks and time commitments.
- Effectively multi-task.
- Adapt to a changing work environment.

Liquor Enforcement Inspector
Critical & Essential Tasks

Agility, Balance, Dexterity and Physical Fitness

- Use hands or feet for self-defense or to maintain physical control.
- Demonstrate cardiovascular endurance (sudden onset, sustained, high-demand physical exertion for longer than three minutes).
- Maintain balance on narrow, uneven or elevated surfaces.
- Dodge or evade blows and thrown objects.

Auditory and Speech Perception

- Detect and understand speech in the presence of a wide range of environmental sounds, including high levels of ambient background noise.
- Understand speech through electronic devices (telephone, cell phone, etc.) in a wide range of conditions.
- Detect and understand faint auditory signals (whispers, transients [clicks, pops, impacts], air movement, etc.).

Awkward Positions (Stoop, Bend, Twist, Crawl, Kneel, Squat)

- Participate in area searches (walking, standing, kneeling, crawling, lifting, bending, etc.). looking for items or persons.
- Crawl over or under obstacles.

Climbing

- Climb through small openings such as windows.
- Climb over or under obstacles.
- Climb up to elevated surfaces with or without a ladder.

First Aid or Public Assistance

- Evacuate people from an area or building.
- Administer first aid, rescue breathing or CPR in a wide variety of environmental conditions.

Hands and Fingers

- Perform repetitive hand movements (typing, mouse, bar code scanning, etc.).

Jumping

- Jump up and down from an elevated surface.
- Jump over obstacles, such as ditches, holes, streams, hazards, etc.

Lifting and Carrying

- Carry or drag heavy objects such as a disabled person or equipment with or without assistance.
- Lift or move heavy objects (cases of beer, kegs, etc.) weighing 50 lbs. or more with or without assistance.

Motor Vehicle Operation

- Drive an agency vehicle while multi-tasking.
- Get in and out of a vehicle (from a standing position or seated position), rapidly at times.
- Drive an agency vehicle in a wide range of routine and emergency conditions.

Olfactory Perception

- Detect and identify faint or odd odors.

Pushing, Pulling, Dragging (with or without assistance)

- Push hard to move objects by hand, including resisting or unresisting persons, with or without assistance.

Restraining and Subduing (with or without assistance)

- Place resisting persons in a building or vehicle with assistance.
- Subdue a resisting or attacking persons by using defensive tools such as a baton, OC spray, etc. with assistance.
- Extract resisting persons from a building or a vehicle with assistance.
- Hold or restrain resisting persons with assistance.
- Mechanically restrain (handcuff) compliant or non-compliant persons with assistance.
- Subdue resisting or attacking persons by using defensive tactics techniques such as pressure points or holds, with assistance.
- Use whatever force is necessary to protect self or others from harm.

Sitting and Standing

- Stand continuously for extended times.
- Sit continuously (car, desk, etc.).

Stress Tolerance

- Cope with physical effects of acute emotional stress, such as fear, anger, etc. (self and family).
- Cope with physical effects of chronic cumulative emotional stress (self and family).
- Cope with the emotional and physical impact of being subjected to verbal threats of violence.
- Cope with the emotional and physical impact of shift work.
- Cope with emotional and physical impact of constant scrutiny and criticism (management, attorneys, judges, the public, etc.).
- Cope with the emotional and physical impact of constant exposure to personal legal liability.
- Cope with the emotional and physical impact of being exposed to hazardous substances (drugs, chemicals, infectious diseases, etc.).
- Maintaining a state of hypervigilance (highly concentrated mental and sensory attention) over a protracted period of time.
- Cope with the emotional and physical results of being exposed to bodily fluids.

Training

- Participate and display proficiency in required training such as self-defense, the use of Oleoresin Capsicum (OC), verbal judo, first-aid, rescue breathing and CPR.

Visual Perception

- Visually detect and identify images, facial features, body features and movement of persons and objects in varying light conditions.
- Accurately determine a full range of colors (clothing, substances, skin tones, etc.) in varying light conditions.
- Possess three-dimensional vision, sufficient for clear depth perception, image placement and location sufficient for complex visual tasks (driving a vehicle in emergency conditions, pursuit of persons over complex surfaces in unpredictable conditions, stairs, steps, obstacles, weapons use, etc.).
- Visually detect and identify transitory and subtle changes in body language (pupil constriction or dilation, skin color, respiration changes, etc.).

Walking and Running

- Walk continuously for extended times.
- Walk over extremely overcrowded locations.
- Walk or move backwards.
- Run on a flat surface.
- Walk or run up or down stairs.
- Walk or run on irregular, potentially hazardous surfaces (slick, muddy, rocks, etc.).
- Run for long distances (greater than 300 yards).
- Run to assist another.
- Walk or run up or down stairs while carrying heavy objects.

DOCUMENT 10.1 Critical and essential tasks.

How to Prepare for the Medical Examination

The only way to prepare for the medical examination is for a candidate to know their medical issues by having an annual complete physical with their physician. The candidate will review the results with their physician and address any issues that are identified. Knowledge is power, and not only will knowing about any medical issues help the candidate prepare for the law enforcement hiring process, it is also essential for a person to know and understand any medical issues they may have. Most law enforcement agencies require their officers to submit to an annual medical examination after being hired, so it is something the candidate should not only prepare for but get used to completing.

SUMMARY OF CHAPTER 10

1. Candidates will understand the medical examination and the different tests that are given during the examination.

2. Prescribed medications that a candidate takes will be evaluated by the physician conducting the medical examination, the psychologist conducting the psychological evaluation, and the background investigator.

3. Candidates should prepare for the medical examination by completing annual medical examinations with their physician so that they know of any issues and are addressing them.

DISCUSSION QUESTIONS

1. What are the different tests that a candidate goes through in a medical examination?

2. How are prescribed medications a candidate utilizes looked at by the hiring agency?

3. How can a candidate prepare for a medical examination?

See Active Learning for the Following:

- Practice quizzes
- eFlashcards
- Video links
- Cognella journal articles
- News clips

References

Department of Public Safety Standards and Training (DPSST). (2016, February 12). *Medical examination for police, corrections, parole & probation officers and liquor enforcement inspectors.*

Hope, C., & Maslin, K. (1990). Random dot stereogram E in vision screening of children. *Australian and New Zealand Journal of Opthamology 18*(3), 319–324.

Good-Lite Company. Retrieved June 2, 2019, from https://www.good-lite.com/Details.cfm?ProdID=107

Segre, L. (n.d.). *What's an eye test? Eye charts and visual acuity explained.* https://www.allaboutvision.com/eye-test/

Image Credits

What Is the Final Interview?

11

"It's not whether you get knocked down, it's whether you get back up."

—Vince Lombardi

KEY TERMS

Final interview: While the initial oral board interview and the final chief/sheriff interview will be similar, they generally have two different purposes. The final interview can also include more difficult questions where the candidate is expected to know more about the hiring agency.

The final interview can be conducted by the chief, sheriff, or any member of the command staff of the hiring agency. The most common focus of the final interview is to give the chief or sheriff or command staff a chance to meet the candidate.

CHAPTER LEARNING OBJECTIVES

After reading the chapter, you should have a good understanding of the following:

- The final interview
- How a final interview is similar to an oral board interview
- How a final interview is different than an oral board interview
- The steps to prepare for a final interview
- Why is it essential to research the hiring agency prior to the final interview
- Why it is essential to go on a ride along with the hiring agency prior to the final interview

What Is the Final Interview?

While the initial oral board interview and the final chief/sheriff interview will be similar, they generally have two different purposes. The **final interview** can also include more difficult questions where the candidate is expected to know more about the hiring agency. The final interview can be conducted by the chief, sheriff, or any member of the command staff of the hiring agency. Therefore, it is important that the candidate can easily identify and refer by rank and last name, the chief or sheriff and command staff members. The most common focus of the final interview is to give the chief or sheriff, or command staff a chance to meet the candidate. *It is not what the hiring agency can do for the candidate but what the candidate can do for the hiring agency.* Every law enforcement agency is different. Some agencies are small and focus heavily on community policing in their daily patrol activities; other agencies are larger and have serious crime issues. Therefore, the most critical part of this process is for the candidate to ensure they understand, know, and have researched what the hiring agency is all about. Can the candidate see themselves working for the hiring agency? What about the jurisdiction that the agency serves is unique? Is the candidate excited about the different departments or divisions the agency has? If the candidate is familiar with the hiring agency, has conducted research into the agency, and is excited at the prospect of having a long career with the agency, then this will show through during the interview.

The candidate should imagine if they were the chief, sheriff, or command staff conducting the final interview and they were looking to hire a new officer for their agency what they would want to hear a candidate say. The make-up of any law enforcement agency is essential. If all the officers get along and have the same goals, then the work environment will be that much better.

The final interview could also include a period where the chief, sheriff, or command staff tell the candidate what is expected of the candidate if hired. It would be a good idea for the candidate to research keywords to help identify what the hiring agency could be looking for in newly hired officers.

Every hiring agency is different, and their needs are unique; therefore, the questions asked during the final interview could vary widely. Some agencies may not even conduct a final interview, depending on the size of the agency. For instance, for a larger agency, it might not be practical for the top cop to interview every candidate.

How to Prepare for the Final Interview

To best prepare for the final interview, the candidate can do the following:

1. Review the chapter in this textbook on the oral board interview and focus on researching the hiring agency and truly knowing and understanding it. Be able to answer all types of questions about the hiring agency and what items about the agency made the candidate interested it. Be prepared to answer questions such as the following:
   a. Where do you see yourself in 5 years?
   b. What kind of relationship does this agency have with the community?
   c. Why should we hire you?
   d. When were you most satisfied with your job?
   e. What motivates you?
   f. What would your coworkers say about you?
   g. How would your friends (or enemies) describe you?
   h. What are your strengths/weaknesses?

2. Go on a ride along with the hiring agency. Question the officers and find out why they like about working for the hiring agency. Prepare the questions ahead of time for the officers. Once on the ride-along use that time wisely to pay attention to everything and be able to utilize the knowledge gained from this process. Candidates should always remember the officers will be watching and reporting on the candidate as well, so candidates should be on their best behavior during the ride-along. Be able to answer such questions as the following:

    a. Why would you want to work at this agency?

    b. Has this agency been involved in any recent controversies in the news?

    c. What size is this agency, and what are the various divisions/departments?

    d. Who does the chief of police (or sheriff) report to?

3. Remember to focus on the fact that it is not what the hiring agency can do for you but what you can do for the hiring agency.

POLICE STORY 11.1 **Being a Gay Police Officer**

by Chief Tighe O'Meara, Ashland (Oregon) Police Department

I knew that I wanted to be a police officer since I was about 15 years old. Growing up in the Detroit, I, along with everyone in my family, were victimized by criminals fairly regularly. I remember that when I was out and about I would always be glad to see a Detroit Police Department vehicle sitting somewhere or cruising by. It made me feel safe for a few minutes. I also knew, from about the same time, that I was different from most people. I was one of the ones who others whispered about and laughed about. I was gay. I knew it but had not come to terms with it.

Now, I grew up in a very liberal family, in a liberal neighborhood and in a (mostly) liberal city, but still, different is different, and no one wants to be different.

So, I went off to college, wanting to be a police officer. I strayed from that desire once or twice but always came back to it, and even served as a reserve officer for a while in college. This was the late 80s/early 90s and the TV show *COPS* was just taking off. I would watch it every Saturday with my friends and loved it!

As I approached the end my time at college I pondered my next move and saw that a large sheriff's office on the west coast was hiring. I bought a plane ticket and flew west to test and explore. I passed all the tests, was offered a job, and told to do a ride-along. I remember talking to the deputy during the ride-along. He asked me if I watched *COPS*. "Sure do," I said. "You know that guy on there a lot?" "Yeah I know who he is." Then, out comes "Well he is faggot."

This took me back. Is this the group I want to get in with I ask myself?

Anyway, off to the background process I go, filling out every last detail of my life. Some of the questions were very personal, along the lines of "Have you ever engaged in anal or oral sex?" "This state's laws," explains the background investigator, "still have it that anything other than regular sex is illegal, so we are allowed to ask."

So, I finish filling it out, keep a good face on, then fly home to Michigan. A couple of days later I call and tell them that I am withdrawing. From my point of view, they had won; they had successfully discriminated me out of a job. They came through loud and clear that I was not welcome.

I got my career anyway. I started off with a job in a small Michigan town, eventually moving on to a slightly larger town. I made good friends and lost them when I came out. I moved back to Detroit and worked at a department I knew would be better and eventually found success as an openly gay officer.

As discrimination goes, I am lucky. There are many gay men who have faced much worse than I have. And, while I have met with success in my career, it is not without its own moments of discrimination and loss because I accept who I am, even if other people and departments may not.

FACT BOX 11.1: CHIEF TIGHE O'MEARA'S FINAL INTERVIEW RECOMMENDATIONS

Chief Tighe O'Meara is a chief of police in Southern Oregon. Watch Video 11.1 to hear his recommendations to candidates on what to expect during the final interview and how to prepare.

Active Learning Video 11.1. Chief Tighe O'Meara final interview recommendations.

POLICE STORY 11.2 Is Fainting Bad?

by Chief Kris Alison, Central Point (Oregon) Police

The chief's interview is one of the most important parts of the hiring process but has the least information on how to approach it. I try to let applicants know that this meeting is a time to get to know each other. I want to emphasize not to be nervous about this meeting and to give me candid answers to my questions so that we know if their employment with the department will be a good fit. Fit is an underrated asset to a police department and is the evaluation on how someone will "fit" in with the other employees and the style of how the department polices the community. An applicant should also be evaluating if they would like to work at the police department and can envision a 20-year career there.

The most memorable applicant in a chief's interview was several years ago when I was not a chief but an observer in the interview. The applicant came into the interview dressed in a suit and was well prepared. The chief did a traditional introduction and asked the applicant to give a brief description of why he would like to work for our police department. I immediately could see the applicant's eyes start to flutter, and he stood up. The applicant looked at the door and the flight-or-fight response was occurring. The applicant collapsed on the floor and passed out due to the nerves and anxiety he had built up prior to the interview. The applicant was embarrassed, and we had to have a medical team come in to assess his ability to continue with the interview. The applicant declined to continue and withdrew from the process later in the week.

I look back at this chief's interview and wished someone could have given advice to this applicant that if you are too nervous to represent yourself, you will never get the opportunity to be a "fit" at a department.

SUMMARY OF CHAPTER 11

1. A final interview is a time where the hiring agency learns more about the candidate. It is not what the hiring agency can do for the candidate but what the candidate can do for the hiring agency.

2. To prepare for the final interview, the candidate should research the hiring agency, go on a ride-along, and understand how to answer various current issue questions about the hiring agency.

DISCUSSION QUESTIONS

1. Do all hiring agencies give a final interview?

2. What is the focus of the final interview?

3. Why should a candidate research the hiring agency and go on a ride-along with the hiring agency?

INTERNET EXERCISE

1. Go to your favorite Internet search engine.

2. Search for a law enforcement agency you are interested in working for.

3. Review current news articles, social media sites, and other related information.

4. Make a list of information about the law enforcement agency.

5. Repeat for two additional law enforcement agencies.

See Active Learning for the Following:

- Practice quizzes
- eFlashcards
- Video links
- Cognella journal articles
- News clips

References

Americans With Disabilities Act of 1990, Pub. L. No. 101-336, 104 Stat. 328 (1990).

Patrol Procedures

Hands-On Police Academy Training

12

"Tell me and I forget, teach me and I may remember, involve me and I learn."

—Benjamin Franklin

KEY TERMS

Firearm safety rules:

1. Always keep firearm pointed in a safe direction.
2. Always keep your finger off the trigger until ready to fire.
3. Every gun is loaded.

AR-15: The AR-15 is a standard law enforcement rifle. AR does not stand for automatic rifle or assault rifle; it instead stands for Armalite rifle, and it is a semiautomatic rifle. Armalite is the manufacturer that is a division of Fairchild Engine and Airplane Corporation. The AR-15 is an essential tool for law enforcement because of how accurate it is at long-distance shooting. The AR-15 is accurate from approximately 100–600 yards, and many models claim its accuracy at 1,000 yards (over half a mile!).

Cartridge: Many people, even law enforcement officers, utilize the incorrect term to describe a cartridge. A cartridge contains the following:

- Bullet
- Cartridge case
- Gun powder
- Primer

Clip: A clip has no springs and does not feed cartridges into a chamber as a magazine does. Clips hold cartridges in the correct sequence.

Deadly force is used to stop the threat: A misunderstood concept is the use of deadly force to stop a deadly threat. Those not in law enforcement often state that law enforcement officers shoot to kill. This is a misnomer since law enforcement officers are trained that if there is a deadly threat and the decision is made to use deadly force, the officer will shoot to stop the threat. As long as the deadly threat continues, the officer is trained to continue firing. Once the threat stops, however, the officer is trained to stop firing.

Drug recognition expert (DRE): Many law enforcement officers are also trained as drug recognition experts (DRE). A DRE is an officer trained in the detection and identification of impairment in drivers. To be certified as a DRE officer takes weeks of training and performs a number of field certifications and can describe the involvement of drugs in impaired driving incidents, name the seven drug categories, be able to recognize their effects, and pass a final written test.

Horizontal gaze nystagmus (HGN) sobriety test: A standardized field sobriety test (SFST) law enforcement officers are trained to give those persons suspected of driving while impaired. The HGN name comes from the "quick movement or jerking of the eye as it moves side to side. The jerking motion, or nystagmus, is an indication of drug or alcohol impairment caused by the brain's inability to properly control the eye muscles" (FieldSobrietyTests.net, n.d.).

Less-lethal firearms: Law enforcement agencies have many options when it comes to less-lethal firearms. First, the firearms utilized are called less lethal because they can be lethal. Training is very essential in less-lethal firearms because the placement of the shot could make it either less lethal or lethal.

Magazine: A magazine holds cartridges under the pressure of a spring.

Most standard primary duty semiautomatic handgun calibers law enforcement officers carry:

- 9mm
- .40 caliber
- .45 caliber

Most standard primary duty semiautomatic handgun manufacturers law enforcement officers carry:

- Beretta
- Colt
- Glock
- Heckler and Koch (H&K)
- Sig Sauer
- Smith and Wesson
- Springfield

One-leg stand sobriety test: A standardized field sobriety test (SFST) law enforcement officers give those persons suspected of driving while impaired.

Shotgun: The most standard type of shotgun carried by a law enforcement officer on patrol is a Remington 870 12-gauge shotgun.

Standardized field sobriety tests (SFSTs): There are many different SFSTs that law enforcement officers learn to conduct during the police academy to determine if a person is driving while impaired. The HGN, walk and turn, and one-leg stand tests are all SFSTs.

Walk and turn sobriety test: A standardized field sobriety test (SFST) law enforcement officers give those persons suspected of driving while impaired.

CHAPTER LEARNING OBJECTIVES

After reading the chapter, you should have a good understanding of the following:

- The most popular calibers and manufacturers of a law enforcement officer primary duty handgun
- The parts of a revolver and semiautomatic handgun
- The various parts of a cartridge
- The history of the AR-15
- Why it is essential to use the correct terminology when identifying a cartridge
- The difference between a semiautomatic rifle and automatic rifle
- What less-lethal firearms are
- The three most standard standardized field sobriety tests (SFSTs)

Hands-On Police Academy Training

One of the best parts of being in law enforcement is the multifaceted training. Law enforcement training can include (not a comprehensive list) the following:

- Firearms
- Less-lethal weapons
- Emergency vehicle operations
- Defensive tactics
- Driving under the influence of intoxicants (DUII)
- Criminal law
- Constitutional law
- Domestic violence
- First-aid/CPR
- Investigations
- Patrol procedures/techniques
- Juvenile law and procedures
- Cultural diversity
- Health and fitness
- Civil/criminal liability
- Human relations
- Community policing
- Stress prevention/management
- Implicit bias

Historically, many law enforcement agencies expected their officers to come into the career with a strong knowledge of many of these areas. More and more agencies are changing their views and have the attitude that they would rather have a novice officer they can adequately train instead of one who needs to relearn how to do something correctly. To correct bad habits can take a lot of hard work; therefore, candidates do not need to worry if they do not have prior law enforcement or military experience, as their hiring agency will ensure they are trained properly.

While law enforcement agencies would rather train a new officer how to do something properly instead of fixing a habit that was learned incorrectly, that does not mean candidates should not be prepared. Candidates can be prepared by knowing and understanding the various parts of law enforcement that do not require hands-on experience. For instance, if a candidate has not ever used a handgun, the hiring agency can look forward to training that candidate on how to shoot their duty handgun; however, the candidate could still study and prepare and understand the different types of handguns and the most standard handguns that law enforcement officers carry on duty. Just because a candidate does not have the knowledge and experience of doing something related to law enforcement does not mean they have to be ignorant about law enforcement–related training.

If this textbook is being used in conjunction with a college class, this is where the professor (who has law enforcement experience) can instruct any of the categories in this chapter. If the professor does not have law enforcement experience, professionals and experts from nearby law enforcement agencies can be contacted to do a guest presentation. Not only will the students enjoy the classes, but they cwill also set the stage for those interested in a career in law enforcement.

Firearms

Firearms are a part of law enforcement. Police officers in the United States who are commissioned or sworn by their state have authority to carry a primary duty semiautomatic handgun, and, depending on the agency, a backup handgun(s) too. If the officer wants to gain further firearms training, they could be a range master or even go into a unit such as SWAT or another specialized unit where firearms are utilized as a part of the daily training and activities.

Caliber and manufacturer differentiate firearms. **The most standard primary duty semiautomatic handgun of law enforcement officers** (the handgun that the law enforcement officer will carry on their duty belt daily) are in the following calibers:

- 9mm
- .40 caliber
- .45 caliber

One of the best calibers of a handgun for new law enforcement officers to learn to shoot is the .22-caliber handgun. The .22 caliber is a smaller caliber and does not have as much kickback when the trigger is pulled, which aids in the learning process.

The most standard primary duty semiautomatic handgun manufacturers of law enforcement officers are as follows:

- Beretta
- Colt
- Glock
- Heckler and Koch (H&K)
- Sig Sauer
- Smith and Wesson
- Springfield

Backup handguns (the handguns that law enforcement officers carry on their body other than their duty belt, such as an ankle holster, hidden somewhere in a bulletproof vest, or carried in a duty bag) can be a variety of calibers and can sometimes either be a revolver or a semiautomatic handgun. It is up to the law enforcement agency to determine and approve the manufacturers and calibers that their law enforcement officers will be allowed to carry either as a primary or as a backup handgun.

Historically law enforcement officers had to purchase their primary duty handgun and backup handguns with their own money. Depending on the law enforcement agency, and their current working contract, many agencies today purchase the primary handgun once a candidate is hired as a law enforcement officer with an agency. However, this means that once the officer retires, the officer must turn in their handgun like any other issued police equipment. Some agencies that do purchase the officer's handgun will allow the officer to purchase the handgun from the agency.

Revolver and Semi-Automatic Handgun

The two most standard types of handguns that law enforcement officers will see during their time working on patrol are the following:

1. Revolver
2. Semiautomatic handgun

Figure 12.1 is an illustration of a revolver. Figure 12.2 illustrates the revolver's main parts. Figure 12.3 is an illustration of a semiautomatic handgun. Figure 12.4 illustrates the semiautomatic handgun's main parts.

FIGURE 12.1 Revolver.

FIGURE 12.2 Revolver parts.

FIGURE 12.3 Semiautomatic handgun.

FIGURE 12.4 Semiautomatic handgun parts.

Armalite Rifle (AR)-15

The **AR-15** is a standard law enforcement rifle. AR does not stand for automatic rifle or assault rifle; it instead stands for Armalite rifle, and it is a semiautomatic rifle. Armalite is the manufacturer that is a division of Fairchild Engine and Airplane Corporation.

The AR-1 was one of the first rifles produced at Armalite's location in Hollywood, CA, and paved the way to the development of the AR-10. All rifles were designated AR, short for Armalite Rifle. Shortly thereafter, Armalite submitted the AR-5, .22 Hornet Survival Rifle to the U.S. Air Force as a replacement for their then-standard survival rifle. The AR-5 was adopted and designated the MA-1 Survival Rifle (Armalite, n.d.).

The AR-15 was developed in the 1950s for the military. It was not very popular, so Armalite sold the design to Colt (manufacturer), and they ramped up the design and made an automatic weapon called the M-16. The M-16 is an automatic rifle, which means when the trigger is pulled, rounds are continuously fired, unlike with the AR-15 where only one round is fired with each trigger pull. Automatic rifles are illegal to own (a citizen cannot simply buy an automatic rifle or handgun at the nearest gun store) unless there is a specific qualification such as being used in the military or law enforcement. The M-16 was a popular rifle in the military; therefore, the AR-15 was re-marketed for law enforcement and the public. Colt's patent for the AR-15 expired in the 1970s, and that is when other manufacturers began producing similar models (Myre, 2018).

Before the terrorist attacks in the United States that brought down the twin towers on September 11, many law enforcement agencies had a small number of AR-15 rifles on patrol. After the terrorist attacks, there were a number of federal grants available for law enforcement agencies to purchase the needed rifles. The AR-15 is an essential tool for law enforcement because of how accurate it is at

long-distance shooting. The AR-15 is accurate from approximately 100–600 yards, and many models claim its accuracy at 1,000 yards (over half a mile!). Many times, it is not safe to get close to a suspect who has a deadly weapon; therefore, the AR-15 rifle allows law enforcement officers to keep a safe distance from a suspect with a deadly weapon, yet still have the option for deadly force. Many semiautomatic handguns law enforcement officers carry as their primary duty handgun cannot be effective at distances greater than 15–25 yards. Figure 12.5 is an illustration of an AR-15 rifle.

FIGURE 12.5 AR-15 rifle.

Shotgun

Historically many law enforcement agencies have had their law enforcement officers on patrol each carry a **shotgun**. The most standard type of shotgun carried on patrol is the Remington 870 12-gauge shotgun.

The shotgun can be fun to learn to shoot and is highly accurate in short distances with a couple of options for shells (shotgun cartridges). The shotgun can also be used as a deterrent to suspects when racking it back. The sound a shotgun makes when it is racked back (this is the motion that loads a shotgun shell into the barrel; it is not what shoots the shotgun) is a very recognizable sound. Figure 12.6 illustrates a Remington 870 12-gauge shotgun.

FIGURE 12.6 Remington 870 12–gauge shotgun.

Less-Lethal Firearms

Law enforcement agencies have many options when it comes to **less-lethal firearms**. First, the firearms utilized are called less lethal because they can be lethal. Training is essential in less-lethal firearms because the placement of the shot could make it either less lethal or lethal. For instance, there are less-lethal shotguns. The shotgun utilized is a Remington 870 12-gauge shotgun; yes,

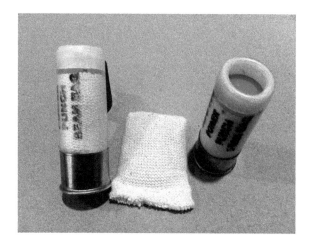

FIGURE 12.7 Less-lethal shotgun bean bag ammunition.

FIGURE 12.8 Less-lethal 40-mm rubber ball launcher.

that is the same shotgun described in the previous section that is a deadly weapon carried by law enforcement officers. However, it is generally painted orange to identify it as the less-lethal option. The shotgun shells utilized are not slugs or pellets, which can have a deadly result. Instead, the ammunition utilized is a type of bean bag that will not penetrate the skin. The intended result is for the person who is struck to feel the bean bag hit (which generally leaves a big welt and bruise) and stop the deadly or threatening behavior or drop the weapon and be injured instead of killed. However, if the bean bag were to hit the suspect on certain parts of the body, the shot could be fatal. Figure 12.7 illustrates the less-lethal shotgun bean bag ammunition.

One other less-lethal firearm option is the 40-mm rubber ball launcher. The 40-mm utilizes a colored rubbery type ball as the shot (the 40-mm ball looks similar to a blue racquetball). Again, it is the same premise for the 40-mm as for the less-lethal shotgun. It is all about shot placement. Figure 12.8 illustrates a less-lethal 40-mm rubber ball launcher.

Less-lethal firearms give more options to law enforcement officers in deadly or threatening situations. However, these tools are expensive, and not every law enforcement agency has the budget

to have every officer on patrol carry all of these tools. More often than not, there will be one or two less-lethal options on each squad. Therefore, they cannot always be utilized depending on where the officer is who has the less-lethal option; and if the officer is on another call, the officer may not be able to make it to the deadly or threatening situation in time to deploy the less-lethal option.

Cartridges (i.e., Bullets)

Many people, even law enforcement officers, utilize the incorrect term to describe a cartridge. The correct term for the item in figure 12.9 is **cartridge**, not bullet. A cartridge contains the following:

- Bullet
- Cartridge case
- Gun powder
- Primer

FIGURE 12.9 Cartridge.

However, all too often, the item in is referred to incorrectly as a *bullet*. For a number of reasons, the correct terminology must be utilized for items found at a crime scene. Imagine a restaurant crime scene where different suspects fired a number of different types of semiautomatic handguns and law enforcement officers, crime scene investigators, and detectives arrived after the incident to find five dead bodies. There would be all types of firearm evidence at the crime scene. If the crime scene investigator labeled every part of the bullet found as only a bullet, it would get confusing for anyone trying to review the reports and evidence found. Was the item in front of one of the dead bodies a bullet or a cartridge? If it was a cartridge, it could mean the suspect's gun jammed or the suspect reloaded

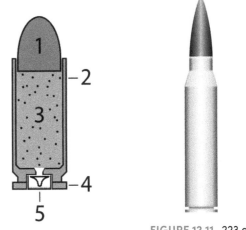

FIGURE 12.10 Cartridge parts.   FIGURE 12.11 .223 or AR-15 cartridge.

the handgun and dropped a cartridge. If it was a bullet, was it a spent bullet that was fired and went through a person and landed on the ground? The improper use of the terminology could lead to a suspect being found not guilty due to all the confusion. It is of the utmost importance that the correct terminology is utilized when referring to the cartridge and the various parts of the cartridge.

Figure 12.10 illustrates the various parts of a cartridge:

1. Bullet
2. Cartridge case
3. Gun powder
4. Rim (some cartridges utilize a rimfire instead of a primer)
5. Primer

Figure 12.11 is a .223 (or AR-15) cartridge, Figure 12.12 is a shotgun slug, and Figure 12.13 is 00 (double-ought) buckshot. The most standard shotgun ammunition law enforcement officers utilize is a shotgun slug or 00 buckshot.

FIGURE 12.12 Shotgun slug.

FIGURE 12.13 Shotgun 00 buckshot.

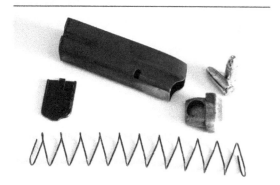

FIGURE 12.14 Magazine.

FIGURE 12.15 Clip.

Magazine or Clip?

A **magazine** holds cartridges under the pressure of a spring. Most semiautomatic handguns utilize a magazine to hold the cartridges. A **clip** has no springs and does not feed cartridges into a chamber as a magazine does. Clips hold cartridges in the correct sequence. Figure 12.14 illustrates a magazine, and Figure 12.15 illustrates a clip.

Firearm Safety

Law enforcement officers not only are around their firearms that they carry on duty, but they also come into contact with many firearms that suspects have illegal possession of or legal firearms other citizens have the officer must check. Law enforcement officers must have a general knowledge of firearms and MUST ALWAYS KNOW, UNDERSTAND, AND PRACTICE FIREARM SAFETY. The following **firearm safety rules** must always be followed:

1. Always keep firearm pointed in a safe direction.
2. Always keep your finger off the trigger until ready to fire.
3. Every gun is loaded.

If thefirearm safety rules are followed the chances of an accidental discharge (AD) are lowered.

Deadly Force Is Used to STOP the Threat

A misunderstood concept is the use of deadly force to stop a deadly threat. Those not in law enforcement often state that law enforcement officers shoot to kill. This is a misnomer since law enforcement officers are trained that if there is a deadly threat and the decision is made to use deadly force, the officer will shoot to stop the threat. As long as the deadly threat continues, the officer is trained to continue firing. Once the threat stops, however, the officer is trained to stop firing. It is not always about how many times an officer shot if the officer continued shooting to stop the threat. Once a bullet enters a human body, no science states it takes so many bullets to stop a person. Many documented gun battles have shown one person shot six times in the upper torso with a large caliber bullet and another person shot one time in the upper torso with a smaller caliber bullet and the second person shot with the smaller caliber bullet dies and the first person lives. Too many factors are in play when a bullet enters a body and the damage that is done; therefore, it is impossible to guess how many shots it will take to stop a deadly threat. **Deadly force is used to stop the threat**.

DUII

DUII or driving under the influence of intoxicants (different acronyms are utilized to describe drinking and driving such as DUII, DUI, and DWI) is another area a candidate can learn about in preparation for a career in law enforcement. DUII training in a police academy setting can last a week or longer as the recruit learns about the effects of alcohol on the body, the effects of alcohol on the body when a person drives, the different clues to look for, and the various **standardized field sobriety tests (SFSTs)**.

The U.S. National Highway Traffic Safety Administration (NHTSA) started researching how to test drivers for impaired driving. There are many different SFSTs NHTSA developed that law enforcement officers learn to conduct during the police academy to determine if a person is driving under the influence of intoxicants (alcohol or drugs) or is impaired while driving. Law enforcement officers do not utilize just one SFST to determine if a person is impaired while driving. Law enforcement officers have many tools to help ascertain if the person is impaired while driving. For instance, the law enforcement officer uses what they see. How is the person driving? Are they going 10 mph under the speed limit? Are they swerving over the center line? Is it dark outside and they do not have their headlights on? Did they fail to signal before changing lanes? The law enforcement officer sees many clues. Many law enforcement officers are also trained as **drug recognition experts (DRE)**. A DRE is an officer who is trained in the detection and identification of impairment in drivers. To be certified as a DRE officer takes weeks of training and requires the officer to perform a number of field certifications, be able to describe the involvement of drugs in impaired driving incidents, name the seven drug categories, be able to recognize their effects, and pass a final written test. By performing a variety of tests on the person, the DRE-trained officer can ascertain if the person is impaired while driving. There are also portable breathalyzer test (PBT) units that can be utilized along with a variety of other SFSTs. While no one SFST can be used to convict a person of driving while impaired, law enforcement officers know how to utilize all the SFST tools to build a case against a person for driving while impaired. Figure 12.16 illustrates how a portable breathalyzer test (PBT) unit is utilized.

The most typically used SFSTs are as follows:

1. **Horizontal gaze nystagmus (HGN) sobriety test**
2. **Walk and turn sobriety test**
3. **One-leg stand sobriety test**

The HGN name comes from the "quick movement or jerking of the eye as it moves side to side. The jerking motion, or nystagmus, is an indication of drug or alcohol impairment caused by the brain's inability to properly control the eye muscles"

FIGURE 12.16 Portable breathalyzer test PBT.

(FieldSobrietyTests.net, n.d.). There are six clues in the HGN, three for each eye. If the subject shows these three clues, they are likely impaired:

1. Lack of smooth pursuit
2. Distinct nystagmus at maximum deviation
3. Onset of nystagmus prior to 45 degrees

Lack of smooth pursuit is where the person conducting the test moves a stimulus (preferably the straight index finger of the person's strong hand since objects such as a pen or pencil can be grabbed and used as a deadly weapon on the person conducting the HGN) smoothly from the left to the right of the subject's eyes. See Fact Box 12.1 for an example of how the HGN sobriety test should be performed. The subject's eyes are being checked to see if they can track the stimulus smoothly. The movement should take approximately 2 seconds for each side. If neither eye can track the stimulus smoothly, then two clues have been exhibited (one per eye). Remember, only three clues are needed to show the subject is impaired.

Distinct nystagmus at maximum deviation is completed after checking for lack of smooth pursuit. The person conducting the test moves the stimulus to the left side of the subject, watching as the subject's eye moves as far to the side as possible. There generally will not be any white showing in the corner of the eye when maximum deviation has been reached. The person will hold the stimulus at maximum deviation for 4 seconds and will watch for nystagmus (movement or jerking of the eye). Repeat the same for the right side, watching the subject's other eye this time. Two clues can be exhibited in this portion (one for each eye).

FIGURE 12.17 Horizontal gaze nystagmus sobriety test.

Onset of nystagmus prior to 45 degrees is where the person conducting the test moves the stimulus toward the subject's right, continuing to move the stimulus to the edge of the subject's shoulder (45 degrees). The movement should take approximately 4 seconds for each side. The subject's eye should be observed during this movement to ascertain when the eye starts jerking. As soon as jerking is seen, stop moving the stimulus to confirm the jerking continues. If jerking continues prior to 45 degrees, then the subject exhibited a clue. Two clues can be exhibited in this portion (one for each eye). Figure 12.17 illustrates an officer administering a horizontal gaze nystagmus sobriety test on a subject.

FACT BOX 12.1: HORIZONTAL GAZE NYSTAGMUS (HGN) SOBRIETY TEST

The horizontal gaze (HGN) sobriety test is relatively easy to learn to use and identify when nystagmus is occurring. To better understand how to conduct the HGN test, you should follow these steps:

1. Go to the Internet.
2. Watch following video on YouTube: https://www.youtube.com/watch?v=ejBEwV_6RQU.

3. Find a family member or friend to practice doing the test and to practice your instructions and demonstration of the test; then look for the following clues as your family member or friend performs the test: (a) lack of smooth pursuit, (b) distinct nystagmus at maximum deviation, and (c) onset of nystagmus prior to 45 degrees.

4. If you are ever in a safe location where an adult (over 21 years of age) family member or friend is legally drinking, ask if you can practice the HGN test, looking for the clues in the previous step. If this is taught in a college class environment, the students could practice doing the test on each other.

DECISION TIME 12.1

The horizontal gaze nystagmus or HGN sobriety test is one of the main SFSTs that law enforcement officers utilize to help them determine if a person is driving while impaired.

You are a police officer and you stopped a vehicle because the driver was driving 20 miles under the speed limit (20 mph in a posted 40 mph speed zone) and failed to signal two times when changing lanes, and when you contacted the driver you noticed it was a friend. You could smell the odor of an intoxicating beverage on your friend when he unrolled his driver's side window. You asked your friend if he had been drinking, and he said he had a work get-together and he drank two glasses of wine in the last hour.

You decided to perform a quick HGN sobriety test while your friend was still seated in the driver's seat of his vehicle. You got three clues, which mean there is a high probability your friend is impaired and driving. What would you do at this point? Would you perform more SFSTs? Would you have your friend call a family member or friend to come to get him and drive him home? Would you arrest him at this time?

The walk and turn sobriety test is a standardized field sobriety test (SFST) law enforcement officers are trained to give those persons suspected of driving while impaired. There is a lot of information and instructions that must be provided to the subject who is going to take the test. The test should be done on even, dry, and hard ground. The person giving the test can use white chalk to draw a straight line or use the lines in a parking lot. Evans (2019) came up with a four-step process:

1. Starting position instructions
2. Basic test overview
3. Demonstration and instructions
4. Head-to-toe instructions

Evans (2019) also gives a quick overview of how the instructions for the walk and turn sobriety test should be demonstrated. The subject starts with their left foot on the line and their right foot directly in front of their left foot touching heel to toe.

1. Start in heel-to-toe position.
    a. Head: Look down at your steps
2. Move and count aloud three heel-to-toe steps ending on the left foot
    a. Mouth: Count the steps out loud
3. Begin taking small steps to turn around with the left foot while keeping the right foot in the same place
    a. Arms: Stay at sides at all times

4. Move and count aloud three return heel-to-toe steps ending on the right foot
    a. Legs: Keep moving once you start until you end
5. Do you understand? (ask the subject)

To watch how to complete the four-step process review Fact Box 12.2.

There are a number of clues the subject might display during the test that the person giving the test must watch for. One clue could be observed multiple times and must be counted as one clue observed, no matter how many times it was observed. Once a subject shows two clues, the subject is likely impaired. If the subject starts displaying a number of clues, the person conducting the test must stop the test immediately for the safety of the subject. The following are the eight validated clues in the walk and turn sobriety test:

1. Starts walking before the person giving the instructions has completed giving the instructions entirely
2. Fails to stay in the starting position of heel to toe
3. Steps off the line
4. Does not step heel to toe (more than .5").
5. Stops while walking
6. Takes an incorrect number of steps
7. Makes an improper turn/loses balance
8. Raises arms (more than 6" from sides)

Figure 12.18 illustrates a 1st Special Operations security forces airman administering a walk and turn sobriety test on a subject.

FIGURE 12.18 Walk and turn sobriety test.

FACT BOX 12.2: WALK AND TURN SOBRIETY TEST

The walk and turn sobriety test takes a little more practice and time to learn to give the instructions, demonstrate the test, and identify the various clues. To better understand how to conduct this test, you should follow these steps:

1. Go to the Internet.
2. Watch the following video on YouTube: https://www.youtube.com/watch?v=MgWxviUYWVk
3. Find a family member or friend to practice doing the test and to practice your instructions and demonstration of the test; then look for the following clues as your family member or friend performs the test: (a) starts walking before the person giving the instructions has completed giving the instructions fully, (b) fails to stay in the starting position of heel to toe, (c) steps off the line, (d) does not step heel to toe (more than .5"), (e) stops while walking, (f) steps an incorrect number of times, (g) makes an improper turn/loses balance, and (h) raises arms (more than 6" from sides).
4. If you are ever in a safe location where an adult (over 21 years of age) family member or friend is legally drinking, ask if you can practice the walk and turn sobriety test looking for the clues in the previous step.
5. Alternatively, if this is taught in a college class environment, the students could practice the test on each other.

DECISION TIME 12.2

You are a new sergeant over patrol. One of your police officers radioed you for assistance on a call. You respond to a traffic stop, where the police officer has pulled over a male for speeding 35 mph in a posted 15 mph school zone. The police officer tells you that when she contacted the driver she could immediately smell the odor of an intoxicating beverage on him. When she asked the driver for identification, the driver gave her a police officer identification card that identified him as a police officer who worked for a nearby police department (which she corroborated through a wants check). Your police officer told you that the driver asked if he could call a friend to come to pick him up and drive his car home, and this would not happen again. The driver was very apologetic. Your police officer did one SFST on the driver before you got there, the walk and turn sobriety test, and the driver showed two clues.

What would you do? Would you perform more SFSTs on the driver? Would you arrest the driver for DUII? Would you call the driver's supervisor at his police department? Would you let the driver have a friend come pick him up and drive him and his car home?

The one-leg stand sobriety test is a standardized field sobriety test (SFST) law enforcement officers give those persons suspected of driving while impaired. There is a lot of information and instructions that must be provided to the subject who is going to take the test. The test should be done on even, dry, and hard ground. Evans (2019) came up with a four-step process (same as with the walk and turn sobriety test):

1. Starting position instructions
2. Basic test overview
3. Demonstration and instructions
4. Head-to-toe instructions

The subject starts with their feet together, heels touching, arms at their sides.

1. When told to start the subject will balance on one foot while raising the other foot approximately six inches off the ground. The subject can raise whichever foot they choose.
   a. Head: Look down at raised foot
   b. Feet: Foot is raised six inches off the ground and parallel to the ground
2. Start counting out loud until told to stop (one-thousand-one, one-thousand-two, one-thousand-three, and so on).
   a. Arms: Stay by sides at all times
   b. Mouth: Count out loud
3. Do you understand (ask the subject)?

To watch how to complete the four-step process review Fact Box 12.3.

There are a number of clues the subject might display during the test that the person giving the test must watch for. If the subject shows two or more of the following clues there is a high probability the subject is impaired:

1. Sways while balancing
2. Raises arms for balance
3. Hops
4. Puts foot down

Figure 12.19 illustrates a staff sergeant administering a one-leg stand sobriety test on a subject.

FIGURE 12.19 One-leg stand sobriety test.

FACT BOX 12.3: ONE-LEG STAND SOBRIETY TEST

The one-leg stand sobriety test takes a little more practice and time to learn to give the instructions, demonstrate the test, and identify the various clues. To better understand how to conduct the one-leg stand sobriety test, you should follow these steps:

1. Go to the Internet.
2. Watch the following video on YouTube: https://www.youtube.com/watch?v=7g7vA_qlcko.
3. After watching the video, find a family member or friend to practice doing the one-leg stand test and to practice your instructions and demonstration of the test; then look for the following clues as your family member or friend performs the test: (a) sways while balancing, (b) raises arms for balance, (c) hops, and (d) puts foot down.
4. If you are ever in a safe location where an adult (over 21 years of age) family member or friend is legally drinking, ask if you can practice the one-leg stand test by giving the instructions and demonstrating as well. Then look for the clues in the previous step.
5. Alternatively, if this is taught in a college class environment, the students could practice the test on each other.

SUMMARY OF CHAPTER 12

1. The most standard calibers and manufacturers of law enforcement officer primary duty handgun.

2. The various parts of a cartridge and why it is essential to utilize the correct terminology when referring to cartridges.

3. The history of an AR-15.

4. How less-lethal firearms can be lethal.

5. The main Standardized Field Sobriety Tests (SFSTs) utilized to identify an impaired driver.

DISCUSSION QUESTIONS

1. What are the various parts of a revolver and semiautomatic handgun?

2. Why is terminology essential when describing a cartridge?

3. Why is AR-15 not an automatic rifle?

4. How do you conduct the three main SFSTs?

CLASSROOM EXERCISES

One of the best parts of the hands-on police academy training chapter is that the student can finally start applying some of the law enforcement officer training that they have read about.

The first classroom exercise is on firearms, actually toy firearms. Obviously, it is not appropriate to utilize real firearms in a college classroom setting. Many colleges are gun-free zones, and the liability for those college campuses that are not would be too high. However, students can learn many of the firearm rules with a toy gun. If this following classroom exercise is done at a college campus, the professor should notify the campus public safety director or university police chief (or other head of safety and security at the college) about the training so as not to alarm other students who may see the training.

Toy gun options: One of the best options on the market today is a plastic toy gun with a laser in it. These laser toy guns have the real weight and feel of a law enforcement officer primary duty handgun, yet they are plastic and, other than the realistic trigger, have no working parts. They are expensive, however, which makes them cost restrictive for some classrooms. However, if they can be purchased, there are a variety of targets that can be purchased as well. For instance, there is a red target block that has circles on it when turned on, and the target registers and sounds when the student shoots and shows the student their shot placement. There are also other targets that can be purchased that sound and register when the student hits the target. It is recommended that there be one to two laser toy guns for every 5–10 students. However, if there is only enough money in a professor's budget to purchase one laser toy gun, then the professor can also purchase different types of cheaper toy guns to ensure student's do not have to wait around to use the one laser toy gun. Laserlyte is one manufacturer of such toy laser guns.

If the laser gun is too cost restrictive, the professor can purchase a variety of toy guns. Nerf toy guns are always good to utilize since they shoot a foam dart and the student can see where their shot lands. There are also a number of targets on the market for the professor to purchase as well. Regular silhouette targets can be utilized as well: Spinning targets, balloons, empty plastic bottles, or empty soda cans can all be placed on a table or shelf to use as targets.

Safety: It is recommended that if the professor utilizes a nerf toy gun or another type of toy gun that shoots any projectile the students wear safety glasses (clear plastic glasses are a good option) just to ensure a rogue foam dart (or another toy projectile) does not injure the eye of a student.

Classroom exercise: First, the professor will go over this chapter and the various sections. Next, the professor will review and write out the three firearm safety rules on a poster board or a regular piece of paper and place one at each station. Then the professor will cover basic shooting stances, how to aim the toy gun, and the proper and slow trigger pull. If the professor does not have fire-arms experience, this would be an excellent time to bring in an expert guest speaker from a local law enforcement agency.

The number of toy guns/types and targets the professor has will determine how many stations the professor sets up. A good guideline is if there are 30 students in the classroom set up six different stations. The professor ill make six groups and place five students in each group.

Each station should have the following:

- A toy gun(s)
- Toy projectiles (if appropriate)
- Target(s)
- Score sheet (depending on the type of target(s) the professor should practice ahead of time to determine a low and high score)

The students would then spend approximately 10–15 minutes at each station. After every student has gone through each station, the professor could have the top student from each station battle it out in a final toy gun shooting competition.

See Active Learning for the Following:

- Practice quizzes
- eFlashcards
- Video links
- Cognella journal articles
- News clips

References

Armalite. (n.d.). *History.* https://www.armalite.com/history/

Americans With Disabilities Act of 1990, Pub. L. No. 101-336, 104 Stat. 328 (1990).

Evans, A. (2019). *DUI training—Walk and turn test.* http://www.bluesheepdog.com/dui-training-walk-and-turn-test/

FieldSobrietyTests.net. (n.d.). *Horizontal gaze nystagmus field sobriety test.* http://www.fieldsobrietytests.net/horizontalgazenystagmusfieldsobrietytest.html

Myre, G. (2018, February 28). *A brief history of the AR-15.* NPR. https://www.npr.org/2018/02/28/588861820/a-brief-history-of-the-ar-15

Image Credits

INDEX

CPSIA information can be obtained
at www.ICGtesting.com
Printed in the USA
LVHW061524221121
R17031400001B/R170314PG703879LVX00001B/1

9 781516 596775